THE MALLEABILITY
OF CHILDREN

THE MALLEABILITY
OF CHILDREN

edited by

James J. Gallagher, Ph.D.
Director
Frank Porter Graham Child Development Center
and
Kenan Professor of Education
University of North Carolina at Chapel Hill

and

Craig T. Ramey, Ph.D.
Director of Research
Frank Porter Graham Child Development Center
University of North Carolina at Chapel Hill

·P A U L·H·
BROOKES
PUBLISHING Co

Baltimore • London

Paul H. Brookes Publishing Co.
Post Office Box 10624
Baltimore, Maryland 21285-0624

Typeset by The Composing Room, Grand Rapids, Michigan.
Manufactured in the United States of America by
The Maple Press Company, York, Pennsylvania.

Library of Congress Cataloging-in-Publication Data
The Malleability of children.
   Includes bibliographies and index.
   1. Adaptability (Psychology) in children.   2. Child development.
I. Gallagher, James John, 1926–   . II. Ramey, Craig T.   [DNLM: 1.
Adaptation, Psychological—in infancy & childhood. WS 105 M252]
BF723.A28M35   1987   155.4   86-32679
ISBN 0-933716-78-8 (pbk.)

Contents

Contributors

Jeffrey Arnett, Ph.D.
Department of Psychology
Oglethorpe University
Atlanta, GA 30319

J. Brooks-Gunn, Ph.D.
Senior Research Scientist
Educational Testing Service (10-R)
Rosedale Road
Princeton, NJ 08541

Bettye M. Caldwell, Ph.D.
Donaghey Distinguished Professor of Education
College of Education
University of Arkansas at Little Rock
Little Rock, AR 72204

Frances A. Campbell, Ph.D.
Coordinator for Psychoeducational Services
Frank Porter Graham Child Development Center
Highway 54 Bypass West 071 A
The University of North Carolina at Chapel Hill
Chapel Hill, NC 27514

Glendon Casto, Ph.D.
Director
Developmental Center for Handicapped Persons
Utah State University
Logan, UT 84322-6800

Victor H. Denenberg, Ph.D.
Biobehavioral Sciences Graduate Degree Program
U-154
3107 Horsebarn Hill Road
University of Connecticut
Storrs, CT 06268

Johanna Freedman
Assistant in Research
The Bush Center in Child Development and
   Social Policy
Yale University
P.O. Box 11A, Yale Station
New Haven, CT 06520-7382

Frank Furstenberg, Jr., Ph.D.
Professor of Sociology
Department of Sociology
University of Pennsylvania
Philadelphia, PA 19104

James J. Gallagher, Ph.D.
Director
Frank Porter Graham Child Development Center
and
Kenan Professor of Education
Highway 54 Bypass West 071 A
Chapel Hill, NC 27514

Nancy C. Jordan, Ed.D.
Head, Special Education Section
Clinical Center for the Study of Development and
   Learning
Biological Sciences Research Center 220H
and
Clinical Assistant Professor
Department of Special Education
School of Education
The University of North Carolina at Chapel Hill
Chapel Hill, NC 27514

Irving Lazar, Ph.D.
Department of Human Service Studies
N.Y.S. College of Human Ecology
Cornell University
Ithaca, NY 14853

Richard M. Lerner, Ph.D.
Professor of Child and Adolescent Development
Department of Individual and Family Studies
S-110 Henderson Human Development Building
The Pennsylvania State University
University Park, PA 16802

Melvin D. Levine, M.D.
Director
Clinical Center for the Study of Development and
   Learning
Biological Sciences Research Center 220H
and
Professor
Department of Pediatrics
School of Medicine
The University of North Carolina at Chapel Hill
Chapel Hill, NC 27514

Robert B. McCall, Ph.D.
Director
Office of Child Development
LRDC Building Room 411

University of Pittsburgh
3939 O'Hara Street
Pittsburgh, PA 15260

John U. Ogbu, Ph.D.
Professor
Department of Anthropology
University of California at Berkeley
Berkeley, CA 94720

Robert Plomin, Ph.D.
Individual and Family Studies
College of Human Development
The Pennsylvania State University
University Park, PA 16802

Craig T. Ramey, Ph.D.
Director of Research
Frank Porter Graham Child Development Center
Highway 54 Bypass West 071 A
The University of North Carolina at Chapel Hill
Chapel Hill, NC 27514

Sandra Scarr, Ph.D.
Chair and Commonwealth Professor of
    Psychology
Department of Psychology
Gilmer Hall
University of Virginia
Charlottesville, VA 22903-2477

Evelyn B. Thoman, Ph.D.
Professor
Infant Studies Laboratory
Biobehavioral Sciences Graduate Degree
    Program, U-154
The University of Connecticut
3107 Horsebarn Hill Road
Storrs, CT 06268

Peter M. Vietze, Ph.D.
Head
Mental Retardation Research Centers
National Institute of Child Health and Human
    Development
Landow Building, Room 7C09
7910 Woodmont Avenue
Bethesda, MD 20892

Edward Zigler, Ph.D.
Sterling Professor of Psychology
Director
The Bush Center in Child Development and
    Social Policy
Yale University
P.O. Box 11A, Yale Station
New Haven, CT 06520-7382

Preface

The issue addressed in this volume is one of the oldest, yet one of the most significant, questions posed about human behavior by many professional disciplines. How plastic is the developing organism? The answers to this question will determine the reasonable parameters of success for the psychiatrist, the educator, the clinical psychologist, the sociologist, the pediatrician, and others who try to improve the human condition. It will also inform the scientist who wishes to understand the nature of the human organism. This volume emerged from a conference on this topic hosted by the Frank Porter Graham Child Development Center at the University of North Carolina at Chapel Hill. The conference was held at the Quail Roost Conference Center at Rougemont, North Carolina, and was sponsored by the Foundation for Child Development.

The two chapters that open the book, written by Richard M. Lerner and Robert Plomin, provide an overview of the issue. On the one hand, Lerner stresses that a probabilistic combination of variables adds up to a complex interaction of genes with biological, psychological, and sociological variables. Lerner reminds us that human beings are the most plastic of all living organisms and testifies to the rewarding nature of constructive intervention, even given the limits set by genetics.

Plomin, on the other hand, points out that behavioral geneticists are interested in variance, while interventionists focus on means or averages. He reminds us that the geneticist focuses on ''what is'' rather than ''what could be,'' and certainly does not address ''what should be.'' He points out that, even with the genetic limitations that are now found to exist in child development malleability, such limitations say nothing about what could be achieved by children given a different or unique set of environmental conditions. This position of the ''potential malleability'' of children and adults is echoed in the chapters by Denenberg and Thoman who present unique environments to animals and infants, respectively, with striking results.

A number of the contributors have mentioned how much more plastic human beings are than animals. The chapter by Denenberg raises some interesting questions about how plastic animals can be under certain circumstances. Animal experimenters, by changing the environment of the animals in unconventional ways, have demonstrated that novel social and physical stimuli during infantile periods can bring about marked changes in behavior patterns, neuroanatomy, brain lateralization, and brain chemistry. This naturally raises the question of the limits of plasticity of human beings under dramatically different environmental settings. Since these environmental conditions also interact with each other to produce results in the animal, it is difficult to project the long-term effects of any single variable. However, maternal behavior, the kind of social interactions experienced, and the timing of these events, have clearly significant impact on later behavior.

Thoman's chapter puts an end to the belief that the young infant is an ''alimentary canal, open at both ends.'' The introduction of the breathing bear and the effects that the bear has on the premature infant show a degree of responsiveness and capability in the infant that would have been thought impossible a generation ago. As demonstrated again, it was not the infant who has changed, it is the level of ingenuity that we have reached in presenting responsive environments to them. The ability of premature infants to show goal-directed motor activity in responding to the breathing bear gives us another indication of the hidden competencies of the infant.

Scarr and Arnett point out the influence of genetics in their "Lessons from Intervention and Family Studies" chapter. They point out that the accumulation of evidence from two sources, twin studies, and the strong relationship between biological mothers and their children even after the children have been adopted in other families, testify to substantial genetic influence.

In this regard, the much maligned IQ score remains a developmental index of some importance. One is forced to ask the question, "If this IQ test score is so susceptible to outside influences of cultural background, motivation, and so on, why is it so hard to change?" The best and brightest of developmental psychologists have spent a generation trying all that they knew to modify that developmental pattern, and the most that seems possible is a very modest change in IQ score of about half a standard deviation. Scarr and Arnett pose the probabilistic epigenesis as a reasonable concept with genetics providing the broad limits, while environment modifies the path slightly within these limits. These forces are accompanied by a self-righting tendency when the child tends to get too far off the original developmental path.

The self-righting tendency is a theme of the McCall chapter. McCall refers to the lack of convergence in the ideas of the developmental psychologist and the intervention psychologist. He poses a series of questions. Why is there a lack of stability of measures on early intelligence, while there is substantial stability from age 6 on? Why does heritability increase with age, and is early intervention really better? He also poses the concept of *canalization* as a possible explanation for these phenomena. The essence of canalization involves the assumption of *creods,* or species-typical paths that all members tend to follow, but that can be disrupted by inappropriate environments. There is a strong self-righting tendency when deviations from this path are temporarily taken.

If early development is highly canalized, then the strong self-righting tendencies will lead to the lack of stability over time. As mental development becomes less canalized, the variation in developmental function increases and individual differences become more stable over time, so that both genetic and environmental correlations with intellectual development increase. If McCall is right, then intervention can be most effective when canalization drops in its developmental influence. Unfortunately, we do not know precisely when that period is, somewhere between 2 and 4 years.

McCall also raises the issue of the importance of family environment in the "discontinuous, nonshared, within-family" environmental effects. Influences within the family differentially affect the children involved. If these factors contribute half of the environmental variance to mental development, as McCall suggests, then we have one more strong argument for further investigations of the family and their complex interactions.

One of the ways to determine the modifiability of children is to adjust one's effort to change them. Zigler and Freedman describe the Head Start experience. This was perhaps the largest effort at social reform since Social Security. In their assessment of the program's impact, they, too, decry the tendency to focus too much on the modification of IQ scores to the detriment of many other dimensions of development that can be influenced through constructive intervention. They point out that many children with early disadvantage in their environment have a sphere of *unused intellect.*

While Zigler and Freedman discuss composite results that come from a nationwide intervention effort where there is inevitably a wide range of program efficiency, Ramey and Campbell report on a specific intervention, the Abecedarian project, which reports on a longitudinal intervention experiment. Their report shows children at risk for low academic adaptability gaining in academic efficiency and showing less grade retention, similar to the findings that the Lazar chapter reports. These authors point out that change in the measured developmental patterns of a child is determined in changing ecology, and that permanent change can likely be obtained only through a permanent change in the ecology surrounding the child. In other words, a burst of ecological enrichment over a 2-year period of time can well be eroded if the unfavorable ecology from which the child has emerged reasserts itself after the special enrichment program is over.

Lazar, in his chapter, reminds us that we have, as child development specialists, often underestimated the capabilities of the young child and infant and are subsequently surprised by the range and level of things that children can do, if we present them with the proper environment to which they can be responsive. He also holds, as do a number of the other contributors, that major changes in environmental stimulation can possibly create the conditions for even greater malleability than was originally projected by current data. Lazar's choice for a significant change in that environment is the computer, which he believes has the capabilities for substantially modifying our educational curriculum by allowing the students to have greater control of the pace, content, and combination of learnings, rather than have them faced with a "fixed" curriculum presented by the teacher. Whether Lazar's concept of the introduction of the computer as a "watershed event" in education is true or not, his concept of the human organism being a remarkably responsive entity, if only we can find the right stimulus, seems clearly true.

Using the new technique of meta-analysis that allows for a statistical analysis of a large number of articles on a given topic, Casto concludes that positive results can be obtained even with moderately and severely handicapped children. His review analysis, however, challenges some often stated elements of intervention programs. He questions whether parent involvement is necessary for gains, or whether early involvement is necessary. He also reminds us that many infants who are severely handicapped have a poor prognosis, even with the best of interventions and most optimal brain development.

While the behavioral geneticists and the developmental psychologists have clearly re-discovered the influence of genetics on human development, it is only natural that the anthropologist, John Ogbu, places the emphasis on cultural influences. If the usefulness of *heritability* is limited to existing environmental conditions, then going beyond standard environments would be helpful in determining plasticity. Ogbu, like Denenberg and Thoman, stresses the interaction of environmental needs and cultural expectations on subgroups, particularly subordinate minorities in a culture. Through numerous examples, he suggests that certain mathematical and artistic abilities emerge and are cultivated in one society or another, leading the children in those societies to be relatively superior in the emphasized skill. In addition, Ogbu raises the interesting hypothesis that in subordinate minorities their resentment of the majority prevents them from taking a full role in that society, or adopting, in the case of the United States, the "white man's role."

Caldwell, in her chapter, reminds us that results obtained at the preschool level often do not carry forward into later childhood, and identifies the ages of 8–10 as a crucial developmental period. During that period, some type of educational or psychological booster shot may be required in order to maintain some of the gains made earlier. She reminds us that this attenuation should not cause us to downgrade the impact of earlier work, but should be viewed as a challenge to see to what extent we can better maintain the gains made through a conceptualization of continued intervention strategies.

In their chapter, Levine and Jordan, like Caldwell, focus on middle childhood as an area of substantial importance. They point out that increasing pressures on the child for sustained attention, ready access to acquired skills, automatization of performance, and so on can cause youngsters who have neurodevelopmental dysfunction to reveal educational problems that might have gone unnoticed at earlier ages where there were less expectations for detailed performance. They point out that the very plasticity of the human being, allowing for adaptation to various dysfunctions, may, in fact, hide the problem. A child with substantial language facility can mask problems in the perceptual area as far as academic performance is concerned. The authors' interests represent an emerging trend to consider much more carefully the middle childhood period that has been largely neglected in the study of malleability of children.

While the majority of the chapters in the volume have dealt with malleability of young children or middle school–age children, Brooks-Gunn and Furstenberg explore the malleability of adolescent mothers in poverty. Although they are dealing with family situations that are least favorable, they still find a major difference in the outcome of the adolescent mothers. While they do report intergenerational transmission of cultural disadvantage, as is often suspected in such situations, they also report that many young girls have been able to escape the cycle of poverty through education. There were identifiable environmental factors that seemed to contribute to success. Adolescent mothers whose parents had more schooling, who were from smaller families, and who were not on welfare as children, were less likely to be on welfare in later life. They make the obvious point that malleability does not end in early childhood and that investments in public policy, aiding adolescent mothers among others, can be profitable to them and to the society.

The last section in the book is devoted to chapters that explore the potential impact on public policy of the knowledge currently available on the malleability of children. Gallagher, in his chapter, presents a model of presumed variance contributions to intellectual performance. On that basis, he presents a model of policy options and decision criteria for the special policy problem of 3- and 4-year-olds. What should be done with the 3- and 4-year-olds in our society given the rapid increase in the population of working mothers?

Peter Vietze, in his chapter, discusses the role of government organization in support of science policy and how that organization can have an impact on policy formulation leading to the investigation of malleability. With his insider's perspective, he discusses the roles played by federal agencies, and the process by which research policy is formulated within that agency, a topic rarely discussed, but clearly important in the evolution of scientific effort on this issue.

The editorial responsibilities for this volume were divided as follows: Craig Ramey organized the conference that was largely the beginning step for this volume. Jim Gallagher was responsible for the editorial work on the volume itself.

We would like to acknowledge the special contribution of the Foundation for Child Development whose support of the conference and manuscript preparation made this volume possible.

THE MALLEABILITY
OF CHILDREN

SECTION I

THEORY

Chapter 1

The Concept of Plasticity in Development

Richard M. Lerner

Over the course of the last decade or so, exciting changes have occurred in those areas of social science that study human development. A growing number of studies of infants and children, of adolescents, and of adults and elderly citizens provide results that challenge several views about the nature of human development; for example, that early experience provides a virtually immutable shaper of the entire life course; that development is essentially a within-the-person phenomenon, largely unaffected in quality or quantity by the context of life; and that, by and large, all people develop in fairly standard, normative manners.

The studies that were conducted in the last decade or so indicate that people are more resilient to early, often quite negative experiences than was previously thought; the events of early life do not necessarily constrain developments later on. These studies also indicate that features of the person's historical setting often shape personality, and social and intellectual functioning, to an extent often much greater than maturational or age-associated changes. General historical events, such as wars, economic privations, or political upheavals—as well as personal events, such as marriage, divorce, illness, death, or career change—are often seen to provide potent shapers of the quantity of life changes and of the quality of the life course. These studies also indicate that there are multiple paths through life. As people age, they become increasingly different from each other and, again, these different life paths are linked to general-historical or personal life events. Finally, the active role of the person himself or herself, in promoting both changes in self and context, has been identified. By influencing their own development directly, and indirectly—by changing the context that feeds back to influence them—people are seen as producers of their own development.

These findings help create a new life-span perspective about human development. This perspective emphasizes that the potential for change exists across life, that, as a consequence of active people reciprocally interacting in a changing world, the life course is always characterized by the potential for *plasticity,* that is, systematic changes within the person in his or her structure and/or function. While not denying that constancies and continuities can, and do, characterize much of many people's life courses, and that plasticity is therefore not limitless, proponents of the life-span perspective hold that many such features of life are not necessary ones. They contend that change and the potential for change characterize life because of the plasticity of the processes involved in people's lives. From the level of biology to that of culture, these processes are presumed to be changeable—on the basis of both their inherent character (e.g.,

The author's work on this chapter was supported in part by grants from the John D. and Catherine T. MacArthur Foundation and the William T. Grant Foundation.

could a life process be adaptive if it were not capable of change?) and their reciprocal relations (their embeddedness) with other processes.

The existence of such plasticity is not a point of minor practical significance. If all levels of analysis are available to be changed, then there is great reason to be optimistic about the ability of intervention programs to enhance human development.

Given its scientific and applied importance, a consideration of the characteristics and bases of human plasticity is both useful and timely. However, complicating this analysis is that the concept of plasticity has been conceptualized in several ways (see Franklin & Doyle, 1982; Gollin, 1981; Sigman, 1982).

For instance, in a discussion of the general meaning of the term, Sigman (1982) notes that

> The concept of plasticity is central to all biological and psychological studies of development. The concept signifies that the living organism can be modified by the environment. Any time we measure development or behavior of a subject in response to a stimulus, we are measuring plasticity. (p. 98)

In turn, Gollin (1981) indicates that plasticity refers to "the possible range of variations that can occur in individual development" (p. 231) or to systematic structural and/or functional changes in a process, and may involve "variations that lie on a continuum of variation around some hypothesized average value, and variations that entail structural and functional changes of a qualitative nature" (p. 237). However, several qualifications need to be forwarded in order to make such general conceptions of plasticity more specific and useful. A means to do this was provided by Maier and Schneirla (1935).

A COMPARATIVE PERSPECTIVE ABOUT THE DEVELOPMENT OF PLASTICITY

In order to provide a criterion by which to discriminate among different species, Maier and Schneirla (1935) focused on ontogenetic dif-

ferences among species. Although some species reached their most advanced level of behavioral organization relatively early in life, their final level of behavioral organization was relatively stereotyped, that is, relatively "sense dominated" (Hebb, 1949). In turn, other species, who took longer chronologically to reach their final level of behavioral organization, were relatively flexible; they could moderate their behaviors—for example, either approaching or withdrawing from a given stimulus—as the circumstances required.

Accordingly, Maier and Schneirla (1935) were able to characterize species differences on the basis of the contrasting capacities of various species to modify their behavior to adjust to new contextual circumstances (cf. Franklin & Doyle, 1982). Plasticity then is a comparative concept for Maier and Schneirla (1935); it serves as a concept summarizing the relative *flexibility,* that is, *the capacity to modify one's behavior to adjust to, or fit, the demands of a particular context,* shown by a species at its most advanced level of development.

Two features of the Maier and Schneirla (1935) conception are important to emphasize here. First, the level of plasticity prototypic of a given species is not preformed; for instance, there is not a gene "coded" for plasticity, such that whatever level of plasticity a species is capable of will be present either congenitally, or inevitably with age progression, in a member of that species (cf. Wilson, 1975). Instead, organisms must develop their plasticity; plasticity is a developmental phenomenon.

Second, a stress in Maier and Schneirla's conception—one that often goes either unrecognized or unemphasized—is that they are describing only *relative* differences among species. For instance, among mammals, rats are more stereotyped and less plastic than are humans, who, in turn, are obviously then less stereotyped and more plastic than rats. But note, however, that these distinctions do not depict rats or humans as either completely stereotyped or completely plastic. In regard to humans, although one may indicate that they develop toward a final level of behavioral organization that shows relatively greater plasticity (or better—as I will explain shortly—flexibility) than do other species, this certainly does not mean that humans are totally plastic. It does not mean that there are no limits on the ability to change the organism across life, or that some unmodifiability—or stereotypy, in Schneirla's (1957) terms—does not remain with the organism across life. Indeed, Maier and Schneirla would be likely to argue that both types of characteristics may, in different circumstances, be useful for the organism: for example, plasticity of response may be useful when the organism behaves in contexts with rapidly changing and/or ambiguous cues for adjustment; response stereotypy may be useful in contexts requiring rapid and/or numerous reflex-like responses for adjustment.

The point made by Maier and Schneirla (1935), that plasticity in any species and, probably, at any point in the life span, is a relative functional feature of an organism, raises some more general points. From a perspective aimed at identifying development or change, the concept of plasticity may be problematic *unless* it is understood as a relativistic phenomenon, that is to say, one that must always be considered in the context of features of the organism that are not plastic. In other words, in order to identify features of ontogeny that qualify to be labeled as "development," and in order to measure change, one needs to have some constancy; this is the case because in order to identify development and/or to gauge change, one needs an invariant and/or a constant (Baltes, Reese, & Nesselroade, 1977; Kaplan, 1983). Similarly, in order to identify and study the plasticity of an organism or a system, one needs some constraints.

And indeed, there are constraints, imposed by the organismic features of the human, by his or her present context, and by his or her earlier experience (see Kendall, Lerner, & Craighead, 1984). Moreover, even in adulthood, an organism's plasticity does not remain constant. For example, whereas evidence can be found for systematic neuroanatomical change across life (e.g., Cotman & Nieto-Sampedro, 1982; Green-ough & Green, 1981; Lynch & Gall, 1979), the character of the changes could best be represented by the concept of "selective preservation" (Greenough & Green, 1981); that is, only some features of the neuronal architecture are preserved, and not all instances of an organism's neuroanatomy show continued growth throughout life (e.g., Buell & Coleman, 1979). Similarly, on the human behavioral level, Baltes and Baltes (1980) have used the concept of "selective optimization" to indicate that in the later years there remains only a subset of cognitive-behavioral functions, which, while formerly available for change, continue to remain so. In short, plasticity is not limitless, although it is ubiquitous in life. While the human organism can be changed across its life, it becomes increasingly more difficult to effect change; change requires a more intensive environmental stimulus. In other words, while present across life, plasticity exists to an increasingly narrower or more circumscribed extent with advancing age, as described by the ideas of selective preservation (Greenough & Green, 1981) and selective optimization (Baltes & Baltes, 1980).

But, it remains the case that humans are relatively more plastic than are other species, and that the level of plasticity that serves to place the human in its location in comparison to other species is the level that is normatively attained in the human's adult period of life. This suggests that humans may possess, through selective preservation and selective optimization, a capacity for systematic change—that humans may retain at least some flexibility—across much if not all of their adult years. Indeed, despite some decline, it may be that the degree to which such flexibility exists across the human life span is greater than many people previously believed.

However, at this point it should be noted that the two issues raised by the Maier and Schneirla (1935) conception of plasticity—the issue of the developmental nature of plasticity and the issue of plasticity being a relativistic and not an absolute phenomenon—themselves raise other issues.

PLASTICITY AS PROCESS
VERSUS PLASTICITY AS PRODUCT

The concept of "levels of organization" has been a useful one in comparative analyses (Novikoff, 1945a, 1945b). In studying the development of an organism, a key issue is how variables and/or processes having their primary loci at one level of analysis relate to variables and/or processes having their main loci at other levels (e.g., Harris, 1957; Lerner, 1976; Nagel, 1957; Schneirla, 1956, 1957). These levels may encompass the physiochemical, physiological, individual-psychological, dyadic, familial or social, physical-ecological, societal, cultural, and historical (see Anderson, 1972).

Schneirla (1957) exemplifies the use of the "levels-of-organization" idea in his call for analyzing behavioral development in a manner that appreciates the relation of one level of analysis to others, and that stresses that the levels of analysis involved in development pertain both to phenomena within the organism and in the context of the organism. He states:

> The critical problem of behavioral development should be stated as follows:
> 1. To study the organization of behavior in terms of its properties at each stage, from the time of egg formation and fertilization through individual life history; and
> 2. to work out the changing relationships of organic mechanisms underlying behavior;
> 3. always in terms of the contributions of earlier stages in the developmental sequence;
> 4. and in consideration of the properties of the prevailing developmental context at each stage. (Schneirla, 1957, p. 80)

As illustrations of the sorts of relations among levels of analysis to which Schneirla (1957) points, consider the studies of the effects of an organism's context on DNA production. For instance, Uphouse and Bonner (1975) assessed the production of DNA by RNA from the brains or livers of rats exposed to either high environmental enrichment (i.e., living in a cage with 11 other rats and having "toys" and mazes available for exploration) or low environmental enrichment (i.e., living in a cage with one other rat but no exploration materials). The RNA from the brains of the environmentally enriched rats showed a level of transcription of DNA significantly greater than that of the other group. No significant differences were found with liver RNA. Grouse, Schrier, Bennett, Rosenzweig, and Nelson (1978) also found significant differences between the brain RNA of rats reared in environmentally rich contexts versus the brain RNA of those reared in environmentally impoverished contexts. In addition, Grouse, Schrier, and Nelson (1979) found that the total RNA complexity of brain RNA was greater for normally sighted kittens than for kittens who had both eyelids sutured at birth. However, the RNAs from the nonvisual cortices and from subcortical structures were not different for the two groups. Grouse et al. (1978) conclude that the normal development of the visual cortex, which is dependent on visual experience, involves a greater amount of genetic expression than occurs in the absence of visual experience. These findings illustrate both the contextual modifiability of genetic material, and the interrelations of levels of analysis that characterize the developmental process.

If we employ Schneirla's use of the concept of levels in the analysis of the development of a species' or an organism's plasticity, our task would become one of:

1. Studying how the properties at each level of analysis contribute to and/or constrain, alone and in combination, the degree of plasticity present in each period of life
2. Assessing how processes at levels of analysis "lower" than the more molar behavioral one may remain constant or change in the means by which they contribute to or constrain plasticity in each successive period of life
3. Determining how antecedent periods of life promote and/or constrain the degrees of plasticity seen at subsequent periods
4. Understanding how the context of the organism limits, induces (Gottlieb, 1976b), or permits the expression and/or further development of plasticity

However, our analytic task is complicated by a limitation in our language. We need to distinguish between the developmental processes that contribute to the organism's plasticity and the outcome of those processes, which is plasticity of behavior. Indeed, because there is no compelling reason to focus only on behavioral organization as our outcome "variable" (we can consider neuronal organization as our outcome and genetic and neurochemical processes as our "antecedents"), we are faced with a situation wherein (a) any of the processes involved in the matrix of developmental covariation influencing an organism can be considered an antecedent of some other level's plasticity *or* as an outcome of other levels' functioning; and therefore (b) the processes that contribute to an organism developing plasticity and to its final level of plasticity may themselves be considered plastic.

Thus, while we may be able to say that plastic processes result in plastic outcomes, to do so does not allow discrimination between antecedent processes and the products of these processes. To circumvent potential confusion, let us use the term plasticity to refer to the evolutionary and ontogenetic processes by which one develops one's capacity to modify one's behavior to adjust to, or fit, the demands of a particular context. In other words, plastic processes contribute to the development of a product, which, instead of also being labeled as plasticity, I will term "flexibility." In short, plastic developmental processes (both within and across time and both within the organism and between it and its context) can produce a flexible behavioral organization, one with the capability (the potentiality) of changing appropriately to meet contextual demands. In addition, we should keep clear that plasticity is a relative concept and that the issue for the study of behavioral development is—to summarize the above—to learn the organismic and contextual conditions that promote and/or constrain systematic change in structure and/or function.

Plasticity and Probabilistic Epigenesis

A similar call about the need to understand how the processes that promote plasticity also promote constraints on change has been made by Gollin (1981), who, similar to the position taken here, adopts a multilevel causal view of the bases of an organism's plasticity. Moreover, and similar to the theoretical stance of Schneirla (1957), Gollin (1981) sees the variables from these bases providing plasticity due to the probabilistic character of their confluence (see also Gottlieb, 1970; Lerner, 1978). Gollin (1981) indicates that:

> The determination of the successive qualities of living systems, given the web of relationships involved, is probabilistic. This is so because the number of factors operating conjointly in living systems is very great. Additionally, each factor and subsystem is capable of a greater or lesser degree of variability. Hence, the influence subsystems have upon each other, and upon the system as a whole, varies as a function of the varying states of the several concurrently operating subsystems. Thus, the very nature of living systems, both individual and collective, and of environments, assure the presumptive character of organic change.
>
> Living systems are organized systems with internal coherence. The properties of the parts are essentially dependent on relations between the parts and the whole (Waddington, 1957). The quality of the organization provides opportunities for change as well as constraints upon the extent and direction of change. Thus, while the determination of change is probabilistic, it is not chaotic. (p. 232)

It is important to underscore here the idea of probabilistic development noted by Gollin (1981). Gottlieb (1970) used the term probabilistic epigenesis

> to designate the view that the behavioral development of individuals within a species does not follow an invariant or inevitable course, and, more specifically, that the sequence or outcome of individual behavioral development is probable (with respect to norms) rather than certain. (p. 123)

Thus, this view of development emphasizes the centrality of interindividual differences as opposed to normative patterns, an emphasis that derives from the reciprocal interaction of the variables causally involved in development *and* the differential timing for different organisms of this interaction (Lerner, 1976, 1978, 1980, 1986). In other words, Gottlieb's conception of probabilistic epigenesis fosters a crucial distinction between normative or generic "developmental trajectories" (Wohlwill, 1973) and individual variation around such trajectories (cf. Plomin, this volume). Many developmentalists theoretically specify and/or empirically search for nomothetic patterns, ones broadly applicable to large segments of the population. Examples are the sequences specified in stage theories of development (e.g., Freud, 1949; Piaget, 1970). However, the idea of plasticity promoted by Gottlieb's (1970, 1976a, 1976b) concept of probabilistic epigenesis involves the development of lawful and inevitable interindividual differences around any normative trajectory, individual differences that derive from the probabilistic confluence of the causal variables involved in development.

Scarr (1982) has also drawn a connection between the ideas of probabilistic epigenesis and plasticity, a connection that emphasizes too that lawful individuality exists along with lawful species commonalities. She notes that:

Development does not merely emerge from the precoded information in the genes. Rather, development is a *probabilistic* result of indeterminate combinations of genes and environments. Development is genetically guided but variable and probabilistic because influential events in the life of every person can be neither predicted nor explained by general laws. Development, in this view, is guided primarily by the genetic program through its multilevel transactions with environments that range from cellular to social. The genetic program for the human species has both its overwhelming commonalities and its individual variability because each of us is both human and uniquely human . . . in this view, humans are made of the newer plastics—they bend with environmental pressures, resume their shapes when the pressures are relieved, and are unlikely to be permanently misshapen by transient experiences. When bad environments are improved, people's adaptations improve. Human beings are resilient and responsive to the advantages their environments provide. Even adults are capable of improved adaptations through learning, although any individual's improvement depends on that person's responsiveness to learning opportunities. . . . One can be optimistic about human development, as early maladaptations do not necessarily foretell lifelong problems. (pp. 852–853)

In short, a focus on the developmental processes that provide the components of human plasticity leads us to emphasize that development is probabilistic-epigenetic in character. This conception of development stresses that in the development of a lawfully distinct individual, the organism's biology and its context interrelate reciprocally, such that biological processes constrain the influence of the environment on the organism at the same time that the environment is influencing biological processes. In turn, environmental processes constrain the influence of biology on the organism, at the same time that biological processes are influencing environmental processes (Gottlieb, 1970, 1976a, 1976b; Lerner, 1976, 1978, 1980). The course of development that derives from such transactions is therefore neither constrained nor unconstrained; it is neither completely plastic nor completely constant. Instead, and as perhaps best depicted by Werner's (1948, 1957) orthogenetic principle, development represents a synthesis of (1) processes that act to make us the same as others, and processes that serve to differentiate us from others; and (2) processes that foster intraindividual continuity through life, and processes that serve to change us continually.

In sum, an emphasis on probabilistic-epigenetic development indicates that the processes that give humans their individuality and their plasticity are the same ones that provide for human commonality and constancies (cf. McClearn, 1981). Indeed, Jack Block (personal communication, 1982) makes this point eloquently when he cautions that when using the term "plasticity," one must not also imply that within the malleable system there is not a structure or structures. He notes:

if individuals are self-initiating, self-organizing systems, responsive in dynamic ways to changing contexts, this is because they have within them various ego structures, cognitive structures, perceptual structures, [and] action or knowledge structures through which experience is apprehended, processed and behavior is forged.

But, these conclusions raise several important issues. If the processes providing bases for the development of flexible behavior organization are plastic ones, and if, as a consequence of their plasticity, constraints currently existing on the actualization of flexibility can be altered, should this be done? Answers to such a question clearly raise issues of values and of ethics. For example, with the virtual explosion in recent years of knowledge and technology pertinent to genetic engineering through recombinant-DNA methodology, scientists and society are faced with dilemmas such as "should we create new forms of life?" and "when, under what conditions, may we scientifically and ethically begin true gene therapy in humans?" (see Anderson, 1982; Anderson & Fletcher, 1980; Hubbard, 1982; Walters, 1982).

Decisions here are complicated by the character of human plasticity as seen from the perspective discussed here. If behavioral flexibility emerges as an outcome of plastic processes involving both the organism and its context, then promotion of a valued change, for example, toward greater flexibility, at the level of the organism, may be associated with an undesired change at other levels of analysis and/or at later developmental periods (cf. Sigman, 1982).

For example, promoting flexibility sufficient to allow a women to meet successfully the demands of the home (e.g., in regard to spousal and parental roles) *and* of the work place (e.g., in regard to professional development) may be a change valued by the woman and by an intervenor; and such changes may be accompanied by other valued ones in the woman (e.g., her self-esteem and her personal income may be increased). However, unanticipated and undesired changes may ensue (cf. Block, 1973). For example, the woman's own parents may disapprove of her working outside the home, and unintended family network conflict may result.

Of course, in addition to unanticipated undesired effects, unplanned and/or indirect effects that may be more positive may occur as well. An excellent illustration of this point can be found in the synthesis of research of Lazar,

Darlington, Murray, Royce, and Snipper (1982). They report the results of a multisample secondary analysis assessing the long-term effects of early childhood education experiences on children from low-income families, children who had been part of one of 12 independently designed and implemented infant and preschool programs begun in the 1960s. In 1976, a collaborative follow-up was conducted of the original subjects, who were 9 to 19 years at the time. With attrition analyses indicating essentially random attrition, Lazar, et al. (1982) concluded that there were long-lasting effects of early education programs for children from low-income families in four areas:

1. Children in these programs were more likely to meet their schools' basic requirements, less likely to be assigned to special education classes, and less likely to be retained in grade than were controls.
2. Children in these programs did better than controls on the Stanford-Binet Intelligence Scale for several years after the program had ended. However, there was no evidence that program participation raised IQ scores. Indeed, Ramey (1982) points out that there was no project that "produced" groups of children who were significantly above average intellectually or, presumably, academically. Indeed, even the children within the projects having the best designs scored considerably below the national average.
3. Nevertheless, despite the failure to boost IQ scores, children who had been in the programs were, when tested in 1976, more likely than were controls to give achievement-related reasons for being proud of themselves.
4. Finally, program participation altered the child's familial context; participation influenced mothers' attitudes toward school performance and about vocational aspirations for the child.

In sum, although not altering IQ scores, these early intervention programs did have long-term effects on the child's school competence and abilities, and his or her attitudes and values, and on the mother's educational and vocational attitudes and aspirations pertinent to the child.

Thus, plasticity as viewed from the present perspective is a "double-edged" sword. The presence of plastic processes holds the promise of potential enhancement of the human condition but also constitutes a danger in that (1) as a consequence of the link between organisms and their contexts, unintended, potentially undesirable consequences of a change on one level may occur at another level, or later at the initial level; and (2) the presence of plasticity means not only that the organism is available to be changed for the better, but also that it is available to be changed for the worse. The recognition of the double-edged character of plasticity itself represents another limit on plasticity. That is, without some way of anticipating the possible, albeit unintentional or undesired effects of an attempt to capitalize on an organism's potential plasticity, scientists and interventionists cannot accurately appraise the cost-benefit ratio of their attempts to foster plastic developmental progressions. As such, scientists and interventionists are in a difficult ethical position about if and how to proceed with their work, and, in my view, only *scientifically* conservative steps are warranted (cf. Anderson & Fletcher, 1980). Such steps do *not* imply inaction, however. Indeed, failure to act is itself an intervention (Lerner, 1984). As such, scientific caution here means that interventions proceed in the context of theoretically guided and methodologically sound and open evaluation. What are some of the key developmental concerns with which one must deal as these interventions proceed?

IMPLICATIONS FOR INTERVENTION

A first developmental concern that may be raised is "when in life is it best to attempt to effect change or to intervene?" The presence of plasticity across life might suggest to some that little investment in childhood is necessary; if one can correct undesired behaviors in later life, if effects of early experience can be counteracted, why be concerned with early life? However, the idea of plasticity as a life-span-ubiquitous but declining or narrowing phenomenon suggests that the childhood years are indeed quite important.

That is, the presence of plasticity across life means that all is not lost for a child if the early years are deficient in important ways (cf. Clarke & Clarke, 1976), and/or if one does not reach the child in his or her early life. But, one must invest in childhood because the costs become increasingly greater to change the child—to actualize his or her potential plasticity; it becomes increasingly more arduous to change the child after early life.

Thus, while Clarke and Clarke (1976) note that all portions of development are important, they also make a point consistent with the idea of "ubiquitous but narrowing (or declining) plasticity" (Baltes & Baltes, 1980; Greenough & Green, 1981; MacDonald, 1985). That is, Clarke and Clarke (1976) point out that:

> It is unclear whether the limits of personal change are the same throughout the period of development, or whether, as we rather suspect, they get progressively smaller as age increases and as personal characteristics in adolescence and young adult life begin to achieve an autonomy and self-perpetuation. This hypothesis is difficult to test because children needing help either do or do not get it rather early in life; and the extreme cases of socialization can scarcely remain undetected beyond the age of school entry. Hence data on comparable environmental changes at very different ages hardly exist. (p. 272)

Similarly, MacDonald (1985) concludes that few, if any, scholars suppose that behavior is either absolutely fixed in early life by genetic factors, or that after a sensitive period it is impossible for behavior to change. On the other hand, there are abundant data speaking against the infinite plasticity of either human or animal behavior. While this evidence does not prevent intervention with people who have suffered early environmental insults, it suggests that the intensity of ecologically appropriate interventions needs to be increased in order to overcome the organism's declining plasticity (MacDonald, 1985). Thus, MacDonald concludes that declining plasticity means that successful interventions are not easily come by.

Parameters of Plasticity

A second set of concerns that may be raised pertains to several fundamental but unanswered questions about the parameters of plasticity. Are processes at different levels of analysis differentially plastic and/or are different targets within levels differentially flexible? For example, while recombinant-DNA technology has put us on the threshold of gene therapy, it may still be the case that selected features of our genotype (e.g., the number of chromosomes we possess) cannot be altered (without, at least, severely damaging our organismic integrity) no matter what the nature of organism-context relations may be. On the other hand, more molar, behavioral features of functioning (e.g., those at the cognitive-behavioral level) may not show such restrictions. For instance, are there limits to the number of languages a person can learn to speak, or the number of names of people a person may know? No current evidence indicates that such limits exist.

In addition to not fully knowing the limits of plasticity that may currently characterize levels of analysis, we do not know what further substantive and technological advances may imply for the future character of these limits. For example, the geneticist D. D. Brown (1981) notes that just a few years ago we could not *imagine* how we could ever isolate a gene. Yet, as noted by geneticist Paul Berg (1981), not only is such identification today quite routine, but the growth in the application of recombinant-DNA methods has been truly explosive.

Thus, if we take the idea of probabilistic epigenesis seriously, and if we recognize that science and technology represent natural parts of the human ecology, then we cannot anticipate where future scientific advances may lead. As a consequence, current limits of plasticity are not necessarily future ones. These limits are themselves plastic, and will likely change in a broader and broader direction in ways that, for some of us, are beyond our imagination (cf. Toulmin, 1981).

Recognition that the limits of plasticity can be altered, however, raises another developmental issue. The actualization of plasticity of course involves change, and change can only be identified over time. Numerous questions exist about the rates of change of plastic processes at the several levels of analysis that transact to provide the bases of behavior. First, it is clear that there is a "non-equivalent temporal metric" across the various levels of analysis (Lerner, Skinner, & Sorell, 1980) involved in person-context transactions. That is, all levels of the context change over time; but time may not have an identical meaning at all the levels.

One way to understand this is to note that the smallest meaningful division of time to detect change differs among levels. If time is one's "X-axis," with the "Y-axis" reflecting levels of one's target process, then reasonable X-axis divisions for detecting infant neuromuscular changes may be as small as weeks, and reasonable X-axis divisions for detecting neurotransmitter changes may be as small as minutes (Hosobuchi, Baskin, & Woo, 1982). However, the smallest reasonable division for detecting social change may be a year. In addition, even within a given level, time may not have an equivalent meaning at different points in development. For example, on the level of the individual, the year between birthdays may seem to a 5-year-old to be a vast length of time; to someone experiencing his or her 39th birthday, the one-year period until the 40th birthday may seem quite short; and to an 85-year-old, having to wait for one year for some important event may again seem quite long.

The import of the nonequivalent temporal metric is that it may be difficult to detect the influence of changes promoted on one level on a different level; for example, a change on the biological level (e.g., from better nutritional programs for children) may be difficult to detect on the societal level. Indeed, if an attempt is made to verify the existence of such an influence, it may be that a long term, perhaps intergenerational, perspective needs to be taken (Sarason, 1973). Or in a within-cohort analysis, it may be that only between-person differences in within-person change, and not within-person change itself, can be assessed. Complicating this issue is that even though the effects of a biological intervention on society may take a long time to detect, there is not necessarily symmetry of influence. That is, "upper level" societal alteration and social change may have relatively rapid and visible impact on "lower level" individual and biological processes. For example, changes in federal government funding programs such as school lunches for the poor, aid to mothers with dependent children, or Medicare and Medicaid for the elderly, may have more immediate impact on health, cognitive, and familial functioning variables associated with an individual.

The issues of the nonequivalent temporal metric and of the assymetry of interlevel influences raise other questions. First, given different levels' rates of change, one needs to know how processes at different levels connect with one another: How do interlevel influences occur? My own work on the "goodness of fit" concept (Lerner & Lerner, 1983) is an illustration of an attempt to answer this question, insofar as one is concerned with the individual and his or her immediate social context (in the case of my research, the child's relations with his or her parents, teachers, and peers). Here the idea is that children whose individual physical and/or behavioral characteristics (e.g., their facial attractiveness or their temperament) conform to the expectations of these significant others, will have better social interactions with them than will children whose characteristics do not afford such a good fit with these social pressures. However, there are perhaps an infinity of possible interlevel relations that may occur and, at this writing, we simply have not devoted enough thought and empirical energies to their investigation.

In turn, the issue of asymmetry of interlevel influence raises similarly, largely unaddressed concerns about efficiency and about cost-benefit ratios. To reach a target at an individual's cognitive-behavioral level, for example, the target of academic achievement, is it more efficient to institute a "bottom-up strategy" (e.g., intervene at the biological level), or a "parallel-level" strategy (e.g., intervene by cog-

nitive-behavioral means), or a "top-down" strategy (intervene by instituting or changing social programs)? Which strategy leads to the most benefits, relative to economic, social, and personal costs? We simply do not know answers to these questions for very many of the potential targets of intervention. As such, research evaluating the relative effectiveness of all three types of approaches seems, in my view, both necessary and useful at this point.

Moreover, a decision about the level of analysis on which to focus one's intervention efforts is complicated by the fact that all levels of analysis are developing and changing over time. While this feature of the human condition permits both concurrent and historical interventions to be possible, it again raises questions of efficiency and cost-benefit ratios. For example, when during the life span is it best to intervene, to optimize a particular target process (and, of course, on what level is it best to focus one's efforts)? Are periods of developmental transition (e.g., puberty or retirement), or are periods of *relatively* more stability, better times within which to focus one's effects? Moreover, do some intervention goals, for example, the elimination of Fetal Alcohol Syndrome (FAS) (Streissguth, Landesman-Dwyer, Martin, & Smith, 1980), require an intergenerational-developmental, rather than an ontogenetic-developmental approach? (In the case of FAS, for instance, may not it be of more benefit to intervene with women who are "at risk" of becoming mothers who use excessive alcohol, even before they become pregnant?) Again, developmental intervention issues such as these have remained relatively unaddressed for most potential targets.

A final developmental issue pertinent to intervention may be raised—one deriving from the point that plasticity is a "double-edged sword," that a system open to change may be altered for better or for worse. If a system remains open to interventions at one point in time, then it may similarly remain open throughout life; as such, one cannot expect an intervention to effect permanent change, when, after the intervention is over, life circumstances may impose numerous, potentially countervailing, unplanned interventions. As a consequence, one must take a life-span perspective toward intervention. Thus, as Sigman (1982) indicates:

> the evidence of continued plasticity cuts both ways. . . . Our awareness of the individual's continued responsiveness to the environment should make us more conservative in our expectation that intervention for a brief period in early infancy will have long-term effects over time. We cannot anticipate that early intervention will be an inoculation against the trauma of all future environments. Although change brought about in the family may have more lasting effects, the family is also responsive to the greater milieu. With both child and family showing significant plasticity, intervention efforts must be sustained. Only by improving living and rearing conditions throughout childhood can we expect to promote continual developmental progress at the optimal level. (p. 112)

In sum, plasticity is both a developmental phenomenon and a feature of the human condition across life. It is a characteristic that derives from a probabilistic combination of variables involving the person's biology, psychology, and social world, and, as such, it is a phenomenon that assures the lawful individuality of each person. In the face of such a phenomenon, interventionists may take comfort knowing that their plans and efforts have, at the very least, a theoretical possibility of success; however, the developmental complexity and contextual embeddedness of the phenomenon should stand as a caution to interventionists that their efforts require multidisciplinary awareness, theoretical precision, and methodological rigor. As attested to by some of the work noted in this chapter, elsewhere in this volume, and in other sources as well (e.g., Brim & Kagan, 1980; Clarke & Clarke, 1976; Lerner & Hood, 1986), such interventions, although few in number, are rich in results and implications. They provide provocative substantiation of the view that investment of resources and efforts into enhancing human functioning within and across all periods of the life span is a scientifically sound and empirically rewarding course of action.

REFERENCES

Anderson, P. W. (1972). More is different. *Science, 177,* 393–396.

Anderson, W. F. (1982). Technical and medical state-of-the-art of gene therapy in human adults and embryos. *Abstracts of Papers of the 148th National Meeting of the American Association for the Advancement of Science,* Washington, D.C.

Anderson, W. F., & Fletcher, J. C. (1980). Gene therapy in human beings: When is it ethical to begin? *The New England Journal of Medicine, 303,* 1293–1297.

Baltes, P. B., & Baltes, M. M. (1980). Plasticity and variability in psychological aging: Methodological and theoretical issues. In G. E. Gurski (Ed.), *Determining the effects of aging on the central nervous system.* Berlin: Schering AG.

Baltes, P. B., Reese, H. W., & Nesselroade, J. R. (1977). *Life-span developmental psychology: Introduction to research methods.* Monterey, CA: Brooks/Cole.

Berg, P. (1981). Dissections and reconstructions of genes and chromosomes. *Science, 213,* 296–303.

Block, J. H. (1973). Conceptions of sex roles: Some cross-cultural and longitudinal perspectives. *American Psychologist, 28,* 512–526.

Brim, O. G., Jr., & Kagan, J. (1980). Constancy and change: A view of the issues. In O. G. Brim, Jr. & J. Kagan (Eds.), *Constancy and change in human development* (pp. 1–25). Cambridge, MA: Harvard University Press.

Brown, D. D. (1981). Gene expression in eukaryotes. *Science, 211,* 667–674.

Buell, S. J., & Coleman, P. D. (1979). Dendritic growth in the aged human brain and failure of growth in senile dementia. *Science, 206,* 854–856.

Clarke, A. M., & Clarke, A. D. B. (Eds.). (1976). *Early experience: Myth and evidence.* New York: Free Press.

Cotman, C. W., & Nieto-Sampedro, M. (1982). Brain function, synapse renewal, and plasticity. *Annual Review of Psychology, 33,* 371–401.

Franklin, M. B., & Doyle, C. L. (1982). Perspectives on plasticity. *Contemporary Psychology, 27,* 694–695.

Freud, S. (1949). *Outline of psychoanalysis.* New York: Norton.

Gollin, E. S. (1981). Development and plasticity. In E. S. Gollin (Ed.), *Developmental plasticity: Behavioral and biological aspects of variations in development* (pp. 231–251). New York: Academic Press.

Gottlieb, G. (1970). Conceptions of prenatal behavior. In L. R. Aronson, E. Tobach, D. S. Lehrman, & J. S. Rosenblatt (Eds.), *Development and evolution of behavior: Essays in memory of T. C. Schneirla* (pp. 111–137). New York: W. H. Freeman.

Gottlieb, G. (1976a). The roles of experience in the development of behavior and the nervous system. In G. Gottlieb (Ed.), *Neural and behavioral specificity: Studies on the development of behavior and the nervous system* (Vol. 3, pp. 25–54). New York: Academic Press.

Gottlieb, G. (1976b). Conceptions of prenatal development: Behavioral embryology. *Psychological Review, 83,* 215–234.

Greenough, W. T., & Green, E. J. (1981). Experience and the changing brain. In J. L. McGaugh, J. G. March, & S. B. Kiesler (Eds.), *Aging: Biology and behavior* (pp. 159–200). New York: Academic Press.

Grouse, L. D., Schrier, B. K., Bennett, E. L., Rosenzweig, M. R., & Nelson, P. G. (1978). Sequence diversity studies of rat brain RNA: Effects of environmental complexity and rat brain RNA diversity. *Journal of Neurochemistry, 30,* 191–203.

Grouse, L. D., Schrier, B. K., & Nelson, P. G. (1979). Effect of visual experience on gene expression during the development of stimulus specificity in cat brain. *Experimental Neurology, 64,* 354–364.

Harris, D. B. (Ed.). (1957). *The concept of development.* Minneapolis: University of Minnesota Press.

Hebb, D. O. (1949). *The organization of behavior.* New York: John Wiley & Sons.

Hosobuchi, Y., Baskin, D. S., & Woo, S. K. (1982). Reversal of induced ischemic neurological defect in gerbils by the opiate antagonist naloxone. *Science, 215,* 69–71.

Hubbard, R. (1982). The ethics and politics of embryo and gene manipulations. *Abstracts of Papers of the 148th National Meeting of the American Association for the Advancement of Science.*

Kaplan, B. (1983). A trio of trials. In R. M. Lerner (Ed.), *Developmental psychology: Historical and philosophical perspectives* (pp. 185–228). Hillsdale, NJ: Lawrence Erlbaum Associates.

Kendall, P. C., Lerner, R. M., & Craighead, W. E. (1984). Human development and intervention in childhood psychopathology. *Child Development, 55,* 71–82.

Lazar, I., Darlington, R., Murray, H., Royce, J., & Snipper, A. (1982). Lasting effects of early education: A report from the consortium for longitudinal studies. *Monographs of the Society for Research in Child Development, 47* (Serial No. 195, Nos. 2–3).

Lerner, J. V., & Lerner, R. M. (1983). Temperament and adaptation across life: Theoretical and empirical issues. In P. B. Baltes & O. G. Brim, Jr. (Eds.), *Life-span development and behavior* (Vol. 5). New York: Academic Press.

Lerner, R. (1976). *Concepts and theories of human development.* Reading, MA: Addison-Wesley.

Lerner, R. M. (1978). Nature, nurture, and dynamic interactionism. *Human Development, 21,* 1–20.

Lerner, R. M. (1980). Concepts of epigenesis: Descriptive and explanatory issues. A critique of Kitchner's comments. *Human Development, 23,* 63–72.

Lerner, R. M. (1984). *On the nature of human plasticity.* New York: Cambridge University Press.

Lerner, R. M. (1986). *Concepts and theories of human development* (2nd ed.). New York: Random House.

Lerner, R. M., & Hood, K. E. (1986). Plasticity in development: Concepts and issues for intervention. *Journal of Applied Developmental Psychology, 7,* 139–152.

Lerner, R. M., Skinner, E. A., & Sorell, G. T. (1980). Methodological implications of contextual/dialectic theories of development. *Human Development, 23,* 225–235.

Lynch, G., & Gall, C. (1979). Organization and reorganization in the central nervous system: Evolving concepts of brain plasticity. In F. T. Falkner & J. M. Tanner (Eds.), *Human growth, Vol. 3: Neurobiology and nutrition* (pp. 125–144). New York: Plenum.

MacDonald, K. (1985). Developmental models and early experience. *Developmental Review, 5,* 99–121.

Maier, N. R. F., & Schneirla, T. C. (1935). *Principles of animal behavior.* New York: McGraw-Hill.

McClearn, G. E. (1981). Evolution and genetic variability. In E. S. Gollin (Ed.), *Developmental plasticity: Behav-ioral and biological aspects of variations in development* (pp. 3–31). New York: Academic Press.

Nagel, E. (1957). Determinism and development. In D. B. Harris (Ed.), *The concept of development* (pp. 15–24). Minneapolis: University of Minnesota Press.

Novikoff, A. B. (1945a). The concept of integrative levels and biology. *Science, 101,* 209–215.

Novikoff, A. B. (1945b). Continuity and discontinuity in evolution. *Science, 101,* 405–406.

Piaget, J. (1970). Piaget's theory. In P. H. Mussen (Ed.), *Carmichael's manual of child psychology* (Vol. 1, pp. 703–732). New York: John Wiley & Sons.

Ramey, C. T. (1982). Commentary to Lazar et al. "Lasting effects of early education: A report from the consortium for longitudinal studies." *Monographs of the Society for Research in Child Development, 47* (Serial No. 195, Nos. 2–3).

Sarason, S. B. (1973). Jewishness, blackishness, and the nature-nurture controversy. *American Psychologist, 28,* 962–971.

Scarr, S. (1982). Development is internally guided, not determined. *Contemporary Psychology, 27,* 852–853.

Schneirla, T. C. (1956). Interrelationships of the innate and the acquired in instinctive behavior. In P. P. Grassé (Ed.), *L'Instinct dans le comportement des animaux et de l'homme* (pp. 387–452). Paris: Masson & Cie.

Schneirla, T. C. (1957). The concept of development in comparative psychology. In D. B. Harris (Ed.), *The concept of development.* Minneapolis: University of Minnesota Press.

Sigman, M. (1982). Plasticity in development: Implications for intervention. In L. A. Bond & J. M. Joffe (Eds.), *Facilitating infant and early childhood development.* Hanover, NH: University Press of New England.

Streissguth, A. P., Landesman-Dwyer, S., Martin, J. C., & Smith, D. W. (1980). Teratogenic effects of alcohol in humans and laboratory animals. *Science, 209,* 353–361.

Toulmin, S. (1981). Epistemology and developmental psychology. In E. S. Gollin (Ed.), *Developmental plasticity: Behavioral and biological aspects of variations in development* (pp. 253–267). New York: Academic Press.

Uphouse, L. L., & Bonner, J. (1975). Preliminary evidence for the effects of environmental complexity on hybridization of rat brain RNA to rat unique DNA. *Developmental Psychology, 8,* 171–178.

Waddington, C. H. (1957). *The strategy of genes.* London: George Allen and Unwin.

Walters, L. (1982). Ethical issues in genetic and reproductive engineering. *Abstracts of Papers of the 148th National Meeting of the American Association for the Advancement of Science,* Washington, DC.

Werner, H. (1948). *Comparative psychology of mental development.* New York: International Universities Press.

Werner, H. (1957). The concept of development from a comparative and organismic point of view. In D. B. Harris (Ed.), *The concept of development* (pp. 125–148). Minneapolis: University of Minnesota Press.

Wilson, E. O. (1975). *Sociobiology: The new synthesis.* Cambridge, MA: Harvard University Press.

Wohlwill, J. F. (1973). *The study of behavioral development.* New York: Academic Press.

Chapter 2

Behavioral Genetics and Intervention

Robert Plomin

Plasticity refers to capacity for change and flexibility in outcomes, as discussed by Lerner in this volume. Although the word carries complex connotations, the core issue is malleability, the extent to which the course of behavioral development can be altered. For this reason, I have chosen to focus on intervention research as a concrete example of research based on the concept of plasticity in order to sharpen the contrast with behavioral genetic research. The thesis of this chapter is that behavioral geneticists and interventionists look at development through different windows, and what they see is so different that the view from one window bears little relationship to the view from the other. Although it is refreshing to see new vistas, it is important to recognize that behavioral geneticists and interventionists are looking at different scenes. This chapter attempts to sketch the view from the behavioral genetics window, highlighting differences from the interventionists' view.

The differences between the two perspectives can be reduced to three major dimensions: means-variances, nature-nurture, and portrayals-potentials.

MEANS AND VARIANCES

When behavioral geneticists look through their window, they see how different children are. Some children are more adept at language than are others; some are better problem solvers than others; and some are more emotional, active, or shy than others. The essence of behavioral genetic research is to study the extent to which these differences among children are related to genetic differences among them or to their experiential differences. In short, behavioral genetics is the study of what makes individuals different. In contrast, interventionists tend to see similarities rather than differences. Interventionists usually look at average differences between groups—typically, differences between experimental and control groups—and the effectiveness of an intervention is judged in terms of its average effect on children. Thus, behavioral geneticists focus on variance and interventionists focus on means. One view is not better than the other, but they are different, and it is important to recognize the difference because variances and means are independent—the description and explanation of one tell us little about the other, as will be discussed later.

Another apparent difference between the two approaches is that intervention research is experimental and behavioral genetic research is correlational, the "two disciplines of scientific psychology" (Cronbach, 1957). However, I suggest that the experimental-correlational distinction is not so important. Be-

The research described in this chapter on the Colorado Adoption Project was conducted collaboratively with J. C. DeFries and has been supported by the National Institute of Child Health and Human Development (HD-10333 and HD-18426) and the National Science Foundation (BNS-8200310).

The helpful comments of Judy Dunn and James J. Gallagher and the excellent editorial advice of Rebecca Miles are gratefully acknowledged.

havioral genetic methodologies involve quasi-experiments in which naturally occurring genetic and environmental manipulations are employed, such as comparisons of the observed similarity of pairs of identical twins, fraternal twins, and adoptees, whose genetic resemblance is roughly 100%, 50%, and 0%, respectively. For the purpose of comparing intervention and behavioral genetic research, the important issue is that behavioral geneticists focus on variance, whereas intervention research focuses on means. Indeed, in the analysis-of-variance approach to the comparison of average differences between groups, individual differences are referred to as *error variance*. Behavioral geneticists would argue that human variation is not error—each of us is a unique genetic and environmental entity, never to be duplicated again. Human variability is not merely imprecision in a process that, if perfect, would generate unvarying representatives of the species type.

McCall (1981) has argued that developmentalists must eventually understand both means (developmental functions) and variances (individual differences). Although it may appear somewhat churlish to refuse an invitation for rapprochement, I believe that, at least from the perspective of behavioral genetics, it is important at this time to keep the two approaches apart, emphasizing their incompatibility rather than their complementarity. I take this boorish stance because, in my experience, failure to recognize the distinction between an individual-differences perspective and a normative perspective is responsible for much misunderstanding about behavioral genetics.

The most important reason for distinguishing between means and variances is that the causes of average differences between groups are not necessarily related to the causes of individual differences within groups. In terms of intervention research, changes in the mean do not usually lead to changes in the rank-ordering of individuals within the group. Furthermore, demonstrating that a particular treatment creates an average difference between experimental and control groups does not imply that the factors involved in the treatment are also responsible for differences among individuals

outside the experimental situation. The converse of this principle is particularly important for understanding the relationship between behavioral genetics and intervention research: The causes of individual differences within groups are not necessarily related to the causes of average differences between groups. As discussed later, substantial genetic influence on individual differences for a particular trait does not imply that heredity is responsible for an average difference between groups for the trait, nor does it limit the creation of average differences by means of intervention.

Finally, I would argue that most socially relevant issues involve individual rather than group differences. McCall (1977) has suggested that a focus on individual differences can obscure important information about developmental functions. The metaphor he uses involves trees: The most interesting fact about the sequoia is that, compared to other tree species, sequoia are much taller on average. Who cares about the differences of a few feet in the height of members of the species when we crane our necks to look up at the towering majesty of the sequoia? No one. However, when the metaphor is extended to the human species, a different conclusion is reached. The most notable facts about the human species, compared to other primate species, include its bipedalism and its use of language and tools. Who cares about differences among members of the species in motor and mental development? We all do. Nearly all questions of societal importance involve individual differences—for example, differences in reading ability, differences in problem solving and reasoning, and differences in personality characteristics such as activity, aggressiveness, and attention span (just to begin an alphabetical list of important personality attributes).

NATURE AND NURTURE

Behavioral geneticists consider genetic as well as environmental sources of variance in a population; interventionists, on the other hand, do not often take genetic influence into account. In this section, the important role that heredity plays in behavioral development will be briefly considered; however, more attention will be given to a discussion of the meaning of genetic influence and, especially, the implications of behavioral genetic research for the study of environmental influence.

Confusion between the individual differences and normative perspectives tends to stoke the ashes of the nature versus nurture controversy. Although it is fashionable to proclaim that issue dead, the mistaken divisive view that pitted nature against nurture is too frequently replaced with the equally mistaken notion that the separate effects of heredity and environment cannot be analyzed. From a normative perspective, both genes and environment are necessary for an organism to develop. From the perspective of individual differences, however, either genes or environment or both can contribute to observed differences among individuals in a population.

For example, if genetic differences among individuals affect phenotypic differences, several predictions follow: First-degree relatives, who are 50% similar genetically, will resemble each other to the extent that heredity is important. However, resemblance of first-degree relatives could be due to the fact that they normally live in the same family; thus, shared family environment could be responsible for their similarity. The adoption design separates the effects of heredity and shared family environment: If heredity is important, first-degree relatives will resemble each other when they are adopted apart and reared in uncorrelated environments. The classical twin design compares the phenotypic similarity of identical twins to that of fraternal twins: If heredity is important, identical twins, who are identical genetically, will be more similar than fraternal twins, who are only half as similar genetically. Details concerning these methods and their assumptions can be found in behavioral genetic textbooks (e.g., Fuller & Thompson, 1978; Hay, 1985; Plomin, DeFries, & McClearn, 1980).

The Importance of Heredity

Behavioral genetic research with nonhuman animals, involving comparisons of inbred strains of mice and selection studies, has demonstrated the ubiquity of genetic influence (e.g., Plomin et al., 1980). Similar results are accumulating for the human species. Recent publications have reviewed the results of family, twin, and adoption studies of general and specific cognitive abilities (Plomin, 1985; Scarr & Carter, 1982) and of personality (Goldsmith, 1983; Plomin, 1986). For IQ scores and some personality traits, the data converge on the conclusion that as much as half of the measured variance can be accounted for by genetic differences among individuals.

For example, recent data from the Minnesota Study of Twins Reared Apart (Bouchard, 1984) for 29 pairs of identical twins adopted in infancy by different families, and tested at the average age of 36 years, yielded a correlation of .58 for Raven's Progressive Matrices. The correlation for 71 pairs of identical twins reared together was .66. Similar results were obtained for self-report personality data: The median correlation for Tellegen's Differential Personality Questionnaire was .65 for identical twins reared apart and .54 for identical twins reared together. Thus, genetically identical pairs of individuals are about as similar when they are adopted and reared by different families in infancy, as when they are reared together in the same family. Heredity, a descriptive statistic describing the proportion of phenotypic (observed) variance that is due to genetic variance, is estimated directly by the correlation for identical twins reared apart— .58 in the case of the Minnesota cognitive data, and .65 for the personality data. The phenotypic correlation for identical twins reared apart in uncorrelated environments directly assesses heritability, because the twin partners are identical genetically, and their covariance thus reflects all sources of genetic variance and no sources of similarity due to shared family environment. The correlation itself, not the square of the correlation, is at issue because the correlation represents the proportion of variance that covaries between the twin partners, rather than the extent to which one twin partner's score can be predicted from the other's score—which would require the square of the correlation.

The Meaning of Genetic Influence

Francis Galton, the father of human behavioral genetics, coined the phrase "nature and nurture" in 1874:

> The phrase "nature and nurture" is a convenient jingle of words, for it separates under two distinct heads the innumerable elements of which personality is composed. Nature is all that a man brings with himself into the world; nurture is every influence from without that affects him after his birth. (p. 12)

This original definition of nature and nurture is not quite what behavioral geneticists mean by the terms "genetic" and "environmental." Galton seems to include prenatal environmental influences under the rubric of nature; nurture is limited to the kind of environmental event "from without that affects him after his birth." In modern behavioral genetics, genetic influences refer to the total impact of variability in DNA products of any kind on behavioral differences among individuals. Genetic effects change throughout development, as genes are turned on and off, and as their effects interact with each other and with the rest of the physiological system. In psychological development, change is just as apparent as continuity, and the subdiscipline of developmental behavioral genetics explores possible genetic sources of change (Plomin, 1983, 1986a). An implication for interventionists is that heritability should not be equated with developmental stability; genes can be responsible for change as well as continuity in development.

In behavioral genetics, "environmental" means "nongenetic," that is, all influences that are not encoded in DNA. This broad definition of environment thus includes the gradients of chemical constituents in the cytoplasm of the egg, as well as psychosocial experiences such as the birth of a sibling. Nongenetic variance also includes error of measurement, although such error can be estimated and considered separately in the behavioral genetic decomposition of variance.

The message of the previous section cannot be overemphasized. Behavioral genetic research only bears upon individual differences in a population. The phrase *significant herita-bility* truncates the more appropriate statement that differences observed among individuals in a specific population are significantly related to genetic differences among those individuals with that population's contemporary genetic and environmental influences. The word *differences* needs to be underlined. Behavioral genetics is the study of genetic and environmental factors that make a difference in behavior. A great deal of DNA is nonvarying for human beings, indeed, for all primates; similarly, many aspects of the environment such as gravity and oxygen are essentially nonvarying. Because such genetic and environmental universals cannot be responsible for differences among individuals, they are not reflected in behavioral genetic analyses.

Because *genetic* in behavioral genetics refers to a source of variance in a population, it implies a probabilistic, not deterministic, relationship between genes and behavior. For example, a heritability of 50% for shyness does not mean that heredity provides half of the reason why a particular child is shy. The child's shyness could be entirely environmental in origin. A heritability of 50% means that, given the genetic and environmental sources of variance in the population, genetic differences account for about half of the observed differences among children in terms of their shyness. A related issue is that heritability does not imply immutability. Genetic influence refers to a probabilistic propensity estimated from existing genetic and environmental variation in the population—if the environment of a particular child is altered, the expression of the child's genetic propensities could be altered. This issue is the focus of the next section.

Another concept germane to a discussion of the meaning of genetic influence on behavior is that genetic effects on such complex behaviors as cognitive abilities and personality are highly polygenic; that is, many genes, each with a small effect, add up to produce observable differences among individuals in a population. This is the essence of quantitative genetic theory, which extends Mendelian genetics to normally distributed characteristics (Fisher, 1918), and which is the foundation for behavioral genetic methodologies. Some single genes can devastatingly disrupt development; for example, over 100 single-gene disorders, such as phenylketonuria (PKU), have been identified that are associated with mental retardation (McKusick, 1983). However, these genetic diseases are rare and thus do not contradict the conclusion that no single gene has been shown to account for even a detectable amount of variation in the normal distribution of any behavioral characteristic. Furthermore, most genes are likely to affect many behaviors; these manifold effects of genes are referred to as pleiotropy. One implication of the polygenic and pleiotropic nature of genetic influence is that a single physiological factor is not likely to explain much variance; the physiological pathways from genes to behavior are likely to be very complex.

This presentation of behavioral genetics should make it clear that genes do not determine one's destiny; genetic influence does not imply hard-wired circuits that create a specific response. Consider alcoholism, for example, for which there is some evidence for genetic influence. This does not mean that there is a gene or a set of genes that determines whether an individual will become alcoholic. No one becomes alcoholic without consuming large quantities of alcohol. However, most individuals in our society are exposed to alcohol and some individuals are genetically predisposed to abuse the drug, for reasons that are not yet understood. Because of the complexities of pleiotropic, polygenic effects, genetic influences are indeed just influences—propensities, or tendencies, that nudge development in one direction rather than another. In other words, genetic influence is not in opposition to such developmental concepts as embeddedness and plasticity. Genetic influence is embedded in the complexity of interactions among genes, physiology, and environment. It is probabilistic, not deterministic; it puts no constraints on what could be.

A discussion of the meaning of genetic influence would not be complete without addressing the possible dangerous implications of finding genetic influence. In accord with the old-fash-

ioned view of a truth-seeking science, I believe that wiser decisions can be made with knowledge than without it. Any important new knowledge is likely to make us re-think issues; this is as true for environmental research as it is for genetic research. Scarr and Weinberg (1978) suggest that the negative effects of environmentalism should not be overlooked when considering the implications of genetic effects:

> Three decades of naive environmentalism have locked most Westerners into wrong-headed assumptions about the limitless malleability of mankind, and programs based on this premise can lead a country into a thicket of unrealistic promises and hopes. The fallacy is the belief that equality of opportunity produces sameness of outcome. Equality of opportunity is a laudable goal for any society. Sameness of outcomes is a biological impossibility. (p. 36)

Awareness of genetic influence leads to a counterintuitive conclusion concerning the effects of equalizing opportunity: It can *increase* heritability. In other words, if an environmental variable that relates to an outcome measure of interest is made to be less variable by distributing the environmental variable more equally, the relative proportion of phenotypic variance that is accounted for by genetic variance will increase to the extent that environmental variance decreases.

The essential worry about genetic influence is that it appears to go against our basic democratic principles. Are not all men (and women) created equal? When our founding fathers proclaimed that principle, they were not so naive as to think that all people are inherently identical. They meant political equality, not an absence of individual differences. In a democracy, we do not treat people equally because they are identical—there would be no need for principles of equality if that were true. The essence of democracy is to treat people equally in spite of their differences. As discussed later, behavioral genetic research describes *what is*, not *what could be*, and certainly not *what should be*. Finding genetic influence in behavioral development is compatible with a wide range of social action, including no action at all.

A related concern about genetic differences is that it just doesn't seem fair that some people are brighter than others, by reason of hereditary endowment, rather than by dint of their own diligence. However, in this sense, life is unfair. The fact is that heredity contributes to differences among people in their behavior as well as their bones.

The Importance of Environmental Variation

To say that genetic influence is important is not to deny the importance of environmental variation. Finding significant genetic influence by no means implies that genetic variance accounts for all observed variation. In fact, genetic variation rarely accounts for more than 50% of the variation of any complex phenotype, which means that environmental variation is usually responsible for the majority of the phenotypic variance. In this sense, behavioral genetic research often provides the best evidence for the importance of the environment. Although this point seems obvious, it is often overlooked. Twenty years ago, it was necessary to argue for the possibility of genetic influence on schizophrenia; now, the evidence for significant genetic involvement (e.g., Gottesman & Shields, 1982) has overshadowed the fact that environmental influences play a larger role than do genetic factors in determining whether individuals become schizophrenic.

I believe that the major contribution of behavioral genetics will be its exploration of environmental influences in development. This may be the best reply to the retort, "Genetic influences may be important, but all we have to work with is the environment." Recognition of genetic influence and methodologies that consider genetic as well as environmental variation will lead to a more complete understanding of how the environment works. This section briefly describes three examples of the potential usefulness of behavioral genetics in helping us to understand environmental influences.

Nonshared Environmental Influence

The most important example involves the partitioning of environmental variation into two classes: environmental variation that makes family members similar (shared), and environmental variation that does not (nonshared). This arbitrary decomposition of environmental variance has always been important in behavioral genetics, because shared environment contributes to the resemblance of relatives; disentangling common influences due to shared environment from the effects of heredity is a primary goal of behavioral genetic research. Among environmentalists, it is often assumed that environmental influences are largely a function of shared environment. For example, most studies of environmental influence obtain some measure of the home environment and relate it to the development of a single child in each family, as if the home environment is monolithic and the children in a family are interchangeable. However, behavioral genetic research consistently leads to the conclusion that most relevant environmental variation, especially for personality and psychopathology, is of the nonshared variety. That is, whatever the salient environmental factors might be, they operate in such a way as to make two children in the same family as different from one another as are children in different families (e.g., Plomin & Daniels, 1987; Rowe & Plomin, 1981). For example, the correlation between measures of a trait in genetically unrelated children adopted into the same home at birth directly estimates the proportion of phenotypic variance that is due to shared environment. For personality and psychopathology, the resemblance of adoptive siblings is negligible. Biological (nonadoptive) siblings resemble each other, but this resemblance appears to be due to heredity, not shared environment.

Until recently, environmental variance that affects individual differences in IQ was thought to fall primarily in the category of shared environment. In 11 studies, the average IQ correlation for pairs of adoptive siblings was .30 (Bouchard & McGue, 1981). Because this correlation means that 30% of the variance in IQ scores covaries for pairs of genetically unrelated children reared in the same adoptive family, 30% of the variance in IQ scores is attributed to shared environmental influences. Adoptive parent/adopted child IQ correlations are lower, about .20, but still suggest substantial influence of shared environment. Not previously noted, however, is the fact that these studies have collected data on adoptive siblings still living at home. An exception was a study of adoptee pairs from 16 to 22 years of age reported by Scarr and Weinberg (1978). This study yielded a correlation of −.03 for IQ. A second study of adoptive and nonadoptive siblings with the average age of 13 years found an IQ correlation of .38 for nonadoptive siblings; however, the IQ correlation for adoptive siblings was −.16 (Kent, 1985). These two studies suggest the important possibility that, although shared environment has a substantial influence on IQ during childhood, its influence fades by adolescence.

The discovery of the importance of nonshared environment has far-reaching implications for the study of environmental influences. Previous studies have been conceptualized in terms of shared influences; approaches to nonshared environment need to be devised. The trick is to study more than one child per family and to explore those aspects of the environment that might make the children different from one another. Any environmental factor can be viewed in terms of its contribution to nonshared environmental variance rather than to shared environment. For example, the HOME (Caldwell & Bradley, 1978) includes scales that assess maternal responsivity and maternal involvement; to what extent do mothers' responsivity to and involvement with their children differ from one child to another? Clearly, nonsystematic, idiosyncratic events such as accidents, illnesses, and other trauma can have a marked effect on development. More interesting, however, are possible systematic sources of differences within families. Family structure variables such as birth order and spacing of siblings are most often studied, although these variables do not appear to account for much variance within families. Studies of differential environments provided by parents and peers and by siblings themselves are more promising (Plomin & Daniels, 1987).

Genotype-Environment Interaction and Correlation   Two quantitative genetic concepts lie at the interface of nature and nurture. Genotype-environment interaction denotes an interaction in the statistical, analysis-of-variance sense of a conditional relationship: The effect of an environmental variable depends upon genotype. Genotype-environment correlation literally refers to a correlation between genetic deviations and environmental deviations as they affect a particular trait; it describes the extent to which children are exposed to environments on the basis of their genetic propensities. Adoption designs make it possible to isolate specific instances of genotype-environment interaction and correlation (Plomin, DeFries, & Loehlin, 1977). Despite the reasonableness of genotype-environment interaction, attempts to isolate specific interactions have so far failed (Plomin, 1986a). Although some examples of interaction have been found (Sameroff & Chandler, 1975; Zeskind & Ramey, 1978), many attempts to find interactions have not been successful (Plomin & Daniels, 1984). For example, educational researchers have put the most effort into finding interactions, specifically interactions involving aptitude and treatment. However, after two decades of research, Cronbach and Snow (1975, p. 492) concluded that "no Aptitude × Treatment interactions are so well confirmed that they can be used directly as guides to instruction."

In contrast, genotype-environment correlation accounts for substantial variance, at least for IQ (Plomin, 1986a). The most important spur for research in this field is Scarr and McCartney's (1983) theory based on three types of genotype-environment correlation, which suggests processes by which genotypes transact with environments during development. Their theory suggests that passive genotype-environment correlation diminishes in importance from childhood to adolescence for IQ, and reactive and active genotype-environment correlations appear to account for substantial variance after childhood.

Genetic Mediation of the Relationship between Measures of the Environment and Measures of Development   Measures of the home environment are measures of parental behavior. This is obviously true for environmental measures such as parental responsivity and involvement, but it is also true

for objective, physical aspects of the environment such as number of books visible in the
home. In nonadoptive homes, in which parents
share heredity as well as family environment
with their children, relationships between environmental measures and measures of children's development could be mediated genetically via parental characteristics. However, in
adoptive homes, adoptive parents share only
family environment with their adopted children; for this reason, correlations between
measures of environment and children's development in adoptive homes cannot be mediated genetically. Thus, if genes underlie relationships
between measures of the home environment
and children's development, environment-
development correlations in nonadoptive homes
will be greater than those in adoptive homes.
The larger the difference between the correlations in the nonadoptive and adoptive homes,
the greater the extent to which the environment-development correlation is mediated genetically.

For IQ, environment-development correlations appear to be substantially greater in nonadoptive than in adoptive families, suggesting
considerable genetic mediation of the relationship between environmental measures and
measures of mental development (Plomin,
Loehlin, & DeFries, 1985). For example, in
the longitudinal Colorado Adoption Project
(Plomin & DeFries, 1985), the HOME correlates .44 with Bayley Mental Development Index scores at 24 months in nonadoptive homes;
however, the correlation in adoptive homes
is .29. Similar results were obtained for language development: The HOME correlates .50
with scores on the Sequenced Inventory of
Communication Development in nonadoptive
homes, whereas the correlation in adoptive
homes is significantly lower, .32.

The most obvious implication of these findings is that, in nonadoptive families, relationships between environmental measures and
measures of development cannot be assumed to
be environmental in origin. It is safer to assume
that when a relationship between an environmental measure and a measure of development
is found in nonadoptive homes, half of the rela-

tionship is due to genetic factors. Another implication is the need for research to isolate parental mediators of genetic influence on
environment-development relationships. All
we know so far is that the answer is not obvious. For example, it would seem likely that
genetic mediation of the relationship between
the HOME and cognitive development would
be due to parental IQ. However, partialing out
parental IQ has little effect on these relationships in either nonadoptive or adoptive
homes.

In summary, behavioral genetic methodologies can do much more than provide estimates of the relative contributions of nature
and nurture. I am confident that the major impact of behavioral genetic research will be in
elucidating the role of environmental influences and the developmental interface between
genes and environment. Recognizing genetic
as well as environmental influences in development might lead to more fine-grained intervention studies.

PORTRAYALS AND POTENTIALS

As indicated earlier, behavioral genetic analyses sketch a portrait of the etiology of individual differences as they exist in a population.
In contrast, intervention studies focus on potential. In other words, behavioral geneticists
consider *what is* in a population (sources of
existing variance), whereas interventionists are
concerned about *what could be*. This is the
major gulf between the two fields. Descrip-
tions of *what is* in a population bear no necessary relationship to *what could be*. Specifically, high heritability does not necessarily limit
the potential for intervention. In fact, even if
heritability were 1.0 for a particular trait, a
novel environmental intervention (i.e., some
environmental factor that has not varied previously in the population) could have dramatic
effects. For example, high heritability for tooth
decay would imply that environmental factors
that currently vary, such as the frequency of
brushing one's teeth, do not account for much
variability in tooth decay. However, a novel
environmental intervention, such as flossing

and staining teeth for plaque deposits, could lead to a dramatic mean reduction in tooth decay. Now that use of preventive dentistry is beginning to vary widely, this intervention has probably increased the relative impact of environmental variance and decreased the influence of genetic variance on individual differences in tooth decay. However, if access to preventive dentistry becomes widespread, this environmental factor will account for less variance and the heritability of tooth decay may increase.

Another example of the lack of relationship between heritability and malleability involves negative genotype-environment correlation: Extra resources could be devoted to children at the lower end of the distribution for a particular trait. Even for highly heritable traits, an environmental intervention that accounts for only a small amount of variance in the population as a whole could substantially raise scores on average for children at the low end of the distribution. To the extent that this example involves negative genotype-environment correlation (that is, children are selected for the environmental intervention on the basis of genotypic differences), phenotypic variance in the population would be reduced; estimates of the relative magnitude of genetic and environmental variance will not be affected.

A relationship between heritability and malleability seems reasonable because high heritability implies that the myriad potential environmental influences that currently vary in the population do not have much of an effect. If that is the case, one might conclude that individual differences in the trait are resistant to environmental influence. However, two arguments speak against making this association. First, heritability never approaches 1.0 for complex behavioral characteristics; rarely does

it exceed .50. Thus, environmental variation significantly and substantially affects all aspects of behavioral development. Second, many interventions (e.g., day care for infants) were novel when they were introduced in that they were not represented among the contemporary environmental variables in the population. In summary, there is no necessary relationship between *what is* and *what could be*.

CONCLUSION

If interventionists focus on normative issues, environmental influences, and *what could be*, behavioral genetic research will be of little relevance. The goal of this chapter is merely to point out the different viewpoints of the two fields. One reason for emphasizing their differing perspectives is that it lessens the likelihood of conflict between interventionists and behavioral geneticists, if they both realize that the results of one type of research do not need to agree with the results from the other. A more positive reason for the tack I have taken is my hope that cross-fertilization between the two fields might result in the synergism of hybrid vigor. Although these "parents" may be too different to produce many fertile "offspring," it is possible that awareness of individual differences and genetic sources of variance in a population will lead to novel types of intervention research. One possible direction along these lines is to consider trait-by-treatment interactions—some individuals might be especially "vulnerable" to the effects of intervention. Other possibilities include intervention research that takes advantage of what we know about the importance of nonshared family environment, genotype-environment correlation, and genetic mediation of environment-development relationships.

REFERENCES

Bouchard, T. J. (1984). Twins reared together and apart: What they tell us about human diversity. In S. W. Fox (Ed.), *Individuality and determinism* (pp. 147–178). New York: Plenum.

Bouchard, T. J., Jr., & McGue, M. (1981). Familial studies of intelligence: A review. *Science, 212,* 1055–1059.

Caldwell, B. M., & Bradley, R. H. (1978). *Home observation for measurement of the environment.* Little Rock: University of Arkansas.

Cronbach, L. J. (1957). The two disciplines of scientific psychology. *American Psychologist, 12,* 671–684.

Cronbach, L. J., & Snow, R. E. (1975). *Aptitudes and*

instructional methods: A handbook for research on interactions. New York: Irvington.

Fisher, R. A. (1918). The correlation between relatives on the supposition of Mendelian inheritance. *Transactions of the Royal Society of Edinburgh, 52,* 399–433.

Fuller, J. L., & Thompson, W. R. (1978). *Foundations of behavior genetics.* St. Louis: C. V. Mosby.

Galton, F. (1874). *English men of science: Their nature and nurture.* London: MacMillan.

Goldsmith, H. H. (1983). Genetic influences on personality from infancy to adulthood. *Child Development, 54,* 331–355.

Gottesman, I. I., & Shields, J. (1982). *Schizophrenia: The epigenetic puzzle.* Cambridge, MA: Cambridge University Press.

Hay, D. A. (1985). *Essentials of behaviour genetics.* Oxford: Blackwells.

Kent, J. (1985). *Genetic and environmental contributions to cognitive abilities as assessed by a telephone test battery.* Unpublished doctoral dissertation, University of Colorado, Boulder.

McCall, R. B. (1977). Challenges to a science of developmental psychology. *Child Development, 48,* 333–344.

McCall, R. B. (1981). Nature-nurture and the two realms of development: A proposed integration with respect to mental development. *Child Development, 52,* 1–12.

McKusick, V. A. (1983). *Mendelian inheritance in man* (7th ed.). Baltimore: The Johns Hopkins University Press.

Plomin, R. (1983). Developmental behavioral genetics. *Child Development, 54,* 253–259.

Plomin, R. (1985). Behavioral genetics. In D. Detterman (Ed.), *Current topics in human intelligence: Research methodology* (pp. 297–320). Norwood, NJ: Ablex.

Plomin, R. (1986a). *Development, genetics, and psychology.* Hillsdale, NJ: Lawrence Erlbaum Associates.

Plomin, R. (1986b). Behavioral genetic methods. *Journal of Personality, 54,* 226–261.

Plomin, R., & Daniels, D. (1984). The interaction between temperament and environment: Methodological considerations. *Merrill-Palmer Quarterly, 30,* 149–162.

Plomin, R., & Daniels, D. (1987). *Why are children in the same family so different from each other? Behavioral and Brain Sciences, 10,* 1–16.

Plomin, R., & DeFries, J. C. (1985). *Origins of individual differences in infancy: The Colorado Adoption Project.* New York: Academic Press.

Plomin, R., DeFries, J. C., & McClearn, G. E. (1980). *Behavioral genetics: A primer.* New York: W. H. Freeman.

Plomin, R., DeFries, J. C., & Loehhlin, J. C. (1977). Genotype-environment interaction and correlation in the analysis of human behavior. *Psychological Bulletin, 84,* 309–322.

Plomin, R., Loehlin, J. C., & DeFries, J. C. (1985). Genetic and environmental components of "environmental" influences. *Developmental Psychology, 21,* 391–402.

Rowe, D. C., & Plomin, R. (1981). The importance of non-shared (E1) environmental influences in behavioral development. *Developmental Psychology, 17,* 517–531.

Sameroff, A., & Chandler, M. (1975). Reproductive risk and the continuum of caretaking causality. In F. Horowitz (Ed.), *Review of child development research* (Vol. 4, pp. 187–244). Chicago: University of Chicago Press.

Scarr, S., & Carter, L. (1982). Genetics and intelligence. In R. Sternberg (Ed.), *Handbook of intelligence.* New York: Cambridge University Press.

Scarr, S., & McCartney, K. (1983). How people make their own environments: A theory of genotype → environment effects. *Child Development, 54,* 424–435.

Scarr, S., & Weinberg, R. A. (1978). The influence of "family background" on intellectual attainment. *American Sociological Review, 43,* 674–692.

Zeskind, P., & Ramey, C. (1978). Fetal malnutrition: An experimental study of its consequences on infant development in two care giving environments. *Child Development, 49,* 1155–1162.

Chapter 3

Developmental Function, Individual Differences, and the Plasticity of Intelligence

Robert B. McCall

It is often said that in the history of thought, major ideas are recycled approximately every 2 or 3 decades. That is, a fundamental theme (e.g., the role of heredity or environment, continuity or discontinuity) dominates thought for several years; it falls into benign neglect or outright disfavor for some years; and then it is resurrected in a form that is close to, but not quite identical to, its previous statement. It is the thesis-antithesis-synthesis conception of intellectual history.

Something like this progression has occurred with respect to thought about mental development over the last few decades. Prior to the 1960s, intelligence was assumed to be essentially fixed, stable, and unchanging—although a few believed otherwise. Then, Hunt (1961, 1963) led the antithetical movement that proclaimed that intelligence was (at least potentially) not fixed and unchanging.

The inherent plasticity, however, was assumed to be limited. That is, the early years were considered formative, so that appropriate environmental interventions could have an effect primarily (or perhaps, only) if they occurred early enough in the child's life. Since milestone longitudinal studies showed that individual differences in IQ stabilized approximately after age 6 (McCall, 1979), it was assumed that intervention had to occur before age 6 (and some proposed before age 3).

The practical deduction from this proposition stated that an appropriate program of enrichment in the early years of life could produce substantial changes in intellectual performance. Although not declared overtly, it became tacitly assumed that such intellectual benefits essentially would be permanent, that no special efforts were needed to maintain those benefits later in childhood and adolescence, and that interventions later in life would not be effective. Viewed in retrospect and with some degree of facetiousness, our thinking became a critical-period or inoculation theory of the environmental effects on intellectual development: a one-shot intervention early in life would produce permanent immunity to subsequent exposure to poor environments.

At the same time some developmental psychologists, usually not those involved in intervention research, were studying the stability of individual differences in mental performance across large segments of the life span. They found that year-to-year correlations in mental test performance were almost 0 during the first 2 or 3 years, and then gradually rose to asymptotic levels at approximately age 6. This fact was used by the interventionists to demarcate the period of plasticity from the period of stability in mental growth.

Ironically, however, the individual-difference scholars and the interventionists interpreted differently the lack of stability in infancy and early childhood. Specifically, the interventionists believed that the lack of cross-age correlations in the early years implied that early mental development was plastic and susceptible to their interventions. In contrast, those who studied the stability of individual differences in mental performance in naturalistic contexts acted as if they did not believe decades worth of their own data. They felt that intelligence was stable from early infancy, and that they simply had not yet discovered the appropriate measurement of the intelligence of those early years. Presumably, once the tools were identified, correlations from early infancy would emerge. So these researchers persisted in their search for early predictors of later IQ (McCall, 1981a). Few seemed to notice the apparent contradiction between these two groups of scholars. Furthermore, few criticized the logic of applying results of observations of samples of middle-class white children to samples of impoverished black children, who had been exposed to an experimental intervention that often consisted of doses of middle-class activities and child-rearing techniques.

Later, the arrival on the scene of behavioral genetics created more contradictions. For example, although the point is disputed (McCall, 1979), the heritability of infant test performance was found to be relatively low, at least substantially lower than it is for IQ at age 6 (Honzik, 1957; McCall, 1979). The interventionists found that information reasonable and reassuring, since it suggested that environmental factors made their contribution early. But if environment's contribution was made early and was relatively permanent, why did the measures of heritability increase during early childhood (Honzik, 1957)? And why do environmental, as well as genetic, factors correlate weakly during infancy and increase with age? Shall we assume that early mental performance is shaped by neither genetic nor environmental factors, and that the influences of both increase with age? But isn't early development largely governed by nature? How can the heritability of a characteristic be weak in infancy but increase with age, when the reverse should be true? Once again, these seeming contradictions apparently bothered no one.

Then, the individual-difference group divided into two parts. One group (e.g., McCall, 1979), for example, decided that 5 decades of research, consistently showing that measures during the first 18 months of life did not predict later IQ, was sufficient grounds for "accepting" the null hypothesis that intelligence undergoes substantial qualitative and quantitative changes early in life. This group emphasized developmental change and urged colleagues to be as vigorous in studying such changes as they had been in pursuing the stability that had eluded them for 5 decades. Just when that admonition began to take hold, the traditionalists reemerged. New data suggested that the faithful were correct, namely, that the early essence of intelligence had been found: Measures of early recognition memory and of responses to new stimuli predicted later intelligence at higher levels than did the earlier infant tests (for a review, see Fagan & Singer, 1983).

By now, the results of long-term prototypical intervention programs are available and mixed (see Chapters 7 through 11 in this volume). Stated simply, a typical enrichment program for disadvantaged children produces IQ gains of approximately 10 to 15 points, but such an advantage seems to last only 2 or 3 years. Moreover, although certain factors (e.g., intensity of program, parent involvement, age of child at entrance [see Ramey, Chapter 11, this volume]) are associated with the extent of the benefits, some very modest interventions have been able to achieve gains of 8 to 10 points, and it appears that entrance into normal schooling is also associated with gains of this magnitude (Caldwell, Chapter 10, this volume). Fortunately, long-term benefits of enrichment programs have shown up in reduced rates of grade failure and of need for remedial services, among other variables (Lazar, Darlington, et al., 1982; Lazar, Chapter 8, this volume; Zigler & Freedman, Chapter 7, this volume). But the effect on IQ has not been as large as anticipated, nor as long lasting as hoped.

Given 1) the failure of enrichment programs to alter IQ permanently, 2) the prediction of intelligence from recognition-memory performance in infancy, and 3) the demonstration of a substantial genetic contribution to IQ, are we on the verge of returning to a belief in a relatively stable, constant IQ that is not easily changed? Probably not. The synthesis, one hopes, will be different from the thesis, otherwise nothing has been learned. As is often the case, what has been learned is not what we set out to find. I would like to discuss a few of these lessons.

METHODOLOGICAL AND CONCEPTUAL STRATEGIES

Many methodological and conceptual strategies have been, or should be, influenced by the recent history of research on early intervention and the plasticity of mental development.

First, we must not put all our research eggs in the basket of one dependent variable—IQ. The IQ test is one of the best single measurements available in developmental psychology. It was foolish, however, to rely so heavily on it in the past as the outcome variable and to pay so little attention to school performance, motivational variables, and intellectual and social behaviors outside the school context, for example.

Second, we must not assume that the human organism can be inoculated forever by a short intervention against the effects of extreme environments. While we had been willing to assume that children were sufficiently plastic to be influenced by our interventions at age 5, why was it so surprising to find that once the intervention stopped at age 6 or 7, and the child was returned to the same environment that contributed to his or her initial pre-intervention status, that IQ also would relapse toward pretreatment levels? Whereas earlier may be easier, is it ever too late? Perhaps, but not at age 3 or 6. Similarly, interventions cannot be terminated abruptly, with no continuing support, if early gains are to be sustained.

Third, intervention programs do not have effects on the child alone. The child belongs to a family context that may have as much or more influence than the intervention program. Bronfenbrenner (1974), warned us of the shortsightedness of ignoring the family and community context; the speculation (Lazar, Chapter 8, this volume) that parents mediate the effects of early intervention programs is consistent with his theme.

Fourth, the interventions themselves must be spelled out in detail, otherwise we will never learn what elements of intervention programs seem to be influential and what elements do not.

Fifth, we must adopt conceptual and methodological strategies that allow us to think about and study nature and nurture as well as individual differences and group changes in a behavior over age within the same conceptual framework. I believe a failure to do so has held us back in several respects. It is this lesson to which I now turn in more detail, because it forms the basis of a synthesis of the theses and antitheses mentioned so far in this chapter.

The Two Realms of Developmental Research

As already described from a historical perspective, research on early mental development has proceeded in two rather independent fashions, one emphasizing the influence of enrichment programs on the average mental performance of a group and the other emphasizing the stability or lack of stability of individual differences in mental performance across age. These contrasting foci parallel the "two disciplines of scientific psychology" discussed by Cronbach (1957) more than 25 years ago, and it is the allegiance to one of these strategies at the expense of the other that may limit our understanding of mental development (McCall, 1981b).

Developmental Function The measured value of a given attribute plotted across age defines the developmental function of that characteristic. The heavy solid line in Figure 1 is an example of a developmental function. It is the group average at various ages, where the group can be a species, a subgroup within a population, or even an individual. Therefore, one can have a developmental function for an entire species, for particular groups (e.g., boys versus girls, treated versus untreated groups) and for individuals. Basically, interventionists have been interested in developmental func-

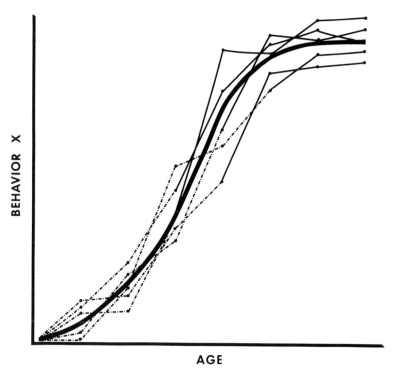

Figure 1.   Hypothetical plot of the development of a behavior X for five subjects, illustrating the developmental function (heavier line) and the stability or lack of stability of individual differences (thinner lines). (From McCall, R. B., Eichorn, D. H., & Hogarty, P. S. [1977]. Transitions in early mental development. *Monographs of the Society for Research in Child Development,* 42 [Serial No. 171], p. 1; reprinted with permission.)

tions; in other words, can an intervention program alter the form of a developmental function for a specific group of children? Piaget, for example, was primarily interested in the developmental function of the human species.

Developmental functions—whether for species, groups, or individuals—are either *continuous* or *discontinuous* (Emmerich, 1964). A developmental function is continuous when changes in it are quantitative rather than qualitative. That is, the fundamental nature of an attribute remains the same over age, but its magnitude increases or decreases. A plot of height over age would be continuous because the fundamental character of these variables is essentially the same at every age. In contrast, a plot of Piagetian sensorimotor development would be discontinuous because its specific behavioral character is different from one stage to the next. Naturally, whether a developmental function is continuous or discontinuous de-

pends partly on how it is measured. Functionally, mental age as measured by an IQ test is continuous, whereas the sequence of Piaget's stages (1952), as measured by appropriate instruments, is discontinuous. Generally speaking, intervention programs have attempted to create changes in a continuously measured variable (e.g., IQ).

Individual Differences   The developmental realm of individual differences typically involves the assessment of the relative consistency of individual differences in a single characteristic over different ages. That is, do individuals maintain the same relative rank ordering within their group at two or more ages, or does the relative rank ordering change from one age to the next?

If individual differences are relatively consistent across age, they are said to be *stable*. If not, they are *not stable*. In Figure 1, the thin lines represent individual subjects. Where the lines are dashed, individual differences are not stable; where they are solid, individual differences are more stable.

The Distinction and Its Implications

Developmental functions refer to group averages and are usually evaluated with statistics that assess the significance of the difference between means. In contrast, individual differences are typically within-group characteristics that are statistically assessed by correlations across age or between variables. In the case of symmetrical distributions, the correlation between two variables is independent of the means of those distributions. Therefore, in principle, the form of a developmental function, or whether it is continuous or discontinuous, does not necessarily say anything about whether individual differences in that attribute are stable or not stable.

This distinction says that information provided in one of these realms does not necessarily provide information about the other realm. It is the failure to appreciate this potential independence that has gotten us into trouble interpreting data in the past. For example, the evidence that individual differences in tested intelligence are not very stable during the early years but become more stable at approximately age 6, says potentially nothing about the possible effectiveness of an intervention program at age 3 or at age 9. More specifically, one often hears that one half of a child's intelligence is established by age 4 (Bloom, 1964). This conclusion was based on the statistical fact that the correlation between IQ at 4 years and at 17 years is approximately .71, which, when squared, is 50%. But this claim for the development of intelligence in general is based solely on the stability of individual differences. It completely ignores that the average child's mental age (i.e., the developmental function) in some sense will increase more than four times during this interval.

Similarly, the study of behavioral genetics is based exclusively on individual differences, yet conclusions are frequently drawn about intelligence in general. The only way to assess the heritability of the species-general developmental function of human intelligence is to use a random sample of animal species. Estimates are that 99% of our genetic material produces species-general characteristics, traits that make humans similar to one another but different from the insects (King & Wilson, 1975; Washburn, 1978). Stated extremely, behavior geneticists may be studying the effects of only 1% of our genetic material, and those effects potentially tell us nothing about how the human species develops intellectually. Given that, however, most people are far more interested in how individuals differ from one another than how man differs intellectually from the apes or the earthworms. The point, however, is that estimates of heritability of intelligence apply to the factors that create individual differences in the sample selected for study, and do not necessarily have implications for the potential of the entire group or species to be improved.

For example, a perfectly heritable trait may be changed by environmental means, and such environmental alterations may even change the heritability from being perfect to being nearly 0. For example, years ago, the disease TB was highly heritable, because the bacillus was endemic and nearly everyone was exposed to it. Therefore, the individual who succumbed had an inherited biological disposition for the disease. With improved hygiene and a better standard of living, the bacillus disappeared from all but the most dismal environments. TB became far less heritable, because one's environment was the greater determinant of whether one came down with the disease. TB, of course, is caused in the same way now as then. Similarly, even though intelligence may be highly heritable, that fact alone does not guarantee that it is immutable. What high heritability does suggest is that *differences in current environments* do not seem to be associated as strongly as differences in genetic circumstances with individual differences in intelligence. But the environment that *everyone* experiences or new environments could have substantial influence on a trait, even though the heritability of that trait is very high.

Similarly, the typical lack of stability of individual differences during the first few years of life may not signal that intelligence is very plastic during this period. Or, just the opposite might be true. For example, everyone might develop essentially the same way according to nature's plan and individual differences might be temporary and inconsequential. Conversely, when individual differences do become stable, that fact alone does not necessarily imply that intelligence is fixed and impervious to change.

It should be noted that individual differences and developmental functions are *potentially* independent; actually they may not be so independent in nature. For example, the discontinuities in Piaget's (1952) theory of sensorimotor development may or may not be accompanied by nodes of instability in individual differences, but at least some data suggest that they are (McCall, 1979; McCall, Eichorn, & Hogarty, 1977). The point is that information in one realm does not necessarily specify information in the other, and associations between realms are empirical issues.

A Broader Perspective

What is needed is a broader perspective—a way of thinking about early mental development that recognizes the distinction between realms, but incorporates both realms into its structure. I have offered one such attempt (McCall, 1981b), which I will describe briefly. This is a way of thinking about mental development and not a formal model to be analyzed and tested.

Canalization   The concept of canalization, described originally by Waddington (1957), and applied to mental development by Scarr-Salapatek (1976), implies a species-typical path, called a *creod,* along which nearly all members of a species tend to develop as long as species-typical, appropriate environments predominate. When such environments exist, development proceeds "normally." Further, there is a strong self-righting tendency in which deviations from the creod are quickly forced back on track. But, when typical environments do not prevail, development can go awry and the self-righting tendency may not be sufficient

to get the organism back on track. Therefore, development that is highly canalized has a wide range of environments that are "typical," the creod is well-defined, and the self-righting tendency is strong and swift. Less canalized characteristics have fewer typical environments, the creod is less well-defined, and there is less self-righting tendency.

Canalization is a crucial concept because it involves both developmental function and individual differences. That is, the creod is a developmental function whereas deviations from the creod represent individual differences. Highly canalized development has a specific developmental function and, because of the strong self-righting tendency, individual differences are not stable.

The Approach   My way of thinking about early mental development can be stated quite simply: Early mental development is highly canalized but becomes less so with age. As such, the developmental function early in life is closely governed by biology, and individual differences are relatively unstable because of the strong, self-righting tendency. As mental development becomes less canalized, roughly between 2 and 6 years of age, the variation in developmental function that can occur in the species increases (e.g., variations in the quantity and quality of intelligence increase), individual differences become more stable over time, and both genetic and environmental correlations increase.

Implications   This approach deals with a number of the thesis-antithesis issues described thus far and has some interesting implications.

First, the proposition that early mental development (e.g., during the first 18 months of life) is highly canalized solves the apparent contradiction between one's intuition that early development must be highly governed by biology and genetics, and the empirical observation that the heritability of early mental development is relatively low (McCall, 1979). Nature does exert strong control over the developmental function; nearly all infants develop the same skills in roughly the same sequence, at roughly the same ages. However, because of the strong, self-righting tendency, individual differences are short-lived (e.g., not stable), and therefore heritabilities, which are based on individual differences, are not substantial.

A second implication is that a self-righting tendency provides blessed forgiveness for those infants who do experience an atypical, deleterious environment early in life. In many cases, if such an infant is restored to species-typical environments, the infant self-rights and recovers from the early apparent deficit.

A third implication is that the skills that are developed during this period are so basic to the functioning and survival of the organism that individual differences may not be very important. For example, the figure-ground distinction emerges, but no one talks about whether one infant has more of this characteristic than another.

A fourth implication of a highly canalized notion of early mental development is that it perplexes researchers. If Piaget is correct in suggesting that the fundamental nature of early mental development is discontinuous, and if early mental development is highly canalized, producing unstable individual differences, then what is a researcher to study if the object of inquiry is both discontinuous and unstable? One describes and perhaps explains the nature of the discontinuity and the instability.

At approximately 18-24 months, canalization begins to weaken. This means that the self-righting tendency slackens, and the number of different creods considered species-typical increases. As a result, individual differences, be they associated with genetic circumstances or environmental ones, become more diverse and more stable. It is in this sense that both environmental and genetic correlates of individual differences increase simultaneously, while nature's hold on a single specific creod decreases.

One implication of this notion is that earlier may not be better as far as intervention is concerned. The optimum time may be that point in development when nature releases its grip on the developmental function and, at the same time, the accumulation of environmental and genetic circumstances has not set the organism off on a path that developmental inertia makes impervious to change. Unfortunately, the age at which this occurs is not known, but it could be approximately age 4, which certainly does not correspond with the notion that earlier is better, but is the approximate age at which many intervention programs have been implemented.

Another implication is that if the fundamental nature of the developmental function is discontinuous, then different skills are acquired at different ages, perhaps as Piaget (1952) proposed. If true, intervention should also be discontinuous, and the appropriate age for one qualitative intervention will be different than for another qualitative intervention. In short, interventions must be matched (Hunt, 1961) with the particular qualitative stage of development. In addition, skills now emerge that do have individual differences, and some individuals reach levels of attainment that others do not (e.g., all children acquire the basic skill of language, but some develop greater fluency than others).

A further implication is that intervention programs may have greater effects on certain kinds of individual differences than on others. For example, individual differences in the age of stage entrance (e.g., rate of development) may be less susceptible to environmental intervention than is the breadth of application of skills typically acquired during a specific stage (e.g., environment may broaden Piaget's horizontal decalage, rather than increase the rate of development).

This approach also suggests that plasticity and change are not impossible, even after the early-childhood period. Whereas it does not deny the possibility that certain well-timed early experiences are more influential than those same events experienced later, intervention in childhood and adolescence may nevertheless be effective. The degree of effectiveness may depend on the extent of developmental inertia set in motion by previous experiences and genetic circumstances, as well as the extent of the match between the intervention and the child's dispositions at the time. This implication will be taken up later when I discuss nonshared, intrafamilial environmental effects.

Perhaps the most important general implication is that factors that influence the developmental function may be different from the factors that influence individual differences. This is especially clear early in infancy when biological heritage closely governs the developmental function, but apparently influences individual differences far less. Similarly, factors that contribute to the developmental function may or may not produce individual differences. Furthermore, from a developmental standpoint, the kind of intervention program required to bring the IQs of disadvantaged children up to an average level (e.g., approximately 100) may be different from the kind of intervention required to raise IQ much beyond 100.

FUTURE DIRECTIONS

Two camps of researchers were described at the beginning of the chapter: the interventionists and those who study the naturalistic development of intelligence. What lies ahead for the interventionists? After 2 decades of intense effort, the next step will probably be to promote specific skills, with interventions matched to the stage of development and the particular skills and interests of the child. Unfortunately, the same fate of enrichment research in animals may befall such study with humans; basically, it died out after the massive-enrichment phase, and few studies were conducted on the specific elements of the enrichment experience. Some ''stimulation'' is ''more equal'' than others, and we need to know what aspects of the massive-enrichment experience are indeed enriching, when that is the case, and for whom.

Research on the naturalistic course of general mental development has hinted at moving toward studying changes in mental performance and the endogenous and environmental factors associated with those changes. I turn to elements of those topics now.

Brain Growth Periodization

Although Piaget (1952) postulated a set of stage transitions that extended into adolescence, the quantitative and qualitative nature of the developmental function for general mental performance has not often been investigated (McCall, 1979; McCall, Appelbaum, & Hogarty, 1973; McCall et al., 1977). Recently, Epstein (1974a, 1974b, 1976, 1978; Epstein & Toepfer, 1978) has suggested that the developmental function for intelligence changes quantitatively in spurts, rather than smoothly, and that such spurts are the result of periodic accelerations in the growth of the brain. Specifically, Epstein proposes that peaks occur in brain growth primarily at 3–10 months; and at 2–4, 6–8, 10–12, or 13, and 14–16 or 17 years of age (Epstein, 1978), and that such spurts in brain growth produce spurts in general mental growth.

Epstein draws several implications from his theory. For example, he suggests that intensive intellectual input should be timed to occur during the periods of rapid intellectual growth (Epstein, 1976). Specifically, Head Start has not been effective because it typically occurs at age 5, which is a period of slow growth, according to his theory. Similarly, the tortuous and unproductive junior high school years also occur during a period of slow brain growth (Epstein, 1978).

The theory has received considerable attention, especially by educators, some of whom have changed curricula to coincide with the hypothesized brain-based periods of accelerated and decelerated learning potential (e.g., Epstein & Toepfer, 1978). Moreover, some have suggested that this theory may rival in importance the discovery of DNA (Toepfer, 1979), and that it could virtually eliminate school failure (Hart, 1981). The appeal to practitioners of a biologically based theory of the developmental function should not be underestimated.

In support of his theory, Epstein (1974a) reviews studies purporting to show that the spurts in both brain size and mental performance are much more likely to occur during specified age periods than between them. The apparent consistency of these several diverse studies with Epstein's theoretical propositions is astounding.

I have recently reevaluated the data Epstein uses as evidence for his theory and do not find such compelling support (McCall, 1985). Neither do Marsh (1985), McQueen (1982), and Hutson (1982a, 1982b). Moreover, in the only study of which I am aware that was specifically directed at testing Epstein's theory, clear support was not found. Specifically, only a few of the hypothesized peaks in mental or brain growth (as indicated by head circumference, a measure of brain size apparently accepted by Epstein) were validated. Further, there was no relationship whatsoever between pattern of head growth and pattern of mental growth, a relationship that had not been tested previously in the same group of subjects and which is crucial to Epstein's theory (McCall, Meyers, Hartman, & Roche, 1983). Therefore, although it is undoubtedly appropriate to match environmental intervention to the particular stages and skills of children, brain growth periodization in this form does not appear to provide a sound basis for such matching.

Discontinuous, Nonshared, Within-Family Environmental Effects on Intelligence

The most frequently mentioned factors in the development of intelligence might include parental encouragement for achievement, exposure to intellectual models, and encouragement to rely on language. They are, in short, aspects of the upper middle-class environment. Indeed, many enrichment programs sought to provide such an environment to disadvantaged children, and many observational studies measure such variables as potential correlates of intellectual growth and achievement. These factors are typically cited as the characteristics that distinguish one family from another, and are presumably responsible for differences in the intelligence of children between families. One would expect, then, that such characteristics would be relatively constant over time and shared by all children within a family. In short, they are between-family, continuous, shared environmental factors.

They are not the only kind of environmental factors. For example, one can have within-family, nonshared, discontinuous environmen-

tal factors. Such factors might include sibling interactions, differential treatment of siblings by parents, birth order and spacing, cohort differences, illness and separation, and the influence of nonfamily members on specific children (e.g., peers, teachers). In addition, environmental events may impinge on all family members but influence individual family members differently and at different ages (e.g., divorce, relocation, death of a relative). Such factors are rarely studied, and certainly not incorporated into intervention programs. However, recent research (e.g., McCall, 1983; Rowe & Plomin, 1981) is consistent with the proposition that 25% of all variation in IQ and half of the environmental variation in IQ may be associated with these within-family, nonshared, discontinuous events. Such factors may be even more influential in personality development (Scarr & Kidd, 1983). This suggests that environmentalists have investigated only one class of environmental factors and have ignored another class that may compose one half of the environmental influences on intelligence.

For example, changes in IQ within individuals, over time, are fairly substantial—averaging 28.5 IQ points by one estimate (McCall, et al., 1973)—and siblings do not have the same pattern of IQ change even when their curves are adjusted to correspond in secular time but not in chronological age (McCall, 1970, 1972). Therefore, whatever is producing these changes appears to transpire within families, not to be shared by siblings within a family, and to occur at one point versus another in development (McCall, 1983).

The only factor of this kind that has received much attention recently is the effect of the birth of a sibling—an event that is obviously not shared by siblings, that occurs within families, and that is discontinuous. The confluence model (Berbaum & Moreland, 1980; Zajonc, 1976; Zajonc & Markus, 1975; Zajonc, Markus, & Markus, 1979) proposes that the birth of a sibling dilutes the intellectual atmosphere of the home at least until the newborn becomes old enough to contribute to that intellectual environment. The result, the confluence model contends, is a decline in the mental performance of the older children in the family. The full confluence model is substantially more complicated than this and is highly controversial. However, in one recent study (McCall, 1984), which was a direct test of this fundamental proposition, the birth of a sibling was found to be associated with a drop of 10 IQ points for the older child during the next 2 years relative to singleton children, and 5.8 IQ points relative to last-born children from families of comparable size. These differences were present but no longer significant at 17 years of age. These results illustrate the possible contribution of at least one within-family, nonshared, discontinuous environmental factor to developmental changes in general mental performance. Many more should be investigated.

CONCLUSION

The era of intervention research has been partly successful in improving the mental performance of disadvantaged children, and it has also suggested some new directions. Among those directions is the need to have conceptual schemes that consider both the developmental function and individual differences in the same structure and to recognize their potential independence. Further, environmentalists have largely ignored the possible contribution of nonshared, within-family, discontinuous environmental factors in mental performance, and recent research suggests that such factors may account for half of all environmental variance.

REFERENCES

Berbaum, M. L., & Moreland, R. L. (1980). Intellectual development within the family: A new application of the confluence model. *Developmental Psychology, 16,* 506–515.

Bloom, B. S. (1964). *Stability and change in human characteristics.* New York: John Wiley & Sons.

Bronfenbrenner, U. (1974). Developmental research, public policy, and the ecology of childhood. *Child Development, 45,* 1–5.

Cronbach, L. J. (1957). The two disciplines of scientific psychology. *American Psychologist, 12,* 671–684.

Emmerich, W. (1964). Continuity and stability in early social development. *Child Development, 35,* 311–332.

Epstein, H. T. (1974a). Phrenoblysis: Special brain and mind growth periods. II. Human mental development. *Developmental Psychobiology, 7,* 217–224.

Epstein, H. T. (1974b). Phrenoblysis: Special brain and mind growth periods. I. Human brain and skull development. *Developmental Psychobiology, 7,* 207–216.

Epstein, H. T. (1976). A biologically-based framework for intervention projects. *Mental Retardation, 14,* 26–27.

Epstein, H. T. (1978). Growth spurts during brain development: Implications for educational policy and practice. In J. S. Chall & A. F. Mikky (Eds.), *Education and the brain: The seventy-seventh yearbook of the National Society for the Study of Education, part II.* (pp. 343–370). Chicago: University of Chicago Press.

Epstein, H. T., & Toepfer, C. F., Jr. (1978). A neuroscience basis for reorganizing middle grades education. *Educational Leadership, 35,* 656–660.

Fagan, J. F., III, & Singer, L. T. (1983). Infant recognition memory as a measure of intelligence. In L. P. Lipsitt & C. K. Rovee-Collier (Eds.), *Advances in infancy research* (Vol. 2, pp. 31–79). Norwood, NJ: ABLEX.

Hart, L. A. (1981). Brain language and new concepts of learning. *Educational Leadership, 38,* 443–445.

Honzik, M. P. (1957). Developmental studies of parent-child resemblance in intelligence. *Child Development, 28,* 215–228.

Hunt, J. McV. (1961). *Intelligence and experience.* New York: Ronald Press.

Hunt, J. McV. (1963). Motivation inherent in information processing and action. In O. J. Harvey (Ed.), *Motivation and social interaction.* New York: Ronald Press.

Hutson, B. A. (1982a, May). Brain-based curricula: Proceed with caution. *Iowa Educational Research & Evaluation Association,* 9–12.

Hutson, B. A. (1982b). Brain-based curricula: Salvation or snake oil? *Midwestern Educational Researcher, 3,* 1–33.

King, M. C., & Wilson, A. C. (1975). Evolution at two levels in humans and chimpanzees. *Science, 188,* 107–116.

Lazar, I., Darlington, R., et al. (1982). Lasting effects of early education: A report from The Consortium for Longitudinal Studies. *Monographs of the Society for Research in Child Development, 47* (No. 195).

Marsh, R. W. (1985). Phrenoblysis: Real or chimera? *Child Development, 56,* 1059–1061.

McCall, R. B. (1970). IQ pattern over age: Comparisons among siblings and parent-child pairs. *Science, 170,* 644–648.

McCall, R. B. (1972). Similarity in developmental profile among related pairs of human infants. *Science, 178,* 1004–1005.

McCall, R. B. (1979). The development of intellectual functioning in infancy and the prediction of later IQ. In J. D. Osofsky (Ed.), *Handbook of infant development* (pp. 707–741). New York: John Wiley & Sons.

McCall, R. B. (1981a). Early predictors of later IQ: The search continues. *Intelligence, 5,* 141–147.

McCall, R. B. (1981b). Nature-nurture and the two realms of development: A proposed integration with respect to mental development. *Child Development, 52,* 1–12.

McCall, R. B. (1983). Environmental effects on intelligence: The forgotten realm of discontinuous nonshared within-family factors. *Child Development, 54,* 408–415.

McCall, R. B. (1984). Developmental changes in mental performance: The effect of the birth of a sibling. *Child Development, 55,* 1317–1321.

McCall, R. B. (1985). Growth periodization in mental test performance. Unpublished manuscript.

McCall, R. B., Appelbaum, M., & Hogarty, P. S. (1973). Developmental changes in mental performance. *Monographs of the Society for Research in Child Development, 38* (No. 150).

McCall, R. B., Eichorn, D. H., & Hogarty, P. S. (1977). Transitions in early mental development. *Monographs of the Society for Research in Child Development, 42* (No. 171).

McCall, R. B., Meyers, E. D., Jr., Hartman, J., & Roche, A. F. (1983). Developmental changes in head-circumference and mental-performance growth rates: A test of Epstein's phrenoblysis hypothesis. *Developmental Psychobiology, 16,* 457–468.

McQueen, R. (1982). *Brain growth periodization: Analysis of the Epstein spurt-plateau findings.* Unpublished paper. Moltromah County Educational Service District Education Association, Portland, OR.

Piaget, J. (1952). *The origins of intelligence in children* (M. Cook, Trans.). New York: International Universities Press.

Rowe, D. C., & Plomin, R. (1981). The importance of non-shared (E₁) environmental influences in behavioral development. *Developmental Psychology, 17,* 517–531.

Scarr, S., & Kidd, K. K. (1983). Developmental behavioral genetics. In M. M. Haith & J. J. Campos (Eds.), *Handbook of child psychology, Vol II: Infancy and developmental psychobiology* (pp. 345–434). New York: John Wiley & Sons.

Scarr-Salapatek, S. (1976). An evolutionary perspective on infant intelligence: Species patterns and individual variations. In M. Lewis (Ed.), *Origins of intelligence* (pp. 165–197). New York: Plenum.

Toepfer, C. F. (1979). Brain growth periodization—A new dogma for education. *Middle School Journal, 10,* 3, 20.

Waddington, C. H. (1957). *The strategy of the genes.* London: Allen & Son.

Washburn, S. L. (1978). Human behavior and the behavior of other animals. *American Psychologist, 33,* 405–418.

Zajonc, R. B. (1976). Family configuration and intelligence, *Science, 192,* 227–236.

Zajonc, R. B., & Markus, G. B. (1975). Birth order and intellectual development. *Psychological Review, 82,* 74–88.

Zajonc, R. B., Markus, H., & Markus, G. B. (1979). The birth order puzzle. *Journal of Personality and Social Psychology, 37,* 1325–1341.

Chapter 4

Animal Models and Plasticity

Victor H. Denenberg

Those researchers who dare to ask serious questions about developmental processes of human beings are confronted with several major dilemmas: the inability to control the environmental context in which their subjects live, the inability to assign individuals randomly to groups, the inability to follow their subjects into adulthood, the inability to intervene physiologically, and the inability to carry out postmortem studies. With such severe limitations on research design, the substantial body of information on human developmental processes is quite impressive.

Fortunately, researchers working with animals are not confronted with these same restrictions, and it is to this group that we turn for fundamental knowledge and theory concerning the concept of plasticity. However, if the information and concepts derived from animal studies are to be useful to those working with humans, it is necessary that those doing human research and those studying animals have an interactive dialogue with each other. Both groups share a common interest in trying to understand how development proceeds, yet each group has its own methodology and body of data. Therefore, by comparing and discussing their findings and ideas, both sets of researchers have the opportunity to extend and enrich their own and their colleagues' depth of knowledge (Denenberg, 1969a).

In this chapter I present a short selective review of studies showing plasticity of the developing nervous system for both behavioral and biological processes. This is followed by comments and speculations on the implications of these findings.

SOME BASIC PRINCIPLES IN ANIMAL RESEARCH

Before reviewing the findings, it may be helpful to describe briefly some of the guiding principles involved in animal research. One critical question revolves around the choice of species. Many factors are considered in deciding upon a species to study. For example, invertebrate species offer the convenience of having simpler nervous systems, so that correlations with behavior may be more easily charted (Fentress, 1976; Kandel, 1974). As another example, there is an enormous literature on the genetics of the fruit fly, and thus this becomes an important animal for those interested in the genetics of behavior (Hirsch, 1963, 1967).

Most researchers studying brain-behavior processes work with vertebrates. The species most often studied include rats, mice, birds, cats, dogs, and nonhuman primates. Thus, it can be seen that mammals are strongly favored over other vertebrates. A major reason for this choice is the reasonable assumption that it is easier to generalize to the human from another mammal, than from species more remote.

Even within these constraints there is a wide variety of choices. One consideration is the specific question under investigation. Thus, if a researcher is interested in the study of human-like communication, it makes more sense to select a higher order, nonhuman primate than a rodent. However, if one is interested in the study of developmental processes, then it is preferable to select a species that matures rapidly and has a short life span. Rats and mice are particularly useful because they become sexually mature by 3 months of age, are easily bred, and have a brief gestation period of about 3 weeks.

A second factor is cost and space. Rodents are inexpensive to house, give birth to 8–16 young, and one female can produce a large number of viable litters. Fruit flies occupy much less space and are much more fecund. In contrast, dogs and nonhuman primates require very large facilities, and the cost of feeding and caring for these species is considerable.

A third reason involves the amount of information available. There is probably more known about the biology and behavior of the laboratory rat than of any other species extant. Thus, this is the favored animal among most researchers.

A fourth factor is that some animals have specialized characteristics that make them eminently suitable for particular studies. Thus, The Jackson Laboratory in Bar Harbor, Maine specializes in producing genetically inbred mice with different forms of neurological or immunological disturbances. These animals, then, become very useful tools for those researchers interested in these specific disease processes.

The final point to note is that, even within a species, there may be rather large variability among strains with respect to the phenomenon under investigation. Thus, different strains of rats or mice, tested under identical conditions, may not yield the same pattern of results. The three most common reasons for these differences are: 1) genetic differences among the strains, 2) differences in the physical and social environment within which the animals were raised, and 3) some interactive combination of conditions 1 and 2. Thus, what appears to be a discrepancy in results when different strains are studied, is actually important information to the researcher indicating that other variables are influencing the phenomenon under investigation. Such findings when pursued, may lead to further insights and understanding concerning the mechanisms and determinants affecting the process being studied.

These principles and restrictions should be kept in mind as we review studies showing

behavioral and neural plasticity in developing organisms.

ANIMAL STUDIES

The field of early experience research has firmly documented that exposing animals to different social or physical events in early life results in major changes in their adult behavior and biology, and, indeed, these effects can be carried over and will affect subsequent generations.

Cross-Species Interaction

One set of studies clearly showing the power of the maternal variable involved cross-species fostering. The rat and mouse are different species, yet there is sufficient similarity in their behavioral patterns and biology that a lactating rat mother is able to raise a newborn mouse pup in a fully adequate fashion (Denenberg, Hudgens, & Zarrow, 1964). In some designs, a complete litter of mice was raised by a foster rat mother, whereas in others, mice were raised by a foster rat mother who was also nursing some of her own offspring. Two different mouse strains were used, thus allowing us to get a rough estimate of genetic-environmental interaction. After weaning, the mice were reared in standard laboratory mouse boxes with other mice. When adult, they were given various behavioral tests.

The C57BL/10 mouse was one of the strains studied. This strain of mouse is an aggressive animal; we were interested in determining whether the experience of being reared with a rat mother would affect this behavior. The results were dramatic: 46% of mice raised by mouse mothers fought when placed into a standardized fighting situation, whereas only 4% of mice reared by rat mothers fought in similar circumstances.

With a finding as startling as this, one immediately becomes worried about artifacts. The obvious artifact in this situation is that the young mice were suckling from a rat mother whose nutritional supply differed from that of a mouse mother. We resolved that problem by the following experiment.

It is known that a virgin rat exposed to newborn pups will quickly become maternal toward those pups and will engage in all of the usual maternal behavior patterns, including retrieving, grooming, and nest building (Rosenblatt, 1967). However, a virgin animal is not capable of lactating. Our procedure, then, was to place a sensitized virgin rat (called an *aunt*) in with a litter of mouse pups and the mouse mother. In this situation, the mouse mother was the source of milk whereas the virgin rat acted as the major caregiver including retrieving, nest building, and grooming. (Indeed, the rat was often seen retrieving the mouse mother as well as the pups.) The key variable has been reduced to that of the behavior pattern of the virgin rat, because the milk is now supplied by the mouse mother. Eleven percent of the mice reared in the presence of rat aunts fight, which is very similar to the 4% figure obtained when mice are reared by rat mothers, thereby establishing that it is the behavior pattern of the maternal caregiver toward the young that critically determines their subsequent propensity to fight (Paschke, Denenberg, & Zarrow, 1971).

In another study we asked the question: Are these animals capable of fighting, or has this behavior dropped out of their response repertoire? We placed rat-reared animals together with aggressive males, and observed the behavior of the fosterlings. Their initial response to an attack was to turn and flee. However, if they were continually pursued and attacked, they turned and fought back. Therefore, we know that the behavior pattern is still present, but has been reduced in rank in the animal's response hierarchy.

A general principle about any biological variable, including plasticity, is that there are limits to it. One limit is set by genetic-environmental interactions. When we repeated these same studies using a different mouse strain (the Swiss Albino), we were not able to reduce aggression at all (Paschke et al., 1971). However, we did find with the Swiss Albino that the experience of being reared with the rat mother or the rat aunt modified the mouse's adrenocortical response. Mice reared with virgin rats had a lesser steroid response than control animals (Denenberg, Rosenberg, Paschke, Hess, et al., 1968; Denenberg, Rosenberg, Paschke, & Zarrow, 1969; Denenberg, Rosenberg, & Zarrow, 1969). This finding shows that the fostering procedure can affect biological variables as well as behavioral ones. In these studies the variable affected was strain-dependent. We have also found that open-field activity is consistently decreased in both mouse strains when a rat mother or a sensitized virgin rat is present during the preweaning interval (Denenberg, 1970).

The final study in this series has to do with a different kind of socialization. In this experiment, we placed weanling mice and rats together in the same cage. Thus we have peer-group interaction rather than mother-young interaction. They remained in these cages for approximately 5 weeks and were then separated. The rats were placed back into a standard rat colony where they lived until adulthood. At that time they, and appropriate controls, were exposed to mice. It is known that rats are muricidal (i.e., are mouse killers) and this is what we found with our controls. In this experiment, 45% of control rats killed the mice to which they were exposed. In contrast, none of the rats that had been reared with mice in early life harmed any of their compatriots (Denenberg, Paschke, & Zarrow, 1968).

In summary, we see from these experiments that modifying the caregiver or one's social mates in early life can have major effects upon behavior patterns that have ethological validity, and on biological patterns that have survival value.

Infantile Stimulation

Giving newborn rodents extra stimulation results in major changes in behavioral and biological processes in adulthood (Denenberg, 1969c, 1975, 1977). The rat is generally used in these experiments. Pregnant animals are checked every day until the litter is born (Day 0). On Day 1 the litter is sexed and culled to 8 pups. At this point the litter is randomly assigned to the control condition or to extra stimulation. *Handling* is the most commonly used procedure for giving pups extra stimulation. This consists of removing the newborn pups from the maternity cage, leaving the mother in the cage, and placing each pup individually into a can containing shavings. The pups remain in these containers for 3 minutes and are then returned to the maternity cage. This procedure is continued from Day 1 through Day 20 of life. The litter is weaned at Day 21. In contrast, the pups in control litters are returned to their maternity cage on Day 1 and are not disturbed thereafter until weaning at Day 21.

This procedure, which appears to be rather innocuous, has pervasive, long-term effects. Animals that have received handling stimulation in infancy, in comparison to controls, are sexually precocious (Morton, Denenberg, & Zarrow, 1963), weigh more in adulthood (Denenberg & Karas, 1959, 1961), are less emotional as measured by activity and defecation in an open field (Denenberg, 1969b; Levine, Haltmeyer, Karas, & Denenberg, 1967), learn better in an avoidance conditioning task (Levine, 1956), are more exploratory and stimulus seeking (DeNelsky & Denenberg, 1967a, 1967b), and have a lesser corticoid response to a novel stimulus (Levine, et al., 1967), but a greater adrenal response to a distinctly noxious stimulus (Haltmeyer, Denenberg, & Zarrow, 1967). Handled animals also have a more lateralized brain than do nonhandled controls. That topic will be discussed in a subsequent section of this paper.

Handling exerts its effects through both physiological and social mechanisms. Physiologically, the handling procedure causes a significant increase in plasma corticosterone in the pups, as a consequence of their being cooled when removed from the nest (Denenberg, Brumaghim, Haltmeyer, & Zarrow, 1967; Schaefer, Weingarten, & Towne, 1962). Socially, the interactions between the mother and her pups are changed when the pups are handled (Denenberg, 1977; Russell, 1971). These changes in the internal chemical environment and the external social environment are the likely causes of the multiple effects of handling.

Postweaning Stimulation

The best way to demonstrate behavioral and brain plasticity after weaning is by use of an enriched environment. This consists of a large enclosure containing toys, ramps, and other playthings. Usually 12 newly weaned rats are placed into the unit (food and water are always available) and stay there for a month or longer. As compared to controls, animals reared in enriched environments were better at problem solving and perceptual tasks; analyses of their brains revealed that enrichment resulted in a greater weight of cerebral cortex, a greater thickness of cortex, and greater total activity of the enzyme, acetylcholinesterase (Hebb, 1949; Krech, Rosenzweig, & Bennett, 1962; Rosenzweig, 1971; Rosenzweig, Bennett, & Diamond, 1972).

Intergenerational Effects

The procedures summarized thus far show that one can manipulate the physical environment (via enrichment), the pups themselves (via handling), or the maternal figure (via cross-species fostering), and obtain long-term consequences. Since handling changes adult behavior and physiology, and since pups are modified by maternal behavior patterns, this suggests that the offspring of handled females may differ from the offspring of nonhandled controls. There are several possible routes by which such changes could occur. Since the female's biology is changed by early stimulation, the interaction between the mother's physiological status and that of the developing embryo-fetus would differ from controls. After birth, the behavior patterns of the two groups of mothers would be expected to differ, and there might also be differences in the milk of the two groups.

The hypothesis that experiences that females receive in infancy will affect the behavior of their offspring was investigated by Denenberg and Whimbey (1963). Handled and nonhandled females either reared their own young from birth to weaning, or else the young were cross-fostered, both within and between handled and nonhandled groups. After weaning, the rats were reared under the same conditions until they were 50 days old, at which point they were given the open-field test. The prenatal natural mother and the postnatal foster mother jointly affected open-field activity scores. The highest score was obtained by the group born of a nonhandled mother and reared by a handled foster mother.

Having found maternal effects, this research was extended yet another generation to investigate grandmaternal factors (Denenberg & Rosenberg, 1967). The initial group of females (the grandmothers) were handled or not handled in infancy. When adult, they were mated and were placed either into maternity cages or enriched environments. The animals born in these units ultimately became the mothers of our experimental subjects. When weaned, the female pups were placed into standard laboratory cages or into enriched environments where they remained until 50 days. At that time, all animals were placed into laboratory cages where they stayed until mature, at which point they were mated. All females gave birth to their offspring (the subjects of the study) in standard maternity cages. At weaning, these pups (who were the grandchildren of the original handled and nonhandled mothers of the study) were tested in the open field. The important finding was that the grandmother-handling variable interacted both with the maternal-preweaning-housing variable and the maternal-postweaning-housing variable to influence their grandpups' open-field behavior.

Early Experiences and Brain Laterality

More recently we have been investigating the effect of early stimulation upon brain laterality in the rat. Handling is always one of the early experience variables. At times postweaning enrichment has been used as well. For purposes of this chapter only the effects of handling will be discussed.

Our general procedure is to take 4 male littermates and subject them to one of four surgical treatments: a right neocortical ablation (i.e., the right cortex was removed), a left neocortical ablation, sham surgery, or no operation. We have never found a difference between the sham-operated and the control animals, and their data have always been pooled. After recovering from surgery, these animals have been given behavioral tests and the pattern of means reveals whether there is any lateralization and, if so, the nature of that lateralization.

The hypothesis we were testing in our first set of studies is that the effects of early experiences are asymmetrically distributed between the two hemispheres of the brain. Several of the key findings are summarized in Table 1.

In order to show that the brain is lateralized, it is necessary that the group with only an intact right hemisphere differ significantly from the group with only an intact left hemisphere. If this is found, then by comparing the means of those two groups to that of the control group, it is possible to make inferences concerning the underlying brain dynamics (Denenberg, 1980, 1981). The first variable listed in Table 1 is open-field behavior. The animals not receiving stimulation in infancy show no evidence of laterality. The two lesion groups have similar means, and both are significantly more active than the control group. In contrast, there is a significant lateralization effect for animals handled in infancy. Those with an intact left hemisphere (i.e., with a right neocortical lesion) were significantly more active than those with a lesion in the opposite hemisphere (Denenberg, Garbanati, Sherman, Yutzey, & Kaplan, 1978).

Open-field activity has been shown to measure two behavioral dimensions, exploration and emotionality (Whimbey & Denenberg, 1967a, 1967b). To determine whether spatial processes were involved in the lateralized, open-field differences found by Denenberg et al. (1978), we conducted an experiment of a somewhat different nature (Sherman, Garbanati, Rosen, Yutzey, & Denenberg, 1980). To test an animal in the open field, the animal is placed into a corner square and a barrier is placed in front of him to prevent his leaving that square. At the end of 10 seconds, the barrier is removed and the animal is free to leave.

Table 1. Summary of experimental findings relating early experiences and brain laterality

Dependent variable[*]	Treatment in infancy	Intact controls	Right hemisphere intact	Left hemisphere intact
Open-field activity	Nonhandled	8.90[a]	27.64	22.33
	Handled	12.51	17.91	36.27[a]
Right-left directionality	Nonhandled	.0305	−1.0268[b]	.5082[b]
	Handled	−.3862[c]	−0.7389	.3300
Taste aversion	Nonhandled	23.9	23.7	23.8
	Handled	28.7[d]	21.7[d]	25.6[d]
Muricide	Nonhandled	96.0[a]	75.0	68.8
	Handled	78.0	94.6[a]	67.6

[*]Measurement units: activity—number of squares entered; directionality—see text; taste aversion—ml of milk ingested; muricide—percentage of animals that killed.
[a]Differs significantly from other values in that row.
[b]Differ from each other.
[c]Differs significantly from zero.
[d]All differences are significant.

In such a situation, the animal will almost inevitably move along one of the two walls and will rarely move directly into the center of the field. Therefore, we recorded whether an animal moved along the left wall or the right wall, upon leaving the square. This was done over 4 successive days, and a laterality index was devised such that negative scores indicated the animal was moving along the left wall, positive scores that he was moving along the right wall, and scores around 0 indicated the animal had equal right and left references.

The second set of data in Table 1 shows that both nonhandled and handled animals are lateralized. For the nonhandled group, those with an intact right hemisphere were more biased to move leftward, when compared to animals with an intact left hemisphere, who typically moved rightward. In contrast, animals with a fully intact brain showed no evidence of laterality. When the left-right choice behavior of the handled animals is examined, it is seen that those with an intact brain have a leftward-going bias. Even though the two lesion groups under these circumstances do not differ significantly, note that there is a greater magnitude of response for those with a left lesion to go leftward as compared to those with a right lesion to go rightward. The patterns from both groups are consistent in showing that if a spatial bias occurs, it is a leftward bias. The effects of handling are to make this bias overt in the intact brain group.

The experiment just described showed that an aspect of exploratory behavior—namely, spatial choice—is lateralized. The second dimension measured by open-field performance is emotionality. We first investigated that by looking at a taste aversion paradigm (Denenberg et al., 1980). In this procedure, animals were given a novel, pleasant-tasting substance (in this instance, sweetened milk), immediately followed by an injection of lithium chloride, which causes a massive gastric upset. Under such conditions, rats are known to avoid the pleasant-tasting substance when exposed to it subsequently, though they will gradually begin to contact and ingest it over repeated trials. The question here was whether this behavior was lateralized to one of the two hemispheres. Table 1 shows that the amount of sweetened milk ingested by nonhandled animals does not differ as a function of brain lesion, whereas all groups differ significantly from each other if they had been handled in infancy. The group that consumed the least of the sweetened milk, and therefore the group with the greatest fear, were the animals that had only an intact right hemisphere, followed by those with only an intact left hemisphere, whereas those with a fully intact brain consumed the greatest amount of the sweetened milk.

The taste-aversion experiment indicated that emotional behaviors were lateralized. This experiment, however, used a learned fear response, whereas the prior experiments involving open-field activity and left-right spatial choice used spontaneously occurring behaviors. Therefore, we decided to select a different measure of emotionality, one that occurs spontaneously. This is muricide (Garbanati et al., 1983). Table 1 indicates that there is no evidence of lateralization for mouse killing among nonhandled animals, although the lesion reduced the incidence of killing for both groups. In contrast, those animals who were handled in infancy showed definite evidence of lateralization: Rats with an intact right hemisphere were more likely to kill mice than those with an intact left hemisphere.

The most general statement that can be made about the data in Table 1 is that the brain of the rat is lateralized, and that spatial and emotional behaviors are primarily to be found in the right hemisphere. What is fascinating about this set of findings is that this parallels what we know about the human brain, where spatial processes and strong emotional behaviors are primarily in the right hemisphere (Gainotti, 1972; Geschwind, 1979). The second general statement to be made is that there is some evidence that the rat's brain is lateralized independent of experience. The right-left directionality data are the basis for this conclusion. The third generality is that early stimulation induces brain lateralization, where it does not otherwise occur. This indicates that brain plasticity, as well as behavioral plasticity, is affected by early experiences, a finding that has been well documented in the literature for many years (e.g., Wiesel & Hubel, 1965).

Finally, the pattern of findings indicates that emotional behaviors are under the control of the right hemisphere, whereas the left hemisphere acts in an inhibitory capacity to reduce the level of emotional reactivity (Denenberg, 1980, 1981, 1984). This again appears to be congruent with what we know about the human brain.

How Does Early Experience Affect Brain Laterality?

The answer to this question is not known as yet, but Denenberg (1981) has hypothesized that the corpus callosum plays a major role in mediating the effects of early experiences on brain laterality. The basis for this thesis is as follows.

First, the corpus callosum is a late-maturing organ with myelination occurring postnatally in the rat (Seggie & Berry, 1972) and the human (Yakovlov & Lecours, 1967, as cited in Davidson, 1978). Thus, it is amenable to the effects of early postnatal stimulation and becomes a prime candidate for mediating the effects of hemispheric specialization.

The relationship between the corpus callosum and hemispheric specialization can be inferred from clinical cases in the human literature involving the condition of agenesis. This is a situation in which the person is born without a corpus callosum. A number of these individuals have been given a battery of tests that are known to reveal impairments in split-brain patients (these patients have had the corpus callosum surgically severed so that severe epileptic seizures would not spread from one hemisphere to the other). The surprising finding is that the agenesis patient does not show any impairment on this test series (Saul & Gott, 1973; Saul & Sperry, 1968). The conclusion from these studies was that the agenesis patient has language represention in each hemisphere and this was what enabled these individuals to perform adequately on the neuropsychology test battery.

Much of the material on agenesis has been recently reviewed (Jeeves, 1979; Milner & Jeeves, 1979). Milner and Jeeves concluded that those with agenesis can read verbal material via either hemisphere, they can identify tactile objects placed in either hand, and their auditory perception for stimuli presented to the left ear equals that of normal persons.

The important point of these findings is that the lack of a corpus callosum appears to result in hemispheres that are redundant rather than specialized (i.e., lateralized), thus arguing that it is presence of the corpus callosum that allows specialization to occur. Denenberg (1981) has hypothesized that competition between the hemispheres, mediated via the corpus callosum, brings about hemispheric specialization.

This hypothesis is concerned with the corpus callosum as the key link in determining brain laterality, but does not deal with the effects of early experience. Thus, it is necessary to propose a second hypothesis: "Stimulation in early life acts to enhance the growth and development of the corpus callosum, just as stimulation of sensory systems leads to their growth and development" (Denenberg, 1981, p. 20). The rationale for this hypothesis comes from the general finding that sensory systems that lack adequate and appropriate stimulation during early development will almost certainly be defective later on. Restrictions in visual stimulation (Wiesel & Hubel, 1965; von Senden, 1960), tactile and proprioceptive stimulation (Nissen, Chow, & Semmes, 1951), or general sensory stimulation (Melzack & Scott, 1957) in early life have been found to cause lasting sensory and perceptual defects. In the context of early experience research, the function of handling in infancy and postweaning environmental enrichment is to provide additional stimulation that will act to enhance the growth and development of the central nervous system, including the corpus callosum.

If the second hypothesis is correct, then one would predict that rats handled in infancy, since their brains are more lateralized, would have a larger corpus callosum than nonhandled animals. This prediction has been confirmed (Berrebi et al., 1985). Berrebi et al. found that adult male rats that had been handled in infancy had a larger cross-sectional area when measured from a central slice of the corpus callosum, as compared to control males. However, this difference was not found with females. Instead, females were found to have a smaller corpus callosum than males, even after adjusting for differences in brain weight between the sexes. The latter finding is interesting because there have been reports that the corpus cal-

losum of the human female is larger than that of the male (de Lacoste-Utamsing & Holloway, 1982; Baack, de Lacoste-Utamsing, & Woodward, 1982), though others have not been able to confirm this report (Demeter, Ringo, & Doty, 1985). If the human findings of a sex difference are confirmed, it becomes of interest to determine where, along the phylogenetic tree, the switch in callosal size occurs, and to try to determine the reasons behind this reversal.

COMMENTS AND SPECULATIONS

It is obviously not possible to take specific procedures and examples from animal studies and translate them directly to human applied situations. However, it is quite apparent that the principles extracted from animal studies are, in most likelihood, also going to be applicable to the human situation.

The rat's brain is much less complex than the human's, yet many researchers have been able to demonstrate that varying social and physical stimuli during the infantile and postweaning periods will readily bring about marked changes in behavior patterns, neuroanatomy, brain lateralization, and brain chemistry. In principle, therefore, one would expect even more powerful and more subtle effects with the human, whose brain is vastly more complicated than that of the rat, and who lives in a much more complex social and environmental milieu. The many findings reported elsewhere in this book, documenting the plasticity of the human infant and child, amply support this general principle.

One major finding from the animal studies is that experience between birth and weaning almost inevitably will affect physiological and behavioral processes involved with affective-emotional characteristics. It is only after weaning that there are major changes brought about in cognitive processes. This suggests that one should consider whether, with humans, it is appropriate to begin manipulating environmental events in the youngest age period to try to influence learning and other cognitive processes. It may well be better to focus on affective behaviors and delay cognitive training until a somewhat later age. With respect to a reference point, Landauer and Whiting (1964) indicate that on a cross-cultural basis, the average age of weaning is two years. That may be worthy of consideration with respect to cognitive intervention programs.

A second major finding from the animal studies is unequivocal evidence of plasticity of the developing nervous system. The social and physical environments in which animals are reared will have a major impact upon the organization of the brain and expression of behavioral processes. Such findings contradict the simple assumption that neural and behavioral processes in animals are governed almost entirely by genetic factors, and that the human is the only species capable of extensive modification of behavior through experience. Genes do not exist in a vacuum, and experiences do not occur in the abstract. Genes can only act when present in a living body, which is continually being modified by its interactive experiences with its internal and external environment. Genes and experience are not separate and independent entities. Neither can exit without the other, and both require living tissue as the milieu for their interactive expression.

There is recent research with humans suggesting that learning difficulties may be associated with immune problems (Geschwind & Behan, 1982, 1984). This opens up a totally new area, which has been called psychoneuroimmunology (Ader, 1981), and suggests that immunological difficulties in early life, or in utero, may have major impact upon subsequent behavioral processes. More recent research indicates that the nervous system may also be affected by immunological processes, and that may be the manner by which the immune determinants affect behavior (Galaburda, Sherman, Rosen, Aboitiz, & Geschwind, 1985; Sherman, Galaburda, & Geschwind, 1983).

Evidence supporting this position has been reported by Geschwind and Behan (1982, 1984) who compared 500 strongly lefthanded persons to 900 strongly righthanded persons. The lefthanders were 10 times as likely to have learning difficulties as the righthanders, and they were 2.5 times as likely to have immune diseases. The lefthanded group also had a greater incidence of migraine headaches, allergies, dyslexia, stuttering, skeletal malformations, and thyroid disorders. These disorders are much more likely to affect males than females. Geschwind and Behan have theorized that some male fetuses either produce too much testosterone *in utero* or else they are highly susceptible to the effects of testosterone. They further hypothesize that the testosterone acts: 1) upon the left hemisphere to slow its rate of growth and development, thus resulting in an increase in lefthandedness and a concomitant increase in language-related problems, and 2) upon the thymus gland, thus increasing the probability of immune disorders. In a major set of papers Geschwind and Galaburda (1985a, 1985b, 1985c) have reviewed the literature on the topics of sex hormones, immune disorders, and neurological diseases as they are related to the issue of brain lateralization, and have presented a broad theoretical perspective on this vast field.

It is evident that to further the depth of our understanding of these serious issues, it remains a necessity that those doing animal studies and those doing human developmental studies maintain a strong interchange for the benefit of all concerned.

Finally, the animal research indicates that strong emotional behaviors are part of the biologic given of an organism, and that they are under the control of an inhibitory process from the left hemisphere. This inhibitory process is the neural analogue of the ''thin veneer of civilization,'' and it behooves us to develop ways to enhance these inhibitory processes in order to maximize opportunities for survival.

SUMMARY AND CONCLUSIONS

The principles involved in behavioral and neural plasticity can best be investigated by conducting experimental studies on infant animals, following them into adulthood, and studying their behavioral repertoire and brain organization. Such studies reveal that adult performance is complexly determined. Some of the critical variables are genetics, maternal behavior, the nature of the physical environment within which the young are reared, the variability and degree of stimulation impinging upon the infant, the kinds of social interactions experienced (over and above that from the mother), and the timing of these events during the course of development. Although each of these classes of variables can separately affect brain and behavioral processes, when they are studied in combination, they are found to interact with each other. Because of this interaction, one must be cautious in trying to draw cause-effect conclusions relating events in infancy to later behavioral outcomes. Indeed, it is questionable whether such models contribute much to our understanding of the processes involved in development.

Recent research was reviewed showing that brain lateralization and behavioral asymmetry are malleable processes affected by the animals's early experiences. Other research found strong associations between the immune system, the nervous system, and behavioral dysfunctions. Theory and data suggest that these associations start in fetal life and affect the entire developmental process.

In order to advance our understanding of behavioral and brain development, it is necessary that those doing experimental studies with animals, those investigating human development, and those working with human clinical cases find ways to maintain contact and to exchange information with each other. The conference on Malleability of Children, which was the basis for this book, is one example of an effective way to achieve this objective.

REFERENCES

Ader, R. (Ed.) (1981). *Psychoneuroimmunology*. New York: Academic Press.

Baack, J., de Lacoste-Utamsing, C., & Woodward, D. J. (1982). Sexual dimorphism in human fetal corpora callosa. *Society for Neuroscience Abstracts, 8*, 213.

Berrebi, A. S., Ralphe, D., Denenberg, J., Friedrich, V. L., Yutzey, D. A., & Denenberg, V. H. (1985). Sexual dimorphism in the corpus callosum of rats. *International Society for Developmental Psychobiology Abstracts*.

Davidson, R. J. (1978). Lateral specialization in the human brain: Speculations concerning its origin and development. *Behavioral and Brain Sciences, 1*, 291.

de Lacoste-Utamsing, C., & Holloway, R. L. (1982). Sexual dimorphism in the human corpus callosum. *Science, 216*, 1431–1432.

Demeter, S., Ringo, J., & Doty, R. W. (1985). Sexual dimorphism in the human corpus callosum. *Society for Neuroscience Abstracts, 11*, 868.

DeNelsky, G. Y., & Denenberg, V. H. (1967a). Infantile stimulation and adult exploratory behavior: Effects of handling upon tactile variation seeking. *Journal of Comparative and Physiological Psychology, 63*, 309–312.

DeNelsky, G. Y., & Denenberg, V. H. (1967b). Infantile stimulation and adult exploratory behaviour in the rat: Effects of handling upon visual variation seeking. *Animal Behaviour, 15*, 568–573.

Denenberg, V. H. (1969a). Animal studies of early experience: Some principles which have implications for human development. In J. Hill (Ed.), *Minnesota symposium on child psychology* (pp. 31–45). Minneapolis: University of Minnesota Press.

Denenberg, V. H. (1969b). Open-field behavior in the rat: What does it mean? *Annals of the New York Academy of Sciences, 159*, 852–859.

Denenberg, V. H. (1969c). The effects of early experiences. In E. S. E. Hafez (Ed.), *Behaviour of domestic animals* (pp. 95–130). London: Bailliere.

Denenberg, V. H. (1970). The mother as a motivator. In W. J. Arnold & M. M. Page (Eds.), *Nebraska symposium on motivation, 1970* (pp. 69–93). Lincoln: University of Nebraska Press.

Denenberg, V. H. (1975). Effects of exposure to stressors in early life upon later behavioural and biological processes. In L. Levi (Ed.), *Society, stress, and disease: Childhood and adolescence* (pp. 269–281). New York: Oxford University Press.

Denenberg, V. H. (1977). Assessing the effects of early experience. In R. D. Myers (Ed.), *Methods in psychobiology* (Vol. 3, pp. 127–147). New York: Academic Press.

Denenberg, V. H. (1980). General systems theory, brain organization, and early experiences. *American Journal of Physiology, Regulatory, Integrative, and Comparative Physiology, 238*, R3–R13.

Denenberg, V. H. (1981). Hemispheric laterality in animals and the effects of early experience. *Behavioral and Brain Sciences, 4*, 1–49.

Denenberg, V. H. (1984). Behavioral asymmetry. In N. Geschwind & A. M. Galaburda (Eds.), *Cerebral dominance: The biological foundations* (pp. 114–133). Cambridge, MA: Harvard University Press.

Denenberg, V. H., Bruhaghim, J. T., Haltmeyer, G. C., & Zarrow, M. X. (1967). Increased adrenocortical activity in the neonatal rat following handling. *Endocrinology, 81*, 1047–1052.

Denenberg, V. H., Garbanati, J., Sherman, G., Yutzey, D. A., & Kaplan, R. (1978). Infantile stimulation induces brain laterality in rats. *Science, 201*, 1150–1151.

Denenberg, V. H., Hofmann, M., Garbanati, J., Sherman, G. F., Rosen, G. D., & Yutzey, D. A. (1980). Handling in infancy, taste aversion, and brain laterality in rats. *Brain Research, 20,* 123–133.

Denenberg, V. H., Hudgens, G. A., & Zarrow, M. X. (1964). Mice reared with rats: Modification of behavior by early experience with another species. *Science, 143,* 380–381.

Denenberg, V. H., & Karas, G. G. (1959). Effects of differential infantile handling upon weight gain and mortality in the rat and mouse. *Science, 130,* 629–630.

Denenberg, V. H., & Karas, G. G. (1961). The interactive effects of infantile and adult experiences upon weight gain and mortality in the rat. *Journal of Comparative and Physiological Psychology, 54,* 685–689.

Denenberg, V. H., Paschke, R. E., & Zarrow, M. X. (1968). Killing of mice by rats prevented by early interaction between the two species. *Psychonomic Science, 11,* 39.

Denenberg, V. H., & Rosenberg, K. M. (1967). Nongenetic transmission of information. *Nature, 216,* 549–550.

Denenberg, V. H., Rosenberg, K. M., Paschke, R. E., Hess, J. L., Zarrow, M. X., & Levine, S. (1968). Plasma corticosterone levels as a function of cross-species fostering and species differences. *Endocrinology, 83,* 900–902.

Denenberg, V. H., Rosenberg, K. M., Paschke, R. E., & Zarrow, M. X. (1969). Mice reared with rat aunts: Effects on plasma corticosterone and open-field activity. *Nature, 221,* 73–74.

Denenberg, V. H., Rosenberg, K. M., & Zarrow, M. X. (1969). Mice reared with rat aunts: Effects in adulthood upon plasma corticosterone and open-field activity. *Physiology and Behavior, 4,* 705–707.

Denenberg, V. H., & Whimbey, A. E. (1963). Behavior of adult rats is modified by the experiences their mothers had as infants. *Science, 142,* 1192–1193.

Fentress, J. C. (Ed.) (1976). *Simpler networks and behavior.* Sunderland, MA: Sinauer Associates.

Gainotti, G. (1972). Emotional behavior and hemispheric side of the lesion. *Cortex, 8,* 41–55.

Galaburda, A. M., Sherman, G. F., Rosen, G. D., Aboitiz, F., & Geschwind, N. (1985). Developmental dyslexia: Four consecutive cases with cortical anomalies. *Annals of Neurology, 18,* 222–233.

Garbanati, J. A., Sherman, G. F., Rosen, G. D., Hofmann, M., Yutzey, D. A., & Denenberg, V. H. (1983). Handling in infancy, brain laterality and muricide in rats. *Behavioral Brain Research, 7,* 351–359.

Geschwind, N. (1979). Specialization of the human brain. *Scientific American, 241,* 180–199.

Geschwind, N., & Behan, P. (1982). Left-handedness: Association with immune disease, migraine, and developmental learning disorders. *Proceedings of the National Academy of Sciences, USA, 79,* 5097–5100.

Geschwind, N., & Behan, P. (1984). Laterality, hormones, and immunity. In N. Geschwind & A. M. Galaburda (Eds.), *Cerebral dominance: The biological foundations.* (pp. 211–224). Cambridge, MA: Harvard University Press.

Geschwind, N., & Galaburda, A. M. (1985a). Cerebral lateralization. Biological mechanisms, associations, and pathology: I. A hypothesis and a program for research. *Archives of Neurology, 42,* 428–459.

Geschwind, N., & Galaburda, A. M. (1985b). Cerebral lateralization. Biological mechanisms, associations, and pathology: II. A hypothesis and a program for research. *Archives of Neurology, 42,* 521–552.

Geschwind, N., & Galaburda, A. M. (1985c). Cerebral lateralization. Biological mechanisms, associations, and pathology: III. A hypothesis and a program for research. *Archives of Neurology, 42,* 634–654.

Haltmeyer, G. C., Denenberg, V. H., & Zarrow, M. X. (1967). Modification of the plasma corticosterone response as a function of infantile stimulation and electric shock parameters. *Physiology and Behavior, 2,* 61–63.

Hebb, D. O. (1949). *The organization of behavior.* New York: John Wiley & Sons.

Hirsch, J. (1963). Behavior genetics and individuality understood. *Science, 142,* 1436–1442.

Hirsch, J. (1967). *Behavior-genetic analysis.* New York: McGraw-Hill.

Jeeves, M. A. (1979). Some limits to interhemispheric integration in cases of callosal agenesis and partial commissurotomy. In I. S. Russell, M. W. van Hof, & G. Berlucchi (Eds.), *Structure and function of cerebral commissures* (pp. 449–474). London: MacMillan.

Kandel, E. R. (1974). An invertebrate system for the cellular analysis of simple behaviors and their modification. In F. O. Schmitt & F. G. Worden (Eds.), *The Neurosciences: Third study program* (pp. 347–370). Cambridge, MA: MIT Press.

Krech, D., Rosenzweig, M. R., & Bennett, E. L. (1962). Relations between brain chemistry and problem-solving among rats raised in enriched or impoverished environments. *Journal of Comparative and Physiological Psychology, 55,* 801–807.

Landauer, T. K., & Whiting, J. W. (1964). Infantile stimulation and adult stature of human males. *American Anthropologist, 66,* 1007–1028.

Levine, S. (1956). A further study of infantile handling and adult avoidance learning. *Journal of Personality, 25,* 70–80.

Levine, S., Haltmeyer, G. C., Karas, G. G., & Denenberg, V. H. (1967). Physiological and behavioral effects of infantile stimulation. *Physiology and Behavior, 2,* 55–59.

Melzack, R., & Scott, T. H. (1957). The effects of early experience on the response to pain. *Journal of Comparative and Physiological Psychology, 50,* 155–161.

Milner, A. D., & Jeeves, M. A. (1979). A review of behavioural studies of agenesis of the corpus callosum. In I. S. Russell, M. W. van Hof, & G. Berlucchi (Eds.), *Structure and function of cerebral commissures* (pp. 428–448). London: MacMillan.

Morton, J. R. C., Denenberg, V. H., & Zarrow, M. X. (1963). Modification of sexual development through stimulation in infancy. *Endocrinology, 72,* 439–442.

Nissen, H. W., Chow, K. L., & Semmes, J. (1951). Effects of restricted opportunity for tactual, kinesthetic, and manipulative experience on the behavior of a chimpanzee. *American Journal of Psychology, 64,* 485–507.

Paschke, R. E., Denenberg, V. H., & Zarrow, M. X. (1971). Mice reared with rats: An interstrain comparison of mother and "aunt" effects. *Behaviour, 38,* 317–331.

Rosenblatt, J. (1967). Non-hormonal basis of maternal behavior in the rat. *Science, 156,* 1512–1514.

Rosenzweig, M. R. (1971). Effects of environment on development of brain and behavior. In E. Tobach, L. R. Aronson, & E. Shaw (Eds.), *The biopsychology of development* (pp. 303–342). New York: Academic Press.

Rosenzweig, M. R., Bennett, E. L., & Diamond, M. C. (1972). Brain changes in response to experience. *Scientific American, 226,* 22–29.

Russell, P. A. (1971). "Infantile stimulation" in rodents: A consideration of possible mechanisms. *Psychological Bulletin, 73,* 192–202.

Saul, R. E., & Gott, P. S. (1973). Compensatory mechanisms in agenesis of the corpus callosum. *Neurology, 23,* 443.

Saul, R. E., & Sperry, R. W. (1968). Absence of commissurotomy symptoms with agenesis of the corpus callosum. *Neurology, 18,* 307.

Schaefer, T., Weingarten, F. S., & Towne, J. C. (1962). Temperature change: The basic variable in the early handling phenomenon? *Science, 135,* 41–42.

Seggie, J., & Berry, M. (1972). Ontogeny of interhemispheric evoked potentials in the rat: Significance of myelination of the corpus callosum. *Experimental Neurology, 35,* 215–232.

Sherman, G. F., Galaburda, A. M., & Geschwind, N. (1983). Ectopic neurones in the brain of the autoimmune mouse: A neuropathological model of dyslexia? *Society of Neuroscience Abstracts, 9,* 939.

Sherman, G. F., Garbanati, J. A., Rosen, G. D., Hofmann, H., Yutzey, D. A., & Denenberg, V. H. (1983). Lateralization of spatial preference in the female rat. *Life Sciences, 33,* 189–193.

von Senden, M. (1960). *Space and sight.* Glencoe, IL: Free Press.

Whimbey, A. E., & Denenberg, V. H. (1967a). Experimental programming of life histories: The factor structure underlying experimentally created individual differences. *Behaviour, 29,* 296–314.

Whimbey, A. E., & Denenberg, V. H. (1967b). Two independent behavioral dimensions in open-field performance. *Journal of Comparative and Physiological Psychology, 63,* 500–504.

Wiesel, T. N., & Hubel, D. H. (1965). Extent of recovery from the effects of visual deprivation in kittens. *Journal of Neurophysiology, 28,* 1060–1072.

Yakovlov, P. I., & Lecours, A. (1967). The myelogenetic cycles of regional maturation of the brain. In A. Minkowski (Ed.), *Regional development of the brain in early life.* London: Blackwell.

SECTION II

EARLY EXPERIENCE AND PLASTICITY

Chapter 5

Self-Regulation of Stimulation by Prematures with a Breathing Blue Bear

Evelyn B. Thoman

This report describes a procedure aimed at improving the quality of life for the youngest infants—those born prematurely. The most important underlying premise for this work is that these infants have complex characteristics of humanness that have not heretofore been given serious consideration.

The earliest postnatal environment provided for premature infants has long been a matter for great concern. Medical advances are permitting survival of ever smaller babies, yet we still know relatively little about the optimal conditions for facilitating their intellectual and emotional development. While the isolette in the neonatal intensive care unit serves to maintain controlled, pathogen-free conditions, it has been described as being *overstimulating,* because of the continuous bright lights, sounds of the isolette motor, and nursery noises; and as being *stimulus-depriving,* because of the constancy of these conditions (Denenberg, 1977; Korner, 1979). Though it is now generally agreed that conditions provided in a neonatal intensive care unit (NICU) play a role in the later developmental difficulties of these infants, there is not agreement on how these conditions can or should be modified.

The seriousness of this issue is highlighted

by growing evidence for long-lasting, developmental sequelae of premature birth (e.g., Bennett, Robinson, & Sells, 1983; Hunt, Tooley, & Harvin, 1982; Knobloch, Malone, Ellison, Stevens, & Zdeb, 1982; Mayes, Kirk, Haywood, Buchanan, Hedvall, & Stahlman, 1985), including greater risk of social problems (Klaus & Kennell, 1982). Improved medical care has apparently affected mortality rates more than morbidity (Davis, 1985). Among the smallest and youngest premature infants (those weighing less than 1,000 grams or less than 30 weeks at birth), the survival rates improve dramatically with increasing weight or age, but the morbidity risk of the survivors remains constant (Horwood, Boyle, Torrence, & Sinclair, 1982; Siegel, 1983; Yu, Orgill, Bajuk & Astbury, 1984).

Despite the statistical evidence for negative sequelae for these small infants, not all show developmental handicaps. The range of outcomes is from severe dysfunction to superior capabilities among individuals (Thoman, 1986). Even more striking is that it is not possible to predict outcome except in cases of severe neurological damage (Cohen & Parmelee, 1983; Hunt, 1981; Mayes, Kirk, Haywood, Buchanan, Hedvall, & Stahlman, 1985). There

This research was supported, in part, by the Crump Institute of Medical Engineering, University of California, Los Angeles, and by Grant No. MH41244, from the National Institute of Mental Health Center for Prevention Research, Division of Prevention and Special Mental Health Programs.

I thank James Garbanati and Lauri Loring, of the Crump Institute of Medical Engineering, for their assistance and valuable suggestions.

simply is not a one-to-one relationship between degree of pre- and perinatal stress and later functional status among prematurely born individuals. Infant outcome is the result of complex interactions of the stress of early birth and other medical complications and a multitude of other factors, including medical care, the physical environment, the infant's genetic background, and the social environment (Murphy, Nichter, & Liden, 1982). In fact, investigators have found that the social environment is a better predictor of infant outcome than perinatal problems (Caputo, Goldstein, & Taub, 1981; Sameroff, 1981; Sameroff & Chandler, 1975). This finding applies to infants where damage to neural circuitry is not extreme, as is the case for the larger number of premature infants. Thus, for most premature infants, environmental circumstances from the earliest days of life can serve to exacerbate or to counteract the effects of early neural trauma (Gorski, 1983).

Such a generalization about the significance of the NICU environment reflects findings from developmental studies of premature infants as well as the growing literature from neuroanatomical studies demonstrating functional plasticity of the immature central nervous system (Schneider, 1979; Thoman, 1982). Premature birth is inevitably a source of central nervous system (CNS) insult. The nature of neural reorganization following such early trauma is a function of the extent and timing (gestational age at birth) of damage to the CNS in interaction with the infant's subsequent experience. Clearly, following premature birth and the attendant perinatal and early postnatal medical complications, there is an urgent need for an environment designed to facilitate development of central integrative controls of adaptive behaviors.

This need is recognized to be of special importance given the unavoidable stresses from medical interventions that are requisite to assure the survival of premature infants. In attempts to make this environment a more optimal one, varied forms of supplemental stimulation have been provided for infants during the preterm period. Rhythmic and nonrhythmic forms of stimulation have been used to provide sensory experience in the auditory (Barnard & Bee, 1983; Burns & Hatcher, 1984; Kramer & Pierpoint; 1976), tactile (Rausch, 1981), vestibular (Neal, 1967; Barnard, 1972; Korner, Schneider, & Forrest, 1983), and visual modalities, given singly or in combination. A more detailed review of intervention research for prematures and the mixed findings effected by the varied environmental manipulations will be given in a later section of this chapter. The guiding premise for most stimulation studies has been that premature birth deprives the infant of specific forms of stimulation that would be available in utero; and the stimulating conditions are designed to compensate for this deprivation, at least in part. However, the nature of stimulation that may be optimal for the infant is still a matter for speculation.

In this chapter, we present a different perspective on providing stimulation for prematurely born infants, one that is based on different premises about the nature of the premature infant.

First, we assume that the premature infant is more than an externalized fetus with the same needs as a fetal organism. With the event of birth, and the associated transformation of cardiopulmonary processes and other biological functions necessary for survival as an autonomous, self-regulating organism, the needs of the premature differ dramatically from those of the fetus. Second, we do not view the prematurely born infant as a passive organism, in need only of having something done *to* him or her. Rather, like the infant born at term, the premature baby is viewed as a competent individual capable of interacting with the environment and thus participating actively in the events that may affect the infant's own developmental processes. It follows from this assumption that the infant's behavior can provide clues to the biological relevance of environmental manipulations.

This view of the baby leads us to postulate that searching for the *best form* of stimulation for premature babies may be an adequate strategy for finding optimal conditions for facilitating their development. It is very clear that a

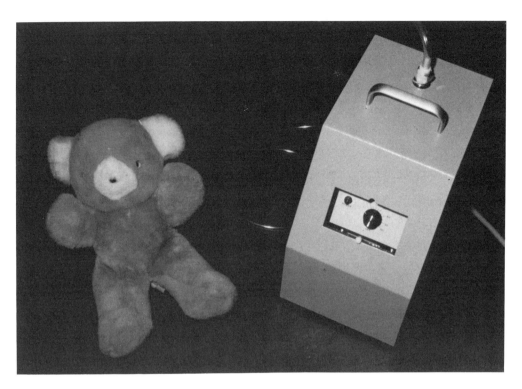

Figure 1.   Breathing Blue Bear with pump.

much more complex approach to the problem of enhancing the environmental circumstances of the premature infant is needed. Accordingly, we propose that premature infants are more competent than previous research indicates, even during the preterm period, and that an opportunity for an interactional experience with the environment may be a critical element for a supportive environment to provide. We suggest that the premature infant is capable of actively seeking sensory stimulation, and the experience of being an active self-regulator of sensory stimulation, rather than a passive recipient, will better facilitate the premature infant's recovery and developmental processes.

The notion of the value of self-regulation of stimulation is not a novel idea. Benson and Uzgiris (1985) found positive effects on performance of self-initiated search activity in 11-month-old infants, in comparison with infants who were passively transported. And, a recent animal study (Porrino et al., 1984) demonstrates that special patterns of glucose utiliza-

tion in the brain are induced as a function of self-stimulation in contrast to effects of stimulation that is passively received.

Consistent with these notions, we have devised a means of making stimulation *available* to preterm infants without *imposing* the stimulation on them. The procedure consists of providing a "companion" for the infant—a stuffed bear placed in the isolette with him or her. The life-like characteristic of the bear is that it "breathes," because it is connected via a plastic hose to a pump outside the crib. The Bear and its pump are shown in Figure 1, and the Bear inside an isolette with a baby is shown in Figure 2.

The presence of the Breathing Bear, which is conceptualized as part of an environmental enrichment procedure rather than a stimulation device, is unique in several ways: 1) the Bear's breathing provides rhythmic stimulation, and the rate of the rhythm is based on a biological rhythm of *infants*, not mothers (or an arbitrary model); 2) the rhythm is individualized for

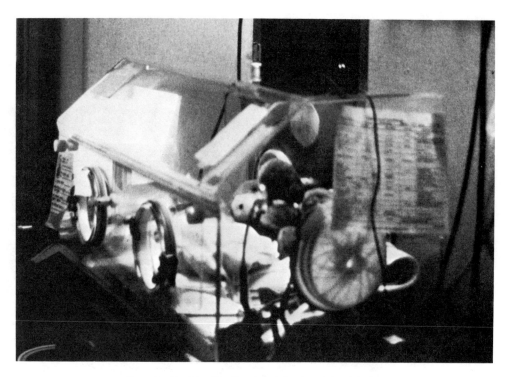

Figure 2.   Breathing Blue Bear in isolette of premature infant.

each infant—the rate of the Bear's breathing is set to match that of the infant during Quiet (Non-REM) Sleep; and 3) the stimulation is *optional* for the infant—each infant regulates the amount and temporal distribution of stimulation received.

The sections that follow describe the animal and human research studies that have provided the rationale for the breathing bear as a device that permits an interactive experience for premature infants, and then discusses the basis for considering the Breathing Bear as a biologically relevant source of stimulation for premature infants.

The conditions provided by the Breathing Bear permit us to a) assess the competence of premature infants to express a stimulus choice; b) assess their performance with respect to modality of stimulation, and intensity and rate of rhythms; and c) assess the consequences of an interactive experience. The results of our first study with these objectives is described. Finally, the implications of this approach for manipulating environmental conditions for

high-risk infants is discussed in relation to the issue of plasticity of the central nervous system.

THE ISSUE
OF STIMULUS DEPRIVATION
OF THE PREMATURE INFANT

Five to seven percent of all newborn infants (more than 150,000 babies) are born prematurely (Goldberg & DiVitto, 1983). Numerous studies have shown these infants to be at greater risk than full-term infants for developmental and social problems (Bennett, Robinson, & Sells, 1983; Hunt, Tooley, & Harvin, 1982; Kitchen et al., 1982; Rothberg et al., 1983; Saigal, Rosenbaum, Stoskopf, & Milner, 1982), including child abuse (Hunter, Kilstrom, Kraybill, & Loda, 1978; Klein & Stern, 1971). Related to these problems are findings that these infants exhibit less social responsiveness (Als & Brazelton, 1981; Als, Tronick, Adamson, & Brazelton, 1976; Barnard, Bee, & Hammond, 1984; Crnic, Rago-zin, Greenberg, Robinson, & Basham, 1983; Field, 1977, 1981); they pay less attention to facial patterns (Field, 1979a; Sigman & Par-melee, 1974), and their state patterns are less appealing to adults (Reich, Maier, Klein, & Gyurke, 1984). In turn, parents of these and other high-risk infants display less holding and less affectionate attention (Bakeman & Brown, 1980; DiVitto & Goldberg, 1979; Field, 1979b; Barnard & Blackburn, 1981).

These commonalities in developmental handicaps are present despite the diversity of prenatal, perinatal, and early postnatal risk fac-tors to which prematures are exposed, and the diversity of home environments in which they are subsequently cared for. It can be argued that a convergence of handicaps derives from some common experiences, and that the major ones are deprivation of the supportive environ-ment found *in utero,* and early postnatal care in an NICU isolette.

In utero the organism is influenced by the mother's physiology, which was shaped by the evolutionary process, to assure the survival and well-being of the fetus. These conditions con-trast with those provided by an isolette, where stimulation is often unmodulated and interrup-tions are primarily for the purpose of medical intervention (e.g., heel sticks for blood sam-ples, removal and replacement of electrodes, injections) and thus are most often stressful. Gorski (1983) has outlined some strategies for improving the care for these infants, including avoidance of repeated, stressful medical inter-ventions. However, the isolette itself can be considered an environment of stimulus excess, because of continuous light and continuous sound (over 80 dB in many instances) from the temperature control mechanism. It can also be considered an environment of deprivation, be-cause there is a deficit of nonstressful dynamic stimulation. Thus, the infant is exposed to the extremes of stimulus excesses and, at the same time, serious forms of stimulus deprivations. The excesses due to medical care are essen-tially unavoidable. However, some excesses, deprivations, and inappropriate forms of stim-ulation in the physical environment and care of

these infants are potentially capable of being remedied.

SENSITIVITY OF THE PREMATURE INFANT

The nature of the deprivation, or, from a positive perspective, the nature of the changes in the isolette environment that would more nearly meet the needs of the premature infant, remains to be determined. Clearly, an under-standing of the infant's needs rests on an under-standing of the infant. Recent research has only begun to provide clues on this issue. A serious consideration on the excess side of designing stimulus conditions for premature infants is that it is not difficult to overstimulate them. They are far less efficient at shutting out intru-sive stimuli than are full-term babies (Field, 1979b; Rose, Schmidt, & Bridger, 1976), and their mechanisms for coping with stress are not well developed. Thus, prematures will decom-pensate physiologically following seemingly mild forms of stimulation (Affonso, 1976; Clark & Affonso, 1976; Sehring, Gorski, Sweet, Martin, & Leonard, 1985). Since rou-tine care of premature infants involves many overwhelmingly stressful events as medical re-quirements, any added stimulation must not increase this load of overstimulation. Over-stimulation is readily identifiable from subtle biobehavioral indicators, such as hiccups, vomiting, change in skin color (reddening, be-coming pale, or mottled), marked change in respiration rate, or occurrence of apneic epi-sodes. Other indicators are not so subtle, such as turning blue, heart rate deceleration, and showing prolonged apneic episodes. Attention to the more subtle clues can permit the timing or modulation of interventions to avoid the more serious stress responses.

These considerations make it clear that ap-propriate stimulation for premature infants in-volves more than merely providing supplemen-tal environmental input. Stimulation that is too intense, too complex, or inappropriately de-signed or timed in relation to the maturity or physiological status, or even the state of the infant, can be as harmful as a lack of stimulation (Blackburn, 1983).

COMPETENCE OF
THE PREMATURE INFANT

Whereas a vast literature has evolved describing the capabilities of the full-term infant, very little attention has been given to the competence of the preterm infant. Hack, Mostow, and Miranda (1976) report evidence for attentiveness in infants as early as 31 weeks. This attentiveness increases steadily in subsequent weeks; Hack concludes that this is one indication of a readiness for interaction with the environment.

Hack's view is further supported by very recent evidence on the experiences and responsiveness of prematures. Prenatally, infants hear sounds from the mother, including her voice, and they acquire a preference for the sound of her voice (DeCasper, 1984). In addition, it has been shown that infant animals can acquire preferences for tastes and odors *in utero* (Smotherman, 1984). Finally, the infant *in utero* is exposed to a variety of biological rhythms, which may serve as *zeitgebers,* or sources of entrainment (Gander, Kronauer, Czeisler, & Moore-Ede, 1984). It is clear that the dynamic uterine environment offers more than variety in forms of stimulation. Rather, it appears that circumstances are appropriate for associations about systematic aspects of the prenatal environment, and such associations are, in fact, being formed.

It is now clear that the issue of prenatal deprivation of the maternal environment is much more complex than a simple deficit of specific forms of stimulation. The infant in the isolette is deprived of a range of experiences and opportunities to form associations about these experiences. Thus, it is reasonable to expect deprivation of the uterine environment, combined with the deficits—and the stresses—of the isolette environment, to have lasting effects on the developing infant.

The issue of deprivation of the uterine experience is even more complex when one considers that the premature infant and the fetus are very different organisms. As already indicated, the process of premature birth results in major changes in the organization of physiological systems, so that the infant breathes, can experience varied visual input, and can move about the crib. Thus, it is reasonable to assume that the needs of extra-uterine life may not be isomorphic with those of a fetus.

PREVIOUS STUDIES
OF STIMULATION
OF PREMATURE INFANTS

Intervention programs have been designed to provide the infant with extra stimulation in the nursery (Kramer, Chamorro, Green, & Knudson, 1975; Solkoff, Yaffee, Weintraub, & Blase, 1969; White & Labarba, 1976), provide extra contact between infant and mother (Barnett, Leiderman, Grobstein, & Klaus, 1970; Brown et al., 1980), or provide long-term support for the mother (Scarr-Salapatek & Williams, 1973). Stimulation studies have also been designed to compensate for sensory impoverishment of the environment (Neal, 1968; Segall, 1972; Barnard, 1973; Barnard & Bee, 1983), to mimic the uterine environment (Hasselmeyer, 1964: Korner, Guilleminault, Van den Hoed, & Baldein, 1978; Korner, Ruppel, & Rho, 1982), or to expose the premature to the experiences of the full-term infant (Segall, 1972; Powell, 1974). The underlying premise of these studies is that some form of additional stimulation may be needed to facilitate the development and organization of the premature's precariously balanced central nervous system.

While some studies have found short-term effects, especially on weight gain and activity levels, the results are not in a consistent direction (Korner, 1985). Nor are there significant long-term effects as a general finding. Barnard and Bee (1983) found that patterned and contingent stimulation given to prematures led to higher mental scores on the Bayley Scales of Infant Development at 2 years, but not at 8 months. And they, like others, did not find any significant effects on the mother-infant interaction. Despite a lack of systematic effects on social interaction, Brown and collaborators (1980) found that parents reported psychological support from intervention. This suggests that the failure to find effects of early interventions on social interaction may be more a problem of lack of measurement, than a lack of impact of the early intervention.

The notion that lasting effects may be present, though not yet measured, derives from extensive animal research on the long-term effects of very early stimulation. These studies indicate that interventions in early infancy, which may appear to be extremely mild in their nature, have effects on the social and emotional behavior of the animals as adults (Denenberg, 1964, 1969, 1975, 1977; Denenberg & Morton, 1962; Denenberg & Zarrow, 1971; Levine, 1969; Levine, Haltmeyer, Karas, & Denenberg, 1967; Levine & Mullins, 1966). It is possible to control the range of confounding variables in animal studies, so that lasting effects are more readily exposed. Although the effects are not so easily exposed in humans, the principle of brain plasticity is well documented at this level. Thus, it is most logical to assume that the infant, and the mother-infant relationship as well, is modified by early interventions that affect the behavior of the infant.

However, it is also clear from the accumulated research on stimulus interventions with premature infants that very few guidelines exist for determining which interventions may be more appropriate for facilitating optimal development.

OPTIONAL STIMULATION AS AN ALTERNATIVE APPROACH

In view of what is known of the needs of premature infants, their extreme sensitivity, as well as their competence, we have proposed that the safest, most appropriate, and possibly most supportive form of stimulation, psychologically and biologically, for these infants is optional stimulation—stimulation that is directly related to the behaviors of the infant. Others have also proposed that premature infants may benefit from exploring and learning about variability in the environment and expe-

riencing the relationship between their own behavior and environmental events (Blackburn, 1983; Hack, 1976). Stimulation that is regulated by the infant rather than imposed by an outside source clearly provides this opportunity. However, it is important to note that not all *contingent* stimulation is *optional*. That is, if the stimulation is imposed on the infant upon the occurrence of an obligatory behavior, such as movement, such stimulation is not optional. The infant must have the alternative of not being stimulated as well as controlling when stimulation occurs, if the conditions are to be considered truly optional for the infant. Optional stimulation for premature infants is provided in the form of the Breathing Blue Bear.

RESEARCH ORIGINS OF THE NOTION OF OPTIONAL STIMULATION

The Breathing Bear, as a source of rhythmic stimulation, is unique in that it provides the opportunity for the infant to seek or not to seek stimulation, and to regulate his or her levels of stimulation. The concept of the stimulation being optional is extended to the auditory realm: The Bear is specially designed to be *silent,* and thus the Bear is not an unavoidable source of sound.

The notion that premature infants should possess the capability of choosing to make contact with a source of rhythmic stimulus derived from early animal research (Thoman & Arnold, 1968), in which infant rats were removed from the mother at birth and placed in an incubator, where they were hand-fed. A "mother surrogate" was placed in the incubator nest. The surrogate was composed of 1¼ inch in diameter visking tubing (which is permeable), through which warm water was pumped in such a way as to create a gentle pulsation of the "mother." From the first hours of life, the animals oriented toward, burrowed under, or climbed on the surrogate, thus receiving its rhythmic stimulation. The research also indicated that rhythmic stimulation even soothes the stress vocalization of infant rats (Thoman & Korner, 1971). Physiologically, the stimulation was important because it elicited urination and defecation in the pups. The mother rat elicits elimination by licking the anogenital area of the pups. Without such stimulation, the pups do not urinate or defecate, and they soon die. The surrogate elicited elimination in the nest, and survival of the pups was dependent primarily on the successes of the hand-feeding procedure. Thus, the animals responded strongly to the surrogate, and, in turn, the surrogate assured their survival and growth.

Since the newborn rat is capable of responsiveness to a biologically relevant source of stimulation, and since the newborn rat is maturationally comparable to a human premature infant of 35 weeks (Himwich, 1971), it was reasonable to expect that the premature infant should have this competence as well.

For the human infant to respond to a surrogate companion requires not only preference but mobility. Fortunately, this is present in the premature infant. During the preterm period, after 34 weeks conceptional age (CA), the premature infant is much more mobile than either the full-term counterpart or the premature at term age (Booth, Thoman, & Leonard, 1980; Prechtl, 1977; Thoman, Waite, & Shafer, 1981). These findings simply confirm the observations of any nursing staff member, namely, that the premature infant can range to all corners of the isolette. Thus, the infants have the requisite mobility. Whether they have the capability of organizing this mobility in a directed fashion is an empirical question that has been addressed.

ENTRAINMENT AS A POTENTIAL MECHANISM FOR MODIFYING CNS CONTROLS OF THE PREMATURE INFANT

Serious consideration was given to the selection of the rhythm at which the Bear would "breathe." With no clear guide in the literature as to choice of rate, it was felt that one of the baby's own biological rhythms would be most appropriate. Since the infant is an independently functioning organism, his or her own rhythms should be more relevant to the

infant than any rhythm of another biological system, namely, the mother. Choosing one of the infant's own biological rhythms eliminates the need to second guess which environmental rhythm might be most attractive as well as facilitative for the infant's central integrative controls.

Respiration during Quiet Sleep is one of the infant's most regular biological rhythms; and it is also one that is disrupted by premature birth. By setting the Bear to breathe at a rate that matches the Quiet Sleep breathing rate of each infant, it is reasonable to expect that the principles of entrainment (Abraham & Shaw, 1982; Gander et al., 1984; Kronauer, Czeisler, Pilato, Moore-Ede, & Weitzman, 1982; Winfree, 1967) will apply, and that the baby's breathing will become more regular as a result. Entrainment refers to the physics principle that two oscillators that have similar rates, if they are in proximity, will come to oscillate in phase with each other. In the case of the bear and the baby, the baby's breathing is somewhat irregular (even in Quiet Sleep), while the Bear's breathing is quite regular. Thus, physical contact with the Bear should *entrain* the baby's breathing so that it assumes (or approaches) the degree of regularity displayed by the Bear. The objective of the Breathing Bear intervention is not to modify the baby's endogenous breathing rate, but to facilitate the maturational organization of controls expressed in greater regularity of breathing.

In their discussions of entrainment of biological rhythms, Abraham and Shaw (1982) point out that the closer the entraining frequency is to the fundamental frequency of the subject, the more optimal are the conditions for the entrainment process. In addition, they posit that "the phases need not be entrained, only the frequencies" (p. 175). The latter premise is important for indicating that one does not need to demonstrate that the baby is breathing synchronously with the Bear, to show that the Bear's regular breathing is entraining the baby's more irregular breathing.

By using an optional source of stimulation, it will be possible to explore empirically whether the infant's contact with the Breathing Bear leads to greater regularity in his or her breathing patterns. In addition, it will be possible to investigate whether infants prefer their own Quiet Sleep respiration rate, or other rates, as well as the consequences of different rates, and the consequences of the opportunity to self-regulate the temporal parameters of stimulation.

Most important, the possibility of overstimulation, with its attendant risks, is minimized by making the Breathing Bear continuously available but not imposed on the infant.

OTHER CONSIDERATIONS IN THE DESIGN OF THE BREATHING BEAR

In designing the Breathing Bear as a stimulating device, other issues were also addressed. As a traditional infant's toy, the teddy bear is highly attractive to both parents and staff: sheepskin feels warm to the touch; is naturally flame resistant; stands up well to repeated use, cleaning and sterilization; and the very thick nap precludes occlusion of the nostrils.

The final major concern in the design of the Breathing Bear was the nature of the pump that would make the Bear breathe. The pump, which is placed outside the crib and is connected to the Bear via a plastic hose, has to meet a number of critical specifications in order that the movements of the Bear's body be precisely controlled. This is important if the stimulation is to be gentle, and if the quality of the Bear's breathing is to reflect the rate and inspiration-expiration characteristics of a baby, but with the precision that is absent in a premature baby's relatively unstable respiratory pattern. Only if the Bear breathes in this manner will it be reasonable to expect the Bear to facilitate regulation of the infant's breathing rhythms. The major specifications for the pump are as follows:

1. It must deliver regularly a controlled volume of air to the bladder within the Bear, and this volume must be adjustable for different sized Bears.
2. The air exchange must occur smoothly, creating a sinusoidal-wave-type motion of the Bear, thus matching the smooth motion of an infant's most regular breathing.
3. It must have a safety release valve to ensure that the Bear is never over-expanded.
4. It must be designed so that the air pressure within the Bear's bladder increases and decreases in a constant fashion, despite any leakage of air from the system.
5. The rate of the Bear's breathing must be adjustable so that it can be set to match the rate of the baby's breathing, or some subhormonic of that rate; once set for any rate, it must maintain that rate with high precision.
6. The air exchange must be achieved with minimal sound, and without any vibratory motion that could be transmitted to the Bear.
7. The pump must be sturdy enough to make the Bear breathe approximately 75,000 times during each 24 hours, and function continuously at that rate for weeks or months without the need for servicing or repair.
8. The pump must be of a small enough size to be reasonably placed in a crowded neonatal intensive care unit.
9. The pump must meet hospital requirements for safety.

These specifications are spelled out in detail, because, as already indicated, they are critical if the Bear's breathing is to have the consistency and regularity required. The objective of providing a gentle, unstressful, smoothly functioning, and adjustable source of stimulation demands a pump that is dependable and that functions with the precision just described. The requirements for the pump's functioning cannot be overemphasized. Pumps can be found on the market, and pumps can be readily constructed. But unless the pump imparts the type of motion to the Bear as specified, and as dictated by the rationale given, predictions for the intervention would be uncertain.

For the current study, we are using a Harvard Apparatus small animal respirator, which functions in accordance with our specifications.

However, it is too large, too heavy, and the motor is noisier than desirable (although the sound of the motor is not transmitted to the Bear). In a crowded, busy NICU, it is important that added equipment be as unintrusive as possible. Thus, size and sound outside the isolette are important considerations. A special pump that fulfills all of the requirements is being designed.

DO PREMATURES RESPOND TO A BREATHING BEAR?

A first study of prematures' responsiveness to optional stimulation has been completed. The design was derived from many months of efforts that did not yield systematic data, but proved enlightening in terms of behaviors of prematures. For example, our initial approach to the problem of assessing their preference behaviors was guided by the notion of introducing the Bear to babies at as advanced a preterm age as possible, preferably 35 or 36 weeks CA, because, we reasoned, the older preterm infant would be more likely to learn that the Bear was present and to seek him out. However, it became apparent that the infants at these ages are not as mobile as younger ones. Thus, they are not as likely to find the Bear by chance initially, and chance contact is the first prerequisite for "knowing the Bear is there."

We also had had plans for a sophisticated research design including the use of each infant as his or her own control, by alternating or randomizing days with and without the Bear. We had intended to alternate the Bear's location from one side of the isolette to the other from day to day. However, the empirical evidence using these procedures did not support our expectations. This was disappointing, because review of the video tape from our preliminary recordings had indicated that the babies could find and cuddle with the Bear. We had consistently found nurses' notes in the babies' hospital records to the effect that the baby "loved the Bear," and parents of babies with the Bear assured us that the baby loved the Bear. We began to suspect that we, and other

adults, were the ones who loved the Bear. Or, that it was not possible to obtain systematic evidence of the babies' responsiveness within the limits of their stay in the hospital.

We then settled on a design that was more consistent with the nature of the babies, namely by starting the intervention with younger infants, by allowing the infants to have access to the Bear continuously, and without changing the location of the Bear from day to day.

This description of our early efforts explains why more elegant experimental procedures were not used. It would have been most desirable to use each infant as his or her own control, rather than having to use group comparisons. This is especially the case given the heterogeneity of premature infants in terms of gestational age (GA) at birth, and other risk factors. However, the design that we have arrived at includes appropriate control procedures so that it is possible to "ask" premature infants about their preferences with respect to parameters of stimulation.

First, we enroll infants at 32 weeks CA, or as soon as the critical medical period is passed, and the infant is considered to be a "growing preemie." Infants are randomly assigned, in sets of three (matched for GA at birth, and birth weight) to one of three groups: 1) infants with a Breathing Bear in the isolette; 2) infants with a nonbreathing Bear in the isolette; or 3) infants with no Bear in the isolette. The Bear is placed against one side of the crib (actually the front or back of the isolette), where it remains throughout the period of intervention—for 3 weeks, or until the infant graduates to a nursery crib. Babies within each set of three are matched also for the side of the crib on which the Bear is placed, and this position is randomly assigned for successive sets of three infants.

Each baby is observed through a period of Quiet Sleep to determine the typical respiration rate in that state, and then the Bear is set to breathe at one half of that rate. We chose this rate rather than actually matching the baby's rate because it was slower and, intuitively, seemed more gentle. In future study, we plan to use the actual rate of the baby's breathing to assess this decision. The two alternatives differ little with respect to the expected effectiveness of entrainment (Abraham & Shaw, 1982).

The baby is continually videotaped with a TV camera mounted over the isolette, using a time-lapse recorder set at a 72:1 ratio. Thus, a 3-day recording is obtained on a 1-hour tape. These tapes are brought to the laboratory, viewed on a video monitor, and scored for each successive 5-second interval (6 minutes in real time) for the following conditions: 1) the baby was in the isolette; 2) the baby was in the supine (tummy) position; 3) the baby was propped; 4) the baby was in physical contact with the Bear (more than momentary, which can occur when the baby is active and crying); 5) an intervention occurred; and 6) the baby was in Quiet Sleep throughout the interval (the baby was almost completely quiescent throughout the 6 minutes, as defined by Anders & Keener, 1985). Exact interval-by-interval agreement between two scorers (one who was experimentally naive) ranged from 92 to 100% on these codes.

The no-Bear infants constitute a group that requires some explanation. This condition was included in order to determine the amount of contact that the babies make with the area in the crib that would be occupied by the Bear, if he were there. That is, we can determine the extent to which contact with the Bear occurs by chance alone. This is a very important control group. In order to measure the amount of contact with the area of the crib occupied by a Bear, the following procedure was used: When the tapes for the babies in the no-Bear group were scored, a paper cut-out, the same size and shape of the Bear (called a Shadow Bear), was placed over the TV monitor to cover the area where the Bear would be if he were in the isolette. Then, the baby's contact with the Shadow Bear was scored in the same manner as for a real Bear.

A baby can only approach and achieve contact with the Bear when the baby is free to move about in the crib (i.e., in the tummy position and not restrained by propping). Thus, for contact with the Bear to be scored for any interval, the baby had to be "available," that is: 1) in the isolette, 2) in the tummy position, 3) not

restrained by propping, 4) no intervention was occurring, and 5) the infant was not placed in contact with the Bear by a member of the nursing staff. All 5-second intervals (6 minutes in real time) that met these criteria were considered to be baby-available intervals. It should be noted that the nurses rarely placed the babies in contact with the Bear, because they had been instructed not to, and they were aware that the video monitored where they placed the baby. However, when this did occur, the segment of contact that followed was not scored.

Each baby's contact time with the Bear was measured as a percentage of baby-available time. Quiet Sleep was also measured as a percent of available time (out of the 3-day recording).

The mean portion of the day spent in available time was 38.1% for the Breathing Bear infants, 39.1% for the nonbreathing Bear infants, and 38.2% for the no-Bear infants. There were no significant differences among the groups on this measure.

The contact date for 18 infants, based on the recordings made over the last 3 days of the 2- to 3-week intervention are presented in Table 1: The percent of available time that each baby spent in contact with the Bear (or the Shadow Bear, for the no-Bear infants).

There is no overlap between the Breathing Bear babies and those in the other two groups with respect to the amount of contact with the Bear. Clearly, premature babies are capable of an approach-response to an available, and apparently attractive, form of stimulation.

With respect to the sleep measure, the infants with the Breathing Bear spent 30.8% of

Table 1. Percent of available time spent in contact with the Bear

Breathing Bear	Nonbreathing bear	No-Bear
57.0	11.6	16.7
60.5	22.7	16.7
96.5	16.5	18.4
56.1	15.5	19.0
45.2	5.9	18.8
65.9	7.6	13.8
$\bar{X}$ 63.4	13.3	17.2
SD 17.5	6.2	2.0

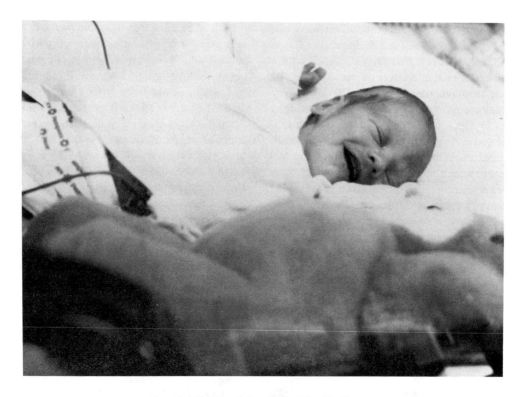

Figure 3.   Premature baby with Breathing Blue Bear.

their available time in Quiet Sleep, compared with 19.5% and 24.1% for the nonbreathing and the no-Bear groups, respectively. The three groups differ significantly ($F = 4.22$, $df = 2/10$, $p < .05$). Furthermore, the Breathing-Bear babies show significantly more quiet sleep than the nonbreathing bear babies ($F = 38.069$, $df = 1/15$, $p < .01$) and the no-Bear babies ($F = 220.226$, $df = 1/15$, $p < .01$). The latter two groups do not differ from each other. These results support our expectation that the experience of self-regulating stimulation from the Breathing Blue Bear should lead to increased Quiet Sleep and, thus, greater amounts of regular respiration.

Figure 3 shows a premature baby, still in the isolette, with a Breathing Blue Bear.

DISCUSSION

Whereas empirical findings may be convincing, nonsystematic observations of individual infant subjects are often most enlightening. Some of our experiences with infants and the Bear have been invaluable and most supportive for us during the long period of data collection, before we had the resources to analyze the tapes and the data.

For example, the parents of one infant subject, a surviving twin, initially showed very little interest in their infant. He had originally appeared to be the one of the two babies who was most critically ill; and, after the first one died, they seemed to assume that he would not live either. Their lack of interest was of concern to the medical staff, because it continued despite the fact that he passed through the critical period and became a stable, growing preemie, and was really beginning to thrive. When we asked the parents for consent to enroll their baby in our study, they agreed readily. We felt they had actually agreed too readily, and that this was possibly because they were detached and still did not expect him to survive; thus, they were not much concerned about what we planned to do. We chose to be very attentive to the baby (not our usual investigators' approach) by a frequent presence in the nursery with him, and reported to the parents with enthusiasm about his responsiveness to the Bear, which was, in fact, remarkably obvious. They became impressed by the fact that the baby was showing an active interest in the Bear. In a very short time, their visits to the baby increased in number and duration; and then others came— grand-parents, cousins, aunts, and uncles from a large, very close-knit family. They all wanted to see the baby and the Bear and to talk with us about the baby and the Bear. We did. It became clear that the entire family now saw the baby as a person about whom they could have expectations for the future. The story had a happy ending, because the baby was discharged without apparently serious handicaps; and from our subsequent informal contacts with him over the past 2 years, he appears to be developing normally.

The medical and nursing staff, as well as parents, are generally enthusiastic about the Breathing Bear. On one occasion, we found in the medical records an entry by an occupational therapist for one of our babies, a statement that she had been ''unable to assess orientation responses since the infant was difficult to alert outside the isolette. However, he was noted to alert nicely to the Blue Bear once back in isolette.''

The findings from this study clearly indicate that the infants are, in some way, aware that the Breathing Bear is there. By 35 weeks conceptional age—5 weeks before they are of full-term age—these small infants are able to seek out and touch the gently moving, furry ''companion.'' By contrast, the furry companion that was motionless (the nonbreathing bear) did not elicit such approach behavior. This organized form of responsiveness reflects a significant form of competence in preterm-period infants that has not heretofore been demonstrated.

The preferences and competence of infants born at full term have been explored extensively. Much less is known about the premature infant. As a consequence, responses to stimuli are often described as being reflexive in nature, and motor activity of pre-term babies is generally viewed as random, uncontrolled, unpatterned movements. It is difficult to conceptualize the organization of motor behaviors required to achieve contact with a surrogate companion as being simply reflexive or as an expression of disorganized activity. The ability of premature infants to show goal directed motor activity clearly contradicts such a view.

With the exception of our early studies of infant rat pups, stimulation during the preterm period, whether for humans or animals, has not been offered as an option; rather it has been provided for the infants with rhythms and intensity levels, and for durations judged to be most appropriate by the provider. The procedure for offering stimulation for the infant, *ad libitum,* provides a tool for determining preferences of infants, and exploring the relationship of preferred stimulus qualities to subsequent development of the infant's adaptive behaviors.

The role of the self-reflecting aspect of the Bear's breathing in eliciting approach from the infant is not yet clear. Nor do we know yet whether a breathing rate for the Bear that differs from the infant's would be more or less biologically relevant in terms of consequences for the infant. Only from studies in which a range of rates are compared will it be possible to confirm our view of the importance of the individualized matching of the Bear's breathing rate with that of the infant.

The finding of increased Quiet Sleep in the Breathing Bear infants provides some evidence on this issue. Our reason for matching Bear with baby was to facilitate the infant's central integrative processes in a way that would lead to a more regular, *not a different,* pattern of breathing. By providing feedback to the infant on his or her own breathing rhythm, it was reasoned that the principles of entrainment would function to increase the regularity of the baby's breathing. And this is precisely what we found: More regular (Quiet-Sleep) breathing in the stimulated infants. Whether there was increased regularity in the pattern of breathing *within* Quiet Sleep is not known. But, clearly, the infants were spending more time sleeping in the state in which breathing is more regular.

The finding of increased Quiet Sleep in the infants with the Breathing Bear has implications for the developing central nervous system of these infants. The organization of sleep-wake states is a direct expression of CNS functioning and an indicator of CNS status (Thoman, 1979; Thoman, 1982; Thoman & Becker, 1979; Thoman, Denenberg, Sievel, Zeidner, & Becker, 1981). The developmental course for this organization includes increasing amounts of Quiet Sleep, from very low levels to approximately 40% of sleep time by full term. Thus, the increased amounts of Quiet Sleep with the Breathing Bear appear to indicate a more advanced maturational status for these infants.

CONCLUSIONS AND SOME SPECULATIONS

We propose that the experience of self-regulating stimulation from the Breathing Bear should have long-term effects on the infant's neurobehavioral functioning. This proposal is offered in spite of inconsistent findings reported in the literature with respect to developmental effects of early stimulation of prematures. In fact, some researchers (e.g., Brown et al., 1980) have concluded that effects are minimal.

Lack of evidence of long-term effects can be for any of several major reasons, including: a) the measures used are not sufficiently sensitive to the effects; or b) the measures were not measuring that which was affected by the intervention; or c) the intervention has, in fact, not made a meaningful difference for the infants' development. It is reasonable to speculate that each of these may be the case to some degree for many of the early intervention studies of prematures.

The notion that lasting effects may be present though not yet measured derives from extensive animal research on the long-term effects of very early stimulation. These studies indicate that interventions in early infancy, which may appear to be extremely mild in their nature, have effects on the social and emotional behavior of the animals as adults (Denenberg, 1964, 1969, 1975, 1977; Denenberg & Morton, 1962; Denenberg & Zarrow, 1971; Levine, 1969; Levine, Haltmeyer, Karas, & Denenberg, 1967; Levine & Mullins, 1966). It is

possible to control the range of confounding variables in animal studies, so that lasting effects can be exposed. This is in marked contrast to the situation at the human level, where there are ongoing, uncontrolled (by the researcher) interactions between an infant and the physical and social environment in which the infant is functioning. However, the findings at the animal level strongly support the expectation of lasting effects of early intervention, to the extent that it becomes possible to measure those effects.

Animal studies also provide the mechanism for such modification in terms of evidence for plasticity of the immature nervous system (Thoman, 1982). Lynch and Gall (1979) summarize a number of studies establishing that the anatomical structure of the brain is plastic in that it can show a remarkable degree of reorganization under certain circumstances, and they conclude that:

> the final architecture of the brain reflects interactions between its neuronal and glial constituents as well as between the organism and its environment. . . . The still evolving concept of anatomical plasticity provides a possible (and at least partial) explanation for the flexibility and adaptability of behavior. . . . If we accept the idea that the environment of the neonate can influence the number of dendritic branches and spines, it would hardly be surprising that early experiences might produce profound and lasting behavioral consequences. (p. 139)

From Huttenlocher's studies of the mechanisms for plasticity in the developing human cerebral cortex (1984), he concludes that plasticity of the brain is greatest during the early postnatal period, that this is the period "during which external stimuli would be most likely to influence the organization of the brain. One might predict that intervention programs, to be effective, would have to be implemented during this early postnatal period. . ." (p. 495).

In our intervention study, the finding of a more mature sleep pattern in the infants exposed to the Breathing Bear permits one to infer modification in CNS controls for state; thus, we would argue that the experience should have lasting consequences that will be revealed with sufficiently sensitive measures.

With respect to lack of evidence of long-term effects from early interventions, research at the animal level again provides guidelines for the parameters of behavior that should be measured to indicate lasting developmental change. It should be noted that preweaning experience in animals has generally been found to affect emotional and social behaviors, rather than intellectual performance (Denenberg, 1977; Denenberg & Thoman, 1976). Thus, mental developmental scores should not be expected to be the most sensitive indices of the effects of very early stimulation. While social and emotional characteristics are not independent of intellectual functioning, the animal findings suggest that more direct focus on these characteristics developmentally should be more fruitful in follow-up studies of very early interventions. An obstacle for such an approach is the dearth of reliable measures of social and emotional functioning of infants during the first months and years of life. However, we have shown that naturalistic observations of infants in their home circumstances can provide highly reliable measures of these characteristics if the observations are of sufficient duration, and if the observations are made on repeated occasions—so that reliability of measurement can be assessed (Thoman, 1981a), and the characteristics of individual infants can be reliably described.

The final issue, that of whether the Breathing Bear intervention should be expected to affect CNS organization and have long-term effects, must be addressed. As in the case of other stimulation programs, this one was planned with this expectation in mind. Once again, we rely on animal research for our most fundamental considerations. Our focus for this purpose is on the greater effectiveness of an *active* experience in contrast to being *passively* stimulated. Held and Hein (1963) compared visual-motor development in kittens as a function of whether early visual stimulation was allowed to vary with their locomotor movements or visual stimulation resulted from their being moved passively through a field. They conclude that their findings provide convincing evidence that "a developmental pro-cess, in at least one higher mammal, . . . requires for its operation stimulus variation concurrent with and systematically dependent upon self-produced movement" (p. 249). Their findings (Hein & Held, 1962; Held, 1961) parallel those with older, immature animals exposed to a free environment with objects to explore and play with, and the general finding "on which all the animal studies agree, (namely) that some form of enriched experience during early development results in subsequent improvement in behaviors involving perceptual and cognitive factors" (Rabinovitch & Rosvold, 1972). These are accompanied by changes in brain development, including greater weight and thickness of the cerebral cortex, increased numbers of glial cells, larger brain cell bodies and nuclei, and increased metabolic activity (Rosenzweig, 1981). The commonality between the early postnatal interventions and those introduced postweaning is the active interaction of the infants with the environment.

The Breathing Bear intervention is consistent with this principle of active participation on the part of the infant. The high level of contact that the infants achieve with the Bear indicates active engagement with the companion, which, in turn, provides feedback to the infant on his or her own biological rhythm of breathing.

In conclusion, we propose that self-regulation of stimulation by the premature infant is a very profound and highly appropriate form of experience for this stage of life, and that such interaction with the Breathing Bear companion should have lasting effects on the infant's developmental course. Some of these effects should be direct, as a function of the experience. Some of these effects should be indirect, as changes in the infant's behaviors in the home after leaving the hospital modify the social system in which the infant is functioning, and through the process of ongoing feedback, these overall system modifications (Thoman, 1980, 1981b; Thoman, Acebo, & Becker, 1983; Thoman & Acebo, 1984) should have further effects on the infant's developmental course.

A FINAL WORD

While the Breathing Bear is a simple device, its design as a therapeutic device for prematures reflects a profound concern and respect for this small infant as a human being—one with competencies, with the capacity for experiencing, and with the capability of expressing feelings and choices. Thus, the Bear is designed as a form of very early environmental enrichment that permits the infant to be an active participant in his or her environmental events.

Such a perspective leads to a very different strategy for designing intensive care environments for these babies. Mainly, it highlights the possibility of choosing among possible forms of stimulation for them by *asking* them what they want; they can *tell* us. It is reasonable to predict that not all forms of special stimulation that have been given these infants are equally appealing, nor are they equally biologically relevant for the infants' growth and development. While infants' preferences for any form of stimulation and the biological relevance of such stimulation may not be perfectly correlated, the possibility of such isomorphism is a reasonable working hypothesis.

REFERENCES

Abraham, R. H., & Shaw, C. D. (1982). *Dynamics—The geometry of behavior*. Santa Cruz, CA: Aerial Press, Inc.

Affonso, D. (1976). The newborn's potential for interaction. *Journal of Obstetrical, Gynecological, and Neonatal Nursing, 5*, 1976, 9–13.

Als, H., & Brazelton, T. B. (1981). A new model of assessing the behavioral organization in preterm and full-term infants: Two case studies. *Journal of the American Academy of Child Psychiatry, 20*, 239–263.

Als, H., Tronick, E., Adamson, L., & Brazelton, T. B. (1976). The behavior of the full-term yet underweight newborn infant. *Developmental Medicine and Child Neurology, 18*, 590–602.

Anders, T. F., & Keener, M. (1985). Developmental course of nighttime sleep-wake patterns in full-term and premature infants during the first year of life. I. *Sleep, 8*, 173–192.

Bakeman, R., & Brown, J. V. (1980). Analyzing behavioral sequences: Differences between preterm and full-term infant mother dyads during the first months of life. In D. B. Sawin, R. C. Hawkins II, L. O. Walker, & J. H. Penticuff (Eds.), *Exceptional infant: Psychosocial risks in infant-environment transactions* (Vol. 4, pp. 271–299). New York: Brunner/Mazel, Inc.

Barnard, K. E. (1972). The effect of stimulation on the duration and amount of sleep and wakefulness in the premature infants (Doctoral dissertation, University of Washington, 1972). *Dissertation Abstracts International, 33*, 2167B. (University Microfilms No. 72-28, 573).

Barnard, K. (1973). The effects of stimulation on the sleep behavior of the premature infant. *Communications in Nursing Research, 6*, 12–40.

Barnard, K. E., & Bee, H. L. (1983). The impact of temporally patterned stimulation on the development of premature infants. *Child Development, 54*, 1156–1167.

Barnard, K. E., Bee, H. L., & Hammond, M. A. (1984). Developmental changes in maternal interactions with term and preterm infants. *Infant Behavior and Development, 1*, 101–113.

Barnard, K. E., & Blackburn, S. (1981, April). Features of the premature infant's animate and inanimate environment in relation to infant activity. In J. L. Gaiter (Chair), *Caregiver-infant interactions and stimulation characteristics of intensive care nurseries*. Symposium conducted at the biennial meeting of the Society for Research in Child Development, Boston.

Barnett, C. T., Leiderman, H., Grobstein, R., & Klaus, M. (1970). Neonatal separation: The maternal side of interaction deprivation. *Pediatrics, 45*, 197–205.

Bennett, F. C., Robinson, N. M., & Sells, C. J. (1983). Growth and development of infants weighing less than 800 grams at birth. *Pediatrics, 71*, 319–323.

Benson, J. B., Uzgiris, I. C. (1985). Effect of self-initiated locomotion on infant search activity. *Developmental Psychology, 21*(6), 923–931.

Blackburn, S. (1983). Fostering behavioral development of high-risk infants. *Journal of Obstetrical, Gynecological, and Neonatal Nursing, 12*(3), supplement, 768–865.

Booth, C. L., Thoman, E. B., & Leonard, H. L. (1980). Sleep states and behavior patterns in preterm and full-term infants. *Neuropediatrics, 11*, 354–364.

Brown, J. V., Larossa, M. M., Aylward, G. P., Davis, D. J., Rutherford, P. K., & Bakeman, R. (1980). Nursery-based intervention with prematurely born babies and their mothers: Are there effects? *The Journal of Pediatrics, 97*, 487–491.

Burns, K. A., & Hatcher, R. P. (1984). Developmental intervention with preterm infants. In W. B. Burns & J. V. Lavigne (Eds.), *Progress in pediatric psychology* (pp. 47–78). New York: Grune & Stratton.

Caputo, D. V., Goldstein, K. M., & Taub, H. B. (1981). Neonatal compromise and later psychological development: A 10 year longitudinal study. In S. L. Friedman & M. Sigman (Eds.), *Preterm birth and psychological development* (pp. 353–386). New York: Academic Press.

Clark, A., & Affonso, D. (1976). *Childbearing: A nursing perspective* (pp. 547–596). Philadelphia: F. A. Davis.

Cohen, S. E., & Parmelee, A. H. (1983). Prediction of five-year Stanford-Binet scores in preterm infants. *Child Development, 54*, 1242–1253.

Crnic, K. A., Ragozin, A. S., Greenberg, M. T., Robinson, N. M., & Basham, R. B. (1983). Social interaction and development competence of preterm infants during the first year of life. *Child Development, 54*, 1199–1210.

Davis, D. H. (1985). *Naturalistic observations of premature and fullterm infants: Comparison of sleep-wake states, infant behaviors, and mother-infant interactions.* Unpublished doctoral dissertation, The University of Connecticut, Storrs.

DeCasper, T. (1984, October). *Do human fetuses eavesdrop in the womb?* Paper presented at the meeting of the International Society for Developmental Psychobiology, Baltimore, MD.

Denenberg, V. H. (1964). Critical periods, stimulus, input, and emotional reactivity: A theory of infantile stimulation. *Psychological Review, 71,* 335–351.

Denenberg, V. H. (1969). The effects of early experience. In E. S. Hafez (Ed.), *The behavior of domestic animals* (pp. 95–130). London: Bailliere, Tindall and Cassell.

Denenberg, V. H. (1975). Effects of exposure to stressors in early life upon later behavioral and biological processes. In L. Levi (Ed.), *Society, stress, and disease: Childhood and adolescence: Vol. 2.* (pp. 269–281). New York: Oxford University Press.

Denenberg, V. H. (1977). Assessing the effects of early experience. In R. D. Myers (Ed.), *Methods in psychobiology: Vol 3.* (pp. 127–147). New York: Academic Press.

Denenberg, V. H., & Morton, J. R. (1962). Effects of environmental complexity and social groupings upon-modification of emotional behavior. *Journal of Comparative Physiology and Psychology, 55,* 242–246.

Denenberg, V. H., & Thoman, E. V. (1976). From animal to infant research. In T. D. Tjossem (Ed.), *Intervention strategies for high-risk infants and young children* (pp. 85–106). Baltimore: University Park Press.

Denenberg, V. H., & Zarrow, M. X. (1971). Effects of handling in infancy upon adult behavior and adrenocortical activity: Suggestions for a neuro-endocrine mechanism. In D. N. Walcher & D. L. Peters (Eds.), *Early childhood: The development of self-regulatory mechanisms* (pp. 40–64). New York: Academic Press.

DiVitto, B., & Goldberg, S. (1979). The effects of newborn medical status on early parent-infant interaction. In T. M. Field, A. M. Sostek, S. Goldberg, & H. H. Shuman (Eds.), *Infants born at risk: Behavior and development* (pp. 311–332). New York: SP Medical and Scientific Books.

Field, T. M. (1977). Effects of early separation, interactive deficits, and experimental manipulations on infant-mother face-to-face interactions. *Child Development, 48,* 763–777.

Field, T. (1979a). Games parents play with normal and high-risk infants. *Child Psychiatry and Human Development, 10,* 41–47.

Field, T. (1979b). Visual and cardiac responses to animate and inanimate faces by young term and preterm infants. *Child Development, 50,* 188–194.

Field, T. (1981). Gaze behavior of normal and high-risk infants during early interactions. *Journal of the American Academy of Child Psychiatry, 20,* 308–317.

Gander, P. H., Kronauer, R. E., Czeisler, C. A., & Moore-Ede, M. C. (1984). Modeling the action of zeitgebers on the human circadian system: Comparisons of stimulations and data. *American Psychological Society, R427.

Goldberg, S., & DiVitto, B. (1983). *Born too soon: Preterm birth and early development.* San Francisco: W. H. Freeman and Company.

Gorski, P. A. (1983). Premature infant behavioral and physiological response to caregiving interventions in the intensive care nursery. In J. Call, E. Galenson & R. Tyson (Eds.), *Frontiers of infant psychiatry, 24,* (pp. 256–263). New York: Basic Books.

Hack, M., Mostow, A., & Miranda, S. (1976). Development of attention in preterm infants. *Pediatrics, 58,* 669–674.

Hasselmeyer, E. G. (1964). The premature neonate's response to handling. *American Nurses Association, 11,* 15–24.

Hein, A., & Held, R. (1962). A neural model for labile sensorimotor coordinations. In E. E. Bernard & M. R. Kare (Eds.), *Biological prototypes and synthetic systems: Vol. 1.* (pp. 71–74). New York: Plenum Press.

Held, R. (1961). Exposure-history as a factor in maintaining stability of perception and coordination. *Journal of Nervous and Mental Disease, 132,* 26–32.

Held, R., & Hein, A. (1963). Movement-produced stimulation in the development of visually guided behavior. *Journal of Comparative and Physiological Psychology, 56,* 872–876.

Himwich, W. (1971, December). Paper presented at Conference on Early Nutrition and Environmental Influences upon Behavioral Development, Seattle, WA.

Horwood, S. P., Boyle, M. H., Torrence, G. W., & Sinclair, J. C. (1982). Mortality and morbidity of 500- to 1,499-gram birth weight infants live-born to residents of a defined geographic region before and after neonatal intensive care. *Pediatrics, 69,* 613–620.

Hunt, J. V. (1981). Predicting intellectual disorders in childhood for preterm infants with birthweights below 1501 grams. In S. L. Friedman & M. Sigman (Eds.), *Preterm birth and psychological development* (pp. 329–351). New York: Academic Press.

Hunt, J. V., Tooley, W. H., & Harvin, D. (1982). Learning disabilities in children with birthweights less-than-or-equal-to 1500 grams. *Seminars in Perinatology, 6,* 280–287.

Hunter, R. S., Kilstrom, N., Kraybill, E. N., & Loda, F. (1978). Antecedents of child abuse and neglect in premature infants: A prospective study in a newborn intensive care unit. *Pediatrics, 61,* 629–635.

Huttenlocher, P. R. (1984). Synapse elimination and plasticity in developing human cerebral cortex. *Journal of Mental Deficiency, 88,* 488–496.

Kitchen, W. H., Ryan, M. M., Rickards, A., Astbury, J., Ford, G., Lissenden, J. V., Keith, C. G., & Keir, E. H. (1982). Changing outcome over 13 years of very low birthweight infants. *Seminars in Perinatology, 6,* 373–389.

Klaus, M. H., & Kennell, J. H. (1982). *Parent-infant bonding* (2nd ed.). Saint Louis: The C. V. Mosby Company.

Klein, M., & Stern, L. (1971). Low birthweight and the battered child syndrome. *American Journal of the Diseases of Children, 122,* 15–18.

Knobloch, H., Malone, A., Ellison, P. H., Stevens, F., & Zdeb, M. (1982). Considerations in evaluating changes in outcome of infants weighing less than 1501 grams. *Pediatrics, 69,* 285–295.

Korner, A. F. (1979). Maternal rhythms and waterbeds: A form of intervention with premature infants. In E. B. Thoman (Ed.), *Origins of the infant's social responsiveness, Johnson & Johnson Baby Products Company*

Pediatric Round Table II (pp. 95–124). Hillsdale, NJ: Lawrence Erlbaum Associates.

Korner, A. F. (1985). Preventive intervention with high-risk newborns: Theoretical, conceptual, and methodological perspectives. In J. D. Osofsky (Ed.), *Handbook for infant development* (2nd ed.). New York: Wiley-Interscience.

Korner, A. F., Guilleminault, C., Van den Hoed, J., & Baldein, R. B. (1978). Reduction of sleep apnea and bradycardia in preterm infants on oscillating water beds: A controlled polygraphic study. *Pediatrics, 61*, 528–533.

Korner, A. F., Ruppel, E. M., & Rho, J. M. (1982). Effects of water beds on the sleep and motility of theophylline-treated preterm infants. *Pediatrics, 70*, 864–869.

Korner, A. F., Schneider, P., & Forrest, T. (1983). Effects of vestibular-proprioceptive stimulation on the neurobehavioral development of preterm infants: A pilot study. *Neuropediatrics, 14*(3), 170–175.

Kramer, L. I., & Pierpont, M. E. (1976). Rocking waterbeds and auditory stimuli to enhance growth of preterm infants. *The Journal of Pediatrics, 88*(2), 297–299.

Kramer, M., Chamorro, I., Green, D., & Knudson, F. (1975). Extra tactile stimulation of the premature infant. *Nursing Research, 24*, 324–333.

Kronauer, R. E., Czeisler, C. A., Pilato, S. F., Moore-Ede, M. C., & Weitzman, E. D. (1982). Mathematical model of the human circadian system with two interacting oscillators. *American Physiological Society*, R3.

Levine, S. (1969). An endocrine theory of infantile stimulation. In A. Ambrose (Ed.), *Stimulation in early infancy* (pp. 45–55). London: Academic Press.

Levine, S., Haltmeyer, G. C., Karas, G. G., & Denenberg, V. H. (1967). Physiological and behavioral effects of infantile stimulation. *Physiology and Behavior, 2*, 55–59.

Levine, S., & Mullins, R. F., Jr. (1966). Hormonal influence on brain organization in infant rats. *Science, 152*, 1585–1592.

Lynch, G., & Gall, C. (1979). Organization and reorganization in the central nervous system: Evolving concepts of brain plasticity. In F. Falkner & J. M. Tanner (Eds.), *Neurobiology and Nutrition: Human growth* (Vol. 3, pp. 125–144). New York: Plenum.

Mayes, L. C., Kirk, V., Buchanan, D., & Stohlman, M. T. (1985). The changing cognitive outcome of preterm infants with hyalin membrane disease. *American Journal of Diseases of Children, 139*, 20.

Mayes, L. C., Kirk, V., Haywood, N., Buchanan, D., Hedvall, G., & Stahlman, M. T. (1985). Changing cognitive outcomes in preterm infants with hyaline membrane disease. *American Journal of Diseases of Children, 139*, 20–24.

Murphy, T. F., Nichter, C. A., & Liden, C. B. (1982). Developmental outcome of the high-risk infant: A review of methodological issues. *Seminars in Perinatology, 6*, 353–364.

Neal, M. V. (1967). The relationship between a regimen of vestibular stimulation and the developmental behavior of the premature infant (Doctoral dissertation, University of New York, 1967). *Dissertation Abstracts International* (University Microfilms No. 70-7342).

Neal, M. V. (1968). Vestibular stimulation and developmental behavior of the small premature infant. *Nursing Research Report, 3*, 2–5.

Porrino, L. J., Esposito, R. U., Seeger, T. F., Crane, A. M., Pert, A., & Sokoloff, L. (1984). Metabolic mapping of the brain during rewarding self-stimulation. *Science, 224*, 306–309.

Powell, L. (1974). Effects of extra stimulation and maternal involvement on the development of low birth weight infants and on maternal behavior. *Child Development, 45*, 106–113.

Prechtl, H. F. R. (1977). Assessment and significance of behavioural states. In S. R. Berenberg (Ed.), *Brain: Fetal and infant* (pp. 79–90). Martinus Nijhoff: The Hague.

Rabinovitch, M. S., & Rosvold, E. (1972). A closed-field intelligence test for rats. In V. H. Denenberg (Ed.), *The development of behavior* (pp. 315–322). Stamford, CT: Sinauer Associates, Inc.

Rausch, P. B. (1981). Effects of tactile and kinesthetic stimulation on premature infants. *JOGN Nursing*, January/February, 34–37.

Reich, J. N., Maier, R., Klein, L., & Gyurke, J. (1984, April). *Effects of infant appearance and state patterns on adult perceptions*. Poster presented at the biennial International Conference on Infant Studies, New York.

Rose, S., Schmidt, K., & Bridger, W. (1976). Cardiac and behavioral responsivity to tactile stimulation in premature and fullterm infants. *Developmental Psychology, 12*, 311–320.

Rosenzweig, M. R. (1981). Effects of environment on development of brain and behavior. In E. Tobach, L. R. Aronson, & E. Shaw (Eds.), *The biopsychology of development* (pp. 303–342). New York: Academic Press.

Rothberg, A. D., Maisels, M. J., Bagnato, S., Murphy, J., Gifford, K., & McKinley, K. (1983). Infants weighing 1,000 grams or less at birth: Developmental outcome for ventilated and nonventilated infants. *Pediatrics, 71*, 599–602.

Saigal, S., Rosenbaum, P., Stoskopf, B., & Milner, R. (1982). Follow-up of infants 501 to 1,500 gm birth weight delivered to residents of a geographically defined region with perinatal intensive care facilities. *The Journal of Pediatrics, 100*, 606–613.

Sameroff, A. J. (1981). Longitudinal studies of preterm infants: A review of chapters 17–20. In S. L. Friedman & M. Sigman (Eds.), *Preterm birth and psychological development* (pp. 387–393). New York: Academic Press.

Sameroff, A. J., & Chandler, M. J. (1975). Reproductive risk and the continuum of caretaking casualty. In F. D. Horowitz (Ed.), *Review of child development research: Vol. 4.* (pp. 187–244). Chicago: University of Chicago Press.

Scarr-Salapatek, S., & Williams, M. L. (1973). The effect of early stimulation on low-birth-weight infants. *Child Development, 44*, 94–101.

Schneider, G. E. (1979). Is it really better to have your brain lesion early? A revision of the "Kennard Principle." *Neuropsychologia, 17*, 557–583.

Segall, M. (1972). Cardiac responsivity to auditory stimulation in premature infants. *Nursing Research, 21*, 15–19.

Sehring, P., Gorski, D., Sweet, D., Martin, J., & Leonard, C. (1985, April). *Bradycardia in preterm in-*

fants: One response to caregiver touch. Paper presented at the meeting of the Society for Research in Child Development, Toronto, Canada.

Siegel, L. S. (1983). Correction for prematurity and its consequences for the assessment of the very low birth weight infant. *Child Development, 54,* 1176–1188.

Sigman, M., & Parmelee, A. H. (1974). Visual preference of four-month-old premature and full-term infants. *Child Development, 45,* 959–965.

Smotherman, W. P. (1984, October). *Fetal learning in utero.* Paper presented at the meeting of the International Society for Developmental Psychobiology, Baltimore, MD.

Solkoff, N., Yaffee, S., Weintraub, D., & Blase, B. (1969). Effects of handling on the subsequent development of premature infants. *Developmental Psychology, 1,* 765–768.

Thoman, E. B. (1979). CNS dysfunction and nonverbal communication between mother and infant. In C. L. Ludlow & M. E. Doran-Quine (Eds.), *The neurological bases of language disorders in children: Methods and directions for research* (pp. 43–54). NINCDS Monograph, Washington, DC: Government Printing Office.

Thoman, E. B. (1980). Infant development viewed within the mother-infant relationship. In E. Quilligan & N. Kretchmer (Eds.), *Fetal and maternal medicine* (pp. 243–265). New York: John Wiley & Sons.

Thoman, E. B. (1981a). Affective communication as the prelude and context for language learning. In R. L. Schiefelbusch & D. Bricker (Eds.), *Early language: Acquisition and intervention* (pp. 181–200). Baltimore: University Park Press.

Thoman, E. B. (1981b). Early communication as the prelude to later adaptive behaviors. In M. J. Begab, H. C. Haywood, & H. Garber (Eds.), *Psychosocial influences in retarded performances: Vol. 2. Strategies for improving competence.* (pp. 219–244). Baltimore: University Park Press.

Thoman, E. B. (1982). A biological perspective and a behavioral model for assessment of premature infants. In L. A. Bond & J. M. Joffe (Eds.), *Primary prevention of psychopathology: Vol. 6. Facilitating infant and early childhood development* (pp. 159–179). Hanover, New Hampshire: University Press of New England.

Thoman, E. B. (1986). Assessment of neurobehavioral stability in infants. In N. A. Krasnegor, T. I. Thompson, & D. B. Gray (Eds.), *Advances in behavioral pharmacology series: Vol. 6. Developmental Behavioral Pharmacology* (pp. 79–97). Hillsdale, NJ: Lawrence Erlbaum Associates.

Thoman, E. B., Acebo, C., & Becker, P. T. (1983). Infant crying and stability in the mother-infant relationship: A systems analysis. *Child Development, 54,* 653–659.

Thoman, E. B., & Acebo, C. (1984). The first affections of infancy. In R. W. Bell, J. W. Elias, R. L. Greene, & J. H. Harvey (Eds.), *Interfaces in psychology I: Developmental psychobiology and neuropsychology* (pp. 17–56). Lubbock, Texas: Texas Tech University Press.

Thoman, E., & Arnold, W. (1968). Effects of incubator rearing with social deprivation on maternal behavior in rats. *Journal of Comparative and Physiological Psychology, 65,* 441–446.

Thoman, E. B., & Becker, P. T. (1979). Issues in assessment and prediction for the infant born at risk. In T. Field, A. Sostek, S. Goldberg, & H. H. Shuman (Eds.), *Infants born at risk* (pp. 461–483). New York: Spectrum.

Thoman, E. B., Denenberg, V. H., Sievel, J., Zeidner, L., & Becker, P. T. (1981). State organization in neonates: Developmental inconsistency indicates risk for developmental dysfunction. *Neuropediatrics, 12,* 45–54.

Thoman, E. B., & Korner, A. F. (1971). Effects of vestibular stimulation on the behavior and development of infant rats. *Developmental Psychology, 5,* 92–98.

Thoman, E. B., Waite, S. P., & Shafer, W. (1981, April). *Motility patterns in pre–term infants.* Paper presented at the biennial meeting of the Society of Research in Child Development, Boston.

White, J. L., & Labarba, R. (1976). The effects of tactile and kinesthetic stimulation on neonatal development in the premature infant. *Developmental Psychobiology, 9,* 569–577.

Winfree, A. T. (1967). Biological rhythms and the behavior of populations of coupled oscillators. *Journal of Theoretical Biology, 16,* 15–42.

Yu, V. Y., Orgill, A. A., Bajuk, B., & Astbury, J. (1984). Survival and 2-year outcome of extremely preterm infants. *British Journal of Obstetrics and Gynaecology, 91,* 640–646.

Chapter 6

Malleability
Lessons from Intervention and Family Studies
Sandra Scarr and Jeffrey Arnett

"'Tis education forms the common mind. Just as the twig is bent, the tree's inclined."

—Alexander Pope

The idea that children's development is shaped by the environment has a long and venerable history in Western thought. Psychologists adopted popular ideas from ages of novelists, poets, historians, and philosophers when they proposed in this century that development is malleable, if not unlimited. Ideas about the effects of the environment on intelligence, as well as on other areas of behavior—especially during the first few years of a child's life—rang true to several generations of social scientists. Early behaviorists, notably John Watson (1928), bragged that any infant could be molded by proper and rigorous training into an adult of any kind—architect, musician, scientist. Though Freud concerned himself with personality and psychopathology, rather than with intelligence, few thinkers are more responsible than he for popularizing the idea that early experience works on the infant as does a sculptor upon an undifferentiated lump of clay, and forms the foundation for all that follows. Both the malleability of children and the importance of early experience are popular ideas rooted in Western culture of the 20th century.

These popular ideas seemed to find an empirical basis in the late 1950s in the work of Hebb (1947), Hunt (1961), and Bloom (1964). Hebb's work in neuropsychology seemed to indicate that an organism's early experience and learning were critical to its ability to learn later in its development. Hunt blended this idea with research based on learning theory and Piaget's theories of cognitive development, and concluded that intelligence is neither fixed nor genetically predetermined, and that early experience offers the hope of salvation for the underprivileged. Bloom asserted that the first 5 years of life were a "critical period," during which intervention was likely to be effective in raising intelligence, after which intelligence could be considered to be fixed. Combined, these ideas created a surge of enthusiasm in the early '60s among psychologists and policy-makers, and led to the creation of several ambitious social programs in that decade, most notably Project Head Start and the Women, Infants, and Childrens' (WIC) Program.

More recent investigations have tempered this optimism, and indeed some investigators have noted that plasticity is a double-edged sword (Sigman, 1982): If development is amenable to environmental improvement, it is also susceptible to environmental damage. There is evolutionary danger in the openness of human beings to experiences that may or may not be beneficial to their development. This caveat has been described by Brim and Kagan (1980):

The belief that early experiences create lasting characteristics, like the belief in biological and genetic determinism, makes it possible to assume that attempts to improve the course of human development are wasted and without consequence. If society believes that it is all over by the third year of life, then it can deal harshly with many people later in life because nothing more can be done, and social programs designed to educate, redirect, reverse, or eliminate unwanted human characteristics cannot be justified. Policies of racial, ethnic, and sex discrimination, incarceration rather than rehabilitation of criminals, ignoring urban and rural poverty, and isolation of the elderly have found shelter in the belief in the determinism of the early years of life. (p. 21)

The extent to which evolution has left human development open to external influences is itself an open question. No one doubts that human development can be damaged by dire circumstances, whether internal (mutations) or external (deprivation of normal experience). Also, there is evidence for plasticity in animal experiments and human studies that show that normal environments following serious deprivations can result in attainment of normal functioning (Clark & Hanisee, 1982; Clarke & Clarke, 1976; Winick, Meyer, & Harris, 1975). Children subjected to extreme nutritional, intellectual, and emotional deprivations in infancy and early childhood have been found to recover and even excel, once their environments have been improved. For example, severely malnourished Asian children, adopted into middle class American families, most often achieve intellectual test scores far above the means of nondeprived American children (Clark & Hanisee, 1982; Winick et al., 1975). But what implications should we draw from such studies for normal human development?

The major challenge to developmentalists is not to establish that there is *some* plasticity everywhere, but to assess how much, in what areas of development, and when. Most authorities on evolution acknowledge some genetic constraints on species' developmental patterns. Without constraints, there would be no species. To argue otherwise is absurd. Similarly, most authorities on the evolution of mammals acknowledge that experience and learning are important to many aspects of behavioral development. Kittens are predisposed to pounce on small moving objects, but they strike more accurately with practice.

Does the kitten need 10, 20, or 250 tries, to reach species-typical accuracy? Will this happen at 4 weeks, 6 weeks, or 6 months? What portion of individual variability in pouncing is due to practice, what portion to genetic individual differences (were mother and father good pouncers?), and what portion to other individual characteristics (does the kitten have good vision?)?

Does the hearing child of deaf parents need 1 hour per day of dialogue with a speaking adult, 2 hours, or 12 hours to become a proficient speaker of the language? How much of the child's language must be developed before 3 years to ensure normal speech; how much can sign language substitute for early language and still guarantee that the child will reach normal levels of language proficiency? The central question about plasticity is: How much experience is necessary, and when, for each aspect of development?

QUESTIONING ASSUMPTIONS

Let us state early on that we doubt that one can conclude anything incontestable about plasticity and the life span (see Gottlieb, 1983). Research on the subject is too diffuse and rudimentary at this point to permit any such attempt. For example, how would one compare the magnitude of malleability in cellular and behavioral events at various points in the life span? Are two more vocabulary words or two more dendrites significantly different in early childhood and late middle age? The mixture of levels of analysis in attempts to form a general theory of malleability obscures the variety of observations that lead to conflicting hypotheses. If one does not differentiate between cells and reading skills, one is likely to confuse the issues about when, where, and how malleability is or is not a property of organisms.

Consider an extreme hypothesis: Perhaps, there *is* no general theory of malleability. Just as it seems we cannot have a general theory of all of the behavior of all of the people all of the time, perhaps one cannot formulate an overarching theory of malleability that subsumes all observations from cellular to social levels of development. To propose that malleability is more a property of younger than older organisms, of behavioral rather than biological levels of development, is mere conjecture and is based primarily on a lack of comparable measurements. It reflects our cultural hopes more directly than our scientific findings.

CLARIFYING THE ISSUES

Plasticity does not imply a lack of organization. Rather, plasticity arises from organized openness to influence by environments ranging from cellular to social. Changes in human development are not random but constrained responses to life events. Constraints come from the genetic program for human development and from the developmental history of the organism. Indeed, the organism's ability to select and make its own environments (Scarr & McCartney, 1983), and its disposition for individual developmental continuities (Brim & Kagan, 1980; Wilson, 1983), argue for a lack of externally orchestrated malleability. What evolution has left open for intervention by externally imposed events, we should all fear.

But we do believe that experientially restricted rodents and humans benefit from exposure to environments with a normal range of variety of opportunity (see Scarr & Weinberg, 1978). Clearly, one cannot select experiences that are compatible with one's developmental level and individual characteristics if the opportunities to gain those experiences are not present. In the vast majority of people's lives, however, a sufficient variety of opportunities are present to permit people to develop as themselves—as their talents, personalities, and interests guide them.

In the following sections, we review briefly several areas of research as they pertain to malleability, including neurophysiological research, early intervention efforts, adoption researching, and twin studies.

NEUROPHYSIOLOGICAL RESEARCH

Traditionally, psychologists have identified three stages of brain development. In the initial, childhood stage, the brain is said to be uniquely receptive to certain experiences at certain times. At the adult stage, the brain retains the capacity to store information from the environment, but the effects of specific experiences are said to be less profound. Finally, during aging, the brain is purported to be less capable of directing many different kinds of mental and physical performance, and has a diminished ability to store and retain information.

But recent research has altered this conception. According to Greenough and Green (1981), a more accurate portrayal of the process is that growth and degeneration occur throughout normal development, though the balance tilts more toward degeneration as development progresses. Young organisms undergo some cell loss continually, and the adult brain is still plastic—experience continues to modify the structure of the brain. Even during aging, the brain retains some flexibility. Thus, adult rats placed in an enriched environment for 30 days have greater complexity of dendritic branching patterns than do controls (Uylings, Kuypers, & Veltman, 1978), and studies of monkeys indicate that noticeable brain changes take place in adults in a naturally occurring environment (Floeter & Greenough, 1979). Among humans, certain areas of the brains of elderly persons are considerably larger and more complex, compared to younger persons. But, though animal studies of adults show that adults in an enriched environment exhibit brain changes, the changes are less than if the animals are placed there immediately after weaning (Rosenzwieg, Bennett, & Diamond, 1972). This research, then, would seem to accord with the assertion that intelligence is malleable, particularly in early development, but later as well.

Much of the neurological evidence for plasticity comes, however, from deprivation experiments with rodents. Not surprisingly, it turns out that animals deprived of species-typical environments develop abnormally, and that supplying them with environments that more closely resemble their normal habitats has beneficial effects on their development. But while these findings might be relevant to the rare human cases of extraordinary deprivation, extrapolating from socially isolated, reared-in-the-dark, caged rodents to human children, even disadvantaged human children, is risky business. It should be done with ample qualifications, where it is done at all.

For humans, the evidence for earlier, greater plasticity is mixed. On the one hand, biologically, cells differentiate and become more rigidly specialized with time; but, on the other hand, it is easier to teach an illiterate adult basic literacy skills than to teach a 2-year old to read. In embryology, the effects of radiation on the developing human depend not on the *earliness* of the teratogen, but on its timing in the course of development (Scarr-Salapatek, 1975). Later effects of radiation are more devastating to the embryo than earlier effects, because what is not yet differentiated cannot be affected by the radiation. The same can be said for other events that can interfere with normal development. Early is not the issue. Timing with respect to development is. The emotional effects of the loss of a parent in the first week of life are surely not as devastating as the same loss at 2 years of age.

EARLY EDUCATIONAL INTERVENTION

In the past 30 years, a variety of efforts have been made to enhance the intellectual abilities of disadvantaged children by exposing them at an early age to an especially enriched and stimulating educational environment. The targets of these interventions have been predominantly minority, urban children. These programs were inspired by beliefs in malleability and early experience, which combined to promise a world of change in disadvantaged children's development. More particularly, the development of intelligence was believed to depend highly, if not solely, on the quality of the environment in which development takes place, and the environment was purported to be especially important in the first 5 years of a child's life. In most cases, however, intelligence proved to be more intractable than initially expected and hoped.

The most vivid illustration of this comes from the Consortium of Longitudinal Studies

(Lazar, Darlington, Murray, Royce, & Snipper, 1982). Follow-up studies were conducted on 11 early intervention projects, in 1975; by then the original participants ranged from 8 to 18 years old. The early intervention programs had differed widely in scope and design. Some had been center-based, some had been home-based, and some had combined the two approaches. In all cases, however, there had been control or comparison groups available, and detailed data had been collected on the children's intelligence and family background, before the intervention had begun.

The consistent result across the studies was that, although virtually all of the children were reported to have had IQ gains immediately following the intervention, in almost all cases this result was followed by a steady decline. Thus, in 1975, 3 or 4 years after the termination of the intervention, the IQs did not differ between the experimental and comparison groups.

This is not to say that the interventions were completely ineffective (Scarr & Weinberg, 1986). The children who had participated in the early intervention programs did perform somewhat better on achievement tests, in general, particularly on the math subtests, than did the children in the control or comparison groups. Moreover, these children demonstrated other noncognitive but academically relevant gains: They were less likely to be in special education or to be retained in grade, and they reported more positive attitudes toward achievement and school. But with regard to intellectual ability, the initial improvements were not sustained.

In the studies in the Consortium follow-up, the interventions were mostly limited to only a few hours daily. Other more intensive projects have produced correspondingly greater results (although elsewhere it has been reported that interventions begun before age 2 are no more effective than interventions beginning in preschool [Ramey, Bryant, & Suarez, 1984]). One exemplary project of this kind is the Abecedarian Project that Ramey and his colleagues (Ramey, this volume, chapter 11; Ramey, Dorval, & Baker-Ward, 1983) have conducted since the early 1970s. The subjects

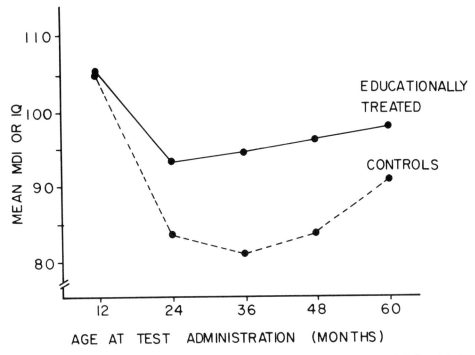

Figure 1. Mean Bayley (12 mo.), Stanford-Binet (24, 26, 48 mo.), and WPPSI (60 mo.). (From Ramey, C. T., Dorval, B., & Baker-Ward, L. [1983]. Group day care and socially disadvantaged families: Effects on the child and the family. *Advances in Early Education and Day Care, 3,* 69–106; reprinted with permission.)

were born to mothers with low incomes, low IQs, and little education. They received educationally based day care from the age of about 3 months, for 5 days a week, all year. Care was provided by a highly trained staff, at staff-child ratios low enough to provide for a great deal of individual attention—1:2 for infants and 1:5 for children aged 2 to 5.

Figure 1 illustrates the results achieved from this intervention. Initially, there is a substantial and dramatic drop in IQ from 12 to 24 months, but over the course of the next several years, the average IQ of the experimental group steadily rises. Curiously, the average IQ of the comparison group also *rises* steadily during this same period, a phenomenon that the authors now attribute to the control group's having had preschool experiences outside of the experimental intervention. Nevertheless, in a follow-up study at age 9, there remains a significant, if less dramatic, difference in IQ between the two groups.

The Milwaukee Project (Heber, 1978) is an-

other example of an intensive and relatively successful intervention. Similar to the Abecedarian Project, children born to mothers of low socio-economic status (SES) received high quality, educationally based day care from infancy, with staff-child ratios of 1:1 at ages 0–2, and 1:4 at ages 2–6. In addition, in this project the mothers were provided with basic education, vocational habilitation and placement, and child-care training.

The results of this study, as originally presented (shown in Figure 2), were impressive and dramatic. However, Flynn (1984) has demonstrated that the high IQ scores reported for the subjects were inflated by the use of obsolete test norms. The adjusted scores are quite similar to those obtained in the Abecedarian Project. Both the original and the adjusted scores are presented in Table 1.

Other studies demonstrate that when a child has suffered deprivation at a young age, maturation alone can lead to a remarkable recovery and advance in intellectual functioning (e.g.,

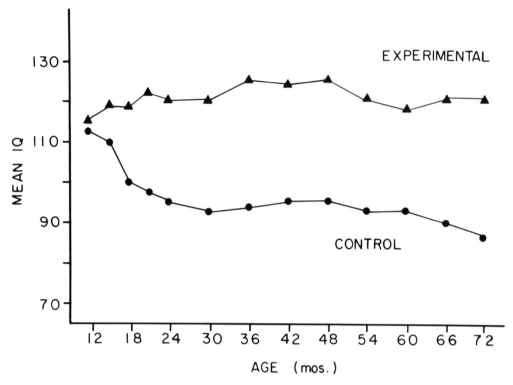

Figure 2. Mean IQ performance for experimental (▲) and control (●) children. (From Heber, R. [1978]. Sociocultural mental retardation: A longitudinal study. In D. Forgays [Ed.], *Primary prevention of psychopathology: Vol. 2. Environmental influences.* Hanover, NH: University Press of New England; reprinted with permission.)

Kagan & Klein, 1973; Werner & Smith, 1982). Kagan and Klein studied children in two Guatemalan villages. The typical infant in these communities received very little cognitive or social stimulation, and they were found to be

Table 1. Heber's experimental group: mean IQ performances with increasing age

Test	Age (years)				
	2–3	4–6	7–9	10–11	12–14
Results as presented					
SB-LM	122	121			
WPPSI		111			
WISC			103	104	100
Results adjusted					
SB-LM	108	107			
WPPSI		105			
WISC			95	96	92

Note: Adapted from "The mean IQ of Americans: Massive gains 1932 to 1978" by J. Flynn, 1984, *Psychological Bulletin, 95,* pp. 29–51. Copyright 1984 by the American Psychological Association. Reprinted by permission of the author.

substantially behind American infants in various aspects of their early cognitive development. But preadolescent Guatemalan children performed similarly to American children on culture-fair tests of specific cognitive abilities, indicating that the differences among the younger children reflected merely a delay in the emergence of certain cognitive abilities for the Guatemalan children, because of their unstimulating early environment, and did not signal permanently catastrophic damage to their cognitive abilities.

In sum, efforts to raise the predicted IQs of disadvantaged children by providing them with high quality early education have achieved mixed success. In most cases, the gains in IQ established during the intervention have faded during the years that follow. The most intensive interventions do appear to produce enhanced intelligence that is both significant and enduring, though even in these interventions, the gains diminish with time.

FAMILY STUDIES

Adoption

One might think of adoption as the ultimate intervention, one that changes the entire social ecology of the child (Scarr & Weinberg, 1976). Adoptive families are usually selected for their salutary characteristics, including above-average SES and benevolent attitudes toward children. Adoptive placements are both continuous and permanent. This is a prime situation for examining the question of whether intelligence is malleable. Two main questions are pertinent. First, do adopted children benefit from the qualities of home environments provided by adoptive families, whose intelligence and life circumstances are, on average, above the population mean? Do adopted children as a group score above average, or, at the level that would be predicted based on their biological parents? Second, do individual differences among adopted children reflect differences in their home environments? That is, do individual children's scores correspond in correlation coefficients to their adoptive parents' scores or other measures of the home environment? To what extent do individual differences correspond to those of their biological rather than adoptive parents?

The two questions, one about average malleability and one about individual variability, are both important and can be answered by adoption studies. The first question of average levels of intelligence can be answered by mean values of adopted children, compared to those of their biological parents and of children in like circumstances. The second can be answered by analyses of covariation between adopted children and their two sets of parents. Because adopted children share none of their genes with their adoptive parents, any similarity between them is likely to be environmental (excluding the effect of selective placement by adoption agencies); and because children given up for adoption have not shared a rearing environment with their biological parents, similarities between adopted children and their biological parents are primarily genetic.

In one of the early adoption studies, Skodak and Skeels (1949) followed children born to mothers with low IQs (a mean IQ of 85.7) and adopted into upper-middle-class families, explicitly selected by the agency for their exceptional quality. The results indicate both genetic and environmental influences: The adopted children had IQs averaging 107 as adolescents, much higher than their natural mothers (but see Jensen, 1973 for a critique). In the adoptive families, however, there were greater similarities between the parents and their natural children, than between the parents and their adopted children.

In seminal studies, Burks (1928) and Leahy (1935), as cited in Scarr and Kidd (1983), showed that although adopted children scored above average for the population, presumably in reponse to their attentive families, they benefited by only about 6 IQ points over the level expected had they been raised by their natural families. More recent studies echo and elaborate these findings. In the Texas Adoption Project (Horn, Loehlin, & Willerman, 1979), 300 adoptive families were studied when the adopted children were, on average, 8 years old. The adoptive families were well above average socioeconomically and intellectually. Table 2 shows the correlations of adoptive and biological parents with their children.

All of the correlations are quite low, but it can be seen that the IQs of the adopted children were correlated more highly with their biological parents than with their adoptive parents, indicating a preponderant effect of genetic influences over environmental differences within this sample of adoptive families. Also, the correlations in IQ scores between biological mothers and their children given up for adoption are as high as the correlations between adoptive mothers and their own children.

Of particular interest is an analysis conducted by Willerman (1979) on two subgroups of the sample. He selected subgroups of biological mothers with the highest (above 120) and lowest (below 95) IQs, and looked at the IQs of their children given up for adoption. The results are shown in Table 3. The substantial difference in IQ between the children of the

Table 2. Correlation of parent's Beta IQ with child's IQ tests

| | Child test | | | |
| | Wechsler performance IQ | | Wechsler or Binet total IQ | |
Correlational pairing	r	N[a]	r	N
Adoptive father and				
biological child	.29	144	.28	163
adopted child	.12	405	.14	462
Adoptive mother and				
biological child	.21	143	.20	162
adopted child	.15	401	.17	459
Unwed mother and				
her child	.28	297	.31	345
other adopted child in same family	.15	202	.19	233
biological child in same family	.06	143	.08	161

Adapted from Horn, J. M., Loehlin, J. C., & Willerman, L. (1979). Intellectual resemblance among adoptive and biological relatives: The Texas Adoption Project. *Behavior Genetics, 9,* 177–207.

[a]Ns refer to the number of pairings (= the number of children)—the same parent may enter more than one pairing. In the case of twins, the second twin was excluded from the unwed mother–other child comparisons.

high- and low-IQ mothers illustrates the differential responsiveness of children to a high quality home environment, depending on their genetic potential.

The Transracial Adoption Study (Scarr & Weinberg, 1976, 1977, 1983) included children of black and interracial parentage who were adopted by white families. It was expected that by being reared "in the culture of the tests and of the schools," these children would have IQs at or above the norm for white children, and well above the norm for black children, thus providing evidence against the claim that there are substantial genetic differences in intelligence between racial groups. This hypothesis was largely supported. The 99 black and interracial children adopted in the

first year of life obtained IQs of 110 on the average, above the norm for the white population. Still, as in the Texas Adoption Study, correlations between biological mothers and their children given up for adoption were as high as for adoptive mothers and their own children, and higher than for adoptive mothers and their adopted children, demonstrating again the influence of genetic differences. Table 4 shows these results.

The Adolescent Adoption Study (Scarr & Weinberg, 1978; 1980) focused on adopted children at the end of the childrearing period, in order to assess the cumulative impact of family environment. In comparison to several other adoption studies of younger children, including those described here, correlations in IQ be-

Table 3. IQs of adoptees as a function of biological mother's IQ

Adoptee's biological mother (Beta)	Adoptive midparent (Beta)	Adoptee (WISC/Binet)	Adoptees >120 IQ	<95 IQ
Low IQ (N = 27; M = 89.4)	110.8	102.6	0%	15%
High IQ (N = 34; M = 121.6)	114.8	118.3	44%	0%

Adapted from Horn, J. M., Loehlin, J. C., & Willerman, L. (1979). Intellectual resemblance among adoptive and biological relatives: The Texas Adoption Project. *Behavior Genetics, 9,* 177–207.

Table 4. Comparisons of biological and unrelated parent-child IQ correlation in 101 transracial adoptive families

	N (pairs)	r
Parents-biological children		
Adoptive mother-biological child	141	.34
Natural mother-adopted child[a]	135	.33
Adoptive father-biological child	142	.39
Natural father-adopted child[a]	46	.43
Parents-unrelated children		
Adoptive mother-adopted child	174	.21 (.23)[b]
Natural mother-biological child		
of adoptive family[a]	217	.15
Adoptive father-adopted child	170	.27 (.15)[b]
Natural father-biological child		
of adoptive family[a]	86	.19

Adapted from S. Scarr and R. A. Weinberg (1983). The Minnesota adoption studies: Genetic differences and malleability. *Child Development, 54,* 260–267.

[a]Educational level, not IQ scores.
[b]Early adopted only (N = 111).

tween adoptive parents and their adolescents adopted in infancy are considerably lower. Wechsler Adult Intelligence Scale (WAIS) IQ score of the adopted children was 106, about 6 points higher than would be predicted based on their natural parents' scores, and about 6 points lower than the biological offspring of the adoptive families. Similarly, the differences in school achievements between adopted and biological children reflected their IQ differences (Scarr & Yee, 1980). Also, in contrast to adoption studies of younger children, which had shown children reared in the same family to be quite similar regardless of genetic relatedness, the IQ correlation of adolescent adopted siblings reared in the same family was 0. The IQ correlation of biological siblings was .35.

These results seem contradictory. How could it be that adopted siblings become *less* similar the longer they live in the same family? Scarr and Weinberg (1978, 1983) hypothesized that the older adolescents are largely liberated from their family's influences and have made choices and pursued courses that are in keeping with their own talents and interests. A further development of this view (Scarr & McCartney, 1983) proposed a progressive developmental change in the degree to which people make their own environments through active genotype → environment effects.

In sum, the adoption studies support the notion that adopted children benefit on average to some extent from their better-than-average home environments (including schools, neighborhoods, and other correlated environments). In this sense, intelligence is malleable. Most adoption studies show the IQs of adopted children to be 6–10 points higher than would have been expected had they been raised by their natural parents. At the same time, the similarity of the IQ correlations of biological mothers with their children given up for adoption indicates the likelihood of a genetic constraint on the degree to which individual differences in intelligence may be influenced.

Twin Studies

Studies of monozygotic (MZ) and dizygotic (DZ) twins also provide information regarding the malleability of intelligence. Although both types of twin share similar rearing environments (Scarr, 1968; Scarr & Carter-Saltzman, 1980), MZ twins are genetically identical, whereas DZ twins share, on average, 50% of their genes. Thus, comparisons of the correlations between MZ and DZ twins illustrate the relative influence of heredity and environment in determining differences in intelligence.

There have been many studies comparing MZ and DZ twins. Nichols (1978) compiled

211 of those that had examined diverse aspects of intelligence, interests, and personality. Taken together, he found that for intelligence the mean correlation for MZ twins was .82, while for DZ twins the correlation was .59. The Louisville Twin Study (Wilson, 1977) compared MZ twins, DZ twins, and non-twin siblings. The IQ correlations for DZ twins were found to be similar to those for siblings, which is not surprising, because in both cases roughly 50% of the genome is shared. MZ twins we again found to be far more similar in IQ than any other sibling pair.

Identical twins reared apart are an intriguing target for twin studies. In three older studies (Juel-Nielson, 1965; Newman, Freeman, & Holzinger, 1937; Shields, 1962) and one ongoing one (Bouchard, 1984), the average IQ correlation of MZ twins reared in different homes was .76, which is higher than for either DZ twins or siblings reared in the same households, and close to the value found for MZ twins reared in the same homes.

In sum, evidence from twin studies generally indicates a substantial genetic influence on intellectual differences among children, adolescents, and adults. The consistently high similarity in intelligence among MZ twins at all ages is striking; it is uniformly higher than the similarity between DZ twins or between biological siblings, and vastly higher than resemblances among adopted siblings reared together from infancy. These results cannot be reasonably explained without invoking a strong genetic influence on variability in intelligence.

In addition, one has to conclude that differences among home environments in the normal range of opportunities for children to express their interests and talents are rather insignificant, accounting for perhaps 10% of the variation in IQ scores among children in the majority American and European cultures. A more important source of environmental variation is *within* families—those unique differences in experience that siblings are provided by their parents (Plomin, 1986; Scarr, 1986). Within-family variance accounts for 30%–40% of the individual variation in intel-

ligence, and can be explained best by recourse to the intrinsic individual characteristics of the siblings, rather than to any differences in their opportunities.

Taken together, the evidence presented here seems to answer the question of whether child development is malleable, with a qualified *yes*. In every area examined, there is some evidence that environmental influences can and do affect the development of intelligence, and equally strong evidence that the effect of the environment is always limited by the genome inherited by the individual from his parents. The idea that anyone could develop high intelligence if provided with an optimal environment does not seem to be warranted, but neither is it reasonable to assert that a person's adult intelligence is fixed from birth and cannot be influenced by environmental factors.

What model best illustrates this evidence? Waddington (1957) proposed the idea of *probabilistic epigenesis* to explain the genetically directed but environmentally variable nature of development. His graphic model of an epigenetic landscape is used to describe the nature of normative development. Development is represented as a ball rolling down a hill into a valley whose contours are defined by the organism's genotype. Environmental factors may act to displace the ball, but unless the forces are strong enough to knock it over the valley wall, it will return to its genotypic path once they are removed. As development progresses, it becomes increasingly canalized, that is, its susceptibility to change by the environment diminishes. Whether early development is more malleable than later development is more of a cultural assumption than a scientific observation. Nonetheless, the idea of a probable developmental course for each individual that is, in part, dependent on the "slings and arrows" of outrageous fortune, is one to which most developmental psychologists today can subscribe.

Waddington's model describes a strong self-righting tendency in organisms, a tendency for development to proceed along a species-typical and individual path and to return to that path even after a period of unusual experience. It explains spontaneous recovery from deprivation; after the deprivation ceases, the organism may rebound to its previous path. The epigenetic landscape of individuals can be said to differ according to their genotypes.

Gottlieb's (1970, 1976, 1983) idea of probabilistic epigenesis follows Waddington. As he describes it, "the behavioral development of individuals within a species does not follow any invariant or inevitable course, and . . . the sequence or outcome of individual behavioral development is probable (with respect to norms) rather than certain" (1970, p. 123). The influence of the genes, then, is to guide development rather than to determine it absolutely.

Another conception is offered by Aslin (1981). He focuses on the idea of a sensitive period to describe experiential influences in perceptual development. Using the analogy of a filter to describe the genetic constraints on development, he begins with several assumptions. The first is that there is a specified range of acceptable environmental inputs. The second is that the height and width of the filter change over the course of development, becoming enlarged during a sensitive period. The function of the sensitive period may be to increase the selectivity of the perceptual system to specific experiences, rather than to experience generally. The third is that changes in the height and width of the filter are determined by the genotype. The idea of a sensitive period—that specific experiences exert a differential effect on development depending on when they occur—might be especially apt in this context. Early development is commonly thought to be more malleable than the other periods of the life span. But what evidence is there that this is true? As noted here, there is some evidence in animal research that an enriched environment is more influential for young animals than for adults. But with regard to human development, very little evidence is available. Calculated attempts to raise intelligence have assumed that early childhood is the most propitious time to intervene, but this idea has yet to rise above the status of an assumption.

The history of Western thought in the last two centuries has led us to believe in the efficacy of intervention and early experience. Perhaps it is also the observation that children develop so rapidly from age 2 to 5 that induces us to think they are especially ripe for environmental influence during that period. But actually, the rapid pace of development then may indicate not an openness to influence, but just the opposite. Perhaps, with so many developmental changes to be achieved in such a short time, nature leaves little room for environmental error, as long as some minimal level of stimulation is provided (Scarr, 1976). One piece of evidence to support this is that children who are born to deaf parents, but have normal hearing themselves, learn to speak at a normal developmental pace, despite being uninvolved in spoken conversation for more than a few hours a week (Schiff, 1979). Perhaps there are other sensitive periods in human development, such as the age of 9 or 10, when children are beginning to learn to define and compare and contrast various concepts; or in early adolescence, when children typically begin to think in less concrete and more abstract terms—the beginning of Piaget's formal operations. But interventions at ages past early childhood, including systematic evaluations, have yet to be tried. Currently there is no evidence indicating whether they would be effective.

Still, the idea of a filter that has limits that are defined by the genome and that can be filled to capacity by stimulation from the environment, seems an apt metaphor for contemporary views of the mutual contributions to development of genetic and environmental influences. Perhaps more apt still is the idea of a reaction range around the developmental path prescribed by the genome. Imagine Waddington's idea of the epigenetic landscape, only with a wider path, so that the ball rolling down it may find itself on one side or another, depending on the influence of the environment. Figure 3 illustrates how this idea might describe a normal population.

Given a normal environment, the phenotypic intelligence of the individual is likely to be at the center of the range. Given an enriched environment, the individual is likely to be at the high side of the range; given a deprived

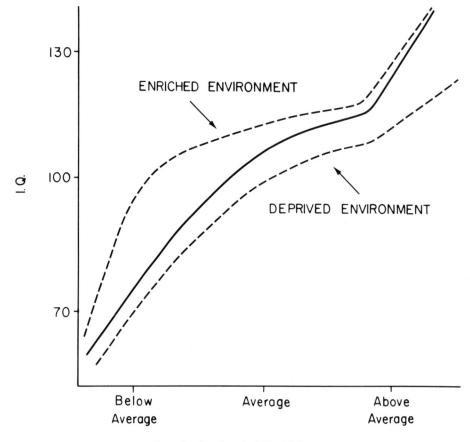

Figure 3.   Genetic potential for intelligence.

environment, at the low side. The range is not equally wide at all points on the continuum; however, at the low IQ end, the possibility of enhancement is greater than the possibility of not reaching the genotypic level, while at the high IQ end, the opposite is true. This takes into account evidence that the IQs of children born to mothers with low IQs are able to be enhanced through intensive early education or through adoption, while the IQs of children born in advantaged environments are not raised even temporarily by educationally based day care.

Intelligence can be said to be malleable, then, but only within certain limits. This may seem to challenge the assumptions of the predominant Western world view that all things are possible to all people—any child can grow up to be President—and of the perfectability of man. But it is certainly a monumental enough task for us to provide the environmental conditions that make it possible for every individual to develop to the limits of his or her own intellectual gifts, whatever those limits might be. The evidence reviewed here reflects a probable heritability for intelligence of .60 or .70— quite high, in other words. But estimates of heritability, and, in fact, all of the evidence presented here, only mean that already existing environmental variations have these limits on how their redistribution can influence intellectual differences. Forms of intervention may yet be discovered that alter our conceptions of how intelligence can be enhanced.

REFERENCES

Aslin, R. (1981). Experiential influences and sensitive periods in perceptual development: A unified model. In R. N. Aslin, J. R. Albert, & M. R. Peterson, *Development of Perception* (Vol. 2). New York: Academic Press.

Bloom, B. S. (1964). *Stability and change in human characteristics.* New York: John Wiley & Sons.

Bouchard, T. J. (1984). Twins reared together and apart: What they tell us about human diversity. In S. W. Fox (Ed.), *Individuality and determinism* (pp. 147–178). New York: Plenum.

Brim, O. G., Jr., & Kagan, J. (1980). Constancy and change: A view of the issues. In O. G. Brim, Jr., & J. Kagan (Eds.), *Constancy and change in human development.* Cambridge: Harvard University Press.

Burks, B. S. (1928). The relative influence of nature and nurture upon mental development: A comparative study of parent–foster child resemblance and true parent–foster child resemblance. *27th Yearbook, National Society for Studies in Experimental Education, 27* (1), 219–316.

Clarke, A. M., & Clarke, A. D. B. (1976). *Early experience: Myth and evidence.* New York: Free Press.

Clark, E. A., & Hanisee, J. (1982). Intellectual and adaptive performance of Asian children in adoptive American settings. *Developmental Psychology, 18,* 595–599.

Floeter, M. K., & Greenough, W. T. (1979). Cerebellar plasticity: Modification of Purkinje cell structure by differential rearing in monkeys. *Science, 206,* 227–229.

Flynn, J. (1984). The mean IQ of Americans: Massive gains 1932 to 1978. *Psychological Bulletin, 95,* 29–51.

Gottlieb, G. (1970). Conceptions of prenatal behavior. In L. R. Aronson, E. Tobach, D. S. Lehrman, & J. S. Rosenblatt (Eds.), *Development and evolution of behavior: Essays in memory of T. C. Schneirla.* San Francisco: W. H. Freeman.

Gottlieb, G. (1976). The roles of experience in the development of behavior and the nervous system. In G. Gottlieb (Ed.), *Neural and behavioral specificity: Studies on the development of behavior and the nervous system* (Vol. 3). New York: Academic Press.

Gottlieb, G. (1983). The psychobiological approach to developmental issues. In M. M. Haith & J. J. Campos (Eds.), *Handbook of child psychology: Infancy and developmental psychobiology* (Vol. 2, pp. 1–26). New York: John Wiley & Sons.

Greenough, W. T., & Green, E. J. (1981). Experience and the changing brain. In J. L. March & S. B. Kiesler (Eds.), *Aging: Biology and behavior.* New York: Academic Press.

Hebb, D. O. (1947). The effects of early experience on problem solving at maturity. *American Psychologist, 2,* 306–307.

Heber, R. (1978). Sociocultural mental retardation: A longitudinal study. In D. Forgays (Ed.), *Primary prevention of psychopathology: Vol. 2. Environmental influences.* Hanover, NH: University Press of New England.

Horn, J. M., Loehlin, J. C., & Willerman, L. (1979). Intellectual resemblance among adoptive and biological relatives: The Texas Adoption Project. *Behavior Genetics, 9,* 177–207.

Hunt, J. M. (1961). *Intelligence and experience.* New York: Ronald Press.

Jensen, A. R. (1973). Let's understand Skodak and Skeels, finally. *Educational Psychologist, 10,* 10–35.

Juel-Neilsen, N. (1965). Individual and environment: A psychiatric-psychological investigation of monozygous twins reared apart. *Acta Psychiatrica Neurologica Scandinavica Monograph, 183,* Supplement.

Kagan, J., & Klein, R. E. (1973). Cross-cultural perspectives on early development. *American Psychologist, 28,* 947–961.

Lazar, I., Darlington, R., Murray, H., Royce, J., & Snipper, A. (1982). Lasting effects of early education: A report from the Consortium for Longitudinal Studies. *Monographs of the Society for Research in Child Development, 47,* (2–3, Serial No. 195).

Leahy, A. M. (1935). Nature-nurture and intelligence. *Genetic Psychology Monographs, 17,* 237–308.

Newman, H. G., Freeman, F. N., & Holzinger, K. J. (1937). *Twins: A study of heredity and environment.* Chicago: University of Chicago Press.

Nichols, R. C. (1978). Heredity and environment: Major findings from twin studies of ability, personality, and interests. *Homo, 29,* 158–173.

Plomin, R. (1986). *Genetics, development and psychology.* Hillsdale, NJ: Lawrence Erlbaum Associates.

Ramey, C. T., Bryant, D. M., & Suarez, T. M. (1984). Preschool compensatory education and the modifiability of intelligence. In D. Detterman (Ed.), *Current topics in human intelligence.* Norwood, NJ: Ablex.

Ramey, C. T., Dorval, B., & Baker-Ward, L. (1983). Group day care and socially disadvantaged families: Effects on the child and the family. *Advances in Early Education and Day Care, 3,* 69–106.

Rosenzweig, M. R., Bennett, E. L., & Diamond, M. C. (1972). Brain changes in response to experience. *Scientific American, 226,* 22–29.

Scarr, S. (1968). Environmental bias in twin studies. *Eugenics Quarterly, 15,* 34–40.

Scarr–Salapatek, S. (1976). An evolutionary perspective on infant intelligence: Species patterns and individual variations. In M. Lewis (Ed.), *Origins of intelligence.* (pp. 165–197). New York: Plenum.

Scarr, S. (1986). Protecting general intelligence: Constructs and consequences for intervention. In R. J. Linn (Ed.), *Intelligence: Measurement, theory and public policy.* Champaign: University of Illinois Press.

Scarr, S., & Carter-Saltzman, L. (1980). Twin method: Defense of a critical assumption. *Behavior Genetics, 9,* 527–542.

Scarr, S., & Kidd, K. K. (1983). Behavior genetics. In M. M. Haith & J. J. Campos (Eds.), *Handbook of child psychology: Infancy and developmental psychobiology* (pp. 345–433). New York: John Wiley & Sons.

Scarr, S., & McCartney, K. (1983). How people make their own environments: A theory of genotype-environment effects. *Child Development, 54,* 425–435.

Scarr, S., & Weinberg, R. (1976). IQ test performance of black children adopted by white families. *American Psychologist, 31,* 726–739.

Scarr, S., & Weinberg, R. (1977). Intellectual similarities within families of both adopted and biological children. *American Psychologist, 31,* 726–739.

Scarr, S., & Weinberg, R. (1978). The influence of "family background'' on intellectual attainment. *American Sociological Review, 43,* 674–692.

Scarr, S., & Weinberg, R. (1980). Calling all camps! The war is over! *American Sociological Review, 45,* 859–864.

Scarr, S., & Weinberg, R. (1983). The Minnesota Adoption Studies: Genetic differences and malleability. *Child Development, 54,* 260–267.

Scarr, S., & Weinberg, R. (1986, November). The early childhood enterprise: Care and education of the young. *American Psychologist 41,*(10), 140–146.

Scarr, S., & Yee, D. (1980). Heritability and educational policy: Genetic and environmental effects on IQ. *Educational Psychologist, 15,* 1–22.

Scarr-Salapatek, S. (1975). Genetics and intelligence. In F. D. Horowitz (Ed.), *Review of child development research* (Vol. 4, pp. 1–57). Chicago: University of Chicago Press.

Schiff, N. (1979). The influence of deviant maternal input on the development of language during the preschool years. *Journal of Speech and Hearing Research, 41,* 348–358.

Shields, J. (1962). *Monozygotic twins brought up apart and brought up together.* London: Oxford University Press.

Sigman, M. (1982). Plasticity in development: Implications for intervention. In L. A. Bond & J. M. Joffe (Eds.), *Facilitating infant and early childhood development.* Hanover, NH: University Press of New England. England.

Skodak, M., & Skeels, H. M. (1949). A final follow-up study of one hundred adopted children. *Journal of Genetic Psychology, 75,* 85–125.

Uylings, H. B. M., Kuypers, K., & Veltman, W. A. M. (1978). Effects of differential environments on plasticity of dendrites of cortical pyramidal neurons in adult rats. *Experimental Neurology, 62,* 658–677.

Waddington, C. H. (1957). *The strategy of genes.* London: George Allen and Unwin.

Watson, J. (1928). *Psychological care of infant and child.* New York: Norton.

Werner, E., & Smith, R. (1982). *Vulnerable but invincible.* New York: McGraw–Hill.

Willerman, L. (1979). Effects of families on intellectual development. *American Psychologist, 34,* 923–929.

Wilson, R. S. (1977). Twins and siblings: Concordance for school-age mental development. *Child Development, 48,* 211–216.

Wilson, R. S. (1983). The Louisville twin study: Developmental synchronies of behavior. *Child Development, 54,* 298–316.

Winick, Meyer, & Harris (1975). Malnutrition and environmental enrichment by early adoption. *Science, 190,* 1173–1175.

Chapter 7

Early Experience, Malleability, and Head Start

Edward Zigler and Johanna Freedman

The question of what aspects of child development are subject to change and at what critical developmental junctures, has been subject to considerable debate. Early in the century, many believed still more strongly than did Freud that biology was destiny. In the words of Hunt (1964):

> During most of the past century anyone who entertained the idea of increasing the intellectual capacity of human beings was regarded as an unrealistic "do-gooder." Individuals, classes, and races were considered to be what they were because either God or their inheritance had made them that way; any attempt to raise the intelligence quotient (IQ) through experience met with contempt. (p. 1)

Since the basic nature of children was thought to be predetermined, few efforts were made to alter the course of their development. By the 1960s, a combination of social change and scientific research had changed the view of development radically. Environmentalism replaced predeterminism, and development was considered almost infinitely open to the manipulation of experts, especially when applied during a "critical period" in development. As is the case with most radical positions, the truth lies between these extremes. Today, children are considered complex beings, with physical, emotional, social, and cognitive aspects, none of which function in isolation, and all of which may be affected by intervention, though to varying degrees. When Head Start began in 1965, the environmental position prevailed. Reliance on IQ as a predictor of life success, paired with the belief that preschool children were at a critical period of development, led some to believe that a short-term intervention would dramatically improve IQ scores, school performance, and, ultimately, the quality of poor children's lives. This overoptimism had serious, nearly fatal consequences for Head Start when these excessive expectations led inevitably to disappointment, disillusion, and near nihilism regarding the possibility of change. A short history will demonstrate.

THE POLITICAL CONTEXT OF HEAD START

Head Start emerged as a social action program at a time in history when social and political forces, as well as intellectual traditions in the social sciences, had come to focus on the problems created by poverty. The story of Head Start's development is an intricate one, with a number of threads running through it. The foremost of these are the revival of scientific interest in the role of environment in human development and the design of educational intervention efforts for children of the disadvantaged. These lines converge rapidly between the fall of 1964 and the summer of 1965, amidst a novel alliance of child development experts and social policy-makers, under whose auspices Head Start grew from an idea to a proposal, and finally to an active program serving over 500,000 children across the nation in Head Start's first summer.

The political vicissitudes that have threatened Head Start's existence, and the strengths that have determined the program's survival and growth, have their roots in the story of its creation. While the 60s were a time of economic prosperity for the majority of Americans, social concern focused on the "other America" (Harrington, 1962)—the one in which a minority of people were economically and socially deprived. According to studies undertaken by the Kennedy administration, 35 million Americans were poor, and the consequences of this poverty were threatening the nation's social and economic well-being.

Searching for new answers to the problem of poverty, the Kennedy and Johnson administrations tended to find those explanations and solutions that would not disturb the consciences, much less the pocketbooks, of middle-class Americans. The Task Force on Manpower Conservation suggested that the inferior living conditions and social behavior that seemed to characterize the poor were passed on from generation to generation in a cycle of poverty. The President's Panel on Mental Retardation (1963) concluded that the persistence of these inferior conditions and behavior patterns meant the economically deprived were somehow "culturally deprived" as well. According to this reasoning, as soon as poor, usually black Americans were skilled and educated for employment, doors would open and they would achieve middle-class economic and social status.

The naive optimism of this view is apparent in hindsight, but when the War on Poverty was declared in 1964, it embodied a basic belief in education as the solution to poverty. The Economic Opportunity Act, passed in August 1964, opened the War on Poverty on three fronts: the Job Corps, to provide education and training for employment; the Community Action programs, to aid communities in planning and administering their own assistance programs for the poor; and VISTA, a domestic Peace Corps.

Both President Johnson and his chief strategist and field commander in the War on Poverty, Sargent Shriver, had personal interests in the issues surrounding education and the disad-

vantaged. Johnson had begun his career as a schoolteacher in rural Texas. Shriver had served for 5 years as the president of the Board of Education in Chicago, where he saw first-hand the problems of a large, inner-city school system. His wife, Eunice Kennedy Shriver, was an active member of the President's Task Force on Mental Retardation. Like many Americans, Shriver and Johnson were amazed and encouraged to learn that what one task force member called "severe degrees of social and cultural deprivation" in children, had apparently been reversed in educational intervention experiments (Davens, 1972). Visions of employing this sort of intervention on a national scale led Shriver to consult child development scholars about proposed social policy.

At the same time, the civil rights movement was burgeoning, having achieved some success with the Civil Rights Act of 1964. These forces, along with the passage of the Economic Opportunity Act in 1964, sparked social unrest. This act provided programs and funds directly to local communities to redress some of the social, political, and economic inequities that had become the focus of public attention. Reformist sentiment was great, legitimated to a large extent by social science theories about the need for political change to counter social injustice (Valentine & Stark, 1979).

Few recall that at the inception of the War on Poverty, Head Start was not an independent program in the Office of Economic Opportunity (OEO), but, as a "national emphasis" program, was part of the OEO's Community Action Program. The Community Action people viewed themselves as poverty warriors, and Head Start was considered only one of the many weapons in their arsenal. Since the most articulate champions for the poor saw participation as a first step toward self-determination and a basic shift in the power structure and the entire political process, such projects mandated "maximum feasible participation" of the economically disadvantaged in program construction. Thus, at its inception, Head Start was regarded as a general remedy to structural racial and economic inequality, to the point that some charged it was less a service program for poor families than a make-work institution for Community Action loyalists (Zigler, 1985).

In the end, though, despite factional battles and conflicting interpretations of its role, Head Start came to be distinguished by its broad developmental approach to early childhood intervention and, if not a complete solution to the problems of poverty, it has proved to be at least a partial amelioration of some of its difficulties.

Because of past misunderstandings about Head Start, it may be helpful to restate the program's seven goals exactly as they were set forth in the recommendations of the planning committee in 1965:

1. Improving the child's physical health and physical abilities
2. Helping the emotional and social development of the child by encouraging self-confidence, spontaneity, and self-discipline
3. Improving the child's mental processes and skills, with particular attention to conceptual and verbal skills
4. Establishing patterns and expectations of success for the child that create a climate of confidence for future learning efforts
5. Increasing the child's capacity to relate positively to family members and others, while at the same time strengthening the family's ability to relate positively to the child and his problems
6. Developing in the child and his family a responsible attitude toward society, and encouraging society to work with the poor in solving their problems
7. Increasing the sense of dignity and self-worth within the child and his family (Cooke, 1965)

Perhaps the most innovative idea found in these recommendations—an idea that continues to be fundamental to Head Start—is that effective intervention in the lives of children can only be accomplished through involving parents and the community in the intervention effort.

IQ VERSUS SUPPORT

Still, Head Start was regarded as an educational effort. As such, unsurprisingly but unfortunately, researchers looked to the IQ test, the traditional measure and predictor of academic success, as an outcome measure. It was all too easy to avoid the rigors of goal-sensitive outcome evaluations, and conclude a program was a success if it resulted in higher IQs, and a failure if it did not.

The problematic nature of the choice of IQ as an outcome measure was increased by the feverish optimism of the times. Some investigators reported that improvement in cognitive functioning could be achieved through early stimulation, in the form of a mobile over an infant's crib. This naive environmentalism was exacerbated by a range of journalists, from popular tabloids to the prestigious *New York Times*, where we were informed that a ''pressure cooker'' approach to early childhood intervention was the solution to the poor school performance of economically disadvantaged children (Pines, 1967). The results of research by trustworthy, careful workers in the field were exaggerated and misrepresented. The widely read *Readers' Digest* advertised a responsible article by Hunt with the banner, ''How to Raise Your Child's IQ.'' In a thoughtful intervention program, the Deutsches, in New York, found a 12-point IQ increase in children over the course of a year-long intervention (Deutsch & Deutsch, 1963). The Herald Tribune proclaimed this finding under the headline, ''Program Increases the IQ One Point a Month.''

This credulous faith in the virtually unlimited potential of intervention was rampant in the early years of Head Start. Originally, the program was designed only as a 6- or 8-week preschool during the summer preceding the child's entry into kindergarten, but many had faith that this minimal effort would solve all of the problems of children from urban and rural slums. We now know that children cannot be inoculated against the ravages of poverty experienced over a lifetime. Fortunately, this was recognized fairly early in Head Start's history. After the first summer, it became a more realistic 1- or 2-year program.

The planners came to realize that even a year or two was insufficient to initiate and support real changes in children and families, and a number of demonstration programs were mounted to provide families with long-term, reliable support.

Project Follow Through, established in 1967 and administered by the U.S. Office of Education, was designed to continue and build on the cognitive and social gains made by children in full-year Head Start programs. The program provided nutrititional and health care, social and psychological services, and special teaching assistance to children during their early years in elementary school.

Parent and Child Centers, launched in 1967, were the first Head Start experimental programs intended to serve young children from birth to age 3 and their families. In 33 urban and rural communities, these centers sought to provide services for over 4,000 children and their families. The centers helped parents learn about the needs of their children and about supportive services available in the community.

Education for Parenthood, a national program jointly sponsored by the Office of Child Development and the Office of Education, played a significant role in Head Start programs for children and families. As part of the program, high school students learned about early childhood experientially, through work with children in Head Start centers. In addition, curricula in child development and parenthood were developed to help train adolescents in the multiple responsibilities of parenting. In what was probably the most complete attempt at providing ongoing support to families, the Child and Family Resource Program (CFRP) provided a variety of services to meet the unique wants of each enrolled family. The services offered by each CFRP supplemented rather than replaced existing community resources. There were four cornerstones to the CFRP approach: 1) an emphasis on support and education for parents; 2) stress on developmental continuity by beginning services before

birth and continuing them into elementary school; 3) an effort to coordinate comprehensive social services by way of direct service provision and referrals; and 4) the attempt to individualize services through needs assessment and goal setting with each family.

Yet, a short Head Start program was consistent with the simplistic and optimistic *zeitgeist* of the early 1960s, and only a few Head Start programs included the demonstration projects. For many, the belief that children were highly malleable and probably perfectable was coupled with a search for some magic period during which a brief intervention could permanently change the course of a child's life.

Across the years, workers have championed a variety of ages as the optimal time for intervention. Some tell us it is the prenatal period. Others view the first year of life, in whole or in part, as a particularly sensitive time, vital to the development of parent-child bonding. White champions the first 3 years of life (1973). Bereiter, once a proponent of preschool education, now believes we should concentrate our efforts on the first 3 years of formal schooling (Bereiter, 1972). Hobbs, basing his thinking on the work of Feuerstein, champions adolescence as the prime period for ameliorative efforts (Hobbs, 1979).

Each of these appeals to some special period is both right and wrong. There is no magic period in the process of development for the simple reason that each and every period is a magical one. Inherent in the view that any one time is especially sensitive relative to others is a concept of development that allows for some discontinuity. A discontinuity position has some heuristic value when applied to qualitative differences in cognitive functioning at different stages. However, we should not be misled by such valuable analytic tools into the belief that development is genuinely discontinuous. Development is incremental and uninterrupted from conception throughout the whole course of life. For each stage there are environmental nutrients that stimulate further development and/or buffer the individual from stress and adverse events. Head Start has been a laboratory in which behavioral scientists increased their knowledge of human development, thereby expanding our understanding of what is appropriate, and when (Zigler & Seitz, 1982).

The optimists of the 1960s were looking for a specific magic period—a time ripe for improving intellectual functioning. Head Start was not so much an outgrowth as a victim of this preoccupation with intelligence. Although a few intervention programs were designed to raise IQ, Head Start was planned by theorists who took a broader developmental view. As seen in the list of goals, their aim was to increase general social competence, defined in terms of physical and mental well-being; and formal cognitive abilities, including language, other intellectual skills, and a variety of motivational variables. Yet, because of the standardized nature of IQ tests, their ease of administration, their predictive value for school performance, and the wish of program administrators to prove Head Start a success, the first evaluations of this and other early intervention projects focused almost exclusively on IQ scores. It was impressive how attractive the IQ became as an outcome measure even to vehement critics of IQ tests, once it became evident that the most common outcome of almost all intervention programs was a 10-point increase in IQ (Eisenberg & Connors, 1966). These evaluations raised great hopes by announcing sizeable gains in IQ after only a few week of intervention.

Head Start was jeopardized, however, when the much publicized Westinghouse Report (Westinghouse Learning Center, 1969) declared that these IQ increases were short-lived. The report was interpreted as a telling indictment of Head Start, despite complaints by a number of workers who addressed biases in the sample selection and defects in design and analysis, such as missing baseline measures and differences in the length and content of programs evaluated (Barnow, 1973; Campbell & Erlebacher, 1970a, 1970b; Lazar, 1981; Smith & Bissell, 1970). Many dismissed Head Start as a failure, ignoring the inappropriateness of the outcome measures.

Matters hardly improved when Jensen (1969) published his monograph on the genetic inflexibility of IQ, opening with the sentence, "Compensatory education has been tried and it apparently has failed" (p. 2). Not long afterwards, the Westinghouse findings were bolstered by the conclusions of one of Head Start's founders, Bronfenbrenner (1974), who declared that the gains in performance attributable to Head Start vanished within 2 years after children entered school.

In fact, there is a disjunction in what is measured in IQ tests at this age, because the child is moving from the preoperational to the concrete-operations stage, or from nonsemantic to semantic conceptualizations, and the drop in IQ is universal. It is possible that more appropriate schooling or more sensitive tests might ameliorate this decrease; in any case, its universality obviates it as proof of the failure of Head Start. Yet, the Westinghouse Report was seen as evidence that the program was ineffective at best, and a misuse of time and taxes. Soon the misguided belief that slum children could be educated to test like the scions of the middle class by a 6–8-week- or even full-year program was replaced by pessimism as to whether they could be helped at all. Before the 70s were over, both the Associated Press and the New York Times ("A New Beginning," 1976) formally reported that Head Start had ceased to exist.

Luckily, this announcement was followed shortly by the Cornell Consortium's report that graduates of early intervention programs showed improvements in social competence that lasted for as long as 13 years (Lazar, Hubbell, Murray, Rosche, & Royce, 1977; Consortium for Longitudinal Studies, 1978). These were not so much IQ increases as gains in the realm of real achievement supposedly predicted by IQ. For example, intervention graduates were less likely to be in special education classes and more likely to be in the correct grade for their age, than were peers who had not received intervention. Without the Consortium's fortuitous presentation of their data, it is quite possible that Head Start's premature obituary would have become fact.

Following the Cornell findings, Head Start received its first budget increase since 1965. Its advocates were also able to keep Head Start out of the newly formed Department of Education (contrary to the wishes of President Carter), ensuring that it would continue to include the extensive services and parental involvement that distinguished it from school programs then current. The loss of these services would have had an impact few recognize. For example, behavioral scientists have generally failed to assess the medical benefits of Head Start. There is no doubt that children who are well-nourished and receive both preventive and immediate medical care can do better on IQ tests and in school than children in poor health.

The Cornell report was just the beginning of a growing number of longitudinal studies that have documented positive, long-term effects of early intervention for overall life adjustment. The Ypsilanti Perry Preschool Project (Berrueta-Clement, Schweinhart, Barnett, Epstein, & Weikart, 1984), whose very early data were included in the work of the Cornell Consortium, is one such encouraging effort. The project, whose clients are now in their late teens and early 20s, describes a successful model for early intervention with poor, low-IQ, at-risk black children; the success of the program is measured in terms of decreased levels of juvenile delinquency, teenage pregnancy, and unemployment in young adulthood. An educational enrichment program for New York, inner-city children also demonstrated positive long-term outcome effects, 20 years later. Benefits were also measured in areas of practical and social importance, such as job status and higher education (Deutsch, Jordan, & Deutsch, 1985). Let us now turn to why early intervention is a failure when it comes to raising IQ scores, but a success in practical terms.

WHAT WE CAN
CHANGE IN CHILDREN

Employing hindsight, we can see why we overemphasized, misinterpreted, and misunderstood the implications of the 1960s reports that dwelled on IQ increases in poor children, following a nursery school experience. We had failed to appreciate the importance of experien-

tial and emotional factors in children's performance.

An IQ score is not a perfect representation of intellectual ability. Rather, performance on an IQ test reflects at least three factors. The first is formal cognitive ability. The second has to do with the child's achievements, which are determined in large part by his or her idiosyncratic experiences. For example, a child may have a formal cognitive system adequate to the task of storing information relevant to the word *gown*. However, if the child has never heard the word *gown*, and you ask what it means, he or she will not be able to answer correctly. The problem here is not a cognitive one, but rather the lack of a particular achievement caused by the nature of the child's experiences. It would be just as erroneous to call this child stupid as it would be to call a middle-class child stupid who has not experienced the particular set of events that includes the definitions of *chitlings* and *wino*. If you are attempting to measure ability, not acculturation, the test is insensitive and invalid. Whereas there are good arguments for providing poor children with mainstream concepts to ensure that they do well with a mainstream curriculum, the question remains one of information, not ability.

The third factor in IQ test performance involves motivation. A young minority-group child confronted by a strange white adult is likely to respond "I don't know" to as simple a query as "What is your name?" In a situation as foreign to a poor black child as intelligence testing, the "I don't know" response is quite likely to become the prevalent one, simply out of fear and a sense of self-protection. Saying nothing may seem the fastest, safest way out of an unfamiliar, frightening situation. Thus, for motivational reasons, performance may be far below that dictated by the child's cognitive abilities and achievements.

Approached in this way, it should be apparent that a change in a child's IQ score does not necessarily indicate a change in formal cognitive ability. It may instead be due to changes in achievement and/or motivation. This line of reasoning can explain the IQ gains apparent after even a brief intervention. Rather than increasing intelligence, per se, intervention programs can provide experiences that enable children to make better use of the cognitive ability they already possess.

This discussion brings us to the issue of the actual degree of malleability of various psychological subsystems. First, to repeat, as is generally recognized today, human beings are a complex combination of emotional, intellectual, and physical subsystems that are intricately co-evolved and are constantly in a state of interaction with one another. Because these systems develop at different rates and in different fashions, it is to be expected that they are differentially sensitive to environmental variation. Some may be highly vulnerable to environmental influences, whereas others are relatively impermeable. The point is that the demonstration of malleability in one system cannot automatically be generalized to another.

Although there are those who argue otherwise, there is strong evidence supporting the view that intelligence is as much influenced by genetic as environmental factors (Scarr & Kidd, 1983; Zigler, 1970). Those who decry preschool intervention as a failure appear to have made their case for the relative unimportance of early experience by concentrating on a subsystem that natural selection may have buffered against the effects of environmental variations (Gamble & Zigler, 1985).

Although the subsystem underlying intellectual development may be a poor candidate for demonstrating sensitivity, other subsystems may be highly influenced by environmental events; these include those subsystems affecting socialization, motivation, and personality development (Zigler, Abelson, & Seitz, 1973; Zigler, Abelson, Trickett, & Seitz, 1982; Zigler & Seitz, 1980; Zigler & Trickett, 1978). Evidence for the greater malleability of these subsystems may be found in the lower heritability ratios reported for socioemotional as opposed to intellectual variables (Kimble, Garmezy, & Zigler, 1984).

It is not my purpose to belittle the role of experience in the development of formal cognition. By all means, let us continue our study of how and when particular experiences influence the development of specific cognitive processes. However, it seems clear that there would be a considerably greater gain if we spent more time in our Head Start centers getting children to use the 10 points of intelligence that motivational factors cause to lie dormant, than in trying to add 10 more IQ points to the child's potential. By working directly on those socioemotional factors that often constitute the roots of a child's ineffectual behavior, we can help the child overcome attitudes that depress performance in school. If our preschool graduates then go off to elementary school equipped not with more intelligence but with a willingness to do the best they can, we will have achieved a realistic and practical goal.

There is no better time than now for those responsible for Head Start to repudiate forever the notion that higher IQ scores are its ultimate purpose. Today's back-to-basics movement and thrust for earlier schooling represent new threats to what is best in Head Start. Insofar as Head Start children are concerned, the back to basics and cognitive emphases are no more than a return to the discredited deficit theory, which proclaimed that more education, sooner, would save economically deprived children from the effects of a life of poverty. A large body of empirical work has now made it clear that poor children are more intelligent than they are often credited with being by those who fail to distinguish between competence and performance (Cole & Bruner, 1971). There is a reservoir of unused intellect in many economically disadvantaged children, and by addressing motivational handicaps, Head Start has been able to unleash this potential. Its success in this realm suggests a course of action for the future: Head Start should continue to tend to the interests and needs of the whole child, in context, confident that cognition will develop as the child develops.

Such a conception is consistent with Bronfenbrenner's (1974) ecological model, which envisions the environment as a set of nested proximal and distal settings within an overall interactive system. If the explanation for certain behaviors lies in the interaction between characteristics of people and their environments, past and present, we must change environments in order to change behavior. A reading of this model suggests that the appropriate focus for intervention efforts is not the child in isolation but the entire family, as is the case in Head Start.

The ecological approach was little understood when Head Start was born. In fact, throughout the 60s and 70s, many interventions treated children in isolation from their families. The techniques used usually consisted of whatever middle-class parents did to raise their children. To the degree that some of these programs enjoyed a degree of success—and some did—an analysis of the program components generally revealed that parents and often other community members were involved, and hence even these programs serve to validate the ecological model embodied by Head Start. The long-term effects of some fairly minimal intervention programs can only be explained in this light. For example, Palmer's (1978) project in which ghetto children received training a few hours per week in the use of prepositions has had long-term outcome effects seemingly out of proportion to the degree and kind of intervention. Participants continue to be superior to comparison children on a number of cognitive and social scales many years later. Such long-lasting effects are comprehensible only if the intervention is assumed to have affected how parents and children enrolled in the program related to each other, and hence set up a consistent and self-perpetuating system of mutually supportive new behaviors.

Happily, there are some encouraging developments in this area. The orientation toward the family as the appropriate unit of intervention is the hallmark of family-support programs, an exciting new grassroots movement. (Pizzo, 1983; Programs to strengthen families, 1983). Head Start has already begun to move away from being a single program toward becoming a center with a variety of programs serving the myriad needs of neighborhood children and families. In constructing such demonstration programs as Project Follow Through,

Parent and Child Centers, Education for Parenthood, and the Child and Family Resource Program, Head Start has evolved in the direction of becoming a general family support system. Head Start should continue this course, offering an assortment of programs designed to strengthen families. It must maintain its commitment to early-childhood intervention but should expand on this commitment. Head Start centers should concern themselves explicitly with 1) general child care, including day care for working mothers; 2) efforts to combat child abuse; 3) parent education and teenage pregnancy programs; and 4) childhood injury prevention programs—to name just a few.

IMPROVING HEAD START

Our errors notwithstanding, the overall history of Head Start has been positive. We must not become sanguine, however; Head Start cannot risk calcification. The project is not a static program, but an evolving concept, an effort that must continue to grow and develop. What then should Head Start consist of?

No evolution or expansion is possible without stemming the erosion of the basic Head Start program that has occurred in recent years. If this disintegration is not halted, it seems likely future evaluations will not show the positive, long-term effects reported by the Cornell Consortium. Head Start's results are dependent on Head Start's retaining its quality as a general support program to children and their families.

One problem in ensuring positive program outcomes is the variability between Head Start programs. There are actually over 2,000 locally administered Head Starts. Some are excellent, some are very poor, and most are between these two extremes. Common sense indicates that if Head Start is to affect all children positively, there must be some mechanism to ensure that every program reaches a minimal level of quality. A committee created for Head Start's 15th anniversary to analyze and improve the program advised restoring and protecting favorable staff-child ratios and class sizes, as well as hours per session (Head Start in the 1980s, 1980). Right now a year in Head Start in many places lasts only 6 months.

At least one worker in every Head Start classroom should have a nationally recognized credential in child development, such as the Child Development Associate (CDA). Far too many Head Start centers are staffed by administrators and caregivers with no training in child care or development.

If there is to be a professional staff, however, it must be paid at a professional rate. This is far from the case at present. In New York State, for example, Head Start workers are required to have the same licensing as those who work in state schools, yet they are paid at half the rate of state workers. As astonishing is that many Head Start workers have never received a cost-of-living increase. Staff should have these increases, as well as salary incentives and employee benefits at least comparable to those of other personnel performing similar tasks in the same community. At every level of the program, job requirements and minimum salaries should be established. At the top, for example, the number of community programs assigned to regional representatives should be reduced, so that they have a more manageable workload, can get to know individual programs well, and can structure the quality of these programs. This attention to the conditions under which Head Start staff work is of paramount importance, because the high turnover rate in many programs undermines an essential element in the young child's development—continuity of care.

This leads to a difficult decision. Will we upgrade the quality of Head Start, or increase the number of families participating in the program? At present, despite being included in President Reagan's safety net, Head Start only serves 16% of all eligible children (U.S. Department of Health and Human Services, 1986). In response to this dearth of services, former Assistant Secretary for Human Development Services, Dorcas Hardy, and the Children's Defense Fund argue that we should increase enrollment.

If such expansion provides services to more children while preserving and upgrading the quality of the current programs, it would be the correct course of action. It is unlikely, however, that this would be the case, because the size of our national deficit precludes the expenditures that would be required. Spending fewer real dollars on increasing numbers of children would reduce the effectiveness of intervention to mere tokenism. The danger of token efforts is less that they damage children than that they give the appearance that something is being done, and thus become a substitute for more meaningful efforts. In consequence, it seems wiser to serve fewer children well than more children poorly.

This of course means that there must be a thoughtful way of deciding which children to include and which to exclude. In current practice, eligibility is almost invariably based on family income, which actually reveals relatively little about the quality of family life. The salient variables of association with a particular ethnic group or geographic location are entirely lost, along with many others. In fact, the poor are an extremely heterogeneous group on a variety of economic, sociological, and psychological dimensions. Use of the family income criterion effectively avoids the vital question of which families can profit most from an expensive intervention such as Head Start. The problem remains, of course, of how to make selections on the basis of more realistic indicators without introducing the counterproductive stigma of labeling, which could work to the detriment of the children and families involved.

It might help to admit that the standard Head Start program is not a panacea required by every child whose family income falls below some arbitrary figure. Poor families, like more affluent ones, face a number of stresses and have a variety of needs and problems. Many economically disadvantaged families do an excellent job of raising their children and have little need for Head Start's services. Others need intervention, and for those the program must be preserved in its most comprehensive form. Still other families need alternate services, services the founders of Head Start did not envision when it began. Head Start must find a way of delivering only those services necessary to those who need and want them.

Some of Head Start's mistakes have been corrected. Some have not. In any case, it is clear that Head Start can and does improve the lives of children and families. In terms of policy directions for the future, Head Start should be preserved as a service institution for high-risk children and their families and as a national laboratory for future experimental programs— optimally under the aegis of a central coordinator, a federal agency that would oversee all programs involving our nation's families. The

research and policy questions of the future will not be whether or not Head Start is beneficial but which children benefit maximally from which types of programs, and, in terms of the development of theory in our field, what particular processes mediate Head Start's long-term effects. We must experimentally isolate the specific emotional and motivational variables that interfere with the child's competence across a wide variety of tasks. We must discover what particular experiences give rise to self-defeating behavior, and most importantly for educators, we must discover those experiences that ameliorate the effects of such negative factors.

REFERENCES

"A new beginning": Education and liberty. (1976, December 17). *New York Times,* p. A22.

Barnow, B. S. (1973). *Evaluating Project Head Start* (Discussion Papers No. 189–73). Madison: University of Wisconsin, Institute for Research on Poverty. (ED106404)

Bereiter, C. (1972). An academic preschool program for disadvantaged children: Conclusions from evaluation studies. In J. Stanley (Ed.), *Preschool programs for the disadvantaged.* Baltimore: The Johns Hopkins University Press.

Berrueta-Clement, J., Schweinhart, L., Barnett, W., Epstein, A. & Weikart, D. (1984). *Changed lives.* Ypslanti, Michigan: High Scope Press.

Bronfenbrenner, U. (1974). *A report on longitudinal evaluations of preschool programs. Vol. 2: Is early intervention effective?* (DHEW Publication No. OHD 74–25). Washington, D C : Office of Human Development.

Campbell, D. T., & Erlebacher, A. (1970a). How regression artifacts in quasi-experimental evaluations can mistakenly make compensatory education look harmful. In J. Hellmuth (Ed.), *Compensatory education: A national debate* (Vol. 3, pp. 185–200). New York: Brunner/Mazel.

Campbell, D. T., & Erlebacher, A. (1970b). Reply to the replies. In J. Hellmuth (Ed.), *Compensatory education: A national debate* (Vol. 3, pp. 221–225). New York: Brunner/Mazel.

Cole, M., & Bruner, J. (1971). Preliminaries to a theory of cultural differences. *American Psychologist, 26*(10), 867–875.

Consortium for Longitudinal Studies. (1978). Ithaca, NY. *Lasting effect after preschool: Summary report of the Consortium Education Commission of the States.* Denver, CO. (ED175523)

Cooke, R. (1965). *Memorandum to Sargent Shriver. Improving the opportunities and achievements of the children of the poor.* Unpublished manuscript.

Davens, E. (1972). Letter to Arturo Luis Gutierrez.

Deutsch, M., & Deutsch, C. (1963). *Report to the Office of the Commission on Education.* Unpublished manuscript.

Deutsch, M., Jordan, T., & Deutsch, C. (1985). *Long-term effects of early intervention: Summary of selected findings.* Unpublished manuscript.

Eisenberg, L., & Connors, C. (1966). *The effect of Head Start on developmental process.* Paper presented at the Joseph P. Kennedy, Jr. Foundation Scientific Symposium on Mental Retardation,

Gamble, T., & Zigler, E. (1985). Effects of infant day care: Another look at the evidence. *American Journal of Orthopsychiatry, 56*(1), 26–42.

Harrington, M. (1962). *The other America: Poverty in the United States.* New York: Macmillan.

Head Start in the 1980s: Review and recommendations. Washington, DC: Office of the Human Development Services, Administration for Children, Youth and Families, Head Start Bureau.

Hobbs, N. (1979). Families, schools, and communities: An ecosystem for children. In H. J. Leighter (Ed.), *Families and communities as educators.* New York: Teacher's College Press.

Hunt, J. M. (1964). The implications of changing ideas on how children develop intellectually. *Children.* Washington, DC: Department of Health, Education and Welfare.

Jensen, A. (1969). How much can we boost IQ and scholastic achievement? *Harvard Educational Review, 31*(1), 1–123.

Kimble, G., Garmezy, N., & Zigler, E. (1984). *Psychology.* New York: John Wiley & Sons.

Lazar, I. (1981). Early intervention is effective. *Educational Leadership, 303–305.*

Lazar, I., Hubble, R., Murray, H., Rosche, M., & Royce, J. (1977). *The persistence of preschool effects: A long-term follow-up of fourteen infant and preschool experiments, summary.* Washington, DC: U.S. Department of Health, Education and Welfare, Administration for Children, Youth, and Families.

Palmer, F. H. (1978). The effects of early childhood intervention. In B. Brown (Ed.), *Found: Long-term gains from early intervention*. Boulder, CO: Westview Press.

Pines, M. (1967, October 15). Slum children must make up for lost time. *New York Times Magazine*, pp. 66–67.

Pizzo, P. (1983). *Parent to parent*. Boston: Beacon Press.

The President's Panel on Mental Retardation. (1963). *Report of the Task Force on Prevention, Clinical services and residential care*. Washington, DC: Public Health Service.

Programs to strengthen families: A resource guide. (1983). New Haven: Yale University and The Family Resource Coalition, Chicago, IL.

Rutter, M. (1982). Social-emotional consequences of day care for preschool children. In E. Zigler & E. W. Gordon (Eds.), *Day care: Scientific and social policy issues*. Boston: Auburn House.

Scarr, S., & Kidd, K. (1983). Developmental behavior genetics. In M. M. Haith & J. N. Campus (Eds.), *Mussen handbook of child psychology, Vol 2, Infancy and developmental psychobiology* (4th ed., pp. 345–435). New York: John Wiley & Sons.

Smith, M. S., & Bissell, J. S. (1970). Report analysis: The impact of Head Start. *Harvard Educational Review, 40*, 51–104.

U.S. Department of Health and Human Services, Office of Human Development Services, Association for Children, Youth, and Families, Children's Bureau. (1986). *Serving the nation's children and families*. Washington, DC: U.S. Department of Health and Human Services.

Valentine, J., & Stark, E. (1979). The social context of parent involvement in Head Start. In E. Zigler & J. Valentine (Eds.), *Project Head Start* (pp. 291–315). New York: Free Press.

Westinghouse Learning Center. (1969). *The impact of Head Start: An evaluation of the effects of Head Start on children's cognitive and affective development*. (Executive summary, Ohio University Report to the Office of Economic Opportunity.) Washington, DC: Clearinghouse for Federal Scientific and Technical Information. (ED036 321).

White, B. L. (1973). *Making sense out of our education priorities*. Harvard University, Laboratory of Human Development. (ED085087)

Zigler, E. (1970). The nature-nurture issue we considered: A discussion of Uzgiris' paper. In H. C. Haywood (Ed.), *Social-cultural aspects of mental retardation* (pp. 81–106). New York: Appleton-Century-Crofts.

Zigler, E. (1985). Assessing Head Start at 20. *American Journal of Orthopsychiatry, 55*(2), 603–609.

Zigler, E., Abelson, W., & Seitz, V. (1973). Motivational factors in the performance of economically disadvantaged children on the Peabody Picture Vocabulary Test. *Child Development, 44*, 294–303.

Zigler, E., Abelson, W. D., Trickett, P. K., & Seitz, V. (1982). Is an intervention program necessary to improve economically disadvantaged children's IQ scores? *Child Development, 53*, 340–348.

Zigler, E., & Seitz, V. (1982). Head Start as a national laboratory. *Annals of the American Academy of Political and Social Science, 461*, 81–90.

Zigler, E., & Trickett, P. (1978). IQ, social competence and evaluation of early childhood intervention programs. *American Psychologist, 33*(a), 789–798.

Chapter 8

Changing Views
on Changing Children
Irving Lazar

Both recent research and older observations suggest ways to reinterpret evidence of the limits of children's malleability. This chapter describes three areas of changing perceptions of children, and suggests some possible consequences of these new understandings.

Although this chapter focuses upon areas of environmental influence and change, it does not deny the role of genetics in limiting the range, directions, and amount of change that can be achieved through environmental manipulation. Just as all traits and behavior are rooted in the potentialities defined by the genes, no genetic potentiality becomes actualized unless, and to the extent that, environmental influences call it forth. However, until the genetic engineers learn a great deal more about the ways in which genetic determinants interact with environmental resources, the principal practical route for improving the lot of children lies in improvements in the child's social and physical milieu.

We are in the midst of a massive change in the way we perceive and understand the development of infants and young children, and the ways in which we are beginning to reinterpret the potentialities of the child, the conditions that facilitate learning, and the roles that adults play in the child's development.

This chapter has been organized around some of the common assumptions that have dominated the accepted views of infant and early growth and development in the U.S., and around some of the instruments used in both deriving and justifying those views.

Let us begin with a simple change that has

already taken place. Until recent observations showed us that we were wrong (Cohen, DeLoache, & Strauss, 1979), child psychologists believed that the immaturity of the central nervous system prevented the infant from being able to distinguish visually between people until the second half of the first year of life. The so-called *10th-month anxiety* was seen as a result of the infant's visual apparatus suddenly revealing a world full of different people, many of them strangers (Spitz, 1945). Furthermore, it was believed, that young infants were so concerned with their own comfort that they could not conceive of themselves as separate from the world around them. With this image of primitive narcissism as the model, research focused upon the mother as the primary molder of the infant's behavior, and saw the infant as a passive vessel, crying out when frustrated, but utterly unable otherwise to control his or her body or life.

It is now known that infants quickly recognize the significant people in their lives and react to them in ways very different than they react to strangers (Cohen et al., 1979). Furthermore, there is now good evidence that there is real interaction between the child and the caregiver, and that the child influences as well as is influenced by the caregiver (Stern, 1974). Communication, though not verbal, is established within days of the child's birth. The infant clearly has many more abilities than had been assumed. Social learning apparently starts immediately after birth.

Partly because many thought the child to be so unaware of the world, and partly out of a cultural romanticism about mothers and children, it has long been believed that only a mother could properly raise an infant, and that separation of the infant from his or her mother, even for only part of each day, would surely damage the child. Spitz's studies of infants subjected to severe emotional deprivation during the first year of life, were used as justification for making group care of infants—and therefore infant day-care programs—illegal in many of the nation's states. Caldwell and her associates disproved this notion, demonstrating that group care of infants could be carried out in ways that clearly did not damage the infant (Caldwell, Wright, Honig, & Tannenbaum, 1970). Indeed, it now appears that, at least for some children, a properly organized group-care situation can foster and support optimal development in ways that are superior to what happens in the child's own home.

And so a second change in our perceptions was established. The infant was not only socially aware, but was more socially adaptable than we had been able to recognize. Whereas there certainly could be deleterious group care, it was no more inevitable than that there are mothers who are dangerous to their infants.

Once it became clear that infants were active participants in social interaction, and that they could and did adapt readily to new situations and to multiple adults, the data-based reasons for objecting to infant care in groups became irrelevant. However, in the United States, a variety of other reasons were at play and resistance to group care of infants is still widespread. (This chapter will not digress into a discussion of the sources of this resistance.) However, the knowledge that group care need not lead to mental illness brought about a third change in how we see small children.

The fourth change is a bit more complicated. The conclusion is simple enough: We now know that the cognitive achievements of children at risk can be positively and permanently increased by educational intervention in the first 4 years of life. Let me briefly describe some of the research that has led to that conclusion.

The idea and work of the Consortium for Longitudinal Studies had its origin as a reaction to a 1975 proposal by the Office of Management and Budget to phase out support for Project Head Start and for the preschool programs financed by the Bureau for the Educationally Handicapped. The reason given for this proposal was the assertion that research had somehow proved, and that expert opinion agreed, that such programs were ineffective. Now, in fact, research had neither proven nor disproven anything about the effectiveness of early intervention. Such data as were available were being interpreted in the light of the ideology of the interpreter.

Perhaps the oldest argument in American education is between the elitist position that some groups were naturally superior and the populist position that interpreted differences as reflections of inequities in opportunities. Head Start and initial efforts to evaluate it simply served as new fuel for this old argument. By 1975, 10 years after the beginning of Head Start—a program that can fairly be described as resting upon populist notions of the malleability of children—the classical elitist positions were in full voice.

With no credible evidence, the American educational literature soon blossomed with a variety of assertions about the noneffectiveness of early education. We were told that black children were genetically inferior (Jensen, 1969), that success was a matter of luck and good connections (Jencks, 1972), that only mothers could educate their young children (Bronfenbrenner, 1974), and that only a total reorganization of the structure of society could help poor children (Ogbu, 1978).

It was against this background that a small group of developmental psychologists decided, in 1975, to take the question of effectiveness out of the realm of debate, by assembling objective data on the actual educational outcomes of children from poor families who had participated in the preschool intervention experiments of the late 1950s and early 1960s. By 1975, these children and their controls were well along in school and their actual school performance could be ascertained without resorting to predictive tests. The original investigators of the 11 largest and best designed of these studies agreed to undertake three tasks:

1. To send their original raw data to an independent group at Cornell for reformatting and reanalysis
2. To work with us in developing a uniform protocol for a follow-up study of their subjects and controls
3. To locate and collect the agreed-upon common data from and about each subject and send it to our central staff for analyses across studies

Each investigator was, of course, free to collect additional data relevant to variables of unique interest to his or her studies, and each was free to publish findings relevant to his or her independent studies. The central group had responsibility for the joint analyses and the dissemination of the pooled findings. The participants in this joint venture are all well known in the field of early childhood research, and each of the studies was independently designed and executed in the first place.[1]

Recovery of subjects was far more successful than was originally contemplated, and data were collected on over 2,100 subjects, or about 72% of the original samples.

Refusals constituted less than 5% of the samples, and attrition analyses demonstrated that the differences between the recovered group and those missing were random.

As outcome measures, we used three easily observable indicators of satisfactory performance in the public schools: whether the child was assigned, at any point, to special or remedial classes; whether the child was retained in grade; and whether the child graduated from secondary school along with his age-mates.

On all three of these indicators, the differences between the experimental and control groups were significant and robust. The differences are of so large a magnitude, and so demonstrably independent of the potential in-

fluences of artifacts that concerted efforts to disavow somehow the findings have, to this date at least, failed. In a sense, this effort represents multiple, independent tests of the same hypotheses, and although the studies differed, the findings did not differ. It is clear that a well-run, early educational experience for preschool children from low-income families can reduce the extent to which they are at risk of educational failure.

The findings were not artifacts of attrition, nor are they the result of teachers somehow knowing which children were in preschool programs. They are not sampling errors, and the differences remain robust after controlling for all of the background and demographic variables that any of us could think of as having even a tangential relationship to school performance. For those interested in a fuller description of both the individual studies and the pooled findings, we have published a volume co-authored by the participants (Consortium for Longitudinal Studies, 1983). An earlier monograph summarizes the findings relevant to academic achievement (Lazar, Darlington et al., 1982).

There are three implications of the findings that are important to our new directions in understanding children. First, many of these children, as preschoolers, had IQs so low they would have been classified as retarded. We found, however, that IQ was not a significant factor in the differences between the program and control groups. Second, it became clear that IQ was not a useful predictor of academic achievement for these children, whose scores tended to fall in the lower end of the continuum. Third, it seems likely that the permanence of the change can very well be accounted for as representing a change in the value placed upon education by both the child and the parent, and that it is this change in values that made the difference. We know, after all, that those cultures and countries that value educa-

[1]Principal members included Susan Gray, Kuno Beller, Martin and Cynthia Deutsch, Ira Gordon, Emil Jester, Merle Karnes, Phyllis Levenstein, Louise Miller, Francis Palmer, Lawrence Schweinhart, David Weikart, Myron Woolman, and Edward Zigler. Joint analytic techniques were devised and supervised by Richard Darlington; Irving Lazar was responsible for overall administration, funding, dissemination and integrative efforts.

tion have highly literate populations; this is true even for such English speaking but multi-ethnic countries as Singapore and New Zealand.

Singapore and New Zealand have taught us that virtually any child can become literate in English; both have achieved literacy rates in excess of 95%. Both have their normal share of children three standard deviations above and below the mean; both have pretty much limited their lists of illiterates to that tiny portion at the bottom of the normal curve.

Let us assume that we are not likely to make massive changes in the teaching behavior of parents; that we can not change values by ukase, and that even if we could, that that would not be enough for most children, let alone the poor, to meet the challenges of our new age. Are there other practical alternatives? It appears that there are. We are in the process of discovering that our children take to computers the way ducklings take to water.

Having demonstrated that the child does not need to a have a single-adult bond, that the child is an active participant in the learning process, and that IQ is neither a fixed quantity, nor even a particularly useful predictor, we can ask whether the conditions of learning are themselves devices that either set or remove barriers to the child's accomplishments. There are a few studies that shed some light on this question.

Some 20 years ago, Steg, at Drexel University, provided a small group of randomly selected 4-year-olds from poor families, access to a computer-directed device called *the talking typewriter,* for a half hour each day for a year and a half. Unlike many later, computer-based learning programs, there was no assumption that the process was in any way connected to the formal precepts of operant conditioning. This was not a Skinnerian program. The children learned by exploration and discovery. There was no effort to break learning into tiny bits, nor to impose a sequence. There was branching, however, that selected new problems based on the child's immediately precedent behavior.

What Steg did was to provide a learning situation that provided instant feedback and was completely under the control of the learner. Even with these very young children, the joy of discovery seemed sufficient reinforcement. What Steg lacked in numbers of subjects she compensated for with extremely detailed observations and analyses of the learning styles of her subjects, both before and after their experience with the computer-assisted program.

Here again it appears that the conventional description of the stages of intellectual development and of the operations of conditioning are insufficient to describe or explain the spurts of learning and the substitution of inductive for deductive logic in problem solving that these children displayed. If children at risk of school failure can apparently skip whole stages of intellectual development while learning to read, with so minimal an intervention as a daily half hour, with a simple teaching machine, what indeed can we look forward to when we really know what we're doing with the new technology?

Twenty years later there are significant differences in the academic histories and life situations of these youngsters and their controls. What sets this study apart from the intervention research discussed earlier is that both the experimental and control groups in this research were also, at the time of the study, enrolled in a high quality preschool program. It appears that, on top of the boost in academic performance that the preschool experience provided, exposure to a new tool for learning made a difference. These findings were reported in 1986 (Steg, 1986).

Let us turn to another study. In a work that has received too little attention, Cunningham (1972) examined the development of intelligence from the perspective of a computer scientist. In this early effort to reconcile information theory, Hebb's work on neurophysiology, and Piagetian developmental theory, he suggested that what Piaget described might hold true for ordinary conditions of stimulation, but probably did not describe cognitive growth as it occurs under the conditions provided by computer-assisted instruction. This observation is being confirmed by people who are working with children and computers in a wide variety of settings. Pappert's widely read account of small children's behavior with a simple computer language (1980) contains the suggestion that the Piagetian stages may not apply when children have access to computers as a tool for discovery and learning (Pappert, 1980). Pappert had been a student of Piaget's, and thus did not make this observation lightly.

It seems possible that we may well have to scrap much of current learning theory. Our present conventional theories are not describing what happens when children get their hands on computers. *Information theory,* or some derivative of it, looks like the next step in understanding the universal process called learning. As we begin to examine learning more carefully, and see it as a product of a dynamic interaction between the learner and his or her world, and less as a matter of skill residing solely within the individual, we can find ways to educate adequately all but the most severely damaged of our populations.

There are now a plethora of studies using computer-assisted programs with preschoolers. Many are reporting high levels of performance by children whose test scores and family situations would suggest that they were at risk of school failure.

What can one conjecture about these studies? If they prove consistent, we will be reaching some very new conclusions about early cognitive development. The Piagetian stages may only apply to the usual situation in which children receive a limited range of information, and in which they have little or no control over either the content or the direction of their learning. When we allow children to control the timing, pace, content and sequence of their learning—which we can do with a computer— it may be that the Piagetian stages collapse and the so-called developmentally determined sequences are no longer fixed.

It appears, further, that the failure of children to learn the basic communication and counting skills is more likely a failure to provide the conditions that allow the learning of these skills, rather than a failure of the child to have the ability to learn them. This reviewer suggests that every child can learn to read if the conditions necessary to his or her own style of learning are available. Among those conditions is an opportunity to use inductive rather than deductive modes of learning.

Enough information is already available to permit a tentative listing of the minimal requirements for optimal learning by very young children:

1. Easy access to all kinds of information, through all of their senses
2. Materials that permit both inductive and deductive discoveries by the child, with no premium placed on either mode
3. Control, by individual children, of the rate, content, and sequence of their learning
4. Immediate feedback to children about the consequences of their efforts to discover and to learn
5. Familial support of and participation in efforts to learn

The use of a computer as the medium for the learning of the basic skills seems to be inevitable and desirable. A computer can more reliably meet the first four of the conditions suggested here than can a classroom.

It is not proposed that children be chained to computer terminals, or that loving interpersonal contact is unnecessary. I am not suggesting that machines can teach everything, or, indeed, much more than basic skills and ways of finding information. Computers will not teach art or literature and will not develop character or values. But the same theoretical structure that has given us the computer is beginning to give us ways of looking at personality and character, at intelligence and discovery, at learning and growth. The change is surely underway: Bronfenbrenner (1979) no longer talks as though mothers have mystic powers, and recent papers use the language and ideas of general systems theory in discussing loss and grief.

What has this to do with malleability? The practical concerns that make this question important have to do with the ability of individuals to meet the basic requirements for adaptation and survival in their society. It seems reasonable to believe that we are approaching a time when the only reason that virtually every child in this society would be unable to learn the skills necessary for survival, would be an unwillingness on the part of society to provide the tools and opportunity for learning those skills.

Will there be children who are smarter or more talented than others? Certainly. But that's not the issue. Need there be children who are not literate? Certainly not. Our newly emerging view of children doesn't imply such limits.

By way of summary, let us consider the infant. He or she is neither helpless nor alone, but is an active participant in a system of social interactions. He or she has strong internal motivation to learn, and requires the freedom to explore, and the freedom to use her own idiosyncratic approaches to learning and discovery. The infant needs immediate feedback about and familial approval of these efforts, and he or she is able to adjust to a wide variety of caregivers and new situations. The basic

skills necessary for participation in modern society are within the means of all but the most damaged of children, and contemporary technology now affords us the means to make it possible for all children to acquire those skills.

As we look at infant care, we can see it changing from a system of simple response to physical needs to a system that provides an environment that promotes and permits types of learning previously reserved for older children. As we look at the future of primary schools, we can see a whole redefinition of their functions, when—within a generation—most children arrive at school already reading, using numbers, directing their own learning, setting their own pace, and selecting their own content and sequence of learning.

As we look at our own theoretical structures, we begin to see a kinship to the same general theories that have been having a major impact on other fields of study and on our technologies. This closer tie among the sciences, which general systems theory is bringing to us, can trigger even more fundamental changes in the next half century.

REFERENCES

Bronfenbrenner, U. (1974). *Is early intervention effective? A report on longitudinal evaluations of preschool programs* (Vol. 2). Washington, DC: Office of Child Development, U.S. Department of Health, Education, and Welfare.

Bronfenbrenner, U. (1979). *The ecology of human development*. Cambridge, MA. Harvard University Press.

Caldwell, B. M., Wright, C., Honig, A. S., & Tannenbaum, J. (1970). Infant day care and attachment. *American Journal of Orthopsychiatry, 40,* 397–412.

Cohen, L., DeLoache, J. S., & Strauss, M. (1979). Infant visual perception. In J. Osofsky (Ed.), *Handbook of infant development*. New York: John Wiley & Sons.

Consortium for Longitudinal Studies. (1983). *As the twig is bent*. Hillsdale, NJ: Lawrence Erlbaum Associates.

Cunningham, M. (1972). *Intelligence: Its organization and development*. New York: Academic Press.

Jencks, C. (1972). *Inequality*. New York: Harper & Row.

Jensen, A. R. (1969). How much can we boost IQ and

scholastic achievement? *Harvard Educational Review, 39,* 1–123.

Lazar, I., Darlington, R. A. (1982). *Lasting effects after preschool. Monographs of the Society for Research in Child Development, 47,* (Nos. 2 and 3).

Ogbu, J. U. (1978). *Minority education and caste*. New York: Academic Press.

Pappert, S. (1980). *Mindstorms: Children, computers, and powerful ideas*. New York: Basic Books.

Spitz, R. A. (1945). Anaclitic depression. *Psychoanalytic Study of the Child, 2,* 313–392.

Steg, D. (1986). Unpublished raw data.

Stern, D. (1974). Mother and infant at play; the dyadic interaction. In M. Lewis & L. A. Rosenblum (Eds.), *Effects of the infant on the caregiver*. New York: John Wiley & Sons.

U.S. Office of Management and Budget, Special Studies, The Budget of the United States. (1975). Washington, DC: U.S. Government Printing Office.

Chapter 9

Plasticity and the Handicapped Child

A Review of Efficacy Research

Glendon Casto

It is important to recognize that an immense galaxy of variables governs human development. These variables can be best understood if we view the developing child as a complex system (Bertalanffy, 1969; Bowlby, 1969; Bunge, 1979; Casto, Biaggio, Hoagland, & Muller, 1976; Denenberg, 1982; Frank, 1966; Ramey, McPhee, & Yeates, 1982). This orientation has important implications for early intervention because it differs from the cause-effect conceptual framework prevalent in the field. According to Frank (1966):

> To advance the study of the infants we may formulate a model of the infant as a General Purpose system. Such a model would recognize the inherited potentialities of the young organism and the basic processes operating in this self-organizing, self-stabilizing, self-directing, largely self-repairing, open system which becomes progressively patterned, oriented, and coupled to the culturally established dimensions of his environment, natural and human. (p. 178)

Systems theory thus regards normal infants as competent organisms equipped with purposive behavior patterns, efficient effectors, and feedback mechanisms that facilitate goal-oriented behavior and adaptation to their environments. For handicapped children, insults to their systems make the development of goal-oriented behavior and adaptation to their environment problematic. We intervene with this population hoping that the cumulative impact of our various interventions and the plasticity of the developing organisms will combine to produce more positive outcomes. We intervene, recognizing that the early-intervention period represents but one link in an involved and intricate chain of development (Kagan, Kearsely, & Zelazo, 1980).

Is early intervention effective? According to previous reviewers of the early-intervention, primary research literature, it is. In a recent review of reviews, White, Bush, and Casto (1985) found that 94% of a sample of 52 previous reviewers had concluded that early intervention had substantial immediate benefits for handicapped, at-risk, and disadvantaged children. These immediate benefits included improved cognitive, language, motor, and social-emotional growth for the children, and improved functioning of the children's parents and their siblings. Although there were reviewers who had reached different conclusions (Ferry, 1981; Gottfried, 1973), the preponderance of previous reviewers seemed to be in agreement that early intervention is effective. In addition, previous reviewers tended to agree on the importance of the four most cited con-

The work reported in this chapter was carried out in part with funds from the U.S. Department of Education (Contract #300-82-0367) to the Early Intervention Research Institute at Utah State University. Portions of the ''Results'' section of this paper also appeared as part of a publication entitled, ''The efficacy of early intervention programs for handicapped children: A meta-analysis,'' in *Exceptional Children*, 1986, volume 52, pages 417–424; reprinted with permission.

comitant variables associated with intervention effectiveness, including:

Parental involvement: 26 out of 27 said "more is better"

Age at start: 18 out of 24 said "earlier is better"

Degree of structure: 16 out of 17 said "high structured is better"

Duration/intensity: 12 out of 17 said "longer, more intense, is better"

Thus, a type of conventional wisdom about early-intervention effectiveness and the variables associated with effectiveness have permeated the early-intervention field. This is disconcerting for two reasons. First, the conclusions drawn about the effectiveness of early intervention have been largely drawn from the studies that utilized at-risk or disadvantaged samples. White and Casto (1985), for example, found that only 20% of the effect sizes in their meta-analysis of early intervention efficacy literature came from studies that utilized handicapped samples, whereas 80% came from studies that utilized at-risk or disadvantaged populations. Second, previous reviewers have based their conclusions on limited numbers of studies. Although White et al. (1985) identified 447 studies that were cited by previous reviewers, the median number of primary research articles cited by previous reviewers was only 15, with a range of 2–76 citations.

The above described limitations in previous review efforts led researchers at the Early Intervention Research Institute at Utah State University to attempt a more comprehensive review of the early intervention research literature. This review was restricted to handicapped populations and included a larger sample of primary research studies. Their findings are reported next.

REVIEW METHODOLOGY

The techniques utilized to integrate the results of previous research were first proposed by Glass (1976) and are referred to as meta-analy-

sis. Briefly described, conducting a meta-analysis requires a) locating either all studies or a representative sample of studies on a given topic, b) converting the results or outcomes of each study to a common metric, c) coding the various characteristics of studies that might have affected the results (e.g., age of children, type and severity of handicap, type of outcome measured), and then d) using correlational and descriptive statistical techniques to summarize study outcomes in ways that allow the examination of covariations of study characteristics with outcomes. In his critique of previous efforts to integrate the findings of research in the social sciences, Jackson (1980) concluded that the "meta-analysis approach is a very important contribution to the social science methodology. It is not a panacea, but it will often prove to be quite valuable when applied and interpreted with care" (p. 455).

Since its introduction, the meta-analysis approach has been used to review and integrate research findings on a wide variety of topics (Glass, Smith, & Miller, 1980; Kavale, 1980, 1982; White & Myette, 1982). Researchers have raised questions about the use and interpretations of meta-analysis (Educational Research Service, 1980; Eysenck, 1978; Gallo, 1978; Mansfield & Bussey, 1977; Shaver, 1979; Simpson, 1979; Slavin, 1984). Some have questioned the results of a specific meta-analysis, others have raised cautions or concerns about the methodology, per se. Most of these criticisms and cautions have been responded to in the literature (Carlberg et al., 1984; Glass, 1978; Glass, McGaw, & Smith, 1981). Previous concerns about meta-analysis methodology suggest that precise implementation of the methodology and appropriate data analysis are key variables. The meta-analysis to be described here incorporated both variables.

PROCEDURES FOR THE INTEGRATIVE REVIEW

Early intervention efficacy studies were located by a detailed search of computerized data bases including ERIC, *Psychological Abstracts, Dissertation Abstracts, SSIE Current Research,* and *Index Medicus.* In addition, letters were written to prominent early-intervention researchers and service providers requesting their assistance in the identification of efficacy research that might not be reported in the professional literature. Previous reviews of the early intervention literature were examined for reports of efficacy research, and efficacy reports referenced in studies already obtained were identified.

Studies were selected for coding that dealt with handicapped preschoolers ages 0–5 and tested some type of intervention. A total of 74 studies were coded.

A coding system was developed to analyze the outcomes and characteristics of each efficacy study identified. Based largely on an analysis of previous reviews of early intervention efficacy literature (White et al., in press), variables in each of the following areas were coded for each study:

1. *Introduction* (5 items, including study ID, year, and source)
2. *A description of the subjects* included in the research (20 items, including demographic variables on both child and family)
3. The type of *intervention* used (37 items, including type of intervention, the setting, child-intervenor ratio, etc.)
4. The type and quality of *research design* employed, including presence of various threats to validity and whether data collectors were "blind" (17 items)
5. The type of *outcome* measured and the procedures used (12 items)
6. The *conclusions* reached by the study including the magnitude of the standardized–mean-difference effect size, the source of that information, and the conclusions of the author (7 items)

For each of the 98 items coded for each study, conventions or definitions were written. For example, degree of parental involvement was coded according to the following guidelines:

Only intervenor: A parent was trained to deliver intervention and received supervision and inservice training, but no one else actually worked with the child.

Major intervenor: To be considered a major intervenor, a parent was responsible for intervention activities 25% or more of the specified intervention time.

Minor intervenor: To be considered a minor intervenor, the parent was responsible for intervention activities 10%–25% of the specified intervention time.

Not involved in intervention: The parent was involved less than 10% of the time in actual intervention activities.

Administrative or training activities were not classified as intervention.

For another example, degree of structure in the curriculum was coded the following way:

1 = *Very structured:* 50% or more of the intervention was based on a detailed set of outcome objectives supported by a task analysis with scripted presentation of activities and procedures and criteria for progressing to new material.

2 = *Somewhat structured:* 50% or more of the intervention was organized around preconceived activities, which were based on explicit scope and sequence charts. The relation of various parts of the curriculum was specified; the interventionists were to follow a preconceived, organized plan of instruction.

3 = *Not structured:* Intervention did not meet the criteria for 1 or 2 above.

= If part of the program was very structured and part of it was not, the item was coded "–" unless one type of "structure" accounted for 80% or more of the total program.

The magnitude of the effect attributed to each intervention was estimated using a standardized mean difference effect size, defined as $(X_E - X_C) - SD_C$ (Glass et al., 1981). This *effect-size* measure is essentially the difference between experimental and control groups measured in Z-score units, and has been widely used in recent years to describe the impact of educational programs (Cohen, 1977; Glass, 1976; Horst, Tallmadge, & Wood, 1975; Tallmadge, 1977). In cases where there was no control group and pre-post designs were used, the standardized–mean-difference effect size was defined as $(X_{posttest} - X_{pretest}) \div SD_{pretest}$ (Glass et al., 1981). In other words, when no control group was utilized, pretest scores provided the best estimate of how subjects would have performed had they not received the treatment.

For some studies, there was insufficient information contained in the reports to code certain items. In those cases, the information was left blank. For example, it was possible to code type of design used for every study included, but the mother's educational level was reported, or could be estimated, in only about 30% of the studies.

It is also important to note that one study could yield multiple effect sizes. For example, a study that compared an experimental group to a control group on language and motor functioning immediately at the conclusion of the intervention program would yield two effect sizes—one for language functioning and one for motor functioning. The coding conventions dictated that only one effect size (ES) be measured for each 12-month period and for each domain (i.e., if two IQ tests were given during the same time period, results from only one of the IQ tests would be used).

Because multiple raters were involved in the study, interrater consistency checks were done for a sample of the studies coded (87% average agreement). Also, all effect-size (ES) computations were independently checked, and a sample of keypunched data was checked against the original coding. More extensive explanation of the procedures utilized in the meta-analysis are available in Casto, White, and Taylor (1983).

CHARACTERISTICS OF THE DATA SET

When the meta-analysis was completed, 215 effect sizes had been computed from 74 primary research studies[1] with handicapped children. Most of the children were categorized as mentally retarded (44%) or as having a combination of handicaps (29%). Orthopedically impaired children (10%) constituted the next most frequently represented group, followed by speech- and language-impaired (8%), emotionally disturbed (4%), generally developmentally delayed (3%), and hearing-impaired (2%).

The effect sizes included in the analysis came from studies conducted from 1937 to 1984; most since 1970. These studies were reported mostly in educational and psychological journals, but substantial numbers came from medical journals, books, ERIC documents, government reports, and dissertations. Not surprisingly, the most frequently measured outcome was IQ. Other child-change measures included language, motor, social-emotional, and self-help measures. Measures of parent attitude, parent skill levels, and such diverse outcomes as amount of mother-infant eye contact, weight gains, and various types of mother-infant interaction measures were also included.

RESULTS

Overall Effect of Early Intervention

The overall conclusion is that early intervention programs do result in moderately large immediate benefits for handicapped populations. These results are evident over a variety of outcome variables including IQ, motor, language, and academic achievement. Unfortunately, there are relatively few results for outcomes such as self-concept, social competency, or family and peer relationships. In addition, few effect sizes have still been included for severely or profoundly handicapped populations, sensory-impaired children, behaviorally disordered children, or speech-impaired children, although the single-subject literature, which is reported elsewhere, included more of these groups. Nonetheless, the data do support the immediate benefits of early intervention programs across a wide variety of children,

---

[1]These research studies included experimental versus control studies, intervention "A" versus intervention "B" studies, and pretest/posttest only studies.

Table 1. Average effect size for intervention versus control early intervention efficacy studies for subgroups of data

	Handicapped		
	ES	S_{es}	N_{es}
All studies	.68	.05	215
Only studies of good quality	.40	.13	13
Only studies of good quality with immediate posttest	.43	.15	20

ES = mean effect size.
S_{es} = standard error of the mean for ES.
N_{es} = number of ESs on which a calculation is based.

conditions, and types of program. Table 1 presents the overall findings for all studies, for all studies with good internal validity indices, and for all studies of good quality with immediate posttests. It should be noted that the effect sizes are considerably lower when only studies of good quality are considered. The findings reported in Table 1 support the notion of plasticity in the handicapped child.

Findings for Key Variables

The data related to the four variables most cited by previous reviewers were then analyzed. These variables were:

Involvement of parents in intervention program
Age at which intervention begins
Degree of structure in the intervention curriculum
The duration/intensity of programs

For each of these variables, a series of analyses were done. These analyses are reported next.

Parent Involvement   The findings from the analysis of parental involvement suggest that parents can be effective intervenors, but that they may not be essential to intervention success. Those intervention programs that utilize parents are not more effective than those that do not. Table 2 presents these data.

Previous reviewers concluded that more parental involvement is better. The meta-analysis results suggested that parents can be effective intervenors, but that they may not be essential to intervention success. Casto and Lewis (1984) concluded that the contradictory findings could possibly be due to four factors. First, the nature of the outcome measures selected to document the effectiveness of parental involvement may be a critical variable, since IQ measures, which were the most commonly utilized outcome measures, may be of questionable utility in this respect. Second, most researchers failed to document the actual amount of parental involvement in their programs, which might mean that parents were not involved to the degree intended. Third, parent involvement resulted in gains for some preschoolers but not for others; as yet we do not know which groups benefited most. Fourth, Halpern (1984) has suggested:

At the most basic level, it is possible that home-based early intervention as a discrete change strategy is not powerful enough to improve, signifi-

Table 2. Average effect sizes for different levels of parent participation in the intervention

Parent participation	Unadjusted				Adjusted for differences of age at start, quality of outcome measure, and time of measurement
	All studies				All studies
	ES	S_{es}	N_{es}	($n_{studies}$)	ES
Minor or not at all	.76	.07	137	(48)	.72
Major or only	.54	.09	70	(27)	.59

ES = mean effect of size.
S_{es} = standard error of the mean for ES.
N_{es} = number of ESs on which a calculation is based.
($n_{studies}$) = number of studies on which a calculation is based.

Table 3. Average effect sizes for different ages at which intervention was begun

| Age at start | Unadjusted | | | | Adjusted for differences on quality of outcome measure, and time of measurement |
| | All studies | | | | All studies |
	ES	S_{es}	N_{es}	($n_{studies}$)	ES
0–6 months	.59	.12	42	(8)	.59
6–18 months	.48	.22	27	(12)	.47
18–36 months	.55	.10	36	(15)	.54
36–48 months	1.06	.14	36	(18)	1.06
48–66 months	.70	.10	47	(15)	.70

ES = mean effect size.
S_{es} = standard error of the mean for ES.
N_{es} = number of ESs on which a calculation is based.
($n_{studies}$) = number of studies on which a calculation is based.

cantly and permanently, child outcomes for even demonstrably high risk infants and toddlers. (p. 40)

Perhaps as Ramey, Bryant, and Suarez (1985) suggest, to demonstrate the impact of parent involvement, high intensity intervention programs are the answer.

Age at Which Intervention Begins
Again, the conclusion is that there are few data to support the notion that earlier is better in starting intervention programs. In fact, there is some evidence for the handicapped population that suggests that children who start later do better. Table 3 presents these results.

Here again, 18 previous reviewers concluded that earlier is better, while the meta-analysis results suggest that there is little data to support this notion. Primary-research studies have examined the effect of age at start, but the age-at-start-comparions have been substantially confounded with other variables such as duration or intensity of intervention. For "confounded" studies (Beller, 1979; Gordon, 1969; Scott, 1974; Strickland, 1971), we computed an average effect size of .16 favoring children for whom intervention was begun earlier.

In two analyses more pertinent to this review, Lazar, Snipper, Royce, and Darlington (1981) analyzed data from the Consortium for Longitudinal Studies, a data set which is included in this analysis, and found a negative correlation between age of entry and program effectiveness ($r = -.56$). Similarly, in analysis of data from the Western Carolina Center Infant Program, Mastropieri (1984) indicated that children who began intervention after 18 months made the most gains on the Bayley Scales of Infant Development.

A final reason for the disparity in age-at-start findings relates to plasticity in development. It may be that the age at which intervention starts should vary according to the type and severity of handicap. Although Bloom (1964) argues cogently for the notion that the first 5 years of life are critical for intellectual development, it is probable that the years from 1 to 5 may have differential importance for children with different handicapping conditions. For example, researchers such as Ramey et al. (1985) believe that for at-risk populations, intervention programs would be more appropriate beginning in the second year of life. Epstein (1980) considers the years from 2 to 4 as being critical for the acquisition of language and intellectual competence, and suggests that rapid brain growth during this period is accompanied by skills and acquisition.

Degree of Structure
A consistent finding with disadvantaged populations is that more highly structured programs are directly associated with more effective outcomes (Casto & White, 1985). This conclusion is not as

Table 4. Average effect sizes for different levels of structure in the intervention curriculum

| Degree of structure | Unadjusted | | | Adjusted for differences on age at start, quality of outcome measure, and time of measurement |
	ES	All studies N_{es}	($n_{studies}$)	All studies ES
Very structured	.82	18	(19)	.88
Somewhat structured	.82	83	(32)	.79
Little or no structure	.83	6	(4)	.76

ES = mean effect size.
N_{es} = number of ESs on which a calculation is based.
($n_{studies}$) = number of studies on which a calculation is based.

well supported by the data from the handicapped population. Table 4 presents these data.

When the data are considered from all studies, there appears to be little difference among programs with various degrees of structure. When the effect sizes are adjusted, there is a trend that favors the more structured programs, but the data are inconclusive.

Intensity/Duration　Again, another consistent finding with disadvantaged populations is that program intensity/duration is not related to intervention effectiveness. The data available for handicapped populations suggest that it

may very well be an important variable for handicapped populations. Table 5 presents these data.

Twelve previous reviews concluded that longer, more intense intervention is better. The meta-analysis results also suggest that duration/intensity is a critical variable for handicapped infants and young children, but not for disadvantaged populations. This same conclusion was reached by Lazar et al. (1981), based on data from the Consortium for Longitudinal Studies.

As Casto and Salehi (1986) have noted, the

Table 5. Average effect sizes for interventions of different intensity

| Total hours of intervention | Unadjusted | | | | Adjusted for differences on age at start, quality of outcome measure, and time of measurement |
	ES	S_{es}	All studies N_{es}	($n_{studies}$)	All studies ES
Less than 50 hours	.56	.16	22	(8)	.45
50–100 hours	.62	.12	21	(10)	.63
More than 100 hours	.86	.12	39	(10)	.88
Intensity/hours per week	ES	S_{es}	N_{es}		
Less than 2 hours weekly	.59	.77	149		
2–10 hours weekly	.71	.77	59		
Over 10 hours weekly	.80	.35	28		

ES = mean effect size.
S_{es} = standard error of the mean for ES.
N_{es} = number of ESs on which a calculation is based.
($n_{studies}$) = number of studies on which a calculation is based.

issue of the optimum intensity and duration required for an intervention program to be effective is important. Cost-effectiveness considerations would suggest that if a program of 2 hours' intensity per day produces the same gains as a program of 6 hours' intensity, then the 2-hour program would be preferred. The data presented in this review suggest tentatively that intensity and duration are important variables to be considered in designing programs for handicapped preschoolers, but are less important when designing programs for disadvantaged populations. Further research that makes direct comparisons of intensity/duration, while controlling for other important variables, will either confirm or refute this conclusion.

In sum, the findings of the meta-analysis, although in agreement with previous reviewers regarding the overall effectiveness of early intervention, contradicts previous reviewers' conclusions about key variables. The possible reasons for this have been discussed. It is now instructive to examine the methodological adequacy of previous reviews as further reasons for these contradictory findings.

Most previous reviewers cited only a small number of articles. The median number of primary-research articles cited in previous reviews was 15. Given the small number of articles cited in many previous reviews, serious questions arise as to the representativeness and objectivity of the findings of many of the reviews.

Another problem is the way data from primary-research studies are reported and summarized in order to draw conclusions. Many of the conclusions of previous reviewers were stated in such vague terms that readers would find it difficult to ascertain the magnitude or importance of the reported conclusions. There were a few exceptions (Ganson & Hubbell, 1984; Gottfried, 1973; Heverly, Newman, & Forquer, 1982; Jason, 1975; Miller, 1968; Murray, 1977) where results were reported in a more understandable fashion. These reviewers were in the minority.

Finally a third problem found in many pre-

vious reviews was the lack of attention paid to the subject of intervention characteristics, which could co-vary with results. For example, to what extent do subject characteristics influence intervention outcomes? J. Gallagher (personal communication, 1986) and associates at the University of North Carolina Research Institute suggest that there should be *goodness of fit* in treatment, and that both subject and family characteristics influence outcomes to a larger degree than previously thought.

TOWARD A TEST OF THE PLASTICITY NOTION

To address the question of plasticity in handicapped populations, we have used indirect comparisons. The age-at-start variable discussed earlier represents one such comparison. Another indirect comparison is whether the benefits of early intervention are maintained over time. Unfortunately, there is little data available on handicapped populations to answer this question. The immediate benefits of early intervention do decline over time, when the outcome measures used in early intervention programs up to this date are considered. For disadvantaged populations generally, the immediate benefits decline rapidly and have largely disappeared after 60 months. For handicapped populations, we have too little longitudinal data to answer the question. Table 6 reports the results.

What few data we have suggest that for handicapped populations the immediate benefits are still apparent as long as 2 years later, but there are too few studies to draw definite conclusions.

A more direct test of the plasticity hypothesis is currently being attempted by the Early Intervention Research Institute at Utah State University with a sample of low-birth-weight (LBW) infants who have suffered intraventricular hemorrhage (IVH), while in intensive care units. Simply described, an intraventricular hemorrhage is the development of a lesion in the germinal matrix, which results in

Table 6. Average effect sizes for various times at which outcome data were collected for handicapped children

Time of measurement in months since completion of intervention	Handicapped					
	All studies				Studies of good quality	
	ES	S_{es}	N_{es}	($n_{studies}$)	ES	N_{es}
0 months (immediate)	.72	.06	179	(65)	.43	20
1–12 months	.16	.14	17	(8)	.13	3
12–24 months	1.16	.42	7	(3)	—	—
24–36 months	1.93	—	1	(1)	—	—
36–60 months	—	—	—	—	—	—
60+ months	—	—	—	—	—	—

ES = mean effect size.
S_{es} = standard error of the mean for ES.
N_{es} = number of ESs on which a calculation is based.
($n_{studies}$) = number of studies on which a calculation is based.

blood entering the ventricular system. The bleeding results in different degrees of neurological damage based on the severity of the hemorrhage (Volpe, 1981).

Approximately 10% of all babies born in the U.S. are LBW, and 35% to 45% of these babies suffer IVH (Ahmann, Lazzara, Dykes, Brann, & Schwartz, 1980). Thus it is readily apparent how IVH has come to be one of the major health problems in the newborn care unit (Pasternak, Groothuis, Fischer, & Fischer, 1983).

With the development of brain-imaging procedures such as ultrasound and computerized axial tomography (CAT) scan, which provide a positive identification of IVH and allow for classification of the hemorrhage into one of four stages of severity, with stage one being the least and stage four the most severe (Papile, Burstein, Burstein, & Koffler, 1978), the technology is available to address the plasticity issue. Given an identifiable insult at birth and a reasonably accurate picture of the areas of the brain affected, some direct inferences about plasticity will be able to be drawn. The Utah State University study, which is addressing age at start as a primary focus, is studying matched groups of IVH infants who have experienced either a 1-year motor intervention program beginning at birth, or a 1-year intervention pro-

gram beginning at age 1. In addition to the primary research question, this study will provide further information as to the ability of the developing brain to overcome a known insult with and without early intervention.

SUMMARY

Early intervention efficacy research provides evidence that early intervention is immediately effective, thus supporting the plasticity construct. The research literature also provides information that demonstrates how little we know regarding the basic parameters of early intervention.

Our findings suggest that both advocates and researchers should be more cautious about asserting that intervention programs should be started as early as possible, should involve parents as much as possible, and that they result in long-term effectiveness. Perhaps the time is appropriate to conceptualize early intervention as but one event in a critical series of events in the life of a handicapped child. Early intervention is important but may not be *all* important.

A final point of view regarding the plasticity of development in the handicapped infant is a general concern as to how much improvement we should expect of participants in early-intervention programs. For many infants, the severity of their condition precludes their making much progress in certain developmental do-

mains. Intervenors should recognize that intervention interacts with the severity of a condition, and that for many infants, the prognosis is poor even with the best of interventions and the most optimal brain development.

REFERENCES

Ahmann, P. A., Lazzara, H., Dykes, F. D., Brann, A. W., & Schwartz, J. F. (1980). Intraventricular hemorrhage in the high risk preterm infant: Incidence and outcome. *Annals of Neurology, 7,* 118–124.

Beller, E. K. (1979). Early intervention programs. In J. Osofsky (Ed.), *Handbook of infant development.* New York: John Wiley & Sons.

Bertalanffy, L. V. (1969). Chance or law. In A. Koestler & J. R. Smythie (Eds.), *Beyond reductionism.* Boston: Beacon Press.

Bloom, B. S. (1964). *Stability and change in human characteristics.* New York: John Wiley & Sons.

Bowlby, J. (1969). *Attachment and loss: Vol. 1: Attachment.* New York: Basic Books.

Bunge, M. (1979). *Anthology II: A world of systems. Vol. 4: Treatise on basic philosophy.* Boston: D. Reidel.

Carlberg, C. G., Johnson, D. W., Johnson, R., Maruyama, G., Kavale, K., Kulik, C-L. C., Kulik, J. A., Lysakowski, R. S., Pflaum, S. W., & Walberg, H. J. (1984). Meta-analysis in education: A reply to Slavin. *Educational Researchers, 13*(8).

Casto, G., Biaggio, M. K., Hoagland, V., & Muller, D. (1976). *Affective behavior in preschool children.* (Final Report, Contract No. 300-75-0254). Washington, DC: United States Department of Health, Education, and Welfare.

Casto, G., & Lewis, A. (1984). Parent involvement in infant and preschool programs. *Journal of the Division for Early Childhood, 9,* 49–56.

Casto, G., & Salehi, M. (1986). *The relationship between program intensity and duration in early intervention.* Unpublished manuscript, Early Intervention Research Institute, Utah State University, Logan.

Casto, G., & White, K. R. (1985). *Final report 1982–83 work scope.* Logan: Early Intervention Research Institute, Utah State University.

Casto, G., White, K. R., & Taylor, C. (1983). An Early Intervention Research Institute: Efficacy and cost studies in early intervention. *Journal of the Division for Early Childhood, 7,* 5–17.

Cohen, J. (1977). *Statistical power analysis for the behavioral sciences.* New York: Academic Press.

Denenberg, V. (1982). Early experience, interactive systems, and brain laterality in rodents. In L. A. Bond, H. Lynne, & J. Joffe (Eds.), *Facilitating infant and early childhood development* (pp. 78–97). Hanover, VT: University Press of New England.

Educational Research Service. (1980, December). Class-size research: A critique of recent meta-analysis. *Kappan,* 239–241.

Epstein, H. T. (1980). Some biological bases of cognitive development. *Bulletin of the Orton Society, 30,* 46–62.

Eysenck, J. J. (1978). An exercise in mega-silliness. *American Psychologist, 33,* 517.

Ferry, P. C. (1981). On growing new neurons: Are ea

intervention programs effective? *Pediatrics, 67*(1), 38–41.

Frank, L. K. (1966). *On the importance of infancy.* New York: Random House.

Gallo, P. S. (1978). Meta-analysis—a mixed meta-phor. *American Psychologist, 33,* 515–517.

Ganson, H., & Hubbell, R. (1984). *The long term effects of Head Start on children's cognitive and socioemotional development: A preliminary report of the Head Start evaluation, synthesis, and utilization project* (Contract No. 105-81-C-026). Washington, DC: Department of Health and Human Services, Administration for Children, Youth and Families.

Glass, G. V. (1976). Primary, secondary, and meta-analysis of research. *Educational Researcher, 5*(10), 3–8.

Glass, G. V. (1978). Reply to Mansfield and Bussey. *Educational Researcher, 7,* 3.

Glass, G. V., McGaw, B., & Smith, M. L. (1981). *Integrating research studies: Meta-analysis in social research.* Beverly Hills: Sage Publications.

Glass, G. V., Smith, M. L., & Miller, T. I. (1980). *The benefits of psychotherapy.* Baltimore, MD: Johns Hopkins University Press.

Gordon, I. J. (1969). Stimulation via parent education. *Children, 16*(2), 57–58.

Gottfried, N. W. (1973). Effects of early intervention programs. In K. S. Miller & R. M. Oregor (Eds.), *Comparative studies of blacks and whites in the U.S.* (pp. 273–293). New York: Seminar Press.

Halpern, R. (1984). Lack of effects for home-based early intervention? Some possible explanations. *American Journal of Orthopsychiatry, 54*(1), 33–42.

Heverly, M. A., Newman, F. L., & Forquer, S. L. (1982). *Meta-analysis and cost analysis of preventive intervention programs.* Philadelphia: EPPI/MCP.

Horst, D. P., Tallmadge, G. K., & Wood, C. T. (1975). *A practical guide to measuring project impact on student achievement* (No. 1, Stock No. 017-080-01460-2). Washington, DC: U.S. Government Printing Office.

Jackson, G. B. (1980). Methods for integrative reviews. *Review of Educational Research, 50*(3), 438–460.

Jason, L. (1975). Early secondary prevention with disadvantaged preschool children. *American Journal of Community Psychology, 3*(1), 33–46.

Kagan, J., Kearsely, R. B., & Zelazo, P. R. (1980). *Infancy: Its place in human development.* Cambridge, MA: Harvard University Press.

Kavale, K. (1980). *Meta-analysis of experiments on the treatment of hyperactivity in children.* Riverside: University of California-Riverside Press.

Kavale, K. (1982). The efficacy of stimulant drug treatment for hyperactivity: A meta-analysis. *Journal of Learning Disabilities, 15*(5), 280–289.

Lazar, I., Snipper, A., Royce, J., & Darlington, R. (1981). Policy implications of preschool intervention research. In M. Begab, H. C. Haymond, & H. L. Garber (Eds.), *Psychosocial influences in retarded performance* (pp. 275–291). Baltimore: University Park Press.

Mansfield, R. S., & Bussey, T. V. (1977). Meta-analysis of research: A rejoinder to Glass. *Educational Research, 6,* 3.

Mastropieri, M. A. (1984). *Age at sart and early intervention effectiveness: A correlational analysis.* Unpublished manuscript, Early Intervention Research Institute, Utah State University, Logan, UT.

Miller, J. O. (1968). *Review of selected intervention research with young children.* Urbana, IL: National Laboratory on Early Childhood Education. (ERIC Document Reproduction Service No. ED 027 091).

Murray, H. W. (1977). *Longitudinal evaluation of education for handicapped infants.* (ERIC Document Reproduction Service No. ED 027 091)

Papile, L. A., Burstein, J., Burstein, R., & Koffler, H. (1978). Incidence and evolution of subependymal and intraventricular hemorrhage: A study of infants with birthweights less than 1500 grams. *Journal of Pediatrics, 92,* 529–534.

Pasternak, J. F., Groothuis, D. R., Fischer, J. M., & Fischer, D. I. (1983). Regional blood flow in the beagle puppy model of neonatal intraventricular hemorrhage: Studies during systemic hypecterism. *Neurology, 33,* 559–566.

Ramey, C., Bryant, D., & Suarez, T. (1985). Preschool compensatory education and the modifiability of intelligence: A critical review. In D. Detterman (Ed.), *Current topics in human intelligence* (pp. 247–296). Norwood, NJ: Ablex.

Ramey, C. T., McPhee, D., & Yeates, K. (1982). Prevent-

ing developmental retardation: A general system model. In L. Bond & J. Joffee (Eds.), *Facilitating infant and early childhood development* (pp. 343–401). Hanover, NH: University Press of New England.

Scott, R. (1974). Research and early childhood: The Home Start Project. *Child Welfare, 53*(2), 112–119.

Shaver, J. P. (1979). The usefulness of educational research in curricular/instructional decision-making in social studies. *Theory and Research in Social Education, 7*(3), 21–46.

Simpson, S. N. (1979). *Comment on "metal-analysis of research on class size and achievement."* London, England: Institute of Education.

Slavin, R. (1984). Meta-analysis in education: How has it been used? *Educational Researcher, 13*(8).

Strickland, S. P. (1971). Can slum children learn? *American Education, 7,* 3–7.

Tallmadge, G. K. (1977). *Ideabook: The Joint Dissemination Review Panel.* Washington, DC: U.S. Office of Education.

Volpe, J. J. (1981). Neonatal intraventricular hemorrhage. *The New England Journal of Medicine, 304*(34), 886–891.

White, K. R., Bush, D., & Casto, G. (1985). Learning from previous reviews of early intervention research. Journal of Special Education, *19*(4), 417–428.

White, K. R., & Casto, G. (1985). An integrative review of early intervention efficacy studies with at risk children: Implications for the handicapped. *Analysis and Intervention in Developmental Disabilities, 5,* 7–31.

White, K. R., & Myette, B. (1982, March). *Drug treatment of hyperactivity: A meta-analysis.* Paper presented at the annual meeting of the American Educational Research Association, New York.

Chapter 10

Sustaining Intervention Effects
Putting Malleability to the Test
Bettye M. Caldwell

I long ago abandoned the immunological model when conceptualizing the impact of early experience on the development of children. It is quite possible that, in a first major effort at developing an early intervention program (Caldwell & Richmond, 1964), I somehow expected that children would be enabled to meet the challenge of formal schooling more effectively, and that the parents would be more consistent supporters of and more effective advocates for quality educational experiences for their children. I never, however, endorsed a simplistic sort of tetanus-immunization model. The cholera model, which calls for a booster whenever exposure or threat is likely, is a more apt description.

Proof of my innocence is the basic conceptualization of the Kramer Project (Caldwell, 1972), which later came to be known as an example of a developmental-continuity, or at least an educational-continuity, model. This program added an early-childhood component to an existing elementary school, thus offering developmentally appropriate education for children from 6 months to 12 years. Its intervention strategy involved early enrichment followed by sustained support through the critical primary-school years. The assumptions that guided the Kramer Project were that certain basic predispositions to relate to the world be produced as a consequence of positive early-childhood experiences: learning to learn and

problem solve, learning how to get information and to acquire skills, finding joy in achievement, acquiring self-confidence, and knowing how to use adults for obtaining needed information. Such achievements, it was hypothesized, would put the children in a better position to function in their subsequent schools. They would be more motivated and be better able to cope with frustration, stress, and their own inadequacies. These achievements would begin in early childhood; the better their primary school, the greater the enhancement effect. Thus gains were presumed to be produced in early childhood and enhanced or sustained during the primary years. In retrospect, relatively little thought was given to the possibility that such gains might be dissipated or obliterated.

The Kramer School was a good environment in which one might be disabused of almost any preconception about factors that influenced development—or anything else, for that matter. Capricious moves of families in and out of the attendance area; herculean struggles of teachers and principal to maintain control of the children's behavior, following the removal of physical punishment as a disciplinary technique; struggles to convert teachers to the philosophy of the project; frequent changes of textbooks; short-term consultations from university professors who liked the idea of access to a social science laboratory like the Kramer School, but not necessarily the hassles associ-

Development of this chapter was supported by a grant from the Foundation for Child Development, New York, New York.

The contributions of Jane Fitzgerald to the project are gratefully acknowledged.

115

ated with direct involvement—such pragmatic events made the hypotheses sometimes seem remote and irrelevant. Nonetheless, we persevered, and the soundness of the basic ideas was reinforced by the early data analyses (Elardo & Caldwell, 1974).

We had no difficulty demonstrating enough benefits to include in our annual reports to the Office of Child Development. But the enhancement effect that I had hoped for seemed to have its limitations.

In most waves of pupils, achievement of those who have spent at least 1 year in the early childhood component would be close to the norm in the first grade, not too far off in the second, but perhaps an entire grade level below norms by the end of third grade. In the spring of 1972, when our first kindergarten class reached the end of second grade, the class mean on the summary achievement score of the Iowa Every Pupil Tests was 2.7. In 1973, at the end of third grade, the mean was 2.8—hardly a dramatic rate of progress. (Please keep in mind that the two groups were not identical in composition at both time points.)

Other changes were noticeable around that same time, which intensified interest in this late primary period. Many of the children began to change in ways that were difficult to put into words. Discipline problems multiplied, and the offenses became more vicious and clearly designed to inflict injury. The affectionate but rational approach to discipline previously used with the children with considerable success seemed to lose its effectiveness. A child caught in the act of hitting another child with a rock might sullenly sit through a session in which we tried to explore other ways of dealing with the conflict, and then, upon release, immediately seek out the intended victim and renew his assault. Free expressions of affection to adults, so common in the school among the younger children, became rare. Being cool seemed to mean a lot more than being good.

These phenomena interested me, and around Kramer School we began to explore ways of focusing on and solving the problems of the third grade. However, it was not until some of our major longitudinal studies matured to the point of providing carefully monitored em-

pirical data that I began to raise scientific questions about whether this age (roughly 8 years), largely ignored by most personality theories, represented something of a critical period in the developmental histories of children. Specifically, I began to question whether social and emotional ferment occurring around this time could cause a dissipation of previous cognitive and academic gains? Or were these changes merely indications that previous gains had been spurious or superficial? Was there a *third-grade slump* that needed to be studied and, if possible, circumvented?

EMPIRICAL SUPPORT FOR EXPERIMENTAL-CONTROL CONVERGENCE

The slump would be more accurately described as a convergence between experimental and control children. A classic example of such a convergence on the Peabody Picture Vocabulary Test can be found in Figure 1, taken from Weikart, Bond, and McNeil (1978). The convergence actually occurs at the end of the second grade in this figure, thus suggesting that my hypothesis about the timing might have been slightly inaccurate. Of particular interest in this graph is the impressive spurt shown by the control children during their kindergarten year—in itself an early-childhood year according to most educational timetables. These data suggest that both groups of children showed a spurt following initiation of enrichment, whether that occurred at 3 years (experimental children) or 5 years (control children). Data based on the Stanford-Binet Intelligence Scale are very similar for children in the Perry Project. As yet we have no accurate way of measuring true academic achievement in preschool children, and it is difficult to scale developments in the socio-emotional area. Accordingly, it is not possible to examine for similar patterns in areas other than intelligence.

The Consortium for Longitudinal Studies

The most impressive data base to examine with regard to this question of convergence is that of the Consortium for Longitudinal Studies

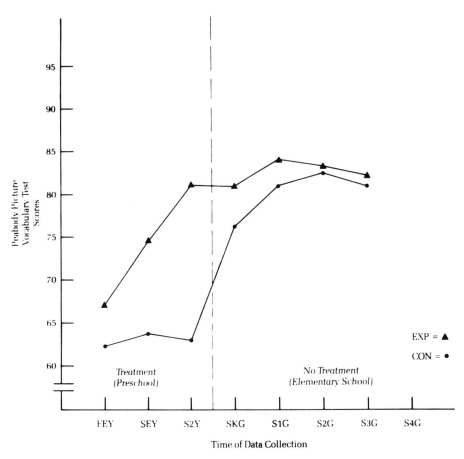

Figure 1. Mean scores on the Peabody Picture Vocabulary Test for experimental and control children in the Perry Preschool Project from age 3 to fourth grade. (From Weikart, Bond, & McNeil, 1978.)

(Lazar & Darlington, 1982). It will be recalled that the Consortium included the Weikart study, from which data in Figure 1 were taken. Figure 2 presents a summary of data on intelligence reported for the Consortium, which bears upon the issue of convergence. Even though the various projects did not use the same assessment procedures or examine the children at identical time points, this study remains a landmark in efforts to understand the long-term effects of early intervention. The data used to compile Figure 2 are found in Tables 14 and 15 of Lazar and Darlington (1982).

When neither background variables nor pretest IQs were controlled, five of the projects found significant experimental-control (E-C) differences in IQ at age 6 (essentially the end of the early enrichment). However, only two of those programs showed significant differences

in favor of the experimental children at age 8 or 10 (Figure 2A). When background variables and pretest IQ were controlled, one additional program found its way into the cell indicating significant differences at both time points (Figure 2B).

As already indicated, achievement data cannot be charted so neatly over time, as baseline measures are probably not very adequate in the first place, and certainly bear little relationship to subsequent achievement. However, cross-sectional data from the Consortium are relevant. In only one of four projects—Levenstein—with data obtained at grade three, was there a significant difference between E and C children ($N = 73$) in reading achievement, and the Levenstein project (with 47 remaining children) was the only one of seven to show a significant difference at grade four. For math

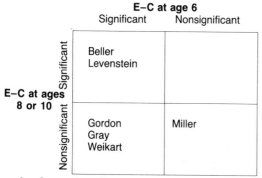

E–C at age 6

A. Comparison of program/control mean IQ scores

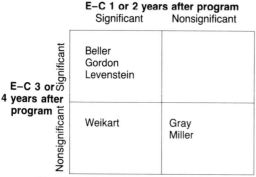

E–C 1 or 2 years after program

B. Comparison of program/control mean IQ scores with background variables and pretest IQ controlled

Figure 2.   Differences between experimentals and controls in intellectual functioning at age 6 and later. (Figure based on Tables 14 and 15, Lazar & Darlington [1982].)

achievement, the Levenstein project also showed a superiority for experimental children at grade three, but only the Gordon project (N = 43), out of six projects, showed a significant difference at grade four.

It should be pointed out here that several of the projects included in the Consortium—most notably the Perry Project headed by Weikart, and the Early Training Project, originated by Gray—have followed their children well beyond the third or fourth grade level. Dramatic differences found for the Perry Project children (Berrueta-Clement, Schweinhart, Barnett, Epstein, & Weikart, 1984) have been widely publicized. Results from this longer follow-up have had a salutary effect on the entire field and have been effective in convincing policy-makers that an investment in high quality, early

childhood programs offers a high rate of return. In this analysis I do not mean to ignore the importance of this longer follow-up. However, in order to examine the issues I was raising, it seemed entirely legitimate to use the third or fourth grade as a temporary terminal and to ignore subsequent follow-ups carried out past that time point.

To summarize data from the Consortium studies, one can conclude that experimental-control differences are, in most studies, attenuated by the third or fourth grade. For the most part, experimental groups were slightly but nonsignificantly higher than the controls. There were a few slight differences in achievement in favor of the controls at grade four, but none of these achieved statistical significance.

Data fron Non-Consortium Studies

In addition to the studies included in the Consortium, there are a number of other early intervention studies that have followed the children to some point near the third grade. Some of these studies lacked the methodological purity necessary to qualify for the Consortium; others were perhaps begun too recently for the children to have reached age levels that would allow comparable analyses, or were perhaps excluded for other unknown reasons. Certainly it is fair to state that finding out about the studies is sometimes more a matter of chance than the result of a systematic literature search. Some very important studies in this area (often with large and impressive sample sizes but nonexistent or poorly chosen controls) have been carried out within the research departments of city school districts or state departments of education. Such research is rarely published in refereed journals, and one simply has to know that it is being done to be able to track it down.

For this analysis I have used nine studies not included in the Consortium. Four of these were carried out from the middle to late 60s: Wisconsin (Heber & Garber, 1975), Florida (Sprigle, 1974; Van de Riet & Resnick, 1973), Illinois (Karnes, Zehrbach, & Tesca, 1974), and Washington, D.C. (Herzog, Newcomb, & Cisin, 1974). Three others were conducted as evaluation projects in large metropolitan areas or as a means of planning a state-wide program: Cincinnati (Nieman & Gathright, 1981), New York State (New York State Education Department, 1982), and Philadelphia (School District of Philadelphia, 1984). The remaining two were different from one another but both more than worthy of inclusion. One is the North Carolina Abecedarian Project (C. Ramey, personal communication, 1985), (see also Chapter 11, this volume) considered by me to be methodologically exemplary and truly a unique project, and the other was carried out in Cali, Colombia (McKay, 1982) as part of a larger study concerned with malnutrition and development.

These studies represent greater heterogeneity in such areas as sample size, assessment techniques, times when evaluations were done, and even research goals, than those included in the Consortium, and are, therefore, more difficult to summarize. Nevertheless, a summary of the data on intellectual functioning available in seven of the studies is presented in Figure 3.

It is obvious that all seven studies reported significant differences between experimental

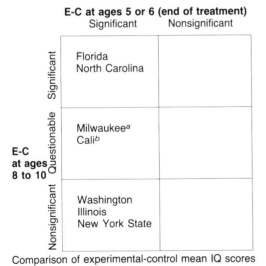

E-C at ages 5 or 6 (end of treatment)

Comparison of experimental-control mean IQ scores

Figure 3. Summary of non-Consortium project data on intellectual functioning. (a Listed as questionable because of challenges to the data and absence of statistical information. b Listed as questionable because, although statistical analysis yields some significant differences among groups representing different intensities of treatment, E children show rather large drops in Stanford-Binet IQ between ages 7 and 10.)

and control children in IQ immediately upon completion of the treatment at ages 5 or 6. At ages 8–10, however, of the seven, only two (Florida, North Carolina) are shown as having significant differences. All others report either questionable or nonsignificant differences between the groups. Actually, a review of research indicates that even the Florida study should be included in the questionable category. In the Sprigle (1974) report, only descriptive statistics are provided, and statistical evidence of significance is minimal in the report by Van de Riet and Resnick (1973).

It is even more difficult to summarize data pertaining to achievement variables examined in these nine studies. However, an overview of the findings is offered in Table 1. Most of the studies collected data on either reading or math in the primary grades and also looked at such indications of scholastic difficulty as retention in grade and utilization of special services. Experimental-control differences were examined for as many of these criteria of achievement as were measured. The upper section of the table deals with the four studies dating back to the late 60s (dates on the references do not accurately reflect the ages of the projects). There were no differences between the groups in the Washington project (probably the oldest of the four), and the once dramatic differences reported for the Milwaukee sample dissipated completely once the children reached the upper primary years. A disturbing finding for the Washington study was the high rate of retention in grade for all of the project children, experimental and control. The Illinois project found the experimental children functioning at a significantly higher level on reading, and the Florida report described their experimental children as consistently higher than controls, but offered no statistical support for the claim.

Only two of the three large scale education studies (Cincinnati and Philadelphia) reported a significant superiority in reading and math for children who had been in early childhood programs. In all three, there was a significantly lower rate of utilization of special services by children who had been in the early-childhood programs. The consistency of this finding

Table 1. Summary of second or third grade achievement data from non-consortium projects

	Reading	Math	Retention in grade	Services
Projects of the 1960s:				
Washington—Howard University	E = C	E = C	1/3 E; 1/2 C	—
Milwaukee	E > C first 2 yrs. Performance of Es has since declined to level of inner-city Milwaukee schools.			
Illinois	E > C	—	—	—
Florida	E group reported to be consistently higher, no statistical evidence.		—	—
Large scale public education studies				
Cincinnati	E > C	E > C	E < C	E < C
New York State	—	—	E < C	E < C
Philadalphia	E > C	E > C	E < C	E < C
Cali, Colombia	Slight association between years of treatment and pass-fail during first 4 years of primary school. Results ambiguous because of nonrandom assignment of children to primary school.			
North Carolina	On achievement variables groups tended to rank as follows: early enrichment-primary enrichment, early enrichment-primary control, with early control-primary enrichment and early control-primary control relatively equal.			

across studies, including the Consortium and the separate analyses for the Weikart project, is impressive and reassuring.

A second grade analysis of the Abecedarian Project was in process at the time this chapter was written, and Ramey (Personal Communication, 1985) was gracious enough to share some of the early results. When the children who had been in the early-childhood program reached first grade, both the experimental and control groups were randomly divided into two subgroups: in one, a home teacher worked with both the children and their parents (primary enrichment); in the other, only the regular first grade program was available to the students (primary control). Table 1 shows that the means for achievement variables ranked themselves from high to low as follows: early enrichment plus primary enrichment, early enrichment and primary control, early control and primary enrichment, early control and primary control. Groups 2 and 3 were very close to one another in mean scores, suggesting the possibility of an enhancement effect during the primary years for those children not previously enrolled in a high quality, early-childhood program.

Achievement data for the Cali, Colombia project were virtually meaningless in that random assignment—assiduously attempted during the preschool years—totally disappeared once the children reached primary school. An attempt was made to enroll the experimental children in one specific primary school which the investigators themselves were planning. This plan fell through, however, after project children had spent varying amounts of time in it. Their analysis was not an experimental-control comparison, as was the case for most of the other studies, but rather an examination of the association between number of years in their early-childhood program and certain criteria of achievement. Some children had been enrolled in the program at 1 year of age, some at 2 years, and so on, until age of admission to elementary school. The only significant finding was a slight association between number of years in the treatment program and pass-fail at fourth grade.

To summarize this section on achievement, it can be said that most of the non-Consortium studies have shown some difference between experimental and control children in the tendency for retention in grade and in the need for special services. Only a few have shown achievement test differences that persisted through the second or third grade. However, it is especially significant to note that the two which did so most impressively (Cincinnati and Philadelphia) were based on programs that would have to be considered regular crops rather than hot house plants! This in itself is most encouraging.

DISCUSSION

At the outset of this discussion, I should like to state that this chapter must be considered preliminary and provisional in that analyses of Head Start data or data from early intervention projects serving primarily handicapped children have not been included. However, on the basis of studies reviewed to date, a few tentative generalizations can be made.

First, as a result of this analysis, I feel no diminution of my enthusiasm for early intervention programs as offering one of the major strategies available to us for facilitating the development of children living in less than optimal environmental conditions. This conviction stands in spite of the evidence presented here that, in many samples, both intelligence and achievement curves from early intervention and control groups do tend to converge during the middle-childhood period.

Perhaps the most parsimonious explanation

of this relates to the immediacy of reaction to most treatments and the subsequent attenuation of treatment effects. It is actually incorrect to refer to *treatment* and *nontreatment* groups in describing the design of early intervention research. All the children in the various control samples received the experimental treatment (intervention)—they all went to school, albeit they entered at a different point along the curve of development of the functions to be assessed as dependent variables. Thus, technically, it would be more accurate to describe experimental subjects as *early intervention,* and control subjects as *subsequent intervention.*

If we conceptualize the treatment groups in this way, then it is logical to expect a spurt in the subsequent-intervention group just as we do in the early-intervention group. Assuming that the maximum response to treatment occurs shortly after treatment begins, we would expect control samples to manifest a spurt around age 6 or 7—that is, during the first year after they begin to receive treatment. As Figure 1 shows, that is indeed the case for many control samples. Because such children have different educational histories, their spurt will not occur at the same time as it will in children who receive intervention at an earlier age. Both groups can perhaps be expected to slow their rates of growth after the initial spurt. Thus, the seeming convergence around the third or fourth grade between children who have and who have not been in early-intervention programs (or who have had early versus subsequent intervention) may represent the fact that the subsequent intervention group is still closer to the spurt phase of its initial reaction to treatment. Rather than representing a stable developmental phenomenon, the convergence may be something of an accident of timing that allows the growth curves of the early and subsequent intervention groups to intersect at that point.

Such a convergence does not in any way minimize the significance of effects of longer-term that have been recently documented (Berrueta-Clement et al., 1984). Rather, it merely offers a challenge to researchers, program designers, and developmental theorists to explain and, if possible, avert it. I shall discuss briefly factors in each of three areas that may help to account for the convergence here described.

Methodological Factors

As is well known, there are major methodological problems associated with most longitudinal research; the studies concerned with the effects of early intervention represent no exception. In spite of help provided by design specialists (Campbell & Erlebacher, 1970; Cook & Campbell, 1979), many researchers in this area may well have gone beyond compromise to capitulation. All the studies included in the Consortium presumably had random assignment of subjects to experimental and control groups, but few researchers can arrange this luxury. On the basis of data already in hand, one could impute as unethical any investigator who deliberately withheld early enrichment from a disadvantaged child in order to help construct a scientifically impeccable control group.

There are many other methodological problems that could be identified. Lack of "blind" assessment in most of the projects is a major one. Typically, this is not even mentioned, from which one can probably conclude that evaluators were aware of the group identity of individual subjects. Somewhat related is the question of whether the instruments used were appropriate measures of the variables under study.

Pedagogical Factors

During the past 20 years or so, there has been a great deal of ferment in the area of curriculum for the early-childhood period. What constitutes an acceptable curriculum? An optimal curriculum? An unacceptable curriculum? In the frenetic period of the mid 60s, most program developers were concerned only with showing that some early-childhood program was associated with developmental advances in the participating children. Soon, however, the game became that of proving that a particular type of curriculum, not just any curriculum, was associated with greater progress. Words began to appear that presumably communicated the essence of different approaches—

terms like *cognitively oriented, learning to learn, ameliorative,* and *parent-mediated* joined already common labels like Montessori and traditional.

There are probably certain features common to all the high quality experimental programs of the 60s and subsequent years: low adult:child ratio, high level of both stimulus and response on the part of teachers and caregivers, heavy emphasis on language development, some attempt to sequence learning activities, parent involvement, high levels of social reinforcement for desirable behavior, hands-on utilization of teaching-learning materials, attempts to foster a positive self-concept, concern with achievement motivation, efforts to foster positive peer interaction, and an orientation toward problem solving and increasing independent behavior. And yet, there are undoubtedly important differences among the different approaches that could and perhaps should produce different developmental outcomes. That the interpretation of such differences is not always easy can be illustrated by two studies carried out by Miller and her colleagues.

Both of the studies (Miller & Bizzell, 1983; Miller & Dyer, 1975), dealt with follow-ups of 214 predominantly black children in Louisville, Kentucky, who had been randomly assigned to one of four prekindergarten groups. Two of these were considered didactic (DARCEE and Bereiter-Engelmann) and two were classified as nondidactic (Montessori and traditional). Immediately at the end of the treatment period, the greatest effect on cognitive variables was found in children in the two didactic programs. However, by the end of second grade, the group that had gained the most (Bereiter-Engelmann) had declined the most. No cognitive gains associated with Montessori had been found at the end of the prekindergarten program, but by the end of second grade the Montessori program was found to have been the most beneficial for males in terms of both IQ and achievement.

The study by Miller & Bizzell (1983) followed the children into the sixth, seventh, and eighth grades. At this point, separate analyses had to be conducted for boys and girls in order to show any patterns. Males from the two non-didactic programs were significantly higher in reading and math achievement, whereas a nonsignificant reversal was found for girls. Trends in IQ from prekindergarten to the eighth grade showed that males in the didactic programs lost an average of 9 points, whereas those in the nondidactic programs lost only 3 points. Females in both types of groups lost an average of 12 IQ points over the same time period.

I have described the complicated findings from these two studies in some detail because they illustrate a most important point about curriculum: The effects of a particular curriculum may vary as a function of the ages of the children at the times of evaluation. A curriculum that appears to be most effective at one developmental period may be less effective—or seem actually inimical to development—at another. There is still a great deal to be learned about which types of curriculum are appropriate for which types of children, and we will not be able to draw any firm conclusions about the limits of malleability until we understand more fully the interaction between type of early-childhood program and pattern of change in the children.

Developmental Factors

The age period with which this analysis is concerned—roughly ages 8 to 10 years—has been relatively neglected by most developmental theories. Perhaps more than anyone, Rogoff and her associates (Rogoff, Newcombe, Fox, & Ellis, 1980; Rogoff, Sellers, Pirrotta, Fox, & White, 1975) have called attention to this neglect. They have reminded us that during this period major transitions occur in such areas as visual/spatial analytic ability, organization of material for recall, understanding of causality, use of conditional reasoning, hypothesis testing, judging intents and motives, differentiation of social roles, and the degree of egocentrism.

In spite of all these important behavioral transitions, little effort has been made to integrate them into an organizing theory of development. Behaviors characteristic of this period might be interpreted as identifying a period of consolidation of previously acquired competencies or of preparation for later changes (such as the development of formal operations coinciding with the onset of puberty). It is quite possible that the educational activities provided children during these years do not permit sufficient rehearsal and practice of newly acquired skills and attitudes to allow consolidation of earlier gains. This might be especially true if, through some sort of intervention program, skill acquisition had been somewhat forced, rather than more spontaneous.

The possibility of biological changes during this period that might influence the curve of acquisition of new skills and the consolidation of those that have been previously acquired must also be considered. The controversial neurophysiological theories of Epstein (1974a, 1974b, 1978, 1979, & 1980) posit spurts in brain growth followed by *fallow* or *trough* periods of brain development, when little new growth occurs. Allowing for individual variations, Epstein suggests that these spurts occur in cycles beginning roughly at ages 3, 7, 11, and 15 years. He coined the term *phrenoblysis* to refer to the correlated aspect of brain and mind growth stages and relates the term to the educational concept of readiness.

A pedagogical implication of the phrenoblysis hypothesis is that intensive teaching should be timed to coincide with periods of spurts in brain growth, and that assimilation and consolidation should be allowed during plateau periods. The third grade will occur for most children during a plateau period. And yet the nature of teaching in most elementary schools at this time might be characterized as spurt-period teaching—the curriculum begins to make more demands on the children for independent work, specialist teachers are introduced, and rather major increments of expected output are added.

It should be stated here that the validity of Epstein's theories and the accuracy of the data upon which they are based have been sharply criticized (McQueen, 1984). Nonetheless, the ideas are mentioned here because of their special relevance for a consideration of developmental factors that may predispose children to an attenuation of cognitive and academic gains acquired during an earlier developmental period.

In sum, in this chapter I have raised the question of whether, during the middle childhood years of roughly 8 to 10, there tends to be an attenuation of cognitive and academic gains acquired as the result of a previous early-childhood intervention program. The analysis has suggested that such an attenuation does indeed occur, albeit not with the precision of timing implied by a term such as the third grade slump. That this attenuation occurs should not be construed as in any way challenging other findings of long-term benefits (such as smoother school careers, with less retention in grade or need for special services, and greater evidence of responsible social behavior). Rather it should be used to challenge researchers to try to understand more fully the important developmental changes of this age period, to devise ways to demonstrate more convincingly changes associated with quality, early-childhood programs, and to design intervention strategies that will maximize the likelihood that gains will be sustained. Data from this analysis in no way suggest that the human organism is not malleable; rather they merely remind us that we have much to learn about how to allow such malleability to become and remain manifest.

REFERENCES

Berrueta-Clement, J. R., Schweinhart, L. J., Barnett, W. S., Epstein, A. S., & Weikart, D. P. (1984). *Changed lives: The effects of the Perry preschool program on youths through age 19*. Ypsilanti, MI: High/Scope Educational Research Foundation.

Caldwell, B. M. (1972). Kramer School—something for everybody. In S. J. Braun & E. P. Edwards (Eds.), *History and theory of early childhood education*. Worthington, OH: Charles A. Jones Co.

Caldwell, B. M., & Richmond, J. B. (1964). Programmed day care for the very young child—a preliminary report. *Journal of Marriage and Family, 26,* 481–488.

Campbell, D. T., & Erlebacher, A. (1970). How regression artifacts in quasi-experimental evaluation can mistakenly make compensatory education look harmful. In J. Hellmuth (Ed.), *Disadvantaged child,* (Vol. 3, pp. 185–210). New York: Brunner-Mazel.

Cook, T. D., & Campbell, D. T. (1979). *Quasi-experimentation: Design and analysis issues for field settings.* Chicago: Rand McNally.

Elardo, P. T., & Caldwell, B. M. (1974). The Kramer adventure: A school for the future. *Childhood Education, 50,* 143–152.

Epstein, H. T. (1974a). Phrenoblysis: Special brain and mind growth periods. I. Human brain and skull development. *Developmental Psychobiology, 7,* 207–216.

Epstein, H. T. (1974b). Phrenoblysis: Special brain and mind growth periods. II. Human mental development. *Developmental Psychobiology, 7,* 217–224.

Epstein, H. T. (1978). Growth spurts during brain development: Implications for educational policy and practice. In J. Chall & A. F. Mirsky (Eds.), *1978 Yearbook of the National Society for the Study of Education.* Chicago: University of Chicago Press.

Epstein, H. T. (1979). Correlated brain and intelligence development in humans. In M. E. Hahn, C. Jensen, & B. C. Dudek (Eds.), *Development and evolution of brain size.* New York: Academic Press.

Epstein, H. T. (1980). EEG developmental stages. *Developmental Psychobiology, 13,* 629–631.

Heber, R., & Garber, H. (1975). The Milwaukee Project: A study of the use of the family intervention to prevent cultural-family retardation. In B. Z. Friedlander, G. M. Sterritt, & G. E. Kirk (Eds.), *Exceptional infant* (Vol. 3). New York: Brunner/Mazel.

Herzog, E., Newcomb, C. H., & Cisin, I. H. (1974). Double deprivation: The less they have, the less they learn. In S. Ryan (Ed.), *A report on longitudinal evaluations of preschool programs* (Vol. I, Publication No. OHD 75–25). Washington, DC: U.S. Department of Health, Education, and Welfare.

Karnes, M. B., Zehrback, R. R., & Teska, J. A. (1974). The Karnes preschool program: Rationale, curricular offerings, and follow-up data. In S. Ryan (Ed.), *A report on longitudinal evaluations of preschool programs* (DHEW Publication No. OHD 74–24, 95–108). Washington, DC: Office of Child Development, Children's Bureau.

Lazar, I., & Darlington, R. (1982). Lasting effects of early education. *Monographs of the Society for Research in Child Development, 47*(1–2, Serial No. 194).

McKay, A. G. (1982). *Longitudinal study of the long-term effects of the duration of early childhood intervention on cognitive ability and primary school performance.* Unpublished doctoral dissertation, Northwestern University, Evanston, IL.

McQueen, R. (1984). Spurts and plateaus in brain growth: A critique of the claims of Herman Epstein. *Educational Leadership, 6,* 66–71.

Meyer, L. A. (1984). Long-term academic effects of the Direct Instruction Project Follow Through. *The Elementary School Journal, 84,* 380–394.

Miller, L. B., & Bizzell, R. P. (1983). Long-term effects of four preschool programs: Sixth, seventh, and eighth grades. *Child Development, 54,* 727–741.

Miller, L. B., & Dyer, J. L. (1975). Four preschool programs: Their dimensions and effects. *Monographs of the Society for Research in Child Development, 40*(5–6, 1–170).

New York State Education Department. (1982). *Evalua-*

tion of the New York State Experimental Prekindergarten Program (Final Report). New York State Education Department. (ERIC Document Reproduction Service No. ED 219 123).

Nieman, R. H., & Gathright, J. F. (1981). *The long-term effects of ESEA Title I preschool and all-day kindergarten: An eight year follow-up.* Cincinnati, OH: Cincinnati Public Schools.

Rogoff, B., Newcombe, N., Fox, N., & Ellis, S. (1980). Transitions in children's roles and capacities. *International Journal of Psychology, 15,* 181–200.

Rogoff, B., Sellers, M. J., Pirrotta, S., Fox, N., & White, S. H. (1975). Age of assignment of roles and responsibilities to children: A cross-cultural survey. *Human Development, 18,* 353–369. Also in A. Skolnick (Ed.), *Rethinking childhood: Perspectives on development and society.* Boston: Little, Brown.

School District of Philadelphia. (1984). *Evaluation of the Prekindergarden Head Start Program* (Report No. 8435). Philadelphia: Author.

Sprigle, H. (1974). Learning to Learn program. In S. Ryan (Ed.), *A report on longitudinal evaluations of preschool programs: Vol. 1. Longitudinal evaluations* (Publication No. (OHD) 75-25). Washington, DC: U.S. Dept. of Health, Education, and Welfare.

Van de Riet, V., & Resnick, M. B. (1973). *A sequential approach to early childhood and elementary education.* Gainesville, FL: University of Florida, Department of Clinical Psychology.

Weikart, D. P., Bond, J. T., & McNeil, J. T. (1978). The Ypsilanti Perry Preschool Project: Preschool years and longitudinal results through fourth grade. *Monographs of the High/Scope Educational Research Foundation.* Ypsilanti, MI: High/Scope Press.

Chapter 11

The Carolina Abecedarian Project

An Educational Experiment Concerning Human Malleability

Craig T. Ramey and Frances A. Campbell

"Every American ought to have the right to be treated as he would wish to be treated, as one would wish his children to be treated. This is not the case."

—John F. Kennedy

The structure and functioning of society is linked to its beliefs about human development. Social and meritocratic democracies tend toward liberal stances on human malleability. That is, they tend toward beliefs that mature accomplishments are, to some degree, related to environmental adequacy. Modern developmental psychology reinforces that view. Yet, the limits of developmental plasticity are unknown.

For the past quarter century the most direct scientific tests of the nature and limits of human malleability have been conducted with young children. Early childhood education has emerged as the major tool of inquiry. Children from socially disadvantaged families have become the major focal point for investigation.

Children from undereducated and poor families are at elevated risk for delayed intellectual development and school failure (Ramey, Stedman, Borders-Patterson, & Mengel, 1978). Minority families who are undereducated have children who are especially at risk for the de-velopment of educational handicaps (Finkelstein & Ramey, 1980). These handicaps are typically detected during the early public school years (Mercer, 1977; Richardson, 1975). The statistical association between social and economic disadvantage and developmental retardation, however, does not elucidate the causal mechanisms between risk factors and outcomes. Nor does it inform us about how changeable the outcomes of these conditions are.

Operating on the assumption that an inadequate early environment had been linked to deleterious effects on subsequent mental development (e.g. Skeels & Dye, 1939), and that children reared in poverty were deprived of crucial experiences necessary for optimal intellectual growth (e.g. Hess & Shipman, 1967), some scientists and educators have supported the efforts of policymakers to institute interventions designed to help children overcome the handicapping effects of nonsupportive early environments. Historically, the most popular intervention strategy has been to intervene early in the life span and to provide for the disadvantaged child a more stimulating educational environment. In the late 1950s and throughout the 1960s, various experimental early education programs were begun to remedy the intellectual deficits and/or delays asso-

This research has been supported by the National Institute for Child Health and Human Development.

ciated with social disadvantage. These efforts culminated in Project Head Start, which has been the largest and longest lasting federally supported program for disadvantaged children. After an initial evaluation of Head Start results, however, there was some disillusionment about the efficacy of this approach to produce durable, long-term intellectual and scholastic benefits (Cicarelli, 1969). Jensen went so far as to argue that compensatory education had been tried and proved a failure because the cognitive gains due to Head Start faded after entry into public schools (Jensen, 1969). Unfortunately, public and professional opinion continues to expect these programs to produce *permanent* elevations in intellectual and scholastic performance. This is unfortunate because no widely accepted modern theory of human development makes such a prediction in the absence of *permanent and developmentally appropriate ecological change*. This expectation of permanent benefits seem to be derived from a public-policy wish to find quick and cheap solutions to one of modern society's most complicated and vexing problems.

Whereas the search for permanent, positive effects may be an unrealistic expectation, it is certainly scientifically appropriate and necessary to examine the short- and long-term benefits of various approaches to early education. In this context it is important to note that a recent and extensive long-term follow-up of 12 early intervention programs by the Consortium for Longitudinal Studies (Lazar, Darlington, Murray, Royce, & Snipper, 1982) concluded that preschool education did have significant and lasting benefits for children who participated. The follow-up revealed significant reduction in retention in grade and special class placements for participating children relative to controls.

Ramey, Bryant, and Suarez (1985) recently reviewed 18 experiments of preschool compensatory education for socially and culturally disadvantaged children that used random assignment to form experimental and control groups. Grouping these educational programs in order from least to most intensive, the authors concluded that the more intense the early

intervention (defined by amount and breadth of contact with the child or family), the greater the demonstrated positive short-term effects upon children's IQ. There was no conclusive evidence, however, that intervention begun in early infancy was superior to that begun in early childhood or at kindergarten. They argued that we need to know more about how early and how long interventions must be conducted in order to have a meaningful impact upon intellectual development and scholastic performance.

The Carolina Abecedarian Project has been concerned with this issue of timing and intensity for the past 15 years, and its methods and results are the subject of this chapter.

THE CAROLINA ABECEDARIAN PROJECT

In 1971, pilot work began on the Carolina Abecedarian Project. (*Abecedarian* refers to one who is learning the rudiments of something such as the alphabet.) The Abecedarian Project is an experimental early education program for young children at risk for developmental retardation and school failure. In 1972, the first official cohort of high-risk Abecedarian children were enrolled. A summary of the methods of the Abecedarian Project and a description of some interim intellectual and academic achievement results follow. The specific aims of the Abecedarian Project are:

1. To determine whether developmental retardation and social failure can be prevented in children from socially and economically high-risk families by means of educational day care
2. To determine whether a follow-through program for early elementary school is necessary to maintain preschool intellectual gains in high-risk children
3. To determine whether school-age intervention alone can significantly improve academic and/or intellectual performance in children who did not have preschool intervention

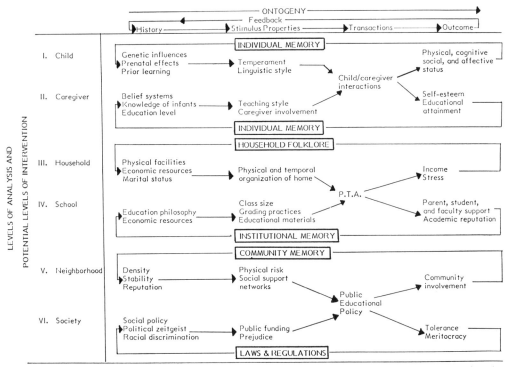

Figure 1. A general-systems model for inquiry into developmental retardation. Flow chart is illustrative but not exhaustive of some important variables and processes. (Adapted from Ramey, C. T., MacPhee, D., & Yeates, K. O. [1982]. Preventing developmental retardation: A general systems model. In L. A. Bond & J. M. Joffe (Eds.), *Facilitating infant and early childhood development*. Hanover, NH: University Press of New England.)

To address these questions, it was necessary to begin mapping the social ecology of economic disadvantage by defining and measuring many factors. These factors include such diverse elements as: the family and home environments, classroom behaviors, social behavior in preschool and elementary school, the language environment at home and at school, physical growth and development, biomedical status, and child and parent beliefs and attitudes toward academic achievement. This wide focus has resulted in an enormous longitudinal data base, comprising over 10,000 bits of information for each child in the sample.

Obviously, in a study of this complexity, there is a risk of finding apparently lawful relationships that may have occurred by chance, or conversely, of failing to identify forces that are in fact important determinants of development. In order to maximize the coherence of the effort, a model derived from general systems theory has been used to guide the search for meaningful and orderly results. This conceptual framework is based upon the work of Bertalanffy (1975) and Miller (1978).

Figure 1, adapted from Ramey, MacPhee, and Yeates (1982), depicts the model as it applies to the present research. The model is concerned with various levels of analysis and potential levels of intervention. It is especially concerned with the historical and psychosocial mediation of intellectual and cognitive outcomes measured at the level of the child. Outcomes can also be identified at the level of caregivers, families, schools, neighborhoods, and society. Hypotheses have been generated by scholars and researchers at every level in this model to explain retarded development and school failure. For example, Jensen (1969) has proposed a genetic explanation; Moynihan

(1969) has proposed a family dynamics explanation; and Ogbu (chapter 13, this volume) has proposed a social-structure explanation. We believe that these and other explanations are not necessarily mutually exclusive. Our model emphasizes that behavior always has multiple causes; that it emerges from an interaction among its underlying components; that any behavior may be analyzed within a hierarchy of complexity; that behavioral systems tend to be relatively stable within a certain range of reaction, and forces that disturb this equilibrium create stress upon that system; that human behavior is continuously regulated by feedback within the system at various levels; and that individuals are actively changing at all times, eliciting responses from the environment while at the same time adapting to its demands.

It is the task of the developmental scientist interested in delayed or retarded development to identify specific sets of variables that are causally implicated. A number of causal hypotheses may be generated, depending on the perspective taken by the individual investigator. Within our framework, we are particularly concerned with the means whereby historical influences, such as biological and social histories, are expressed as observable stimulus properties that potentially affect intellectual and educational outcomes. Further, we have pursued this issue with an experimental method that incorporates educational intervention at the levels of the child, the child's caregivers, and the child's schools. Through our experimental manipulations we hope to obtain a clearer understanding of causal mechanisms underlying academic and intellectual competence.

RESEARCH METHOD

Participants

In order to identify a sample of families at high risk for having a developmentally retarded child, a High Risk Screening Index (Ramey & Smith, 1977) was developed. This index, shown in Table 1, included factors judged on the basis of the developmental literature to be associated with poor intellectual and scholastic progress. Each factor was assigned a weight based upon professional consensus as to its likely importance in determining intellectual and scholastic outcomes. For example, in assigning a value to mother's educational level, fewer years of education were given a higher weight. A total of 13 factors were included such as paternal and maternal education, family income, absence of father, evidence of retardation among other family members, indications of family disorganization, a history of maladaptive and/or antisocial behavior within the family, and unstable job history.

If a family obtained 11 or more points on the High Risk Index, that family was judged to be at elevated risk and eligible for inclusion in the study. Characteristics of the 109 families eventually enrolled in the study are given in Table 2. As may be seen in Table 2, the families in the sample were predominantly black (98%); were headed by a single female (72%), who was young (mean age: 20 years) and who had less than a high school education (mean number of years: 10.23). Not included in the table are figures on income, because the modal earned income, reported by 65% of the sample, was none. Of those families who reported earned income, the modal category was $2,000 to $3,000 per year. The average High Risk Screening Index Score was an astounding 21 points.

It is a special feature of the Abecedarian project that assignment of participants to either the preschool experimental educational treatment group or to the control condition was random. As families were identified and invited to participate in the research, they were informed of the condition of random assignment. Of the 122 families contacted for Abecedarian recruitment, 121 agreed to particpate, and 109 accepted their assignments and actually took part. These 109 families had 111 children, including one set of twins and two siblings. Fifty-seven children were randomly assigned to the preschool experimental group, 54 to the preschool control group. Assignment was accomplished by matching pairs of children on the High Risk Index scores, and, using a table of random

Table 1. High-Risk Index

Factor	Weight
Mother's educational level (last grade completed)	
6	8
7	7
8	6
9	3
10	2
11	1
12	0
Father's educational level (last grade completed)	
6	8
7	7
8	6
9	3
10	2
11	1
12	0
Family income (per year)	

Size	1–2	3–4	5–6	7–8	9–10	11–12	
Annual	2,000	4,500	7,000	7,500	8,000	8,500	8
gross	3,000	5,500	8,000	8,500	9,000	9,500	7
income	4,000	6,500	9,000	9,500	10,000	10,500	6
	5,000	7,500	10,000	10,500	11,000	11,500	4
	6,000	9,500	12,000	12,500	13,000	13,500	1

Factor	Weight
Father absent for reasons other than health or death	2
Any member of mother's or father's immediate family required special services in school (special class placement, repeated school failure)	3
Any member of mother's or father's immediate family required special community services provided for mentally disabled persons (training school, disability payments, institutionalization, sheltered workshop)	3
Siblings of school age who are one or more grades behind age-appropriate grade or who score equivalently low on school administered achievement tests	3
Payments received from welfare agencies within past 5 years	3
Record of father's work indicates unstable and unskilled or semiskilled labor	3
Records of mother's or father's IQ indicate scores of 85 or below	3
Records of siblings' IQ indicate scores of 85 or below	3
Relevant social agencies in the community indicate that the family is in need of assistance	3
One or more members of the family has sought counseling or professional help in the past 5 years	1
Special circumstances not included in any of the above that are likely contributors to cultural or social disadvantage	2

Criterion for inclusion in High Risk sample is a score ≥ 11.

numbers, assigning one member of each pair to the experimental condition. Ninety-six children remained in the study to be randomly assigned to a school-age treatment group.

At public school entry, Abecedarian children within the two preschool groups were rank-ordered according to 48-month Stanford-Binet IQs, and each consecutive pair was randomly assigned to either the school-age experimental group or the school-age control group.

All families accepted their new assignment, but three children assigned to the preschool control–school-age experimental condition (CE) moved away, and did not actually participate in the school-age phase.

Design

Figure 2 gives the overall design of the Abecedarian study, including the preschool and school-age treatment programs, and the

Table 2. Entry level demographic data for experimental and control families

Variable	Group		
	Experimental (n = 55)	Control (n = 54)	Total (N = 109)
1. Mean High Risk Index	20.08 (5.72)	21.41 (5.88)	20.75 (5.81)
2. Mean maternal age (years)	19.62 (3.87)	20.28 (5.77)	19.94 (4.89)
3. Mean maternal education (years)	10.46 (1.75)	10.00 (1.89)	10.23 (1.83)
4. Mean maternal IQ (WAIS Full Scale)	85.49 (12.43)	84.18 (10.78)	84.84 (11.61)
5. Percent female headed family	78%	65%	72%
6. Percent black families	96%	100%	98%

Numbers in parentheses are standard deviations.

numbers of children randomly assigned to each condition. The Abecedarian study can be conceptualized as a 2 × 2 factorial design. The factors are preschool educational treatment versus no preschool treatment, and school-age educational treatment versus no school-age treatment. Thus, there were two preschool groups, the experimental (E) and control (C) groups, and four school-age conditions: preschool experimental–school-age experimental (EE), preschool experimental–school-age control (EC), preschool control–school-age experimental (CE), and preschool control–school-age control (CC). These groups varied in the intensity (defined as number of years) of intervention: 8 years for the EE group, 5 years

for the EC group, 3 years for the CE group, none for the CC group.

Preschool Treatment

The preschool program may be characterized as a whole-child program. The aim was to create a rich, stimulating, yet orderly environment in which the children could grow and learn. The curriculum was designed to enhance cognitive and linguistic development and to provide the children with many opportunities for successful mastery experiences. The curriculum materials included those for infants and preschoolers developed by Sparling and Lewis (1979). In addition, there were many attempts

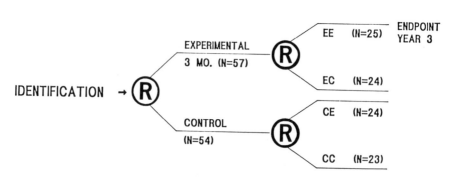

Figure 2. Research design of Carolina Abecedarian Project.

to provide an enriched language environment that was responsive to the child's needs and interests (Ramey, McGinness, Cross, Collier, & Barrie-Blackley, 1982).

In many ways the program was not unlike other high quality, infant day care and pre-school programs. Child:caregiver ratios ranged from 1:3 for infants to 1:6 for 4-year-olds. Teachers typically had early childhood education experience and participated in an extensive in-service education program. The children's experiences became increasingly more structured over the preschool years, eventually coming to include pre-phonics programs and science and math experiences, in addition to the emphasis on language and linguistic development. The presumption was that when the child left the preschool, he or she should be able to make a smooth transition into kindergarten.

Children attended the preschool program beginning somewhere between 6 weeks and 3 months of age. Entry before 6 weeks was not permitted, in order to avoid possible health risks associated with immaturity of the immunological system. The family was encouraged to enroll the child by 3 months of age, because one of the experimental questions was whether intensive and systematic educational intervention beginning in early infancy could *prevent* developmental retardation. Children attended the day-care program 5 days per week, 50 weeks per year. The center was open from 7:30 am to 5:15 pm. Free transportation to and from the center was provided for families who needed it. Almost all of the children were transported by center staff. Children in the experimental group also received their primary medical care on site and were permitted to attend the center when sick, except if they had measles or other potentially serious communicable diseases.

In order to control for the impact of non-educational factors upon intellectual development within the control group, efforts were made to ensure comparable nutrition and medical care in both groups. Children in the control group were provided free, iron-fortified formula for the first 15 months of life. Low-cost or free medical care was available locally for their families. The original plan had been for the center to provide primary pediatric care for both groups, but this proved impractical. Instead, families of control-group children were assisted in enrolling at a primary care clinic at the local university-affiliated hospital, which many did. Preliminary examination of medical records of children in the control group has shown that there does not appear to be a major difference in health outcomes for the two groups at age 5, but there is no question that children in the experimental group had unusually close health monitoring and treatment.

School-Age Program

The school-age intervention program began at kindergarten entry. It consisted of providing a home/school resource teacher to each child and family in the two Abecedarian school-age experimental groups (EE and CE), shown in Figure 2. These teachers filled many roles. They were curriculum developers who prepared an individualized set of home activities to supplement the school's basic curriculum in reading and math; they taught parents how to use these activities with their children; they tutored children directly; they met regularly with classroom teachers to ensure that home activities matched the skills being taught in the classroom; they served as a consultant for the classroom teacher when problems arose; and they advocated for the child and family within the school and community. They thus facilitated communication between teacher and parent, providing an important support for high-risk parents who frequently lacked the skills and confidence needed to advocate for their children within the school system, an institution seen by many as both monolithic and difficult to comprehend. Each home/school resource teacher had a caseload of approximately 12 families per year. Over the years, 6 home/school teachers participated in the program. Home/school resource teachers were experienced educators familiar with the local school system.

The supplemental curriculum delivered as home activities concentrated on two basic subjects: reading and math. These subjects were emphasized because it seemed likely that high-risk children might need extra reinforcement of these basic concepts to master them. The program sought to provide such reinforcement, presuming that scholastic performance would best be enhanced by direct teaching and practice of needed basic skills. The curriculum packets contained teaching activities that parent and child could share and enjoy. In addition, work sheets to give extra drill and practice were often included.

Home/school teachers made approximately 17 school visits per year for each child. During these visits they met with the classroom teacher to identify the skills currently being taught and to learn which areas needed extra work or review. A variety of specialists within the system were contacted as necessary, including special education resource personnel, reading teachers, or school counselors. Every effort was made to coordinate the child's program and to make sure the best available resources were being used.

The home visits were equally frequent. Home visits were made about 15 times each school year. A typical visit lasted approximately 30–45 minutes, with the mother being the most likely participant. Teachers reviewed the classroom situation and showed the parent the materials in the activity packet, explaining the purpose and directions for each activity. The child was present and participated in about one fourth of the home visits; this was often helpful because it allowed the teacher to demonstrate how an activity was to be carried out. Parents reported spending an average of 15 minutes a day working with their child on home activities. Parent response to the activities was very positive; very few reported that they failed to use the activities.

Many forces other than intellectual ability and encouragement to learn can have an impact on a child's scholastic performance: emotional upset at home, parental unemployment, the death of a family member, or instability of living arrangements, to name a few. Home/school resource teachers sometimes attempted to help families deal with personal crises, which resulted in extra home visits.

Home/school teachers also helped to give the children a variety of summer experiences: providing summer activity packets, helping to arrange summer camp experiences, arranging trips to the public library, and most intensive of all, tutoring some children in reading for 6 weeks.

Results

The results to be included in this chapter cover the intellectual and academic outcomes for Abecedarian children through the first 2 years in public school. Many other results are available, but these have been chosen for focus because they represent the outcome of the primary hypotheses under investigation.

Figure 3 gives the IQ scores for Abecedarian children from infancy through age 6½ years (78 months). In Figure 3, the mean standardized IQ scores are graphed according to preschool group up to the age of 60 months and according to school-age group thereafter. The scores are Bayley Mental Developmental Indices at 3, 6, 9, 12, and 18 months (Bayley, 1969); Stanford-Binet IQs at 24, 36, and 48 months (Terman and Mervill, 1972); Full-Scale IQs on the Wechsler Preschool and Primary Scale of Intelligence, at 60 months (Wechsler, 1967); and the Wechsler Intelligence Scale for Children Revised at 78 months (Wechsler, 1974).

All tests were administered by trained examiners under standard conditions. For children up to the age of 60 months, tests were administered with the mother present. Half the children at 36 months were tested by an examiner who was "blind" to the child's group assignment. Practical considerations made it impossible to achieve this for all assessment occasions; however, the evaluation staff was separate from the preschool and school-age intervention staff, and specific results of tests were not shared with preschool teachers. This was an attempt to

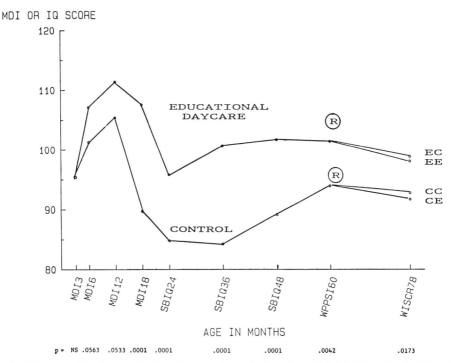

Figure 3.   Mean mental development (MDIs) and IQ scores for randomly assigned, high-risk children from 3 to 78 months of age in the Abecedarian Project.

reduce the chance of the teachers "teaching the test."

The preschool intervention had a positive effect upon intellectual development of the high-risk children in the experimental group, as may be seen in Figure 3. Throughout the preschool period, at every testing occasion after 12 months, significant mean differences on standardized test scores were found between the two Abecedarian preschool groups (Ramey & Campbell, 1984). The primary form of this effect was to reduce the drop in mental test scores in the experimental as opposed to the control group. It is now apparent that this preschool effect persists up through 78 months. A 2×2 analysis of variance using preschool and school-age assignment as independent variables, and 78-month, Full Scale IQ on the Wechsler Intelligence Scale for Children Revised (Wechsler, 1974) as the dependent variable, revealed a significant positive effect for

the preschool program, $F(1, 86) = 5.89$, $p < .02$. There is no evidence, however, that the school-age intervention had significant impact on children's intellectual performance during the first year and half of public school. No signficant effect of the school-age program was found at 78 months. Thus, regardless of school-age intervention status, the two groups who had preschool intervention maintained their relative superiority in tested intelligence over children who were preschool controls.

Academic Achievement

Figure 4 contains box and whisker plots (Tukey, 1977) for total raw scores on the Peabody Individual Achievement Test (PIAT) (Dunn & Markwardt, 1970) administered in the spring of the first and second years to children in the four school-age groups. These plots depict, by group, the median, the interquartile range, and the full range for total raw scores on

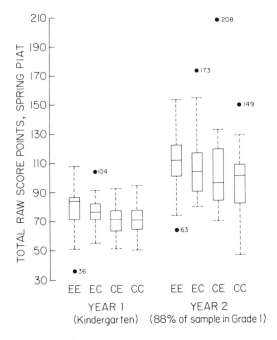

Figure 4. Box and whisker plots for total raw scores on the Peabody Individual Achievement Test, first and second years, all four school-age groups.

the PIAT. Inspection of the figure suggests the following trends: that children with early and continued intervention (EE) outscore the other three groups; that a lasting effect of the preschool intervention on school achievement may be seen into the second school year for children not receiving school-age intervention (EC), that children with no intervention at either age (CC) are lowest in performance.

A multivariate approach to repeated measures analysis of covariance was employed to determine whether the four school-age treatment groups' mean scholastic performance, as measured by total raw score on the spring-administered PIATs, showed group and/or time effects across groups. The issue of interest was whether the preschool or school-age treatment conditions affected the level and/or patterns of academic performance, when effects due to age at school entry were removed. Age at school entry was used as a covariate because preliminary analyses had shown that child age at school entry was positively related to scholastic attainment in both the first and second years in public school. The results of this anal-

ysis suggested that group membership affected the *level* of academic performance, but did not differentially affect the *pattern* of academic performance over time. Group membership was significantly associated with the academic achievement averaged over time, $F(3, 82) = 3.10$, $p < .04$). Post hoc Dunnett's contrasts compared each treatment group's mean with the control group's (CC) mean. The contrasts showed that, averaged over 2 years, the EE and EC groups' means were significantly higher than that of the CC group, but that the CE group did not differ significantly from the CC group. Thus it appeared that preschool treatment status did affect the level of academic outcomes, but that school-age treatment status did not, at least during the first 2 years of the program.

Predictably, time effects were observed. There was a significant linear trend in the data, indicating an increase from the first to the second year's total; $F(1, 82) = 465.68$, $p < .0001$. The Time $\times$ Group interaction did not attain statistical significance. Hence, it appears that preschool treatment effects were maintained through the second year of school, since the rate of gain was not significantly different among the four groups.

Figure 5 describes the PIAT in terms of age-referenced percentile scores. Examination of this figure reveals that the preschool experimental groups are near national average, whereas the preschool control groups are below national average. This figure also buttresses the earlier point that during the first 2 years in public school, all groups made similar academic gains.

Collectively, these results suggest that although the treatments did not affect the rate of academic growth in these children in the first two grades, it did affect the level of academic achievement. Thus, during the first 2 years in public school, positive preschool treatment effects on academic achievement were observed.

Retention in Grade

Figure 6 presents the percentage of children retained in either kindergarten or first grade for each of the four experimental conditions. In North Carolina, children are retained in the ear-

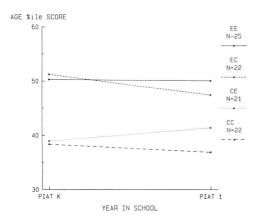

Figure 5. Mean age-referenced percentile scores on the Peabody Individual Achievement Test by year in school, for the groups in the Abecedarian Project.

apparently reducible through intensive early education. Such a high retention rate also strengthens the initial judgement that these children were indeed at elevated risk for school failure.

DISCUSSION

Together, the data on IQ scores, academic achievement, and retention in grade suggest that preschool intervention exerts an influence on intelligence and school success in the first 2 years of public school. Preschool intervention supplemented by continued help in the early grades via a home/school-resource-teacher program was the most effective intervention. This intensity of effort apparently enabled the high-risk children in this sample to maintain a level of achievement near the national average. In addition, the likelihood of being retained in grade was less by a factor of approximately 3 for children who had early and continued educational intervention.

One of the puzzling aspects of the Abecedarian Project concerns the level of intellectual performance of the control group across time. We have been delighted that these children have performed better than we had initially ex-

ly elementary grades if they have not mastered the core curriculum. Approximately 16% are typically retained in kindergarten, first grade, or second grade. One eighth, or 12%, of the children in the EE group were retained in grade, compared to approximately one-third in the other three groups. Although it is very early in these children's public school careers, it is remarkable that the academic failure rate is so high in the groups that did not receive early and continuing supplemental education. The one-third–grade-retention rate is clearly costly and

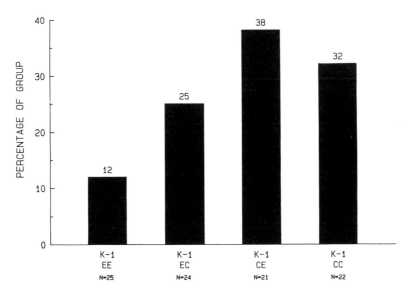

Figure 6.   Percentage of high-risk children retained in grade as a function of 4 experimental conditions.

pected. We have considered several possible explanations for this pattern of development. The first possiblity is that our high-risk identification procedures were not as stringent as they might have been and, thus, many of these families were not really at elevated risk levels. We are inclined to doubt this possibility given the entry characteristics of the families. These families were seriously disadvantaged and quite far out of the mainstream of society both locally and in terms of national standards.

The second possibility is a psychometric one. The norms of the Bayley, Stanford-Binet, and Wechsler scales are now becoming quite dated. Thus, it is possible that the scores obtained by all groups were overestimates of their relative levels of performance based on the current national population. Current work on renorming the Stanford-Binet, for example, may yield some insights into this possibility.

A third explanation concerns the community in which this project is being conducted. The people in this university community are affluent and well-educated; there is much local support for disadvantaged families. The town contains a university teaching hospital, an excellent public education system, and many social services. In fact, when the program began in 1972 there were 67 identifiable local agencies or groups specifically concerned, at least in part, with disadvantaged children and families. Thus, the town and county evidenced a high degree of social concern and had many more resources than a more typical town in the Southeastern United States. These resources may, therefore, have had a direct and positive effect on the development of these children. A related observation that bolsters this possibility concerns attendance by control-group children at other preschool programs and intellectual performance during the preschool years. Breitmayer and Ramey (1986) and Burchinal, Lee, and Ramey (1986) have reported a positive association within the control group between duration of attendance at other preschool centers and IQ. Although selective placement of abler control group children into preschool cannot be ruled out as an alternative explanation for this finding, it does raise the intriguing possibility that, as a group, the development of these disadvantaged children was enhanced over what it might have been without the availability of other preschool programs.

SUMMARY

We have been pursuing and continue to pursue the prevention of developmental retardation within a general systems theory framework. Our educational interventions have occurred at the levels of the child, the caregiver, and the school. It now appears that systematic early education can reduce the incidence of underachievement and delayed intellectual development—outcomes that are theoretically and educationally important. The intellectual and academic achievement results suggest to us that a preschool comprehensive program coupled with a school-aged follow-through program contains much promise. We are currently in the process of analyzing data for the final year of the school-age intervention. When those analyses are completed and we have systematically examined the family, school, and child factors associated with academic performance, we hope to have a better understanding of the forces associated with the academic performance of children from disadvantaged families and the ability of educational intervention to moderate those forces.

REFERENCES

Bayley, N. (1969). *Bayley scales of infant development.* New York: The Psychological Corporation.

Bertalanffy, L. V. (1975). *Perspectives on general system theory.* New York: George Braziller.

Breitmayer, B. J., & Ramey, C. T. (1986). Biological non-optimality and quality of environments as co-determinants of developmental outcomes. *Child Development, 57,* 1151–1165.

Burchinal, M., Lee, M., & Ramey, C. T. (1986, August). *Daycare effects on preschool intellectual development in poverty children.* Paper presented at the annual convention of the American Psychological Association, Los Angeles.

Cicarelli, V., (1969). *The impact of Head Start: An evaluation of the effects of Head Start on children's cognitive and affective development.* Athens, OH: Westinghouse Learning Corporation.

Dunn, L. M., & Markwardt, F. C. (1970). *Peabody Individual Achievement Test.* Circle Pines, MN: American Guidance Service, Inc.

Finkelstein, N. W., & Ramey, C. T. (1980). Information from birth certificate data as a risk index for school failure. *American Journal of Mental Deficiency, 84,* 546–552.

Hess, R. D., & Shipman, V. C. (1967). Cognitive elements in maternal behavior. In J. P. Hill (Ed.), *Minnesota symposia on child psychology,* (pp. 52–81). Minneapolis: University of Minnesota Press.

Jensen, A. R. (1969). How much can we boost IQ and scholastic achievement? *Harvard Educational Review, 39,* 1–123.

Lazar, I., Darlington, R., Murray, H., Royce, J., & Snipper, A. (1982). Lasting effects of early education: A report from the Consortium for Longitudinal Studies. *Monographs of the Society for Research in Child Development, 47* (2–3, Serial No. 195).

Mercer, J. R. (1977). Cultural diversity, mental retardation and assessment: The case for nonlabeling. In P. Mittler (Ed.), *Research to practice in mental retardation: Vol. I. Care and intervention.* Baltimore: University Park Press.

Miller, J. G. (1978). *Living systems.* New York: McGraw-Hill.

Moynihan, D. P. (Ed.). (1969). *On understanding poverty; perspectives from the social sciences.* New York: Basic Books.

Ramey, C. T., Bryant, D. M., & Suarez, T. M. (1985). Preschool compensatory education and the modifiability of intelligence: A critical review. In D. Detterman (Ed.), *Current topics in human intelligence* (pp. 247–296). Norwood, NJ: Ablex.

Ramey, C. T., & Campbell, F. A. (1984). Preventive education for high-risk children: Cognitive consequences of the Carolina Abecedarian Project [Special issue]. *American Journal of Mental Deficiency, 88*(5), 515–523.

Ramey, C. T., MacPhee, D., & Yeates, K. O. (1982). Preventing developmental retardation: A general systems model. In L. A. Bond & J. M. Joffe (Eds.), *Facilitating infant and early childhood development* (pp. 343–401). Hanover, NH: University Press of New England.

Ramey, C. T., McGinness, G. D., Cross, L., Collier, A. M., & Barrie-Blackley, S. (1982). The Abecedarian approach to social competence: Cognitive and linguistic intervention for disadvantaged preschoolers. In K. Borman (Ed.), *The social life of children in a changing society* (pp. 145–174). Hillsdale, NH: Lawrence Erlbaum Associates.

Ramey, C. T., & Smith, B. (1977). Assessing the intellectual consequences of early intervention with high-risk infants. *American Journal of Mental Deficiency, 81,* 318–324.

Ramey, C. T., Stedman, D. S., Borders-Patterson, A., & Mengel, W. (1978). Predicting school failure from information available at birth. *American Journal of Mental Deficiency, 82,* 525–534.

Richardson, S. A. (1975). Reaction to mental subnormality. In M. J. Begab & S. A. Richardson (Eds.), *The mentally retarded and society: A social science perspective.* Baltimore: University Park Press.

Skeels, H. M., & Dye, H. B. (1939). A study of the effects of different stimulation on mentally retarded children. *Proceedings of the American Association on Mental Deficiency, 44,* 114–136.

Sparling, J., & Lewis, I. (1979, February). Six learning games to play with your baby. *Parents,* pp. 35–38.

Terman, L. & Merrill, M. (1972). *Stanford–Binet Intelligence Scale.* Boston: Houghton Mifflin.

Tukey, J. W. (1977). *Exploratory data analysis,* Reading, MA: Addison-Wesley.

Wechsler, D. (1974). *Wechsler Intelligence Scale for Children Revised.* New York: The Psychological Corporation.

Wechsler, D. (1967). *Wechsler Preschool and Primary Scale of Intelligence.* New York: The Psychological Corporation.

Chapter 12

Neurodevelopmental Dysfunctions

Their Cumulative Interactions and Effects in Middle Childhood

Melvin D. Levine and Nancy C. Jordan

The years from 11 to 14 comprise a revealing transitional phase in human development. Middle childhood is an opportune time in which to examine the tentative outcomes of life's first decade of transaction between environmental conditions and events and evolving endogenous capacities (Levine & Satz, 1984). At the same time, it is a critical period in the pathogenesis of functional morbidity. Although seeds of maladjustment and failure may be sown early in life, the middle-childhood years are a period of germination for potentially catastrophic and increasingly prevalent negative consequences, among which are delinquency, adolescent depression, substance abuse, teenage pregnancy, and school dropout. In recent years there has been growing interest in linkages between these outcomes and chronic academic underachievement. The latter has been increasingly associated with learning disabilities or low severity–high prevalence handicaps representing dysfunctions in the neurological development of children. These neurodevelopmental dysfunctions offer a revealing window through which to view the interplay between endogenous predispositions, life experience, and adult expectations of children.

This chapter examines neurodevelopmental dysfunctions as they constitute endogenous and evolving risk factors for poor school-related performance in middle childhood. Additionally, it considers the ways in which a range of historical factors foster resistance or create inordinate susceptibility to the negative effects of these dysfunctions.

ACADEMIC EXPECTATIONS

Through the elementary school years, there is a steady progression in the maturation of the central nervous system coinciding with the enhancement of its processing and production functions. Neurodevelopmental progression takes place in a historical context of evolving expectations imposed upon children. Growing demands from parents, peers, siblings, and teachers have the potential for testing and straining evolving capabilities. The expansion of academic demands is probably the most conspicuous and reciprocally interactive with the differentiation of central nervous system capabilities.

Scholastic requirements in middle or junior high school differ substantially from those in early elementary school. Basic reading, writing, and mathematics skills introduced during the primary grades must now become tools for the acquisition of new knowledge in content subjects. As students approach middle or junior high school, content-area teachers frequently assume that they have acquired a repertoire of abilities to meet these new challenges. The following interrelated assumptions are among the most relevant and important in understanding the pathogenesis of academic failure in middle childhood.

Sustained Attention to Detail

By middle childhood it is assumed that students will be able to focus attention on salient details in their learning environments, filtering out distraction and concentrating for a sufficient length of time to extract information and/or create high quality products. At the same time, they must be reflective in their cognitive behaviors, allowing for planning, organization, and self-monitoring.

Ready Access to Previously Acquired Skills and Knowledge

In the early elementary grades, recognition and paired associative learning are stressed. As children progress into middle childhood, however, the emphasis shifts to the rapid and simultaneous retrieval of previously acquired skills and information. For example, composition writing requires students to retrieve letter formations; spelling; rules of capitalization, punctuation, and grammar; and vocabulary—all at once.

Automatization of Performance

During middle childhood, an increasing amount of material must be processed and recalled automatically, with little or no expenditure of cognitive effort. In the example cited above, it may be that letter formations from motor memory are encoded automatically, thus sparing cognitive energy for other aspects of the writing challenge (such as verbal expression and creativity). Likewise, fundamental reading skills must be sufficiently automatic to allow students to read for knowledge acquisition rather than to confirm what they already know.

Sophistication of Language Processing and Production

Students in middle childhood should be capable of processing, interpreting, and creating increasingly complex linguistic structures. They must process language at a sufficient rate with adequate precision to keep pace with verbal instructions and explanations in a classroom. Further, they must find appropriate words and formulate sentences with accuracy and speed to carry on social and school-related discussions. It is assumed that students can formulate sentences with grammatical sophistication, and that the effort required to express ideas is not so great that the quality of the content is sacrificed.

Synchrony of Skills

Content-area learning often requires synchrony of subskills. In expository or creative writing, for example, an appropriate synchrony between graphomotor fluency, verbal fluency, and ideational fluency is assumed. Thus, it is expected that the flow of motor movements will be able to keep pace with that of thought processes or linguistic encoding.

Flexible Application of Higher Cognitive Processes

As the sophistication of concepts and ideas grows in middle childhood, students are expected to become proficient problem solvers. This requires flexibility, the ability to seek alternative solutions to problems and to design effective approaches to task simplification. Children must monitor their ongoing performance and make appropriate methodological changes or modifications. In addition, they must be capable of dealing with symbolization, abstraction, superordinate categories, figurative language, and the versatile applications of rules and generalizations.

The capacity of children to meet these expectations is dependent in large part upon the integrity of a range of neurodevelopmental functions (Levine, 1987). Clearly, students with impairments in these areas are at risk of academic failure as they fall short of evolving expectations.

NEURODEVELOPMENTAL DYSFUNCTIONS

Much recent psychological research has included consideration of specific information processing models (Siegler, 1986; Sternberg, 1982). The various neurodevelopmental dysfunctions can be thought of as gaps along information processing and production pathways.

Whereas a broad spectrum of neurodevelopmental dysfunctions have the potential to impede academic performance in middle childhood, we shall limit our discussion to four components of information processing and production that are commonly involved: namely, attention, memory, neuromotor output, and language. Gallagher (1984) makes the useful distinction between developmental and educational learning disabilities. What follows are examples of the former; their impacts upon skills and knowledge acquisition constitute educational learning disabilities.

Attention

The process of selective attention occupies a prominent place in any clinically relevant conceptual model of information processing. This function is often depicted as the portal of entry feeding into information processing and production systems (Anderson, 1985; Lindsay & Norman, 1977). It is through this process that internal and environmental stimuli undergo ordering by priority. The most salient stimulus sets are selected for further evaluation, utilization, and/or memorization, whereas less relevant ones are discarded as distraction. This determination of saliency requires sufficient alertness or arousal as well as effective control over various central nervous system subprocesses.

Selective attention clearly does not operate autonomously; it is at least in part monitored by language, memory, and higher order reasoning. However, clinical evidence suggests that some children experience primary problems with attention without indications of additional processing weaknesses (Douglas, 1983; Levine, Busch, & Aufseeser, 1982). Further, selective attention has some relatively independent neurophysiological underpinnings (Raskin, Shaywitz, Shaywitz, Anderson, & Cohen, 1984), so that the existence of discrete attention deficits is not surprising. Studies of learning disorders continually reaffirm that attention deficits are common among school children with behavioral and academic difficulties (Ross & Ross, 1982). They tend to affect boys more than girls, although females with attention deficits have been discussed in the literature (Berry, Shaywitz, & Shaywitz, 1985). These children manifest a fairly consistent cluster of symptoms that includes difficulties with concentration, various forms of distractability, excessive daydreaming, and a high level of impulsivity (Levine, Brooks, & Shonkoff, 1980; Levine & Melmed, 1982). In some cases these traits are accompanied by motor overactivity, but often the motor manifestations are absent. Symptoms of attention deficits range in severity, so that some students have difficulty only under circumstances requiring intensive concentration on detail, whereas others reveal a diffuse focus and poor control in widely diverse contexts.

In middle childhood, certain elements of the symptom complex are accentuated (Levine, 1984; Levine & Zallen, 1984): Affected children have significant difficulties focusing on precise detail at a time in their education when there is an exponentially expanding amount of such detail upon which to focus. In addition, they exhibit marked performance inconsistency, applying a particular skill competently on one day, only to reveal a notable lack of proficiency for the same skill on a subsequent day. Impulsivity at this age is associated with disorganization, poor planning, lack of effective problem-solving, failure to deploy mnemonic strategies, and deficient self-monitoring. Children with attention deficits often are poor at proofreading or exercising other forms of self-monitoring, which compromises the quality of their work and sometimes of their behaviors and social interactions.

The physiological bases for attention deficits have received considerable scrutiny by neuroscientists (Porges, 1984). Some children with attention deficits endure a chronic imbalance between sleep and arousal. This has led to the underarousal hypothesis; namely, the notion that at least some affected individuals are experiencing a form of cognitive fatigue in the classroom. They are not sufficiently alert and aroused to remain "tuned in." Therefore, they experience particular problems with passive listening, which demands keen alertness. Many such students yawn and stretch frequently throughout the school day. In addition, they are predisposed to the free flight of ideas or distraction by free associations.

From a neuroanatomical standpoint, the reticular activating system has been implicated (Cooper, Bloom, & Roth, 1978). This region of the brain stem is thought to exert control over sleep and arousal. Abnormalities in the metabolism of critical brain stem neurotransmitter substances (generally catecholamines) may be associated with attention deficits (Raskin et al., 1984). Frontal lobe dysfunction has also been linked to some forms of attentional disorder. The frontal lobes are known to play a role in stimulus selectivity as well as in the planning and organization of activity.

The precise manifestations of children's attentional dysfunctions vary and are likely to be shaped by multiple other factors, including the presence or absence of discrete strengths or deficits in other cognitive domains. In our clinical studies (Levine et al., 1982), we found that during middle childhood, approximately 60% of the children with diagnosed attention deficits had no evidence of other forms of processing weakness. The remaining 40%, however, exhibited what has been described as *attention deficit plus*. The latter included children who had attentional weaknesses, along with language disabilities, visual processing dysfunctions, deficiencies of sequential organization, or other forms of low severity cognitive impairment. These children may have become *secondarily* inattentive as a direct result of their processing deficiencies. Thus, a child with substantial language disabilities may experience inordinate difficulty assimilating linguistic data in class. That student, whose attention goes unrewarded, consequently becomes increasingly less attentive to detail, more distractible, and evermore susceptible to fatigue.

Attention deficits create a major gap between capacity and day-to-day performance. Often, but by no means always, they are asso-ciated with signs of behavioral maladjustment. Conduct disorders, delinquent behaviors, and difficulties employing social skills are frequent concomitants (Howell, Huessy, & Hassuk, 1985). Children with attention deficits also are prone to substance abuse, school dropout, and automobile accidents (Satterfield, Hooper, & Schnell, 1982; Tarter, McBride, & Bounpane, 1977). Other associated clinical disorders include adolescent depression (unipolar and bipolar), Tourette's syndrome, and certain seizure disorders (Herskowitz & Rosman, 1982). However, in most cases, attention deficits seem to occur as isolated phenomena with no known etiology or associated psychopathology.

Memory

Earlier in this chapter it was stated that a key assumption regarding middle childhood abilities is that students are capable of markedly increased memorization and recall. Dysfunctional memory in middle childhood therefore constitutes a likely predisposition to academic underachievement. Multiple subtypes of memory dysfunction have been documented in learning-disabled students (e.g., Torgeson, 1985). Some of the more common and relevant ones include the following:

Retrieval Memory A series of studies have suggested that retrieval memory develops progressively during elementary school, whereas recognition remains relatively static (Kail, 1984). Not surprisingly, many learning disabled children perform more poorly than normal achievers on a range of retrieval tasks, including rapid naming (Denckla & Rudel, 1976; Wolf, 1984) and free recall (Torgeson, 1977). Students with retrieval difficulties are at a distinct disadvantage in content-area classes, often being unable to keep pace with increased expectations for precise and fast factual recall. Their problems are characterized by vagueness and prolonged latencies of response time. Retrieval difficulties may engender frustration during class discussions, essay writing, or social encounters.

Active Working Memory Active working memory entails the capacity to work on one aspect of a process while temporarily storing in short memory other essential components of the same task (Baddeley, 1981). Commonly, children with active working memory deficits fail to reason and remember simultaneously during certain endeavors. Many are prone to difficulties in mental arithmetic. For example, Brainerd (1983) demonstrated that children with active-working-memory problems often understood mathematics concepts, but had trouble completing various computations; while working on one aspect of a mathematical problem they lost track of what they had already completed or were intending to accomplish next. Active working memory capacity also plays an important role in reading comprehension (Daneman & Carpenter, 1980). Affected students may have problems retaining the beginning of a paragraph while reading the end of it. In addition, this troublesome inability to hold constituent elements ''on a screen'' in one's mind while manipulating them, can create difficulties with writing and the acquisition of a foreign language.

Modality-Specific Functions Modality-specific memory functions are well documented in the cognitive sciences (e.g., Baddeley, 1976; Margrain, 1967; Murdock & Walker, 1969). It is not surprising then that certain forms of memory disorders are limited to specific channels of processing. For example, some students have particular problems with verbal memory but no difficulty at all in the recall of visual/nonverbal configurations. Others experience discrete deficiencies in revisualization, often manifested in dyseidetic (phonic-equivalent) spelling errors. A study conducted by Fletcher (1985) provides empirical evidence that the performance of learning disabled students varies according to the nature of the learning problem and the stimulus mode. He found that arithmetic-disabled children performed more poorly than did normally achieving controls on nonverbal memory tasks, but the two groups did not differ on verbal ones. In contrast, reading-disabled subjects differed from controls only on verbal memory exercises.

Mnemonic Strategies A number of studies have demonstrated that older children differ from younger children in their use of mnemonic strategies to aid rehearsal, consolidation, and retrieval (e.g., Ornstein, Naus, & Liberty, 1975). It has been found that children with learning problems often fail to use effective strategies to aid recall (Bauer, 1979; Dallago & Moely, 1980; Torgeson, 1980). Even when taught these, there is a reluctance to apply them or a general lack of flexibility in their utilization. In addition, many lack *metamemory,* or an ability to gain insight into the workings of their own memories, thereby to facilitate processes of memorization.

Other memory disorders may be specific to certain content areas especially those in which students lack prior knowledge or have not fully assimilated previous learning (Ornstein & Naus, 1986). This phenomenon also relates to students who are slow to automatize. Their prior learning is poorly consolidated, such that previously acquired skills cannot be retrieved unconsciously (Sternberg & Wagner, 1982). This means that inordinate effort may be required to accomplish expository writing, reading for content, or the completion of mathematics problems under timed conditions. Many such students eventually will achieve automatization of subskills. However, not infrequently, one encounters youngsters in middle childhood who are not automatic in one or more areas of skill and who will require at least several years to acquire this level of proficiency. They are particularly vulnerable, because the inordinate effort required to complete tasks can lead to secondary amotivational states, attentional fatigue, and a precipitous decline in self-esteem.

Neuromotor Output

The increased demand for written output in middle childhood renders conspicuous various forms of neuromotor dysfunction relevant to the control of a writing utensil. Specific fine motor weaknesses commonly create a gap between ideational and verbal fluency, on the one hand, and graphomotor fluency on the other. Students with such impairments are often adept at taking in and processing information, but they may have significant problems with productivity. As a result, their writing tends to be unsophisticated, inconsistently legible, and sparse. The act of writing demands too much effort, thereby obliterating other higher level functions, such as analytic reasoning and sophisticated language expression. This phenomenon has been described as *developmental output failure* (Levine, Oberklaid, & Meltzer, 1981), a condition in which the processing of information is relatively intact, but the products are poor (particularly on paper). Children experiencing developmental output failure often are considered to be lazy or unmotivated.

Four forms of fine motor dysfunction are most commonly discernible among these children:

Eye-Hand Coordination Students with eye-hand coordination problems show generalized clumsiness and have particular difficulties employing visual/spatial data to guide fine motor actions. Often they have a long history of trouble copying from the chalk board, completing artwork, and meeting the visual-mechanical challenges of everyday life (Gordon, 1977). Additionally, they may have been slow to acquire self-help skills (such as tying shoelaces and dressing independently).

Proprio-kinesthetic Feedback (Finger Agnosia) Efficient and legible writing, like other complex motor movements, is dependent upon constant nonvisual feedback emanating from proprioceptive and kinesthetic nerve endings in the distal joints of the fingers (Luria, 1980). This provides a steady flow of information back to the motor analyzer in the central nervous system, allowing for the continuous changes of direction required for implementation of an ideomotor plan during writing. There is a group of children who manifest varying degrees of finger agnosia or difficulties with nonvisual finger localization. While writing, they must engage in meticulous monitoring, which tends to be overly mechanical, slow, and imprecise. The laborious nature of their writing frequently results in highly abbreviated output.

Motor Praxis Praxis entails the capacity to implement a motor plan. Some children appear to have difficulty at this level of operation.

They cannot execute "timed, sequential, detailed movements," possibly as a result of left hemispheric impairment (Denckla, 1985). This obviously has a devastating impact upon writing, such that their graphomotor fluency is significantly impeded. Many such students also have an oral dyspraxia and may have trouble articulating certain complex speech sounds.

Motor Memory Luria (1980) described in detail various aspects of motor memory in older patients. He further wrote of the production of motor engrams or kinetic melodies, constituting the blueprints for various forms of complex fine motor output. Among the more sophisticated engrams are the letters of the alphabet, particularly as they are deployed in cursive writing. One portion of the middle childhood population suffers to varying degrees from a motor-memory dysfunction. Affected children fail to establish and readily retrieve motor engrams in a consistent manner. This results in poor recall of letter formation, inconsistent legibility, and a reduced rate of writing.

The above forms of fine motor dysfunction occur either in isolation or in clusters. When found in combination with other developmental dysfunctions, the results can be particularly devastating, culminating in underachievement and failure in multiple academic domains.

Language

Over the past decade, a significant body of research has suggested that subtle deficiencies in language ability are associated with academic underachievement in the elementary and junior high school grades (e.g., Wiig, Lapointe, & Semel, 1977). Such weaknesses can occur along a number of linguistic dimensions, including phonology, syntax and morphology, semantics, and pragmatics. Each will be discussed briefly:

Phonology A series of studies have demonstrated that a weak sense of phonology is often related to a delay in the acquisition of sound/symbol associations or basic decoding skills for reading (Liberman, Liberman, Mattingly, & Shankweiler, 1980; Liberman,

Shankweiler, Liberman, Fowler, & Fisher, 1977). Often this deficit persists throughout the elementary grades, resulting in a slow, and labored reading style. Since so much effort is devoted to sounding out unknown words, students with inadequate decoding skills have few residual resources to allocate to a text's meaning. Many children with weak phonological awareness also have trouble with spelling, often producing bizarre dysphonetic errors (Fox & Routh, 1983).

Syntax and Morphology Poor appreciation of syntax and morphology constitute signs of dysfunction in many learning disabled students (e.g., Goldman, 1976; Vogel, 1974; Wiig, Semel, & Crouse, 1973). Some have particular problems processing the increasingly complex syntax that emerges progressively during the school years; they have difficulty dealing with embedded clauses, the effects of altered word order, and other elements of grammatical structure. These weaknesses are reflected in an inability to understand verbal explanations, to follow instructions, and to develop adequate reading comprehension skills. Others may experience rate-dependent problems; that is, they have trouble keeping up with the speed of language input rather than with its linguistic complexity and sophistication per se. Denckla (1978) notes that such slow processors may "blow a fuse" in the classroom if bombarded with too much verbal information too quickly.

Sentence production problems also exist in a group of disabled learners. For example, Fry, Johnson, and Muehl (1970) found that learning disabled children were less proficient than their normally achieving counterparts in spontaneous grammatical construction, verbal fluency, and general narrative organization. Such students tend to have trouble with reading resynthesis and summarization, written expression, and class discussions—all critical prerequisites for academic achievement in middle childhood.

Semantics Vocabulary becomes increasingly abstract during the middle childhood years with the advent of content subjects such as history, geography, and the natural sciences (Chall, 1983). Students encounter many unfamiliar words in their textbooks and must understand and apply their meanings rapidly to aid comprehension as well as to acquire new concepts. In addition, they must be able to retrieve these words automatically for class discussions, written reports, and timed essay tests. Empirical evidence has indicated that poor learners are inferior to normal learners in a number of semantic areas, including vocabulary size (McLeod, 1965), the ability to derive meanings from context (Merrill, Sperber, & McCauley, 1981), and, as noted previously, automatic word retrieval (Denckla & Rudel, 1976; Wolf, 1984).

Pragmatics Verbal pragmatics—language use in social/communicative context—has received considerable attention in the psycholinguistic literature (Wiig & Semel, 1984) and has important implications for the student with learning problems. As children progress through elementary and junior high school, their worlds become increasingly verbal, both in and out of the classroom setting; they must engage in social conversations on the playground, in corridors, and over the telephone.

Bryan (1978) provides empirical evidence that a group of learning disabled students with concomitant expressive language disorders have trouble adapting their language and communicative style to the needs of a particular listener. When asked to teach a game to a peer and a much younger child, these students performed less competently than nondisabled controls; that is, they could not match the level of linguistic complexity employed with the age level of the listener. It has been suggested that such difficulties may contribute to observed social interaction problems among learning disabled children (Bryan & Bryan, 1978; Pearl, Donahue, & Bryan, 1986).

Children with language-related dysfunctions are at a distinct disadvantage in our society. Clinically, it is not at all unusual to encounter a child whose language dysfunctions are accompanied by real strengths in the visual/spatial domain. Such a student may have excellent nonverbal cognition but nevertheless be failing academically. This is particularly ironic, because so many vocations in the adult world reward good visual/spatial and fine-motor abilities, whereas academic expectations during middle childhood demand linguistic proficiency far more than they tap nonverbal talents. As a result, some significant mismatching of aptitudes with expectations occurs during middle childhood, a time when the language demands of school intensify dramatically.

CLUSTERS AND COMPLEXES

Single neurodevelopmental dysfunctions are common among children who are succeeding academically. In many such cases, sufficient compensatory strengths may foster resiliency and malleability so as to minimize or overcome the effects of an isolated deficit. Our community studies (Levine et al., 1983) revealed that on direct examination, nearly half of the school-age children with adequate academic performance exhibited at least one area of neurodevelopmental dysfunction and one fifth exhibited three or more such areas. What commonly differentiated successful subjects with dysfunction from those with academic failure was the precise combination of dysfunctions and/or the coexistence of cumulative stressors.

The severity of individual dysfunctions is also clearly an important determinant. However, drawing the line can be quite difficult; some students appear to be inordinately affected by comparatively mild dysfunctions, whereas others display enormous resiliency in the presence of a substantial problem with processing or production. This makes it especially difficult to determine precise thresholds or establish stringent criteria for normalcy or delay in any single area of developmental function. Each of the dysfunctions described in the previous section falls on a continuum. Even a condition such as finger agnosia, which may appear to represent an all-or-none phenomenon, is encountered in varying degrees of severity. At the less severe end of the clinical spectrum, fewer children are likely to be handicapped by the problem, but nevertheless some students will be adversely affected even by such mild problems. These

variable impacts make it exceedingly difficult to compile reliable prevalence figures for any single deficit.

Relationships between dysfunctions and levels of academic competency deserve continuing study to define sources of what might be called "deficit resistance" or the capacity to mitigate the impacts of dysfunctions. In a sense, this may be an analogue of what Garmezy and Tellegen (1984) call "stress resistance," the ability to withstand detrimental environmental forces.

In a series of important longitudinal studies, Werner and Smith (1982) discovered a substantial group of children who were performing well in life despite the presence of very serious environmental disadvantage. They aptly described such children as "vulnerable but invincible."

Rutter (1984) described a related phenomenon in his concept of "catalytic factors." As he stated: "The concept is one of factors that are largely inert on their own but, when combined with environmental stresses or hazards, either increase their effect (so-called vulnerability factors), or decrease their impact (so-called protective factors)" (p. 329). In this context, we can view mild, isolated, or benign clusters of neurodevelopmental dysfunctions as capable of catalyzing catastrophic outcomes in the presence of longstanding exposure to exogenous stressors. Analogously, important neurodevelopmental strengths may be thought of as protective factors, perhaps even conferring invincibility on some children.

Investigations of early adolescent juvenile delinquents offer a vivid demonstration of multiple susceptibility. These studies have documented the almost universal presence of longstanding academic failure among 11- to 14-year-old incarcerated subjects (Meltzer, Levine, Karniski, Palfrey, & Clarke, 1984; Murray, 1976). Further, certain *lethal clusters* of neurodevelopmental dysfunction seem to differentiate delinquents from controls in the same communities. For example, Karniski, Levine, Clarke, Palfrey, and Meltzer (1982) showed that combined dysfunctions of expressive language, attention, and memory were most predictive of middle childhood delinquent behavior.

Clusters of neurodevelopmental dysfunctions in the presence of exogenous stressors almost universally characterize the population of juvenile delinquents. The former are more likely than controls to endure poverty, health problems, family disruption, and other major life setbacks, in addition to their dysfunctions (Levine, Karniski, Palfrey, Meltzer, & Fenton, 1985). We have termed such aggregations of negative cumulative effects *risk factor complexes,* analogous to the immune complexes operant in a number of recently recognized physical illnesses. Such risk factor complexes in middle childhood delinquents in all likelihood constitute burdens that thwart resiliency and malleability. In other words, there is simply too much adversity to bypass and perhaps too much damage to repair.

DEVELOPMENTAL IMPLICATIONS

As we have suggested, a child's neurodevelopmental profile present or latent at birth, interacts over time with environmental, historical, and physiological factors in the genesis of tentative outcomes at middle childhood. The endogenous neurodevelopmental profile and its capacity to satisfy expectations is a major determinant of school-related performance during this period. However, the profile itself is susceptible to flux over time, as likely to be influenced by experience as to influence experience. For example, language abilities are richly fortified through reading (Chomsky, 1972). Children with neurodevelopmental dysfunctions that impede reading are likely to read less than their peers during the early school years. Consequently, a test of language ability at age 12 might reflect a lack of reading experience as much as or more than an indication of an endogenous language dysfunction. By middle childhood, performance also reflects the cumulative effects of other interactive forces, including parental nurturance, the socio-cultural milieu, various critical life events (both positive and negative occurrences), the modeling effects of peers and siblings, physical

health (the presence or absence of chronic disease, neurotoxic exposures, or serious acute illness), the quality and intensity of the child's educational experience (both at home and in school), temperament, and other variables depicted in Figure 1. These influences to varying degrees affect and are sometimes affected by the evolving neurodevelopmental profile.

At the same time, three modulating phenomena further influence outcome: 1) *stabilization* (analogous to McCall's notion of canalization; see chapter 3, this volume), or a tendency for a child's neurodevelopmental profile and patterns of behavior and learning to remain constant or predictable over certain time spans; 2) *resiliency* or self-righting, the capacity to recover spontaneously from setback (stress resistance) and/or to compensate for personal deficiencies (deficit resistance); and 3) *malleability,* the extent to which educational and/or therapeutic efforts adaptively shape the neurodevelopmental profile itself, as well as its relationships to performance outcomes. Ideally, we anticipate that a healthy child will stabilize positive attributes, recover spontaneously from injurious critical life events or environmental deterrents, compensate for endogenous deficits, and strengthen his or her neurodevelopmental profile through educational experience.

FUTURE DIRECTIONS

Cumulative environmental effects, evolving neurodevelopmental profiles in juxtaposition with societal expectations, the modulation of resiliency, malleability and propensities toward stability over time create a puzzling network of transactions through the course of development. Clinicians and investigators are faced with a formidable challenge in characterizing or generalizing in the face of such phenomenological complexity and diversity. There is clearly little uniformity of impact such that poverty, chronic illness, family disruption, and peer pressure are likely to affect different children differently. Any one effect undergoes substantial dilution amid multiple coexisting effects and the passage of time.

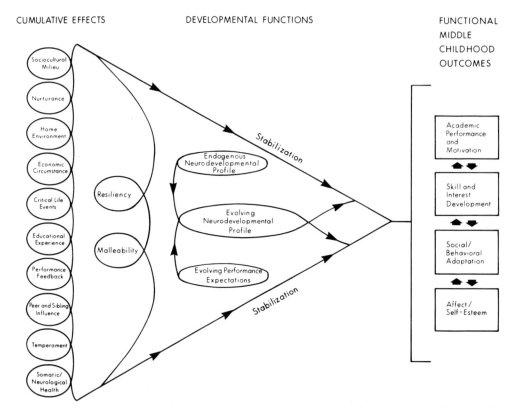

Figure 1.   This diagram portrays the multifactorial processes that shape the tentative functional outcomes of middle childhood. On the left side of the figure, it can be seen that 10 overlapping circumstances, events, and forces interact like coils in a spring to exert a net cumulative effect on the developing child. The impacts of these factors modulate and are modulated by another pair of coils, namely the child's resiliency (i.e., self-righting in the face of stress or deficiency) and malleability (i.e., susceptibility to educational/therapeutic change). A neurodevelopmental profile (i.e., the distribution of central nervous system strengths and deficits) evolves over time through a series of transactions between its endogenous capacities (present or latent at birth) and the expectations imposed upon them. The evolving neurodevelopmental profile ultimately makes a major contribution to behavioral and academic performance in middle childhood, but the extent to which the neurodevelopmental profile governs functional outcomes is determined by the cumulative effects and the child's resiliency and malleability. At different points during childhood and to degrees varying from child to child, relative stabilization occurs, such that functional outcomes become somewhat transfixed and reliably observable at the same time that they become cumulative effects, themselves perpetuating future outcomes.

Traditional diagnostic and statistical approaches run the risk of masking essential factors operant in individual children. Consequently, a multifactorial perspective is now essential for valid research and responsible clinical activity. To meet this challenge, the following hierarchical approach merits consideration.

1.   Further research and interdisciplinary dialogue should help to delineate more comprehensively the individual neurodevelopmental dysfunctions and their relevant subcomponents (developmental learning disabilities), as well as their relationships to various forms of failure to meet educational expectations (educational learning disabilities).

2.   There is a need to study the ways in which dysfunctions interact to nullify, intensify, or otherwise modify each other's effects. To do so, it is important to demonstrate predictable academic impacts of specific clusters of dysfunctions and to differentiate between academically lethal and benign clusters.

3.   It will be useful to identify neurodevelopmental protective factors that modify prognoses. Certain neurodevelopmental strengths may be especially likely to override the effects of deficits. For example, a child with superior

language skills may suffer less academically from an attention deficit than would a peer who additionally manifests normal or delayed linguistic facility. On the other hand, visual perceptual strengths may do little to facilitate learning in a child with generalized–retrieval-memory dysfunction in middle childhood, a period when sophisticated appreciation of spatial relationships is not especially germane in formal education.

4.   Neurodevelopmental profiles (dysfunctional clusters and associated strengths) need to be examined with respect to their interactions with other cumulative risk and/or environmental protective factors to generate outcomes. This may require new analytic methods and mathematical models that avoid artificial reductionism and foster a holistic portrayal of the developing child. At the same time, techniques sensitive to small but important effects of single factors should be applied.

5.   Future studies of resiliency and malleability should determine the extent to which children with specific neurodevelopmental profiles and risk factor/protective factor complexes are more or less capable of adaptive change. Such research should include consideration of the possibility that patterns of central nervous system dysfunction and environmental circumstance vary in natural history and prognosis. We might then be capable of making prognostic distinctions that are commonly applied in dealing with other clinical conditions as exemplified by the following categories:

a.   Benign and self-limited
b.   Threatening but curable
c.   Threatening but manageable
d.   Threatening and treatment-resistant

The above distinctions could have profound implications for resource allocation. One might, for example, be inclined to fund service delivery for b and c and to encourage more basic research into d, while investing considerably less in patterns subsumed under a.

6.   The period of middle childhood provides a convenient probe point for developmental research. Longitudinal, cross-sectional, or epidemiological studies of this age group can document critical linkages between clusters, complexes, and expectations. The occurrence of various forms of maladaptation in later adolescence can serve as important indicators of outcome. Furthermore, the surge in complexity of expectations in this age group may precipitate some "sleeper" effects, whereby early life stresses or endogenous vulnerabilities do not exert their major effects until middle childhood. Similarly, the positive influences of early life interventions may become most evident as children demonstrate their resiliency in the face of middle childhood demands.

7.   Clinical research into the effectiveness of specific interventions will be strengthened significantly when samples can be characterized more accurately with regard to neurodevelopmental profiles and the presence or absence of risk factor complexes/protective factors. The greater appreciation of subgroups within such samples will enhance replicability as well as the applicability of investigations. For example, abundant studies have shown the effectiveness of stimulant medication in children with attention deficits, but reports of such research characteristically fail to take into account the diversity of subjects with respect to associated information-processing problems, motor dysfunctions, critical life events, and other environmental forces. It may be that neurodevelopmental and environmental factors relatively independent of the attention deficits themselves are powerful predictors of drug response.

Several public-policy implications are clearly discernible in the study of neurodevelopmental progression and performance during middle childhood. First, communities will need to ensure prompt detection of functionally lethal neurodevelopmental clusters within risk factor complexes. Second, there is a need for greater accountability, for taking stock of the readiness of children in middle childhood to deal effectively with the expectations and temptations of adolescence. Third, diagnostic labels that oversimplify children and deny the multifactorial bases of failure to justify service delivery should be reexamined in light of research that demonstrates the diverse sources and manifestations of failure. And finally, we need to demonstrate that the recognition and management of risk factor complexes in middle childhood can abort the need for more extensive and costly interventions in later life.

As our knowledge grows so should the impetus for further research based upon definable clinical variations in central nervous system development. Neurodevelopmental dysfunctions and the diversity of their impacts and manifestations in individual cases constitute valuable models for the study of normal developmental forces, as well as the pathogenesis of childhood performance failure. Ultimately, the goal should be the creation of informed practices and policies that lessen the impacts of troublesome patterns of neurodevelopmental dysfunction and deter the formation and stabilization of risk factor complexes. Such goals, if reached, should reduce the prevalence of negative functional outcomes in middle childhood as well as the occurrence of their potentially catastrophic social complications.

The message for practitioners (both clinicians and educators) is clear. Classrooms and diagnostic settings must become increasingly attuned to childhood developmental diversity. Curricula need to take into account varied neurodevelopmental profiles and learning styles within specific age groups. Techniques must be enhanced, so that children can continue learning despite the presence of significant clusters of neurodevelopmental dysfunction. This means that there must be effective strategies devised to bypass deficits. In addition, students with notable neurodevelopmental strengths need to have an opportunity to enhance these capacities, even if they are irrelevant to the academic expectations of the moment. Children can be presumed to have a right to exhibit their assets, to practice their innate specialties at any age, and to be spared public humiliation over their endogenous deficiencies. In diagnostic settings, the narrow use and interpretation of standardized tests must give way to broader perspectives capable of characterizing risk factor complexes, diagnosing strengths as well as weaknesses, and formulating interventions that meet diverse needs of children whose problems are multifactorial in origin. For both teachers and clinicians, there is a compelling need for training in modern child development. It is important that such education cover the full span of childhood to communicate emphatically that significantly endogenous and exogenous effects condition change throughout a child's educational career. The price for such altered perspectives and alteration of practices will be high, but not nearly as high as the costs to children and society of developmental needs that are neglected.

REFERENCES

Anderson, J. R. (1985). *Cognitive psychology and its implications.* New York: W. H. Freeman.

Baddeley, A. D. (1976). *The psychology of memory.* New York: Basic Books.

Baddeley, A. D. (1981). The concept of working memory: A view of its current state and probable future development. *Cognition, 10,* 17–23.

Bauer, R. H. (1979). Memory, acquisition, and category clustering in learning-disabled children. *Journal of Experimental Child Psychology, 27,* 365–383.

Berry, C. A., Shaywitz, S. E., & Shaywitz, B. A. (1985). Girls with attention deficit disorder: A silent majority? A report on behavioral and cognitive characteristics. *Pediatrics, 76,* 801–809.

Brainerd, C. J. (1983). Young children's mental arithmetic errors: A working memory analysis. *Child Development, 54,* 812–830.

Bryan, T. H. (1978). Social relationships and verbal interactions of learning disabled children. *Journal of Learning Disabilities, 11,* 107–115.

Bryan, T. H., & Bryan, J. H. (1978). Social interactions of learning disabled children. *Learning Disabilities Quarterly, 1,* 33–38.

Chall, J. S. (1983). *Stages of reading development.* New York: McGraw-Hill.

Chomsky, C. (1972). Stages in language development and reading exposure. *Harvard Educational Review, 42.*

Cooper, J. R., Bloom, F. E., & Roth, R. H. (1978). *The biochemical basis of neuropharmacology* (3rd ed.). New York: Oxford University Press.

Dallago, M. L., & Moely, B. E. (1980). Free recall in boys of normal and poor reading levels as a function of task manipulations. *Journal of Experimental Child Psychology, 30,* 62–78.

Daneman, M., & Carpenter, P. A. (1980). Individual differences in working memory and reading. *Journal of Verbal Learning and Verbal Behavior, 19,* 450–466.

Denckla, M. B. (1978). Minimal brain dysfunction. In J. S. Chall & A. F. Mirsky (Eds.), *Education and the brain* (pp. 223–268). Chicago: University of Chicago Press.

Denckla, M. (1985). Motor coordination in dyslexic children: Theoretical and clinical implications. In F. H. Duffy & N. Geschwind (Eds.), *Dyslexia: A Neuroscientific approach to clinical evaluation* (pp. 187–196). Boston: Little, Brown.

Denckla, M. B., & Rudel, R. (1976). Rapid automatized naming (R.A.N.): Dyslexia differentiated from other learning-disabled children. *Neuropsychologia, 14*, 471–479.

Douglas, V. I. (1983). Attentional and cognitive problems. In M. Rutter (Ed.), *Developmental neuropsychiatry* (pp. 280–329). New York: Guilford Press.

Fletcher, J. M. (1985). Memory for verbal and nonverbal stimuli in learning disability subgroups: Analysis by selective reminding. *Journal of Experimental Child Psychology, 40*, 244–259.

Fox, B., & Routh, D. (1983). Phonemic analysis and severe reading disability. *Journal of Clinical Child Psychology, 12*, 28–32.

Fry, M., Johnson, C., & Muehl, S. (1970). Oral language production in relation to reading achievement among select second graders. In D. Bakker & P. Satz (Eds.), *Specific reading disability* (pp. 123–148). Amsterdam: Rotterdam University Press.

Gallagher, J. J. (1984). *Unthinkable thoughts: Educational policy and learning disabilities*. Paper presented at the Association for Children with Learning Disabilities International Conference, New Orleans.

Garmezy, N., & Tellegen, A. (1984). Studies of stress-resistant children: Methods, variables, and preliminary findings. In F. Morrison, C. Lord, & D. Keating (Eds.), *Advances in applied developmental psychology* (Vol. 1). New York: Academic Press.

Goldman, S. R. (1976). Reading skill and the Minimum Distance Principle. *Journal of Experimental Child Psychology, 22*, 123–142.

Gordon, N. S. (1977). The clumsy child. In C. M. Drillien & M. B. Drummond (Eds.), *Neurodevelopmental problems in early childhood: Assessment and management*. Oxford: Blackwell Scientific Publications.

Herskowitz, J., & Rosman, N. P. (1982). *Pediatrics, neurology and psychiatry—Common ground*. New York: Macmillan.

Howell, D. C., Huessy, H. R., & Hassuk, B. (1985). Fifteen-year follow-up of a behavioral history of attention deficit disorders. *Pediatrics, 76*, 185–190.

Kail, R. V. (1984). *The development of memory in children*. New York: W. H. Freeman.

Karniski, W., Levine, M. D., Clarke, S., Palfrey, J., & Meltzer, L. J. (1982). A study of neurodevelopmental findings in early adolescent juvenile deliquents. *Journal of Adolescent Health Care, 3*, 151–155.

Levine, M. D. (1984). Cumulative neurodevelopmental debts: Their impact on productivity in late middle childhood. In M. D. Levine & P. Satz (Eds.), *Middle childhood: Development and dysfunction* (pp. 227–244). Baltimore: University Park Press.

Levine, M. D. (1987). *Developmental variation and learning disorders*. Cambridge, MA: Educator's Publishing Service.

Levine, M. D., Busch, B., & Aufseeser, C. (1982). The dimension of inattention among children with school problems. *Pediatrics, 70*, 387–395.

Levine, M. D., Karniski, W., Palfrey, J., Meltzer, L. J., & Fenton, T. (1985). Risk factor complexes in early

adolescent delinquents. *American Journal of Disabilities of Children, 139*, 50–56.

Levine, M. D., & Melmed, R. D. (1982). The unhappy wanderers: Children with attention deficits. *Pediatric Clinics of North America, 29*, 105–119.

Levine, M. D., Meltzer, L., Busch, B., Palfrey, J., & Sullivan, M. (1983). The PEEX: Studies of a neurodevelopmental examination. *Pediatrics, 71*, 894–900.

Levine, M. D., Oberklaid, F., & Meltzer, L. (1981). Developmental output failure: A study of low productivity in school-aged children. *Pediatrics, 67*, 18–25.

Levine, M. D., & Satz, P. (Eds.). (1984). *Middle childhood: Development and dysfunction*. Baltimore: University Park Press.

Levine, M. D., Brooks, R., & Shonkoff, J. P. (1980). *A pediatric approach to learning disorders*. New York: John Wiley & Sons.

Levine, M. D., & Zallen, B. G. (1984). The learning disorders of adolescence: Organic and nonorganic failure to thrive. *Pediatric Clinics of North America, 31*, 345–369.

Liberman, L. Y., Liberman, A. M., Mattingly, I. G., & Shankweiler, D. (1980). Orthography and the beginning reader. In J. F. Kavanagh & R. L. Venezky (Eds.), *Orthography, reading, and dyslexia* (pp. 207–225). Baltimore: University Park Press.

Liberman, I. Y., Shankweiler, D., Liberman, A. W., Fowler, C., & Fisher, F. W. (1977). Phonetic segmentation and recoding in the beginning reader. In A. S. Reber & D. Scarborough (Eds.), *Toward a psychology of reading: The proceedings of the CUNY conferences* (pp. 207–225). Hillsdale, NJ: Lawrence Erlbaum Associates.

Lindsay, P. H., & Norman, D. H. (1977). *Human information processing*. New York: Academic Press.

Luria, A. R. (1980). *Higher cortical function in man*. NY: Basic Books.

Margrain, S. (1967). Short-term memory as a function of input modality. *Quarterly Journal of Experimental Psychology, 25*, 109–114.

McLeod, J. A. (1965). A comparison of WISC subtest scores of preadolescent successful and unsuccessful readers. *Australian Journal of Psychology, 17*, 220–228.

Merrill, E. C., Sperber, R. D., & McCauley, C. (1981). Differences in semantic encoding as a function of reading comprehension skill. *Memory and Cognition, 9*, 618–624.

Meltzer, L. J., Levine, M. D., Karniski, W., Palfrey, J., & Clarke, S. (1984). An analysis of the learning styles of adolescent delinquents. *Journal of Learning Disabilities, 17*, 600–608.

Murdock, B. B., & Walker, K. D. (1969). Modality effects in free recall. *Journal of Verbal Learning and Verbal Behavior, 8*, 665–676.

Murray, C. A. (1976). *The link between learning disabilities and juvenile delinquency: Current theory and knowledge*. Washington, DC: U.S. Government Printing Office.

Ornstein, P. A., & Naus, M. J. (1986). Effects of the knowledge base on children's memory-strategies. In H. W. Reece (Ed.), *Advances in child development and behavior* (Vol. 19). New York: Academic Press.

Ornstein, P. A., Naus, M. J., & Liberty, C. (1975). Rehearsal and organizational processes in children's memory. *Child Development, 46,* 818–830.

Pearl, R., Donahue, M., & Bryan, T. (1986). Social relationships of learning-disabled children. In J. K. Torgeson & B. L. Wong (Eds.), *Psychological and educational perspectives on learning disabilities* (pp. 193–224). New York: Academic Press.

Porges, S. W. (1984). Physiological correlates of attention: A core process underlying learning disorders. *Pediatric Clinics of North America, 31,* 371–385.

Raskin, L., Shaywitz, S. E., Shaywitz, B. A., Anderson, G., & Cohen, D. J. (1984). Neurochemical correlates of attention deficit disorder. *Pediatric Clinics of North America, 31,* 387–396.

Ross, D. M., & Ross, S. A. (1982). *Hyperactivity: Current issues, research, and theory.* New York: John Wiley & Sons.

Rutter, M. (1984). The family, the child, and the school. In M. D. Levine & P. Satz (Eds.), *Middle childhood: Development and dysfunction* (pp. 293–343). Baltimore: University Park Press.

Satterfield, J. H., Hooper, C. M., & Schnell, A. M. (1982). A prospective study of delinquency in 110 adolescent boys with attention deficit disorder and 88 normal adolescent boys. *American Journal of Psychiatry, 139,* 795–798.

Siegler, R. (1986). *Children's thinking.* Englewood Cliffs, NJ: Prentice Hall.

Sternberg, R. J. (Ed.). (1982). *Handbook of human intelligence.* New York: Cambridge University Press.

Sternberg, R. J., & Wagner, W. J. (1982). Automatization failure in learning disabilities. *Topics in Learning and Learning Disabilities, 1,* 1–11.

Tarter, R. E., McBride, H., Bounpane, N., & Schneider, D. U. (1977). Differentiation of alcoholics. *Archives of General Psychiatry, 34,* 761–768.

Torgeson, J. K. (1977). Memorization processes in reading-disabled children. *Journal of Educational Psychology, 69,* 571–578.

Torgeson, J. K. (1980). Conceptual and educational implications of the use of efficient task strategies by learning disabled children. *Journal of Learning Disabilities, 13,* 364–371.

Torgeson, J. K. (1985). Memory processes in reading-disabled children. *Journal of Learning Disabilities, 18,* 350–356.

Vogel, S. (1974). Syntactic abilities in normal and dyslexic children. *Journal of Learning Disabilities, 7,* 103–109.

Werner, E. E., & Smith, R. S. (1982). *Vulnerable, but invincible: A longitudinal study of resilient children and youth.* New York: McGraw-Hill.

Wiig, E. H., Lapointe, C., & Semel, E. M. (1977). Relationship among language processing and production abilities of learning disabled adolescents. *Journal of Learning Disabilities, 10,* 292–299.

Wiig, E. H., & Semel, E. (1984). *Language assessment and intervention for the learning disabled.* Columbus, OH: Charles E. Merrill.

Wiig, E. H., Semel, E., & Crouse, M. (1973). The use of English morphology by high-risk and learning-disabled children. *Journal of Learning Disabilities, 6,* 457–465.

Wolf, M. (1984). Naming, reading, and the dyslexias: A longitudinal overview. *Annals of Dyslexia, 34,* 87–115.

Chapter 13

Cultural Influences on Plasticity in Human Development

John U. Ogbu

Plasticity, according to Lerner (1984), encompasses the "systematic changes within the person in his or her structure and/or function" (p. vi). These changes occur throughout the life span to some degree. They are found at all levels, from the biological to the cultural. Lerner points out that the existence of plasticity is significant for intervention. As he puts it, "The existence of plasticity is not a point of minor significance. If all levels of life are open to change, then there is a great reason to be optimistic about the ability of intervention programs to balance human development" (p. vii).

Anthropologists have been interested in human malleability and development as far back as the early part of the 20th century, when Malinowski (1927, 1929) questioned the universality of the Oedipus complex postulated by Freud, and Mead challenged the assertion of American and European psychologists that certain problems of adolescence were biologically based (Mead, 1928; Suarez-Orozco, 1985). Malinowski, who studied matrilineal Trobriand Islanders, claimed that he found no evidence of an Oedipus complex, but instead a kind of matrilineal complex. Mead, who studied adolescence in Samoa, suggested that Samoan adolescent girls did not manifest the type of crisis usually found among their American and European counterparts. Socio-cultural anthropologists before and after Malinowski and Mead have documented variability in human behavior and personality, and their work can be interpreted as evidence of cultural influences on human plasticity in development.

At the same time, it should be made clear that the influence of culture on plasticity in human development has not been a focused topic of explicit anthropological study. The evidence that culture does use human malleability to shape development for its own purpose is indirect. One kind of evidence is the cross-cultural differences in human competence; another is the effect of culture change on human competence. Cross-cultural differences in human competence are made possible by human plasticity, and are adaptive responses to differences in cultural tasks requiring different competencies. Later in this chapter the focus is on the problem of intervention. At the outset, the main point is that, at the cultural level, the relationship between plasticity and intervention is a complex matter, especially when intervention means that dominant-group members define the problems of and solutions for minority cultures.

Some clarifications are necessary. The first has to do with the meaning of *culture;* the second is the distinction between psycho-biological–maturational versus cultural outcomes of development.

CULTURE

Nonanthropologists studying human development, and those involved in intervention programs tend to define culture narrowly. Perhaps, partly because their work focuses on individuals or on individuals in family situations, or partly because of their disciplines' perspectives on human functioning, they assume that culture is made up of family environment or family characteristics caused by the socioeconomic status of parents. Occasionally, they include community environment and social norms, but they rarely show how the latter enter into development.

Culture embraces more than what is in the person's immediate environment or family. Culture is a way of life shared by members of a population. It is the socio-cultural adaptation or design for living that people have worked out in the course of their history. The culture of a people includes institutionalized public behaviors or customs, as well as thoughts and emotions that accompany and support those public behaviors (LeVine, 1974a); it also includes things people make and have made that bear symbolic meanings. Of particular significance for this chapter is that culture includes economic, political, religious, and social institutions—the *imperatives of culture* (Cohen, 1971)—which form a recognizable pattern guiding behaviors of members of the population in a fairly predictable manner. The cultures of different populations vary.

MATURATIONAL VERSUS CULTURAL OUTCOMES IN HUMAN DEVELOPMENT

Psycho-biological–maturational outcomes are not the same as cultural outcomes in human development. An example of a maturational outcome is Piaget's idea of stages in cognitive development. The goal of psycho-biological–maturation here is the individual's attainment of the final stage postulated by Piaget, namely, the stage of formal operational thinking. In order to reach this stage, the individual's physical systems—the brain and central nervous system—must be fully developed for the kind of thought and language characteristic of the formal operational stage (Ginsburg & Opper, 1979).

There is no evidence that there are any human populations or cultures where people do not reach this physical-systems maturity. That is, there are no reports of populations where people do not have fully developed brains and fully developed nervous systems that enable formal operational thinking. On the other hand, there are reports of cultural differences in formal operational thinking (Berry & Dasen, 1974; Dasen, 1977). It appears that in some populations, such as the middle class in various Western nations, cultural tasks require formal operational thinking to a large extent (Dasen, 1977; Greenfield, 1976; Vernon, 1969). In these cultures, attaining formal operational thinking is likely to net adaptive cultural outcomes, and the cultures are likely to provide mechanisms, such as middle-class type of schooling, to facilitate the development of the operational thinking. In some other cultures, such as various ethnic groups in Central Africa and New Guinea, where cultural tasks do not call for much formal operational thinking in the Western middle-class sense, the development of this kind of formal operational thinking is probably not an adaptive cultural outcome and therefore there would be little or no cultural provision to facilitate the development of operational thinking (Kelly, 1977; Laurendeau-Bendavid, 1977). The psycho-biological foundation for human development is probably present cross-culturally, as is human malleability. However, what develops depends on cultural requirements, resulting in patterned adaptive cultural outcomes that vary cross-culturally.

CULTURAL INFLUENCES ON PLASTICITY: SOME CROSS-CULTURAL EVIDENCE

In exploring cultural influences on plasticity in human development the primary concern is with how cultures take advantage of human malleability to achieve desirable outcomes. Cultural outcomes in development are both to ensure the physical survival of children (LeVine, 1974a), and to ensure that children grow up with appropriate skills, beliefs, and behaviors or competencies—social-emotional, cognitive, and practical—that will make them competent adult members of their society, who will contribute to its survival (Fishbein, 1976; Ogbu, 1981). The focus in this chapter is on development of competence, especially cognitive competence, rather than on physical survival of children. Given common psycho-biological potential for development of competence, plasticity makes it possible for different cultures to use the potential to achieve their particular development goals. Competence is defined as a set of social-emotional, cognitive, and practical skills that are necessary to perform cultural tasks (Connolly & Bruner, 1974; Ogbu, 1981). Competence is, therefore, a set of functional or instrumental skills in a culture.

Why do cultures differ in their goals of cognitive competence, or any other domain of competence? To answer this question, it is necessary to return to the definition of culture as encompassing *cultural imperatives*. These cultural imperatives, or the economic, political, social and religious institutions and activities within a given culture or society, require and facilitate the form of competencies characteristic of members of the society.

Although all populations face certain common problems in life, such as how to make a living, how to reproduce, how to maintain order within their boundaries and defend their members against outsiders, different populations have solved these problems differently. The varying solutions arose, for example, because different people occupy different physical and social environments with different resources, or because they have diverse histories that influence their perceptions of and relationships with their environments and with one another. Thus, cultures vary in the tasks of making a living (economic and technological activities), of governing themselves (political), of organizing domestic life for reproduction (family and childrearing), and of maintaining relationships with the supernatural (religious). Each domain of cultural task both requires and promotes a repertoire of skills and capabilities, that is to say, human attributes or competencies. Because the cultural tasks in a given domain (e.g., subsistence tasks, tasks connected with domestic organization) vary from culture to culture, the repertoire of competencies that they require and promote also varies from culture to culture. Therefore, in any culture people tend to value and foster the development in children of the adaptive, functional, or rewarding repertoires of competencies that are required by the cultural tasks of adult existence. Parents and other socialization agents do not usually encourage children to develop competencies in the abstract—competencies that have no bearing to their way of life. Furthermore, competencies that are useful in the most intensely involved and valued cultural tasks are likely to permeate other areas of life.

The intent is not to deny the biological basis of competencies, nor is it to advocate an extreme relativism in human development of competence. Rather, attention is called to the influence of culture on the development of human competencies, and caution urged against hasty biological interpretations of observed differences in competencies. Indeed, the choice to illustrate the relationship of culture and human malleability by discussing cognitive competencies or intelligence is a response to extreme biological and Western-centric interpretations. The choice to focus on cognitive competencies also has to do with a long-standing aim of intervention programs to improve the cognitive skills of disadvantaged children in contemporary urban industrial societies.

One important distinction suggested as a prerequisite for proper interpretation of cross-cultural differences in cognitive skills is the distinction between cognitive capacities and cognitive skills or competencies (Scribner & Cole, 1973; Vernon, 1969). Cognitive capacities—the ability to remember, form concepts, generalize, operate with abstraction, reason logically—are found in all human populations or all cultures. They are universal and probably biologically based. Cognitive competencies or cognitive skills, on the other hand, arise from the different ways different populations use the common human cognitive capacities to solve specific cognitive problems they face in their particular environments and in their historical experiences. That is, the patterns of cognitive skills found in different cultures are the different ways in which members of the cultures have fashioned the universal capacities to solve unique problems they confront as a result of their unique historical and ecological experiences. In one population, for instance, the main cultural task or problem may require and facilitate a high degree of verbal skills; in another population, the major cultural task may require and encourage numerical or mathematical skills (Ginsburg, 1986; Saxe & Posner, 1983); yet in a third population, spatial-perceptual skills may be most essential and therefore prominent (Seagrim & Lendon, 1980). In still another population, the cultural task may require and promote some combination of these and other cognitive skills. Furthermore, how members of a given population remember, how they generalize, or how they reason logically may depend on their historical and ecological experiences. Cognitive competencies or cognitive skills are, therefore, not universal but may vary from culture to culture.

The cognitive skills of the contemporary Western middle class are not more functional than the cognitive skills of other people, if evaluated against the background of the cultural tasks faced by respective populations, nor are they due to superior genetic endowment. Rather, they are products of particular historical cultural developments and cultural tasks. Both Baumrind (1976) and Vernon (1969) have speculated that the development of industrialization, urbanization, and bureaucracy as well as the development of formal education in the West gave rise to new cultural tasks that required and encouraged the contemporary Western middle-class mode of thought, with its emphasis on ability to absorb complex information, manipulate abstract concepts, and grasp relations. In other words, new cultural tasks resulting from industrialization, urbanization, bureaucratization, and formal education gave rise to new cultural outcomes in cognitive competence for the Western middle class, and human plasticity made it possible for the middle class involved in these activities to develop appropriate cognitive competencies.

IQ tests measure aspects of these new mid-dle-class cognitive competencies; they do not measure some universal property that is biologically determined. IQ tests, however, measure only a part of the middle-class cognitive competencies, the part selected for specific purposes or for specific cultural tasks. In particular, the cognitive competencies tapped by IQ test items are deliberately and carefully selected to predict success at specific, middle-class cultural tasks—namely, academic and job performance (Travers, 1982; Vernon, 1969; Wigdor & Garner, 1982). Furthermore, IQ test scores predict well the academic performance of the middle class because the test items selected measure cognitive skills that are a part of the middle-class cognitive repertoire, emphasized both in childrearing practices and school curricula. These cognitive skills are emphasized in both middle-class child-rearing practices and formal schooling because they are required by the cultural tasks of the middle class.

It is instructive that although IQ test scores predict the academic performance of white middle-class children, they do not generally predict the academic performance of some minority children, such as black children. They also do not predict well the academic performance of non-Western children who attend Western-type schools (Serpell, 1982).

Other cultures have also taken advantage of human plasticity to develop the specific configurations of cognitive competencies that meet their cognitive needs. The first cross-cultural example comes from the work of Gay and Cole (1967) who studied cultural influences on cognitive skills among the Kpelle of Liberia. One set of skills they investigated involved estimating various types of quantities. They found that the Kpelle were particularly good in estimating things dealing with their everyday activities. For example, illiterate Kpelle were better than American college students in estimating the number of stones in a pile, but did worse than the Americans in estimating lengths of objects by hand spans. Gay and Cole (1967) explained the difference by saying that the Kpelle estimated well the number of stones in a pile because they commonly use stones to tally the number of cups in a container of rice, an important staple food among them. On the other hand, the Kpelle did poorly in measuring lengths by hand spans and foot lengths because their culture does not have a system for length that uses interchangeable units like 1 foot = 12 inches.

Studies of cognitive skills associated with art experience constitute a second example. These studies measure children's ability to reproduce patterns as depicted in the Goodenough-Harris Drawing Test. Dennis (1970) analyzed and summarized the results of these studies in 52 different cultures, and his findings are instructive. Generally, children's performance depends on the art experience of the people in their culture or the culture's involvement with modernization. That is, children from cultures with visual art (i.e., woodcarving, sculpture, decorative art, pottery, masks, and sandpainting) usually scored high. Among the high-scoring groups are Native Americans in the U.S. Southwest and Japanese villagers in rural art centers in Japan. There were rarely sex differences, except in two high-scoring groups. Among Japanese villagers, where women rather than men were highly involved with art work, girls scored higher than boys; whereas in the Native American groups, where men rather than women were involved with art work, boys scored higher than girls. Zhov (1980) recently reported a similar influence of sex-typed art activities on test scores for rural Ngoni children in Central Africa.

The final example is the influence of cultural tasks on mathematical skills. Posner (1982), and Saxe and Posner (1983) have reported this phenomenon for two West African cultures whose economic activities differed in the extent to which they used numerical skills. In one group, the Dioula, the people are merchants whose principal economic activities require extensive use of numerals; their culture not only values mathematical skills but provides children with many opportunities to practice and develop these skills. In the second group, the Baoule, the people are subsistence farmers whose major economic activities do not depend on numerical skills, and who, therefore, do not value these skills strongly enough to stress

them for their children to the same degree as the Dioula. Children from the two groups, who had not been to a Western-type school, performed differently when tested for mathematical skills. Dioula children, the merchant group, were superior. Saxe and Posner (1983) summarized the differences between the two groups by saying that the unschooled Dioula children "adopt more economic strategies than their unschooled Baoule, the agricultural group, counterpart. In particular, they use a greater number of memorized addition facts and regrouping by tens ($7 + 5 = 10 + 2$), as compared to the Baoule" (pp. 302–303).

In other studies where investigators took into consideration indigenous cultural activities and familiarity with test materials, test results generally suggest that cognitive skills are influenced by cultural tasks. Examples include conservation studies (Bovet, 1974; Price-Williams, Gordon, & Ramirez, 1969); studies of spatial tasks, such as rotation and horizontality (Berry & Dasen, 1974); and studies of classification (Kellaghan, 1968; Okonji, 1971; Price-Williams et al., 1969). Human malleability enables each culture to meet its needs for cognitive competence in selected areas of interest or focus.

Cultures are able to meet their unique needs for cognitive competence because of human plasticity. When cultures change and new cultural tasks arise, giving rise to new cultural demands for cognitive competence, human plasticity also makes it possible for the new outcomes to be reached. A few examples follow.

A good example is the change that occurred in the cognitive skills of the Western middle class as a result of the emergence of bureaucratic urban industrial economy and formal education. Today in the United States some further changes are appearing in middle-class cognitive competencies because of emerging computer technology and "high-tech" jobs with their emphasis on *cognitivism*. The cognitive skills required by the new computer technology include "precise definitions, linear thinking, precise rules and algorithms for thinking and acting" (Committee of Correspondence on the

Future of Public Education, 1984). Middle-class Americans are acquiring the new cognitive skills by learning about computers at home, school, and work; they are also encouraging and enabling their children to acquire the new competencies. American schools are rewriting their curricula and modifying their instructional techniques, in response to public pressures to emphasize cognitive skills compatible with computer thinking and with emerging cultural tasks relying on computer literacy.

Another sign of changes in cognitive competencies can be found in studies among Third World people (Cole, Gay, Glick, & Sharp, 1971; Cole & Scribner, 1974; Greenfield, 1966; Lancy, 1983; Scribner & Cole, 1973; Seagrim & Lendon, 1980; Sharp, Cole, & Lave, 1979; Stevenson, 1982). Under the impact of Western technology, emerging cash economy, bureaucratic organization, urbanization, and Western-type schooling, Third World people appear to be experiencing some kind of *cognitive acculturation*. They are increasingly acquiring the cognitive skills characteristic of Western middle-class people as they become involved in Western middle-class types of cultural tasks. Their new cognitive skills include Western middle-class skills, such as those for absorbing complex information, manipulating abstract concepts, and grasping relations. Furthermore, as in the case of the Western middle class, these new cognitive skills are increasingly permeating the daily cultural activities of the Third World middle class, outside of the school and work settings where people first encounter and use them.

Moreover, Third World individuals who participate in the new technology, economy, education, and urban culture—and thereby acquire the new cognitive skills—become differentiated from those who are not yet involved in these new cultural tasks and life situations. This generational differentiation in cognitive skills can be illustrated with Scribner's study of sorting tasks in Liberia among Kpelle high school students and nonliterate adult "bush" villagers (Cole & Scribner, 1974). Scribner found that the high school students were not

only superior in the sorting tasks but also superior in verbal explanations of what they did. Cole and Scribner summarize the generational difference in verbal explanations as follows:

> High-schoolers almost always gave a category label to their groups ("these are clothes") or expressed their category status by some statement referring to a common attribute of the group members ("you can bunt with these"). In sharp contrast, 70 percent of the bush villagers gave reasons that had nothing to do with the properties of the objects they were grouping: most of their explanations were arbitrary statements, such as "I like them this way" or "my sense told me to do it this way." (p. 20)

What is to be learned by examining cultural uses of plasticity? What is learned is that cultures differ in their goals for cognitive competencies, and that they generally appear to meet their goals because human plasticity permits them to develop cognitive repertoires or configurations most appropriate for their needs. Similarly, when cultures change and new cognitive needs arise, plasticity makes it possible to develop new adaptive cognitive skills.

CULTURE, PLASTICITY, AND INTERVENTION

The optimism for "intervention programs to balance human development" because of human plasticity throughout life (Lerner, 1984, p. vii) was noted earlier. Intervention for disadvantaged children, for instance, should no longer be limited to early childhood, as it has been in the past. Previously, intervention was based on the paradigm of early experience that assumed that there were "direct and causal linkages between early experiences and subsequent intellectual functioning" (Ramey & Suarez, 1985, p. 3). The paradigm of early experience is now seen as inadequate, partly because intervention programs based on it have not proven particularly effective over time, partly because it is now known that development continues beyond the early childhood period, and partly because the existence of plasticity throughout life means that intervention can take place after early childhood.

As already stated, intervention programs based on the early experience hypothesis, or the *failure-of-socialization hypothesis* (Ogbu, 1979), have not been particularly effective over a long period, especially for some minorities like black Americans (see Ogbu 1974, 1978, 1981). One reason has to do with the assumption about origins of the deficits in the cognitive and social development of disadvantaged children that the programs intended to eliminate; another is the failure of these programs to distinguish between different types of disadvantaged children and their unique problems and intervention needs. A good paradigm for intervention must make a distinction between the cultural-ecological basis for the presence or absence of any set of skills in a given population *and* the formulas or mechanisms for inculcating, transmitting, and acquiring the functional/instrumental skills. The paradigm must also distinguish between different types of disadvantaged groups, because, as will be suggested later, the disadvantages of some minority groups are not merely those caused by poverty or rural living or biological risks. These minorities have other disadvantages that arise from cultural and psychological responses they have developed to cope with generations of structural and psychological subordination by the dominant group, responses that have come to make intercultural learning, crossing cultural/language boundaries, and school learning problematic. These two points are discussed in detail in the next section.

Intervention versus Cultural Formulas for Development of Competencies

Preschool education is good for children, including poor and minority children. That is, it is good for so-called disadvantaged children to participate in preschool programs. Disadvantaged children who participate in good preschool and related intervention programs benefit especially from the nutrition and health components of the programs. Furthermore, some of the children learn skills that eventually help them succeed academically. But intervention programs will not necessarily produce significant and lasting changes in many poor mi-

nority children's cognitive skills as measured by IQ. The reason for this is that the programs make some incorrect assumptions about the reasons the minority children lack white, middle-class cognitive skills.

As noted previously, cognitive competencies change in response to cultural demands. They do not change simply because people change their early experiences or child-rearing practices. *No population has ever achieved significant social, economic, and political advancement by first changing its child-rearing practices* (Kaplan & Manners, 1970; Ogbu, 1978, 1981). In fact, the reverse is usually true. Socialization or child-rearing practices, and even preschool education, are formulas invented by members of a society to ensure that their children will acquire the adaptive or instrumental competencies necessary to become competent, contributing adult members of their society (Fishbein, 1976; LeVine, 1974b; Ogbu, 1979, 1981, 1982).

The formulas consist of teaching children directly and indirectly, consciously and unconsciously, the instrumental skills or competencies *already existing* in the population, because they are required by the cultural tasks of the members of the population. Parents do not invent the knowledge, beliefs, skills, and behaviors they teach their children. These already exist. Except in a period of rapid social change, the competencies parents and other agents of socialization teach children are more or less preordained within their environment. This is not a matter of what should be; it is, in any human society, including the United States, what is. For example, the competencies that contemporary, middle-class Americans teach their children, such as self-direction, initiative, independence, competitiveness, and certain cognitive and communicative skills (Connolly & Bruner, 1974; Kohn, 1969; Leacock, 1969; Vernon, 1969), are not inventions of individual middle-class parents; rather, these are competencies that are adaptive to high-level, high-paying, middle-class occupations and social positions (see also Seeley, Sim, & Loosley, 1956). Parents in hunting and gathering societies or in peasant communities teach their children other types of competencies more adaptive or useful in their activities, and such other competencies are prevalent and valued amongst them.

The formulas work because parents and other socialization agents in a population or society use *culturally standardized techniques* of child rearing, which time and experience have shown to be effective. It can be argued that contemporary, white, middle-class Americans share some standardized knowledge, skills, and practices of raising children—practices that time and experience have shown to be effective in producing the kinds of competencies adaptive to middle-class occupations and cultural tasks. It is true that some middle-class parents rely on experts' advice (e.g., Dr. Spock and contemporary child developmental psychologists). But, from an anthropological point of view, these "experts" are cultural role-players in a constantly changing culture. Their approved role is to study changes in middle-class cultural tasks, especially in techno-economic domains, and devise and pass on to the general population (though mainly to the middle class) appropriate changes needed in child-rearing techniques, so that children will learn the requisite new competencies (Ogbu, 1981). The point here is not that child development experts think of themselves as playing the role in cultural separation or cultural integration. In fact, they are probably not aware that they are playing such a role; but they are.

Why cleave to these formulas? Parents use the formulas because there are rewards for compliance and penalties for noncompliance. The incentives for using culturally prescribed child-rearing practices to teach adaptive competencies can be understood through the concept of *status mobility system* (LeVine, 1967a). Members of each population usually share some common idea of how to succeed in their cultural tasks and in their reward system. How one gets ahead is defined differently in different populations. The status mobility system theory encompasses the range of cultural tasks and status positions available, their relative importance, the competencies essential for attaining and performing the cultural tasks, the strat-

egies for obtaining higher status position, and the expected societal rewards and penalties for success or failure. Parents employ the formulas because they want their children to become competent and successful adults. As children themselves grow older and become aware of the status mobility system of their population, they, too, actively seek to acquire the competencies that are functional in their culture. Role models or cultural images of successful members of the population, living or dead, guide child-rearing agents in their tasks and also influence the growing children's responses to the efforts of these agents.

Previous intervention programs have erred in at least two respects. One is that they have incorrectly traced the origins of cognitive competencies or skills for middle-class types of cultural tasks and positions simply to childrearing formulas; they confuse the process or formulas for inculcating functional cognitive skills with the reason for the presence of skills in middle-class American society in the first place. Second, intervention programs have tried to teach these middle-class types of cognitive skills to disadvantaged children in the abstract. The programs assume that disadvantaged children will have access to middle-class types of cultural tasks after they have developed middle-class skills. Under certain circumstances, this may be a good route or strategy for advancement into middle-class positions. But cross-cultural studies indicate that, as already noted, people often first gain access to middle-class types of positions, schooling, and jobs before they develop middle-class types of cognitive and other skills (Clignet, 1967; Inkeles, 1955; LeVine, 1967b). Furthermore, as noted in the next section, some groups who do not have the white middle-class type of early experience do quite well in the public school.

The Special Case of Caste-Like Minorities

Another criticism of the theory underlying previous early-intervention programs is that it did not explain why there are differences in school performance between different groups of disadvantaged minorities. For example, some minority-group children are academically successful even though they have all the characteristics that the early-experiences hypothesis would label *disadvantages;* characteristics that researchers tend to correlate with school failure. Moreover, these successful minorities do not raise their children as white middle-class parents raise their children (Gibson, 1983; Ogbu, 1984; Ogbu & Matute-Bianchi, 1986). The early-experiences paradigm also does not explain why children and adults in non-Western societies who come to Western-type schools and a Western techno-economic system after childhood are able to acquire and manifest Western-type cognitive skills.

We need to recognize different kinds of disadvantaged groups and their distinctive circumstances and disadvantages. First, some white Americans are disadvantaged because they are poor or because they are poor and live in rural areas. Second, there are other Americans who are disadvantaged not only because they are poor or rural-poor, but also because they are minorities. Their minority status has some added disadvantages for human development and education. But there are also different types of disadvantaged minorities. Minority groups who are immigrant are usually more successful in school than minorities who are nonimmigrant, even though the two minority types face somewhat similar disadvantages, namely, poverty, parents with little or no formal education, parents with low-status jobs, little or no proficiency in standard English, a cultural tradition different from mainstream American culture, lack of mainstream child-rearing practices or early experiences, and discrimination and barriers in adult opportunity structure (Gibson, 1983).

The differences in the school performance of the two types of minorities arise partly from differences in the quality of relationship between the minorities and the dominant group and the consequences of that relationship. Disadvantaged immigrant minorities, although they may have other unmet needs, are not usually targets of intervention programs to raise their children's IQs to facilitate their school success. The reasons for the relatively good school success records of the immigrants in spite of their disadvantages have been explained elsewhere (Fordham & Ogbu, 1986; Gibson, 1983; Ogbu, 1983, pp. 185–190; Ogbu, 1984; Ogbu, 1985c, p. 862; Ogbu & Matute-Bianchi, 1986, pp. 99–111). As suggested next, additional but as yet unrecognized disadvantages of nonimmigrant minorities are an important reason for their persistently disproportionate school failure; these disadvantages make them candidates for intervention efforts.

Disadvantaged nonimmigrant minorities are people we have classified as *subordinate* or *caste-like minorities* (Ogbu, 1978, 1984, 1985b). They are people who were initially incorporated involuntarily and permanently into American society (or into any other society, for that matter) and then relegated to menial positions through legal and extra-legal devices. Black Americans are a good example of this, although Native Americans, Mexican Americans, and Native Hawaiians also share certain important features of caste-like minority status (Berreman, 1967; Myrdal, 1944). Native Americans, the original owners of the land, were conquered and then subjugated on reservations (Spicer, 1962). Mexican Americans, too, were conquered and then displaced from power in the Southwestern United States. Mexicans who later immigrated from Mexico were treated like the conquered group (Acuna, 1972; Schmidt, 1970). There are examples of caste-like minorities in other countries, such as the Korean Japanese and the Buraku outcasts in Japan (DeVos & Wagatsuma, 1967; Lee & DeVos, 1981; Rohlen, 1983), or the Maoris in New Zealand (Metge, 1967; Ogbu, 1978).

Special problems for caste-like minorities arise from the fact that under caste-like stratification (a) the minorities are largely excluded from the more desirable cultural tasks that demand and promote the cognitive and social competencies of the middle-class members of the dominant group; (b) generations of the minorities are relegated to menial cultural tasks that require and promote other non-middle-class competencies and different perceptions and interpretations of how one gets ahead in society; and (c) the minorities tend to respond to their subordination and exploitation by developing an oppositional social identity and an oppositional cultural frame of reference. As a result, the minorities may consciously and unconsciously develop beliefs, competencies, and behaviors that then make it difficult for them to learn things that they associate with their "oppressors," or to learn skills that they think make them act like members of the dominant group.[1]

Before the 1960s, most blacks and similar subordinate minorities in the United States were excluded from jobs and other positions requiring and promoting middle-class cognitive skills (Ogbu, 1974, 1978). Thus, if in the 1960s, when intervention programs began on a large scale, blacks did not demonstrate white middle-class types of cognitive skills, it was because blacks were denied jobs and other positions where such cognitive skills were functional; and if blacks did not work hard or persevere in school or prolong their education, it was probably because they realized that they did not have the opportunity to get jobs and wages commensurate with their educational accomplishments, as did their white counterparts. Many blacks diverted their time and talents and invested them in other, survival strategies (Ogbu, 1985b).

But the treatment of blacks and similar minorities was more than denial of instrumental opportunities, and it elicited from the minorities more than instrumental responses. One response pertinent to the issue of intervention and development is that subordinate minorities developed a strong distrust for members of the dominant group and for the institutions they controlled, such as the schools. Two other responses more germane are that subordinate minorities developed a complex collective or social identity system that they perceived as oppositional to the social identity of white Americans; and that subordinate minorities developed a cultural frame of reference or ideal way of behaving *in selected areas of life* that they also perceived as oppositional to the cultural frame of reference of the whites.

Oppositional cultural frame of reference means that the minorities have come to regard certain behaviors, activities or events, and symbols as not appropriate for them because those behaviors, events, and symbols are characteristic of white Americans. At the same time, the minorities emphasize other behaviors, events, and symbols as more appropriate for them because these are *not* a part of the white American way of life. Oppositional cultural frame of reference is applied selectively by black Americans and similar minorities. Endeavors traditionally defined as the exclusive province of white people are repudiated by blacks, as part of this oppositional cultural frame of reference. Examples are areas where criteria of performance have been established by whites, competence in performance is judged by white people or their representatives, and reward for performance is determined by white people according to white criteria. Intellectual performance or academic learning and high-status jobs in the mainstream economy fit this paradigm (Ogbu, 1986c). It appears that caste-like minorities perceive success in mainstream educational and economic institutions as something that depends on competencies derived from a white cultural frame of reference. It appears, too, that the minorities consciously or unconsciously interpret the ac-

---

[1]An important challenge in comparative study of minority education is to explain the variability in the school performance of minority groups. In the United States, for instance, several minority groups speak their own languages or dialects; have their own cultures; and have experienced economic discrimination, political subordination, and other forms of adverse treatment at the hands of the dominant group. Yet, some of these minorities have done relatively well in school; others have not. A comparative analysis shows that those minorities who are academically successful and those who are not academically successful differ in some other important ways: they differ in how they became minorities, in their folk theories of getting ahead, in their interpretation of economic and other forms of discrimination by the dominant group, in types of cultural and language differences that characterize them, in collective identity, and in interpretation of and responses to schooling. Detailed analyses are available elsewhere of these complex factors and their possible differential influences on various types of minorities and their schooling outcomes (see Fordham & Ogbu, in press; Ogbu, 1978, 1983, 1984, 1985c; Ogbu & Matute-Bianchi, 1986).

quisition of those competencies as incompatible with their own cultural frame of reference and with their sense of identity and security. To them it means acting white. The black community apparently perceives black executives and academically successful black students as people who have learned to act white. Thus, Brown and Ford (1975) report that a prerequisite for making it in the mainstream economy or institutions and in white corporations is often too high a price to pay for most blacks who would like to be successful in major white corporations. Other black authors note that for a black child to succeed academically he or she must first submit to a process of resocialization or reenculturation, which eventually alienates him or her from black culture and identity (Boykin, 1986; Cary, 1976; Fordham, 1984).

It is therefore important to understand that the cultural frame of reference of blacks and similar minorities is emotionally charged because it is closely tied to their sense of collective identity and their sense of security. Therefore, individuals who try to behave like whites or who try to cross cultural boundaries or to act white in forbidden domains face opposition from their peers and probably from their community. Their peers construe such behavior as trying to ''join the enemy'' (DeVos, 1967). Individuals trying to cross cultural boundaries may experience stress, what DeVos (1967, 1984) calls *affective dissonance,* because they share their group's sense of collective oppositional identity, a belief that may cause them to feel that they are betraying their group and its cause. They also may experience stress because they are uncertain about being accepted by whites, even if they succeed in learning how to act white (Ogbu, 1986a, 1986c). Learning itself may arouse a sense of ''impending conflict over one's future identity'' (DeVos, 1984). Of course, not everyone feels this way. Some black Americans do not identify with the oppositional identity and cultural frame of reference; some do so only marginally.

What has been said here should not be interpreted to mean that blacks and other minorities do not want to succeed in school. They do indeed want to succeed academically and to be able to obtain good jobs with good wages in the mainstream economy. But, at the same time, participant-observation studies of actual attitudes, perceptions, and behaviors of black students (as distinct from studies of attitudes obtained through questionnaires) show that blacks do not invest enough time and effort, do not persevere in pursuing their educational goals, and do not strive at test-taking. All of these behaviors entail acting white.

Preliminary studies among upper elementary school children and junior and senior high school students in the inner-city reveal that black students have classified the following attitudes and behaviors as white, not black: speaking standard English, being on time, being serious about school, following standard classroom practices that enhance academic success, and even getting good grades or doing well on tests (Fordham & Ogbu, 1986; Ogbu, 1974; Petroni, 1970). It appears that many black and similar minority students who are failing in school or scoring low on various tests have the ability to do better. However, because they identify academic attitudes and behaviors, as well as academic success, consciously or unconsciously, as white, many intellectually able students do poorly in school because of the cultural dilemma they face.

Some black students resolve the dilemma by camouflaging their real academic attitudes and efforts to avoid peer criticisms and pressures, at the cost of academic success. Other black students adopt the immigrant's approach to schooling, which is to distinguish school learning for credentials and future employment from learning that leads to acculturation into a white cultural frame of reference. Still other black students consciously or unconsciously choose to act white and to repudiate black identity and culture and to assimilate. These strategies help many students succeed in school. But many more do not resolve the dilemma and fail (Fordham, personal communication).

Socialization and Development

From an anthropological perspective, black children, like children in every culture, learn from their parents and other socialization agents the collective perceptions and interpretations of their people's history; they are taught black people's collective sense of social identity vis-a-vis white American social identity. The children also are taught and learn a black as opposed to a white American cultural frame of reference. Comparative studies of subordinate minorities in the United States and elsewhere suggest that children acquire the oppositional identity and cultural frame of reference as they grow up through socialization and peer pressures (DeVos, 1967, 1984; Ogbu, 1981, 1986c).

Socialization begins with the family, but learning also takes place in other settings. Parents often unconsciously teach their children, beginning at a very early age. Peer group pressures ensure that as the individual child develops, he or she learns to conform to what is defined as appropriate for minorities. In the case of inner-city black children, they learn these things not only in the home but also in the street. Children's participation in the street culture and learning environment begins before they go to school (Ogbu, 1981; Young, 1970). The street has its own culture and language that the children learn as a part of acquiring social, linguistic, and cognitive competency in the community. The actual techniques by which the group's oppositional identity and oppositional cultural frame of reference are transmitted and acquired are varied (Ogbu, 1981, 1986a). The point to stress is that as the children get older, their awareness that they share an oppositional identity increases (Cross, 1985; Spencer, 1985). The children also increasingly acquire more and more knowledge and skills that enable participation in the distinctly black cultural frame of reference.

IMPLICATIONS FOR
FUTURE INTERVENTION

A number of important factors should be considered before undertaking future intervention efforts. They are listed below.

1. Different populations and their distinctive features and needs should be recognized.

More specifically, different types of minorities should be distinguished and their different needs for intervention identified. For example, subordinate or caste-like minorities like black Americans differ in many respects from immigrant minorities like Chinese Americans.

2. There should be continued vigorous effort to enable blacks and similar minorities to have unimpaired access to jobs and other positions or cultural tasks requiring and promoting middle-class cognitive and social competencies and school success.

3. Elimination of instrumental barriers in areas of jobs, wages, education, and politics will not necessarily automatically eliminate gaps in academic performance, because of factors related to identity and cultural frame of reference. Since these factors are rarely recognized and taken into account by minority and majority reformers, they tend to persist after instrumental barriers are removed and thus perpetuate inequality to some extent. Therefore, these elements should be recognized as a part of the problem and taken into account in future reform policies and programs.

4. A good understanding of the special forces—historical, structural, cultural, and psychological—that influence the academic orientation and behaviors of subordinate minority students should enable school officials and interventionists to design better programs to help minority students. For example, programs based on an understanding of the oppositional process described in this chapter can include ways to help minority students learn to separate the benefit of academic pursuits from the anathema of acting white.

5. A good paradigm for future intervention should not merely aim to balance assumed biological factors with factors of early experience. It should also consider the nature and meaning of early experiences for different groups of disadvantaged children, especially for subordinate minority children.

6. The subordinate minority community has an important part to play. It should find ways to help its children learn to stop equating academic pursuits with one-way acculturation into a white frame of reference. It should find

ways to reward more visibly its children who are academically successful, so as to instill that academic success is one of its cultural values. On the whole, subordinate minorities should adopt a perspective on school learning similar to that of immigrant minorities, which is that academic success and associated attitudes and behaviors are not incompatible with ethnic identity and security; in fact, they can reinforce ethnic identity and security.

REFERENCES

Acuna, R. (1972). *Occupied America: The Chicano's struggle toward liberation*. San Francisco: Canfield Press.

Baumrind, D. (1976). *Subcultural variations in values defining social competence: An outsider's perspective on the black subculture*. Unpublished mauscript, University of California, Institute of Human Development, Berkeley.

Berreman, G. D. (1967). Concomitants of caste organization. In G. DeVos & H. Wagatsuma (Eds.), *Japan's invisible race: Caste in culture and personality* (pp. 308–324). Berkeley: University of California Press.

Berry, J. W., & Dasen, P. R. (Eds.). (1974). *Culture and cognition: Readings in cross-cultural psychology*. London: Methuen & Co.

Bovet, M. G. (1974). Cognitive processes among illiterate children and adults. In J. W. Berry & P. R. Dasen (Eds.), *Culture and cognition: Readings in cross-cultural psychology* (pp. 311–334). London: Methuen & Co.

Boykin, A. W. (1986). The triple quandary and the schooling of Afro-American children. In U. Neisser (Ed.), *The school achievement of minority children: New perspectives* (pp. 57–92). Hillsdale, NJ: Lawrence Erlbaum Associates.

Brown, H. A., & Ford, D. L. (1975). Blacks in the management profession: The recent MBA graduate. *Contact, 7*, 12–19.

Cary, W. M. (1976). *Worse than silence: The black child's dilemma*. New York: Vantage Press.

Clignet, R. (1967). Environmental change, types of descent, and childrearing practices. In H. Miner (Ed.), *The city in modern Africa*. New York: Praeger.

Cohen, Y. A. (1971). The shaping of men's minds: Adaptations to the imperatives of culture. In M. L. Wax, S. Diamond, & F. O. Gearing (Eds.), *Anthropological perspectives on education* (pp. 19–50). New York: Basic Books.

Cole, M., Gay, J., Glick, J. A., & Sharp, D. W. (1971). *The cultural context of learning and thinking: An exploration in experimental anthropology*. New York: Basic Books.

Cole, M., & Scribner, S. (1974). *Culture and thought: A psychological introduction*. New York: John Wiley & Sons.

Committee of Correspondence on the Future of Public Education. (1984). *Education for a democratic future: A manifesto*. New York.

Connolly, K. J., & Bruner, J. S. (1974). Introduction. In K. J. Connolly & J. S. Bruner (Eds.), *The growth of competence* (pp. 3–7). London: Academic Press.

Cross, W. E., Jr. (1985). Black identity: Rediscovering the distinction between personal identity and reference group orientation. In M. B. Spencer, G. K. Brookins, & W. R. Allen (Eds.), *Beginnings: Social and affective development of black children* (pp. 155–171). Hillsdale, NJ: Lawrence Erlbaum Associates.

Dasen, P. (1977). Introduction. In P. Dasen (Ed.), *Piagetian psychology: Cross-cultural contributions* (pp. 1–25). New York: Gardner Press.

Dennis, W. (1970). Goodenough scores, art experience, and modernization. In Ihsan Al-Issa & W. Dennis (Eds.), *Cross-cultural studies of behavior* (pp. 134–152). New York: Holt, Rinehart & Winston.

DeVos, G. A. (1967). Essential elements of caste: Psychological determinants in structural theory. In G. A. DeVos & H. Wagatsuma (Eds.), *Japan's invisible race: Caste in culture and personality* (pp. 332–384). Berkeley: University of California Press.

DeVos, G. A. (1984, April). *Ethnic persistence and role degradation: An illustration from Japan*. Paper presented at the American-Soviet Symposium on Contemporary Ethnic Processes in the USA and the USSR, New Orleans, LA.

DeVos, G. A., & Wagatsuma, H. (Eds.). (1967). *Japan's invisible race: Caste in culture and personality*. Berkeley: University of California Press.

Fishbein, H. D. (1976). *Evolution, development and children's learning*. Pacific Palisades, CA: Goodyear Press.

Fordham, S. (1984, November). *Ethnography in a black high school: Learning not to be a native*. Paper presented at the 83rd Annual Meeting of the American Anthropological Association, Denver, CO.

Fordham, S. (1985). *Black student school success as related to fictive kinship*. Final Report to the National Institute of Education, Washington, DC.

Fordham, S., & Ogbu, J. U. (1986). Black students' school success: Coping with the "burden of 'acting white.'" *The Urban Review, 18*(3), 1–31.

Gay, J., & Cole, M. (1967). *The new mathematics and an old culture: A study of learning among the Kpelle of Liberia*. New York: Holt, Rinehart & Winston.

Gibson, M. A. (1983). *Home-school-community linkages: A study of educational equity for Punjabi youth*. Final Report. Washington, DC: National Institute of Education.

Ginsburg, H. P. (1986). Rethinking the myth of the deprived child: New thoughts on poor children. In U. Neisser (Ed.), *The school achievement of minority children: New perspectives*. Hillsdale, NJ: Lawrence Erlbaum Associates.

Ginsburg, H., & Opper, S. (1979). *Piaget's theory of intellectual development: An introduction*. Englewood Cliffs, NJ: Prentice-Hall.

Greenfield, P. M. (1966). On culture and conservation. In J. S. Bruner, R. R. Oliver, & P. M. Greenfield (Eds.), *Studies in cognitive growth* (pp. 225–256). New York: John Wiley & Sons.

Greenfield, P. M. (1976). Cross-cultural research and

Piagetian theory: Paradox and progress. In K. Riegel & J. Meacham (Eds.), *The developing individual in a changing world*. The Hague: Mouton.

Hickerson, R. (1980). *Role models in the ghetto*. Unpublished manuscript, Department of Anthropology, University of California, Berkeley.

Inkeles, A. (1955). Social change and social character: The role of parental mediation. *Journal of Social Issues, 11,* 12–23.

Kaplan, D., & Manners, R. M. (1970). *Culture theory.* Englewood Cliffs, NJ: Prentice-Hall.

Kellaghan, T. (1968). Abstraction and categorization in African children. *International Journal of Psychology, 3,* 115–120.

Kelly, M. (1977). Papua New Guinea and Piaget—An eight-year study. In P. Dasen (Ed.), *Piagetian psychology: Cross-cultural contributions* (pp. 169–203). New York: Gardner Press.

Kohn, M. L. (1969). Social class and parent-child relationships: An interpretation. In R. L. Coser (Ed.), *Life cycle and achievement in America* (pp. 21–48). New York: Harper & Row.

Lancy, D. F. (1983). *Cross-cultural studies in cognition and mathematics.* New York: Academic Press.

Laurendeau-Bendavid, M. (1977). Culture, schooling and cognitive development: A comparative study of children in French Canada and Rwanda. In P. Dasen (Ed.), *Piagetian psychology: Cross-cultural contributions* (pp. 123–168). New York: Gardner Press.

Leacock, E. B. (1969). *Teaching and learning in city schools.* New York: Basic Books.

Lee, C., & DeVos, G. A. (Eds.). (1981). *Koreans in Japan: Ethnic conflicts and accommodation.* Berkeley: University of California Press.

Lerner, R. M. (1984). *On the nature of human plasticity.* Cambridge, England: Cambridge University Press.

LeVine, R. A. (1967a). Father-child relationship and changing life-styles in Ibadan, Nigeria. In H. Miner (Ed.), *The city in modern Africa*. New York: Praeger.

LeVine, R. A. (1967b). *Dreams and deeds: Achievement motivation in Nigeria*. Chicago: University of Chicago Press.

LeVine, R. A. (1974a). Child rearing as cultural adaptation. In P.H. Leiderman, S. R. Tulkin, & A. Rosenfeld (Eds.), *Culture and infancy: Variations in the human experience* (pp. 15–28). New York: Academic Press.

LeVine, R. A. (1974b). Parental goals: A cross-cultural view. *Teachers College Records, 76* (1), 226–239.

LeVine, R. A. (1974c). *Culture, behavior, and personality*. Chicago: Aldine.

Malinowski, B. (1927). *Sex and repression in savage society*. London: Routledge & Kegan Paul.

Malinowski, B. (1929). *The sexual life of savages*. New York: Harcourt, Brace & World.

Mead, M. (1928). *Coming of age in Samoa*. New York: William Morrow.

Metge, J. (1967). *The Maoris of New Zealand*. New York: Humanities Press.

Myrdal, G. (1944). *An American dilemma: The Negro problem and modern democracy*. New York: Harper & Brothers.

Ogbu, J. U. (1974). *The next generation: An ethnography of education in an urban neighborhood*. New York: Academic Press.

Ogbu, J. U. (1978). *Minority education and caste: The American system in cross-cultural perspective*. New York: Academic Press.

Ogbu, J. U. (1979). Social stratification and socialization of competence. *Anthropology and Education Quarterly 10*(1), 3–20.

Ogbu, J. U. (1981). Origins of human competence: A cultural-ecological perspective. *Child Development, 52,* 413–429.

Ogbu, J. U. (1982). Socialization: A cultural ecological approach. In K. M. Borman (Ed.), *The social life of children in a changing society* (pp. 253–267). Hillsdale, NJ: Lawrence Erlbaum Associates.

Ogbu, J. U. (1983). Minority status and schooling in plural societies. *Comparative Education Review, 27*(2), 168–190.

Ogbu, J. U. (1984). *Understanding community forces affecting minority students' academic effort*. Unpublished manuscript, prepared for the Achievement Council of California, Oakland, CA.

Ogbu, J. U. (1985a). A cultural ecology of competence among inner-city blacks. In M. B. Spencer, G. K. Brookins, & W. R. Allen (Eds.), *Beginnings: Social and affective development of black children* (pp. 45–66). Hillsdale, NJ: Lawrence Erlbaum Associates.

Ogbu, J. U. (1985b). *Schooling in the ghetto: An ecological perspective on community and home influences*. (ERIC Document Reproduction Service No. ED 252-270)

Ogbu, J. U. (1985c). Cultural-ecological influences on minority education. *Language Arts, 62*(8), 860–869.

Ogbu, J. U. (1986a). *Cross-cultural study of minority education: Contributions from Stockton research*. Paper presented at the 23rd annual J. William Harris Lecture, School of Education, University of the Pacific, Stockton, CA.

Ogbu, J. U. (1986b). Class stratification, racial stratification, and schooling. In L. Weis (Ed.), *Race, class and schooling* (pp. 6–35). Special Studies in Comparative Education #17. Comparative Education Center, State University of New York at Buffalo.

Ogbu, J. U. (1986c). *Identity, cultural frame, and schooling among subordinate minorities*. Working Paper #4. Unpublished manuscript, University of California at Berkeley, Department of Anthropology.

Ogbu, J. U., & Matute-Bianchi, M. E. (1986). Understanding sociocultural factors in education: Knowledge, identity and adjustment. In *Beyond language: Social and cultural factors in schooling language minority students* (pp. 72–143). Sacramento: California State Department of Education, Bilingual Education Office.

Okonji, O. M. (1971). A cross-cultural study of the effects of familiarity on classificatory behavior. *Journal of Cross-Cultural Psychology, 2,* 39–49.

Petroni, F. A. (1970). "Uncle Toms": White stereotypes in the black movement. *Human Organization* 29(4), 260–266.

Posner, J. (1982). The development of mathematical knowledge in two West African societies. *Child Development, 53,* 200–208.

Price-Williams, D. R., Gordon, W., & Ramirez, M. (1969). Skills and conservation: A study of pottery-making children. *Developmental Psychology, 1,* 769.

Ramey, C. T., & Suarez, T. M. (1985). Early intervention and the early experience paradigm: Toward a better framework for social policy. *Journal of Children in Contemporary Society 7*(1), 3–13.

Rohlen, T. (1983). Education: Policies and prospects. In C. Lee & G. A. DeVos (Eds.), *Koreans in Japan: Ethnic conflicts and accommodation* (pp. 182–222). Berkeley: University of California Press.

Saxe, G. B., & Posner, J. (1983). The development of numerical cognition: Cross-cultural perspectives. In H. P. Ginsburg (Ed.), *The development of mathematical thinking* (pp. 291–317). New York: Academic Press.

Schmidt, F. H. (1970). *Spanish surname American employment in the Southwest.* Washington, DC: U.S. Government Printing Office.

Scribner, S., & Cole, M. (1973). Cognitive consequences of formal and informal education. *Science, 182,* 553–559.

Seagrim, G. N., & Lendon, R. J. (1980). *Furnishing the mind: A comparative study of cognitive development in Central Australia Aborigines.* New York: Academic Press.

Seeley, J. R., Sim, H. A., & Loosley, E. W. (1956). *Crestwood Heights: A study of the culture of suburban life.* New York: Basic Books.

Serpell, R. (1982, July). *Intellectual handicap in a cross-cultural perspective.* Paper presented at the Sixth International Congress of the International Association for Cross-Cultural Psychology, University of Aberdeen, Scotland, U.K.

Sharp, D., Cole, M., & Lave, C. (1979). Education and cognitive development: The evidence from experimental research. *Monographs of the Society for Research in Child Development, 44* 1–2, (Serial No. 178).

Spencer, M. B. (1985). Cultural cognition and social cognition as identity correlates of black children's personal–social development. In M. B. Spencer, G. K. Brookins, & W. R. Allen (Eds.), *Beginnings: Social and affective development of black children* (pp. 215–230). Hillsdale, NJ: Lawrence Erlbaum Associates.

Spicer, E. H. (1962). *Cycles of conquest: The impact of Spain, Mexico and the United States on the Indians of the Southwest, 1533–1960.* Tucson: The University of Arizona Press.

Stevenson, H. (1982). Influences of schooling on cognitive development. In D. A. Wagner & H. W. Stevenson (Eds.), *Cultural perspectives on child development* (pp. 208–224). San Francisco: W. H. Freeman.

Suarez-Orozco, M. (1985, May). *Opportunity, family dynamics and achievement: The socio-cultural context of motivation among recent immigrants from Central America.* Paper presented at the University of California Symposium on Linguistic Minority Education, Tahoe City.

Travers, J. R. (1982). Testing in educational placement: Issues and evidence. In K. Heller (Eds.), *Placing children in special education: A strategy for equity* (pp. 230–261). Washington, DC: National Academy Press.

Vernon, P. E. (1969). *Intelligence and cultural environment.* London: Methuen & Co.

Wigdor, A. K., & Garner, W. R. (Eds.). (1982). *Ability testing: Uses, consequences, and controversies* (Part II: Documentation). Washington, DC: National Academy Press.

Young, V. H. (1970). Family and childhood in a Southern Negro community. *American Anthropologist, 72,* 269–288.

Zhov, P. J. (1980). *The effects of father-absence on boys in an African patrilineal society.* Unpublished master's thesis, University of Zambia, Lusaka, Zambia.

Chapter 14

Continuity and Change in the Context of Poverty
Adolescent Mothers and Their Children

J. Brooks-Gunn and Frank F. Furstenberg, Jr.

The ways in which developmentalists study the individual across the life span have been changing in the last decade, in part because of accumulating evidence about the flexibility of the organism to respond to environmental alterations and to reorganize behavior in response to internal and external challenges. The ability to adapt to different contextual factors always has been a feature of developmental conceptualizations, as is illustrated by the inclusion of accommodation as well as assimiliation in Piagetian theory (1937, 1952), the interactive nature of Werner's conceptualizations (1948, 1957), and the early (and continuing) debates about the relative contribution of early environment to cognitive functioning (Brooks-Gunn & Weinraub, 1983; Crissey, 1937; Skodak, 1939). However, systematic study of the environment by psychologists did not become a primary research focus until the late 1960s, as development typically was considered to be relatively inflexible and primarily controlled by maturation, or malleable only at very early ages.

The methodologies used, the topics chosen, and the conceptual models offered were constrained by the following three beliefs about development (Lerner, 1985). First, the early experience of the organism shapes an individual in such a way that later change, although possible, was believed difficult to initiate and not likely to be enduring. The seminal work of Bloom (1961), Hunt (1961), and others not only reinforced this notion but in part also led to proportionately more research on early childhood than on any other life phase. Second, development was seen as essentially a within-the-person phenomenon, with contextual features having a relatively small impact. Research concentrated upon cognition, language, and neuromotor growth, especially as age-graded and physiologically linked, rather than on environmental effects. Third, development was thought to proceed in a fairly standard sequence for all persons; individual differences in life courses and the existence of various multidetermined developmental paths were not a focus of study. One of the most important contributions to developmental research has been a critical examination of these three beliefs, as well as the methodologies and models underlying them. Research has demonstrated that change occurs across the life span, that developmental life courses are not entirely determined by early childhood experiences, and that contextual features both enhance and constrain

The research reported in this chapter was supported by a grant from the Commonwealth Fund, whose assistance is greatly appreciated. A complete accounting of the Baltimore Study may be found in Furstenberg, Brooks-Gunn, and Morgan (1987). *Adolescent mothers in later life*. New York: Cambridge University Press.

the potential for change, the end result being an alteration in all three beliefs (Baltes & Brim, 1979, 1980, 1981; Baltes & Nesselroade, 1973; Brim & Kagan, 1980; Gollin, 1981).

Today, development is more likely to be characterized as an interaction between the organism and the environment and as a process with elements of both continuity and discontinuity. Plasticity in development is no longer believed to occur only in the early years. Furthermore, the conditions under which change is possible are being systematically studied, specifically in models focused on the interaction of person characteristics and environmental characteristics (Bronfenbrenner, 1985). Finally, the limitations of plasticity also are being explored, as the idea that constraints on change may buffer the individual from negative consequences gains acceptance. Our current conceptualization of development, especially as plasticity is concerned, is exemplified by the following statement (Scarr, 1982):

> Human beings are made neither of glass that breaks in the slightest ill wind nor of steel that stands defiantly in the face of devastating hurricanes. Rather, in this view, humans are made of the newer plastics—they bend with environmental pressures, resume their shapes when the pressures are relieved, and are unlikely to be permanently misshapen by transient experiences. When bad environments are improved, peoples' adaptations improve. Human beings are resilient and responsive to the disadvantages their environments provide. Even adults are capable of improved adaptations through learning, although any individual's improvement depends on that person's responsiveness to learning opportunities. (p. 853)

PLASTICITY AND CHILDREN IN POVERTY

The life-span approach is of great relevance to those who study families of poverty, and who wish to ameliorate developmental delay or enhance child competency via specific, directed interventions. At the heart of the matter is no longer whether change is possible in childhood or adolescence, but (1) how much change is likely to occur, (2) in which behavioral domains change is most likely, (3) what contexts are most likely to promote change, (4) what

circumstances are necessary in order to maintain change, and (5) which individuals are likely to benefit from a specific context or intervention strategy. Put more succinctly, the challenge is to understand the range of plasticity across age, functions, and structures (Lerner, 1985).

Systematic attempts to alter cognitive functioning of disadvantaged individuals have focused on early childhood, in part because of beliefs about plasticity in this age group. Several approaches to studying plasticity have been taken. Perhaps the most pragmatic and most significant have been the heroic efforts to alter the incidence of developmental delays in disadvantaged children at risk of such delay. Since social service programs do not engage in what is often considered to be a radical intervention, that of ameliorating poverty, services are provided in order to make poverty less onerous for families (for example, the Special Supplemental Food Program for Women, Infants, and Children [WIC program], Aid to Families with Dependent Children [AFDC], food stamps) or to prevent poverty from repeating itself across generations (for example, Head Start, Title IX). In neither case are families given the means to move out of poverty. In terms of prevention of the intergenerational transmission of poverty, the cognitive functioning of the child is the focus, in the hope that academic success, completion of high school, and entrance into the work force will occur.

Programs are targeted toward the parent, the child, or the interaction between the two. Programs may attempt to alter maternal internal resources for coping with an impoverished existence (i.e., programs focusing on decision-making strategies, maternal self-esteem, efficacy), they may try to urge the mother to move toward self-sufficiency (via schooling, job training, or entrance into the work force), or they may operate in an advocacy role to obtain more services for the family (or, in ideal circumstances, to help the mother be a better consumer of the myriad of social service programs). Child-oriented approaches provide a substitute experience for the child, typically in terms of enriched environments, caregiver interactions more akin to those practiced by the middle class, and better nutrition. These experiences almost always occur in the context of day care. Strategies for influencing the mother's child-directed behaviors include programs to teach her how to interact with her child in more middle-class ways, to alter her expectancies for child achievement, to provide knowledge about child-rearing practices, and to encourage maternal participation in child-care programs. Most early-childhood programs include aspects of maternal-, child-, and interaction-oriented strategies, in order to maximize success in preventing developmental delay. However laudatory in terms of helping children, such an approach makes it difficult and almost impossible to estimate the relative efficacy of the various strategies (see, as an exception, the recent meta-analysis of Head Start programs, McKey et al., 1985). Thus, although we know that early intervention programs may reduce the incidence of developmental delay, we do not know under what conditions or for what children this change takes place.

Another approach to understanding plasticity in the disadvantaged child is to elucidate the environmental factors associated with developmental delay, rather than providing experiences to prevent its occurrence. Myriads of studies have looked at the relationship between child competencies and environmental characteristics. Studies range from a focus on only a few factors, to a focus on the interplay between all of the contexts in which the child operates; they range from simple correlational, to causal modeling analyses; and from single studies to meta-analyses. Structural measures typically include ethnic, economic, educational, and marital status. Familial measures are primarily assessments of the home environment (e.g., crowding, provision of educational materials, safety, opportunities for interaction with adults), of maternal behaviors (e.g., responsivity, control, warmth, verbal discourse, punitiveness), and of family composition (presence of male adult, number of siblings, number of persons in the home, movement in and out of the home). This vast literature allows for some estimates

of the relative effects of certain factors upon child functioning but does not give much insight into differences in outcomes among the disadvantaged. Why do some children from poor families do better than their neighbors, who are also in dire straits? Borrowing from the developmental psychopathology literature, we may ask why some children are resilient and some vulnerable to adverse circumstances, and what individual and familial characteristics make it possible to overcome potentially negative circumstances, or make it possible to benefit from a particular educational intervention. The use of a life-span–developmental approach allows for an examination of these examination of these questions.

To effect a change in any organism is difficult. Developmental trajectories, once set in motion, must encounter a significant force to alter them. This may be particularly true in early childhood, when growth may be more canalized or determined than in later childhood (McCall, Hogarty, & Hurlburt, 1972; Scarr & McCartney, 1983). Indeed, if growth is more canalized, the gains of intervention programs are particularly impressive but also may explain why so many gains are short lived. Later in life, individual proclivities may play a larger role in the alteration of an individual's developmental trajectory. Such changes, although still requiring a significant force, may be more long-lasting in that the individual is able to alter his or her circumstances in order to maintain the change. The older child may be able to select actively certain environments and may evoke certain responses from others. The young child, not having as much control over his or her environmental contexts, may find maintenance of a new trajectory difficult, unless it is congruent with his or her characteristics, both acquired and inherited (such as curiosity, inherent ability, developed skills), or results in a change in the significant others who control resources and environmental circumstances.

As an example of the potential usefulness of a life-span approach in understanding the possibility for change in the young child (in this case amelioration of highly probable developmental delays) and the efficacy of intervention to effect such change, we present findings from a 17-year follow-up of teenage mothers and their children—referred to here as the Baltimore Study. Our goal was to examine those situations, individual characteristics, and life events occurring after early parenthood that enhanced the young women's chances of succeeding, or, in very unambiguous terms, of finishing high school, being employed fairly continuously, and being well-off economically. Overall, the life chances of the teenage mother are reduced, compared to young women who postpone parenthood. Indeed, one of the more well-known and early statements about the ill effects of teenage childbearing is as follows (Cambell, 1968):

> The girl who has an illegitimate child at the age of 16 suddenly has 90 percent of her life's script written for her. She will probably drop out of school; even if someone else in her family helps to take care of the baby, she will probably not be able to find a steady job that pays enough to provide for herself and her child; she may feel impelled to marry someone she might not otherwise have chosen. Her life choices are few, and most of them are bad. (p. 238)

This passage probably is a gross overestimate of the lack of plasticity in life courses, even for disadvantaged teens for whom an early pregnancy adds appreciably to their burden in finishing school and obtaining a job. The stereotype of the teenage mother as being on the dole with lots of children belies the diversity in outcomes as well as strategies for overcoming an unplanned and potentially disruptive life event.

The mother's struggle to overcome the additional burden of having a child when she is attempting to finish school and enter the job market may affect her child's life chances as well as her own. For example, the young mother may not have much time available to spend with her child; she may need to piece together complex child-rearing arrangements; she may not be the most competent of parents, due to her own immaturity; her knowledge about child-rearing in general may be inadequate; and of course, she may be economically disad-

vantaged. Such conditions are believed to place the *children* of teenage parents at risk for developmental delays, social and emotional problems, and early childbearing themselves, thus helping to perpetuate a cycle of disadvantage. On the basis of rather little evidence, the supposition that disadvantage is transmitted intergenerationally in families with teenage parents has been accepted by the public and portrayed in the media. The impoverished lives of the teenage mother and the conditions in which her children grow up are believed to contribute to high rates of school failure and juvenile delinquency. In short, the children are seen as ill-fated.

In fact, very little is known about the life course of the children of adolescent mothers or the mothers themselves, except over the short term. In addition, how early parenthood affects their life chances is poorly understood. Whether early parenthood per se results in deleterious outcomes through some unspecified pathway, or whether the children of early childbearers and the childbearers themselves are only worse off because of their disadvantaged status, has not been determined. The 17-year follow-up of Baltimore Study participants was designed in order to examine the mother's life course and the potential for change in eventual economic and academic success, as well as the effect of maternal life-course decisions upon children's development.

TEENAGE PARENTHOOD: THE PROBLEM THAT WON'T GO AWAY

Teenage childbearing has always been common in America but was not considered a social problem until the 1960s. Indeed, the fertility rate among teenagers has declined over the past 25 years, as illustrated in Figure 1. However, the relative share of births born to teenage as opposed to adult women increased substantially, from 12% in 1955 to 16% in 1979, and 29% of all first births were to teenagers in 1979. This is because the absolute number of teenagers is large (due to the baby boom) and because fertility rates for women in their 20s have declined even more rapidly than those for

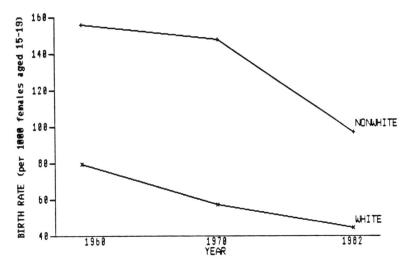

Figure 1.   Birth rates in the United States for 15- to 19-year-olds by race and year. (From Brooks-Gunn, J., & Furstenberg, F. F., Jr. [1986]. The children of adolescent mothers: Physical, academic and psychological outcomes. *Developmental Review, 6;* reprinted by permission.) Sources: Adolescent Pregnancy and Childbearing: Rates, Trends and Research Findings: Collaborative Perinatal Study, NICHD, October, 1984; United States Bureau of the Census, Current Population Reports, Series P-20, No. 385; (National Center for Health Statistics Annual Volumes).

teenagers. Perhaps the most pressing problem is that more and more babies are being born out of wedlock today than ever before. Out-of-wedlock fertility rates have soared; the percentage of all births to teenagers that were out of wedlock jumped from 14% in 1955 to 53% in 1983. The costs of supporting a family, the high rates of unemployment among young adult males, and the likelihood of high-school dropout in almost one half of all teenage mothers all have made early family formation—which may have seemed ill-advised even in the 1960s—all the more misguided in the 1970s and 1980s. Much of the concern is centered on the fact that a large proportion of unmarried young mothers receive Aid to Families with Dependent Children (Moore & Burt, 1982). And, of the out-of-wedlock births, almost half are to adolescents.

Not surprisingly, in short-term comparisons with teenagers who do not become mothers, early childbearers are much more likely to drop out of school, have difficulties in the job market, and become reliant on public assistance. In the face of these dismal facts, it is easy to abandon hope that the life courses of teenage mothers will change, via intervention or the mothers' own efforts, and to forget that great diver-

sity exists among teenage mothers. Virtually all existing studies show tremendous variation in the short-term outcomes of early parenthood. In addition, the focus of existing studies is on the years immediately following the birth of the first child. Taking a reading of a young parent's adjustment shortly after the transition to motherhood and during the often troubled adolescent years may provide an especially negative impression of her eventual capacity as a mother and a productive member of society.

THE BALTIMORE STUDY

The Baltimore Study was initiated in order to remedy two limitations of our current knowledge about the effects of teenage parenthood. By following 300 teenage mothers into their mid and late 30s, the changes in their social and economic circumstances in the 12 years between the 5- and 17-year follow-ups were charted. This study is the only investigation to date that has traced the life course of adolescent parents from first pregnancy to later adulthood, looking both at childbearers and their offspring.

The purpose of the study was to explore the following five questions: (1) What is the extent to which poverty and lower socioeconomic status persist over the life course of young mothers and their children? (2) How and why are certain teenage mothers able to escape poverty? (3) What are the long-term effects, if any, of comprehensive prenatal care, postnatal family planning and attendance at a special high school for teenage mothers? (4) Does disadvantage seem to persist in certain families; that is, is there any evidence for the belief in the intergenerational transmission of poverty? and (5) How do the children of teenage parents fare as they enter their own adolescent years?

The Baltimore Study was initiated in 1966 as an evaluation of one of the first comprehensive care programs for adolescent mothers in the country. At Sinai Hospital, adolescent mothers received comprehensive prenatal and postnatal care either in a clinic tailored to teenage mothers' special needs, or in the regular hospital clinics via random assignment. The evaluation eventually led to a 5-year follow-up of a cohort of some 400 adolescent mothers and their first-born children. The study contrasted their transition to adulthood with the experiences of their classmates who had delayed childbearing. Individual differences in the adaptation to early parenthood were explained as a function of participation in the Sinai program, characteristics of the young parents, assistance provided by their families and friends, and services offered by welfare agencies and a special school for pregnant teens in Baltimore (see Furstenberg, 1976 and Furstenberg, Brooks-Gunn, & Morgan, 1987, for a complete description of the 5-year and 17-year follow-up, respectively).

The participants in the Baltimore study were seen five different times, as shown in Table 1, which depicts the design of the study. In 1972, about 5 years after the first child was born, 331 of the young mothers were interviewed and their children's social and cognitive functioning was assessed. In 1983, we attempted to locate the 400 families. Almost 90% were found, and 81%, or 324 families, were interviewed at that time.

Perhaps a critical factor in the success of this project was the location of 89% of the original Baltimore-Study families. The Institute for Survey Research in Philadelphia is to be com-

Table 1. Design of the Baltimore Study, 1966–1984

Interview schedule	Interview dates	Participants	Attempted interviews	Completed interviews[a]	
				N	%
Time 1: during pregnancy	1966–1968	Adolescent mothers, grandmothers	404 379	404 350	100 92
Time 2: 1 year after delivery	1968–1970	Adolescent mothers	404	382	95
Time 3: 3 years after delivery	1970	Adolescent mothers,[b] classmates	404 361	363 268	90 74
Time 4: 5 years after delivery	1972	Adolescent mothers, children of adolescent mothers, classmates	404 331 307	331 306 221	82 92 72
Time 5: 16–17 years after delivery	1983–1984	Adolescent mothers or surrogates	404	289 33	80
		Children of adolescent mothers	392	296	76
		National Survey of Children (blacks, 14–16 years old)		450	

From: Furstenberg, F. F., Jr., Brooks-Gunn, J., & Morgan, P. (1987). *Adolescent mothers in later life.* New York: Cambridge University Press; reprinted with permission.

[a]This category includes a small number of interviews that were excluded from the analysis because of a large amount of missing or falsified information.

[b]Interviews were also obtained with about one third of the fathers at this time.

mended for their devotion to the tracing effort. Of course some attrition did occur, primarily in white families and in families who had left Baltimore in the years immediately following the birth of the child. Thus, our findings apply to urban blacks, who contribute disproportionately to teenage fertility in the United States, but who do not make up the majority of adolescent parents.

Possible limitations of the study design could restrict the generalizability of the conclusions, over and above the fact that the findings focus on urban blacks. The participants in the Baltimore Study were not selected at random but were recruited from a hospital clinic. As best we could determine, participants were similar to the general population of blacks in Baltimore. Also, our results were similar to those from several cross-sectional national surveys of black women in their middle 30s (see Furstenberg, et al., 1987). Nevertheless, our data are based on a single cohort, which, as is always the case, has a unique historical experience. The women came of age in the era of the Great Society and as such received a fairly generous amount of public support. At the same time, they may have been the last cohort of teenagers to believe that early marriage is a viable strategy for responding to premature parenthood. A substantial number left school in order to marry as soon as possible. Their daughters, who became early childbearers, may respond differently than their mothers did, especially in terms of marriage.

In this chapter, we focus on three time periods of the child's life—birth, the 5th year, and the 16th year. From the perspective of the mother, the focus is on the pregnancy, the early 20s (when child-rearing was still a predominant life task), and the mid to late 30s (when child-rearing was ending).

The Mother's Life Course

Based on the findings of the 5-year follow-up concluded in 1972, we had expected to discover a certain amount of variation in the life courses of the women in our study in 1984. The earlier statement that 90% of a teenage mother's life script is written appeared to be something of an exaggeration on the basis of what we already knew (Furstenberg, 1976). However, we were unprepared for the extent of diversity that emerged when the results of the 17-year follow-up were examined, or for the improvement seen over time between 1972 and 1984. We illustrate this diversity by presenting findings for fertility, education, jobs, welfare, and marital status (see Furstenberg et al., 1987, for a comprehensive discussion of these results).

Between 1972 and 1984, 56% of the women in the study reported that they attended school at least part of 1 year. A sixth of the women completed high school in the 12 years, or one third of all of those who had not graduated by the time of the 5-year follow-up. A substantial proportion of those women had dropped out and subsequently returned to get a high school diploma or GED. By the 17-year follow-up, 30% of all the women in the sample had received some postsecondary education, and 5% had completed college.

Only 9% of the women in the study had not been employed in any of the 5 years preceding the 1984 follow-up, and 60% had been employed all 5 of those years. At the time of the 1984 interview, more than two thirds were currently employed and over three fourths had worked in the past year. Most current job-holders had been regularly employed for a number of years and were earning between $10,000 and $20,000 annually. Two thirds of the participants had not received any public assistance in any of the preceding 5 years, whereas 13% were on welfare more or less continuously during that period. At the 17-year follow-up, about a quarter of the sample were presently receiving public assistance, though some of these women also held part-time jobs and were only receiving supplementary payments (see Figure 2).

The sample divided almost evenly into four distinct economic subgroups: those on welfare, the working poor with family incomes under $15,000 per year, those women with moderate incomes between $15,000 and $24,999, and the economically secure whose family incomes exceeded $25,000. In view of the conventional

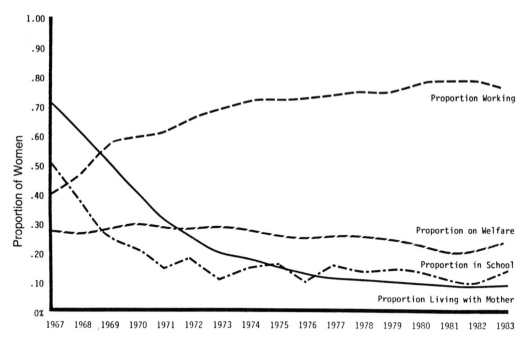

Figure 2.   Proportions working, on welfare, in school, and living with mother by calendar year following first birth (N=290). From Furstenberg, F. F., Jr., Brooks-Gunn, J., & Morgan, P. (1987). *Adolescent mothers in later life.* New York: Cambridge University Press; reprinted with permission.

stereotype of the teenage mother, it is surprising to discover that only a minority, albeit a significant one, were on welfare, and that a quarter had incomes that placed them clearly in the middle class.

The majority of those doing well financially were currently married or living with someone of the opposite sex. With few exceptions the single mothers did not earn enough from their own employment to place them in the top quartile. Virtually none of the married women were currently receiving welfare. Thus, marital and economic status were closely linked.

Almost four fifths of the sample had been married, but only about a third were currently married, and just a quarter were still in first marriages. Two thirds of the first marriages had already ended in separation or divorce, and just over half of the second marriages had dissolved.

Many women actually had had fewer children by 1984 than they had either desired or expected in 1972. About one fifth never had had another birth, and an additional two fifths had had only one more birth. Thirty-one percent had had two births after the study child,

and only 8% of the women had three or more subsequent births. The mean number of children was 2.2. Close to two-thirds of all the births after the study child occurred within the first 5 years of the study. This unexpected pattern of birth spacing suggests that the women became acutely conscious of the costs of additional children over time and made strenuous efforts to curtail their fertility in their 20s and 30s. The remarkable and unanticipated slowdown in the pace of family building was primarily achieved by voluntary sterilization. By 1984, 57% of the women in our sample had been medically sterilized, a figure that exceeds the national average for women in their middle 30s.

Whereas the adolescent mothers in our study fared much better in later life than many observers would have predicted, they unquestionably remained at a disadvantage compared to women who postponed childbearing until their 20s. The blacks in the Baltimore sample were compared to black women between 29 and 36 years of age, with at least one child, who were either early or later childbearers in several other surveys (the 1983 Current Population

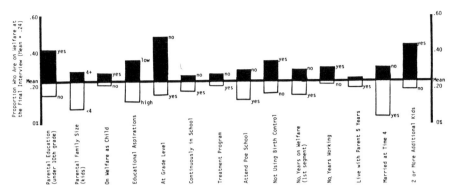

Figure 3.   Predictors of economic dependence in 1984. From Furstenberg, F. F., Jr., Brooks-Gunn, J., & Morgan, P. (1987). *Adolescent mothers in later life.* New York: Cambridge University Press; reprinted with permission.

Survey, a study carried out by the Census Bureau, which focused on fertility and childbearing experience; the 1980 National Longitudinal Survey; and the 1982 National Survey of Family Growth). The results revealed that the Baltimore mothers were less likely to achieve educationally, less likely to be employed, more likely to be receiving welfare, and less likely to be currently married than the later childbearers in the national studies. Disparities in family size did not occur.

Predicting Economic Success and Failure

How do we account for the differences in the mother's adaptation to early childbearing? Some of the major determinants of whether mothers were currently on welfare or whether they had achieved economic security (i.e., a family income of $25,000 or more) in 1984 were examined in separate log linear regressions. We examined a large number of variables that measured the young mother's personal attributes, her family background, the availability of social support, her involvement in two social programs that were designed to provide assistance, and the effect of different career decisions following the birth of her first child.

A summary of the results for predicting economic failure is presented in Figure 3, which illustrates the relative effects of 14 factors upon welfare dependency in 1984, controlling for all other factors. We may ask the question, what proportion of the teenage mothers would have been on welfare in 1984, if all of the mothers had had a certain characteristic? For example,

if *all* of the mothers had gone to the special school for pregnant teens, what proportion of the sample would have been on welfare in 1984? From Figure 3 it is clear that instead of 22% being on welfare, only 15 percent would have been on welfare. As another example, if all of the teenage mothers' parents had had less than a 10th grade education, 42% as opposed to the actual 22% would have been on welfare. And, if none of the teenagers' parents had had less than a 10th grade education, 18% as opposed to the actual 22% would have been on welfare. Thus, Figure 3 presents a summary of the direct effects of 14 factors and allows for a comparison of their relative effects on eventual economic dependency. The same procedure was used to summarize the results of economic security (defined as incomes of over $25,000; see Furstenberg et al., 1987).

Before turning to the factors listed in Figure 3, we must stress that many features of the family of origin, such as the marital status of the teenage mother's parents, whether her mother was employed, or her mother's age were not directly linked to welfare dependency or economic security. The quality of the adolescent's emotional relationship with her parents had no important effect on her adjustment to early childbearing, nor did her initial response to the pregnancy or her age at first pregnancy.

Several early familial factors did have an effect on economic outcome, namely education of the teenager's parents, the size of the family of origin, and their welfare status. Parental education was the most powerful determinant of these factors. Parents with limited education and with more children are probably less capable of assisting their pregnant daughters in remaining in school, and may also be less willing and able to provide emotional and material support to further the educational goals of their children, thus affecting economic security by limiting the educational attainment of their daughters.

Whether or not the adolescent was behind in school (had repeated a grade) at the time of the pregnancy was a powerful determinant of her economic position in later life. Her educational ambitions also were predictive of later economic outcome, independent of parental education and her own grade repetition. Completing high school also is one of the essential keys to economic independence and security. Adolescents who had completed high school before the 5-year follow-up were half as likely to be receiving public assistance and twice as likely to be economically secure in 1984. A substantial number of the adolescents in our study attended the Edgar Allan Poe School, a special educational program for pregnant teenagers, which provided instruction, counselling, childcare assistance, and education during pregnancy, and helped students return to their regular classes following delivery. Attendance at the Poe School significantly reduced the proportion of women on welfare in adulthood. In brief, the educational factors together were the strongest predictors of welfare dependence, as well as of economic success.

Both the probability of receiving welfare and of achieving economic security were strongly influenced by the number of additional births that had occurred in the 5-year period after the birth of the study child. Women who had had two or more additional children by the 5-year follow-up were almost four times more likely to be on welfare at the 17-year follow-up. The teens who were enrolled in the Sinai Hospital comprehensive care program were more likely to have avoided economic dependency in later life, in large part because they had practiced birth control in the year following delivery of their first child.

An important pathway away from economic dependency is marriage—that is stable marriage. Women who had remained with their families for at least 5 years after their first child was born were less likely to be economically secure and more likely to be on welfare in adulthood. Thus, living with one's parents, although important in the early years when child care is necessary in order to finish school or obtain work, can hamper independence later in life.

This summary does not include the indirect paths of influence upon eventual economic success. In the complete model presented in *Adolescent Mothers in Later Life* (Furstenberg et al., 1987), these effects are considered. For example, if the young mothers had had low educational aspirations, they were less than half as likely to have attended the Poe School; they were about 30% less likely to have stayed in school during and after the pregnancy; they were over four times as likely *not* to have finished high school by the 5-year follow-up; and they were almost two and one-half times as likely to have had two or more children, be unmarried, and be on welfare at the 5-year follow-up. However, inclusion of such indirect effects (and the most indirect effects were seen for educational aspirations) does not alter the findings presented in this chapter, given that these indirect effects were controlled in these analyses.

The Children's Life Course

The long-term costs of teenage motherhood to the women were considerably less than we had anticipated, even given the tremendous diversity of outcomes seen at the 5-year follow-up. However, the costs to the children may be considerably more. In order to see whether this was true we reconstructed the life courses of the children from the mothers' reports, from interviews with the children themselves at the 17-year follow-up, and from cognitive assessments at the 5-year follow-up. The children were between 16 and 17 years of age in 1984; their academic achievement, misbehavior in school, and sexual experiences give an idea of whether or not they will finish school, enter the work force, or avoid early parenthood. We may ask, which children perpetuate or break the cycle of disadvantage, and how much influence did the mother's life-course decisions have on the children's ability to succeed?

The complexities of the mothers' lives, as they juggle child care, schooling, jobs, and relationships with men, are mirrored in the potentially significant events in their children's lives, such as separations from the mother, child-care arrangements, and living with an adult male figure. One third of the children had been separated from their mothers at least once for 2 months or more (excluding summer vacation) during their lives. The most common reasons were disciplinary problems, mother's difficulties taking care of the child, and mother being out-of-town. Most typically, the children were living with their grandmother, and to a lesser extent, with their father. Somewhat surprisingly, separations were more common in the teenage than the early- or late-childhood years, perhaps because the mother and adolescent were going through a tumultuous time in their relationship.

Merely because mother and child resided together continuously is not necessarily an indication that the mother was the primary caregiver, however. Many children (40%) had another adult as a primary caregiver during early childhood, as their mothers finished school or worked. In some cases, child care was shared, as in the case where the mother and child lived with the child's grandmother (25% of the families); in others, the child was taken to the grandmother or another relative during the day. However, the majority of mothers were actively involved with their children, and were satisfied with the child-care arrangements. Shared caregiving seemed to be a good compromise between the mother's desires to further herself (and ultimately make a better life for her children) and to provide high quality care for her offspring.

The high rate of marital dissolution, the relatively large number of women who never married, and the frequency of short-term cohabitation relationships translate into the fleeting and unpredictable presence of adult men for the children. With the exception of 9% who had never lived with an adult male (father, step-father, or boyfriend), all of the children had spent some time with a male figure in the household. However, only a handful (16%) were living with the biological father as teenagers. The comparable figure for black children of later childbearers in a national survey is 38% (Furstenberg, Nord, Peterson, & Zill, 1983). A third of the Baltimore teenagers were living with a stepfather. Movement of adult figures in and out of the household was common, so that only 29% of the children lived more than three quarters of their lives with a male figure in the household.

Turning to the academic status of the teenagers, we may look at cognitive functioning at the 5-year follow-up and school failure at the 17-year follow-up. As preschoolers, the children were given the Caldwell Preschool Inventory; one half of the children were functioning above the 50th percentile and one half below, similar to other samples of black urban preschoolers seen in the 1970s. However, their scores were lower than a black, middle-class sample attending preschool in Philadelphia, and lower than a small sample of Baltimore children whose mothers had delayed childbearing until their 20s. Thus, whereas the Baltimore children were not faring as well as more advantaged preschoolers, the differences were not great.

The story is quite different when we turn to the children's high school experience. What we see can only be described as massive school failure. Half of the sample had repeated at least one grade during their school career—59% of the males and 39% of the females. Seventeen percent were currently enrolled in remedial classes, with twice as many boys as girls being so enrolled.

Another perspective on the level of school functioning is provided by examining the record of adjustment in school as reported by adolescents and their parents. According to the adolescents themselves, in the past year, 36% report that because of a behavior problem, their parents were brought to school; 34% of the students have skipped school; 28% have fought at school; and 4% have damaged school prop-

Table 2.   School-related behavior of black adolescents, ages 15–16, by mother's age at first birth: The Baltimore Study, 1984, and The National Survey of Children, 1981

	Baltimore childbearers 14–19 (202)[a]	NSC: Early childbearers 14–19 (35)	NSC: Late childbearers 20 and over (61)
I. School achievement			
Child repeated a grade, ever	53.0[b]	42.9[c]	19.7
Standing in class (% above average)	26.4	29.4	31.0
II. School problems			
Child reports			
Parents brought to school because of student behavior in the past year	40.9	40.0	16.9
Skipped school in the past year	28.5	28.6	9.9
Fought at school in the past year	27.6	37.1	16.9
Damaged school property in the past year	3.4	17.1	2.8
Parent reports			
Parents received note from school about behavior problem in the past 5 years	55.9	54.3	22.5
Child suspended/expelled from school in the past 5 years	48.8	37.1	22.5

From Furstenberg, F. F., Jr., Brooks-Gunn, J., & Morgan, P. (1987). *Adolescent mothers in later life.* New York: Cambridge University Press; reprinted with permission.
[a]Base N's in parentheses.
[b]All numbers are percentage of total. "Don't know" and "No answer" responses eliminated from sample score.
[c]NSC percentages weighted to correct for oversampling.

erty. Fifty-two percent of the parents in the past 5 years have received a note from the school about a behavior problem, and 44% have had children suspended or expelled.

Are the problems seen in this sample of teenagers typical of those seen in other samples of teenagers who were not born to teenage mothers? As a partial answer to this question, the responses from the Baltimore sample were compared with those from the National Survey of Children. Comparisons include only the black adolescents who were 15 to 16 years of age in the Baltimore and National Survey of Children samples. As can be seen in Table 2, school-related problems seen in the adolescents of early childbearers in the Baltimore Study were similar in magnitude to the problems of the teens of early childbearers seen in the National Survey of Children. Both differed substantially from the children of late childbearers, who were having less difficulty in the academic areas. For example, whereas over half of the Baltimore adolescents and 43% of the NSC adolescents of early childbearers had repeated a grade, only 20% of the black adolescents born to later childbearers had done so. In other words, twice as many adolescents whose mothers were early childbearers had repeated a grade as those adolescents whose mothers were later childbearers.

Perhaps the greatest concern of public and policymakers alike has to do with the specter of the children of children perpetuating the cycle of early childbearing. Indeed, even teenage mothers themselves worry about what one of our Baltimore Study mothers, no doubt having read the term in the media, called "the cycle of having babies." Does being raised in a family where teenage parenthood has occurred influence sexual decisions of the next generation of teenagers? To explore this issue, we return to the National Survey of Children, comparing the black 15- to 16-year-olds whose mothers were teenagers or older at the time of their first child's birth. Having a teenage mother increases the likelihood of starting to have intercourse as an adolescent: 39% of those adolescents whose mothers were late childbearers have had intercourse versus 57% for those whose mothers were early childbearers. The same-aged Baltimore adolescents were even more likely to be sexually experienced than their peers in the National Survey of Children; 78% reported having had intercourse already. This percentage is similar to that reported by Zabin and her colleagues (Zabin, Hardy, Streett, & King, 1984) for Baltimore youth.

As might be expected from the large differentials in the incidence of intercourse between teenagers born to early and late childbearers, it comes as no surprise that the former are also more likely to become pregnant. In the National Survey of Children, 11% of the adolescents whose mothers were early childbearers, as opposed to none of the adolescents whose mothers were older childbearers, reported a pregnancy (or getting a girl pregnant). In the comparable subsample of Baltimore teens, the incidence was 14%. For the total sample, 16% reported a pregnancy—25% of the girls and 6% of the boys.

In brief, the mothers' struggles to avoid poverty levied a cost on their children, as measured by academic achievement and management of sexuality. The amount of time available, the need for complex child-care arrangements, the absence of the father, lowered educational attainment, and in some cases, reduced economic circumstances, all are part of the adolescent mothers' experiences. Even with the help of family and friends in child rearing, these obstacles were not (and probably could not) be totally overcome.

We wish to stress that mothers were not indifferent to their children. In fact most mothers felt they have done a good job, in less than ideal circumstances. At the same time, the mothers were very realistic about the consequences of early parenthood for themselves and potentially for their children. The mothers knew that avoiding pregnancy, completing school, and postponing marriage are most likely to ensure later success; these three factors were, in fact, the best predictors of their own economic achievement. As one mother said when asked what she wanted her daughter to do, "I wouldn't want her to have a child early; I wouldn't want her to marry early, and I wouldn't want her to be a secretary."

Interconnections between the Maternal Life Course and Child Outcomes

By examining the occurence, timing, and sequencing of multiple events in the mother's life course, we were able to explain some of the variability in the women's economic status and fertility at the 17-year follow-up. We also asked whether or not variability in the children's outcome could be understood in terms of the timing and sequencing of maternal life events. Of specific interest are the role of environment upon child competence and the degree of continuity or discontinuity in the developmental trajectories from the preschool to the high school years.

Continuity has perhaps been the central theme in developmental longitudinal research since the publication of *Birth to Maturity* (Kagan & Moss, 1962) and perhaps even earlier (see Brim & Kagan, 1980). Continuity typically is believed to be domain-specific, to be mediated by environmental events, to be fairly elusive from the infancy years onward (with the exception, perhaps, of development in certain risk groups), to become stronger in the preschool years, and to be stronger for cognitive rather than social development (an exception might be preschool behavior problems; Rutter, 1979). Given that we had information on the children at three time points (infancy, preschool, and adolescent years), it was possible to see the degree of continuity characteristic of child behavior in three domains—academic, behavior, and personality. Moderate to high continuity for academic and behavior problems was seen, in keeping with other studies (see also Kellum, Ensminger, & Turner, 1977). For example, a one standard deviation change in the Preschool Inventory increased the likelihood of having failed a grade by 80%. Cross-domain continuity was not found.

Clearly, then, once a trajectory was set, in terms of preschool academic or behavior problems, it was likely to continue. But what of environmental effects? We know that maternal characteristics are related to preschool functioning (Wachs & Gruen, 1982), and our findings are no exception. For example, a child whose mother was not married, was on welfare, had three or more children, and was not in school at the 5-year follow-up, had a Preschool Inventory score 30 points lower than a child whose mother was married, was not on welfare, was in school, and had less than three children. And, as adolescents, having a mother with these four characteristics (replacing not being in school with not being a high school graduate) increased the likelihood of grade failure 11 times over a child whose mother did not have these characteristics (see Table 3).

It is critical to remember, however, that negative environmental conditions do not always relate to deleterious child outcomes. This is illustrated by looking at behavior problems. In the preschool years, maternal ratings of problems (as uncooperative, rude, or disobedient) are strongly linked to welfare status, weakly linked to family size, and unrelated to the mother's marital and school status. At the high school follow-up, recent welfare experience and mother being unmarried are related to

behavior problems such as being expelled from school, stealing, being stopped by police, and running away. Family size and maternal education were *not* associated with these child outcomes. Thus, at both ages welfare is related to behavior problems, maternal education is not; family size is at 5 years, and marital status is at 16 years.

Thus far, our analyses are similar to other cross-sectional and longitudinal studies (see also Garmezy & Rutter, 1983; Kagan & Moss, 1962; Kellum et al., 1977; Rutter, 1979). What is unique about this study is the attempt to interconnect the life decisions of mothers and their children's developmental trajectories. Many mothers altered their life-course trajectories over the 17 years. How did this affect their children's life chances? Four different models were tested, one in which mother's life course did not affect child outcome, one in which the maternal status had an influence in the early years of life only, one in which the influence was in the adolescent years only, and one in which maternal influences occurred at both time points. Not surprisingly, perhaps, the most predictive model was contingent upon the maternal characteristic and child behavior under examination. Thus, environmental effects are fairly specific, rather than diffuse, and also are contingent on age of the child and behavioral domain under consideration.

Consider the example of academic success. Maternal welfare status influences schooling in preschool and high school. A trajectory for academic failure is set in motion by early welfare experiences, which limits preschool functioning. However, moving off welfare will reduce the likelihood of subsequent grade failure, even though grade repetition is related to low preschool scores. In contrast, current marital status and educational status influence school performance in the adolescent but not in the preschool years, suggesting that later maternal events, independent of their earlier occurrence, may influence behavior.

Finally, high fertility is a negative predictor of academic performance in preschool but not in adolescence, suggesting that rapid subsequent fertility reduces time and resources spent

Table 3. Percent of adolescents who failed a grade by maternal characteristics

Maternal characteristic	Yes	No[a]
Married at 5-year follow-up	37	57
On welfare for 5–15 years	71	43
3+ children ever born by 5-year follow-up	58	45
Completed high school	43	65

[a]All χ^2 values are significant at the .05 level.

on the first child. Later births have less of an effect on young children, perhaps because of the primacy of time demands in the first years of life.

Using behavior problems as the child outcome, a different set of trajectories is found. Early, not late, welfare experiences influence behavior problems; the early effect is still seen in adolescence because of strong life-course trajectories in behavior problems. In contrast, marital status in the adolescent but not in the preschool years is associated with behavior problems, just as it was in academic problems. Since family support was more available in the early years to young mothers, perhaps not having a father in the household at that time is offset by the presence of other adult relatives (see Kellum et al., 1977). By the adolescent years, such support is less likely to be forthcoming, so that shared caregiving arrangements are rarer and adolescents in single-parent households have fewer adults to which they can turn. Finally, maternal education has little effect at either age point, suggesting the importance of separating out effects of maternal education, single parenthood, family size, and welfare status.

In brief, then, clear connections between the life courses of mother and children exist. And, environmental effects are seen on academic and behavior problems. *However, no single model describes the impact of maternal decisions upon children's developmental trajectories.* Although most life-span developmentalists will not be surprised by this finding, few studies have examined developmental trajectories in terms of changes in the maternal life course.

THE LONG TERM: POLICY IMPLICATIONS

Perhaps the most striking result of the Baltimore Study is the tremendous diversity in the long-term adaptation to early childbearing. Adolescent mothers do not do as well in later life as women who postpone parenthood, but many manage to offset partially the handicap of giving birth as teens. The invidious stereotype

of the adolescent childbearer may underestimate young mothers' chances of recovery. Ironically, part of the handicap of being a teenage mother may come from the belief that opportunities in later life may be severely curtailed. Those teens who do succeed are not socially visible, whereas the failures are quite prominent because of their reliance on social services. Service providers are likely to see those who have not succeeded, or those who are experiencing a temporary setback, thereby reinforcing the impression that a young mother's chances of recovery are limited. Even our media images of the teen parent take a short-term perspective, reinforcing the notion that the young mother's life script is not amenable to change, that avenues of opportunity are not open. Instead, a variety of strategies to overcome poverty not only exist but are actively attempted. The beliefs that life chances are foreclosed after childhood and that individuals may not alter their trajectories via chance or effort are not limited to social scientists. Indeed, one of our tasks may be to demonstrate new conceptualizations of development, especially those demonstrating malleability across the life span, to those outside of our respective disciplines.

The experience of our participants shows that some mothers are more at risk for long-term disadvantage than others. Mothers whose parents had limited schooling, who were from large families, and who were on welfare as children were more likely to rely on public assistance and less likely to exit from the welfare rolls in later life. The intergenerational transmission of cultural disadvantage has been thought to follow this pattern—families on welfare begetting a disproportionate number of future welfare recipients.

However, the group is relatively small, smaller than is generally believed by most observers, and even in these high-risk families, many offspring manage to escape the cycle of poverty, especially through education. Although they constitute a small group, pregnant girls from welfare families are at high risk of reduced life chances. They may also be the group for which intervention is most difficult to implement and maintain. However, the ability to identify the highest risk group is important from a policy standpoint for several reasons. First, programs may be tailored to the specific needs of this group. Second, more intensive and comprehensive programs may be designed for this group. Third, more systematic recruitment and maintenance efforts may be mounted, in order to capture what may turn out to be a very elusive group of girls. Strategies to enhance motivation and ultimately compliance must be developed, especially to assist what we have termed the high-risk teenage parent. Whereas this group may be the most difficult to serve, it is also the group for which the payoff is highest. Because high risk teens probably receive a disproportionate share of the resources directed toward the adolescent parent, any positive change could make a substantial difference in resource expenditure. The same is true for their children.

Even more important than family background in escaping poverty are the academic interests and abilities of the teenager herself. In addition, those adolescents who are less academically competent may be at higher risk of early parenthood than those who are more competent or motivated. It may be desirable to implement special educational programs, especially for students with low motivation or repeated school failure, to ease the transition to early childbearing as well as to prevent early pregnancies. Regular school may not be a wise choice for the low-ability teenage mother, given her previous school history. A program emphasizing basic skills and their usefulness in a job environment may be more successful with such students.

It has been difficult to demonstrate that special educational and family planning programs are effective tools for ameliorating the adverse consequences of early childbearing. Despite the fact that hundreds of programs exist around the country for pregnant teens and young mothers, very few systematic evaluations have been carried out. The best of these studies have produced only weak support for the value of services. We suspect that some of these studies have underestimated the benefits of programs, given our findings on the long-term effects of comprehensive prenatal ser-

vices and educational programs. Thus, more attention should be given to the question of how to intervene more effectively rather than whether or not to intervene.

In addition to positing the need for improving services and for differentiating between those services that produce results and those that do not, our results suggest that more aggressive prevention programs are an absolutely essential part of any general attack on the problem of teenage childbearing. It is probably desirable to direct the most energetic efforts to high-risk populations, especially those children who come from poverty and those students who are behind in school. Programs that provide remedial training for children at risk of school failure could be one of the most effective ways of combatting early childbearing, as well as enhancing the adjustment of teens who do bear children.

In addition, we need to become more sensitive to developmental strategies that are designed to reach different categories of the disadvantaged at different points in the life span. Many young mothers may willingly give up public assistance when their children enter school and no longer require day care. In short, not all teenage mothers will pursue the same strategy of recovery and many are not ready to avail themselves of opportunities until later in life. Bridges of opportunity may be necessary for adults who may not have made use of ameliorative services offered to them earlier in life.

Finally, we should be designing programs that reach the next generation, the offspring of the adolescent childbearers. Whereas it would be ill-advised to single out the children of teenage mothers for special services, it is possible to develop programs for neighborhoods and schools where rates of early childbearing are especially high. Preventive programs aimed at reducing school failure are particularly promising.

In summary, what do these results tell us about plasticity and its limitations in disadvantaged women and children? First, the poor are not all the same. Social service programs for and research on children do not always reflect this obvious point. Children (and mothers) likely to benefit from a particular intervention may possess specific characteristics or have experienced particular life situations that make them likely to benefit from a particular intervention. Second, the mother's life circumstances must be examined, not only in terms of static structural characteristics, but in terms of her potential for change and her particular life choices. A mother who is on welfare or has shared child-care responsibilities for her child in order to obtain additional schooling, is very different from a mother who is on welfare, not in school, and rearing her child alone. Third, adverse circumstances may be overcome; as the mother's life changes are enhanced, so too are her children's. This is perhaps the most convincing reason to direct early-childhood services toward mothers as well as children. The children of teenage mothers who are likely to succeed as adults are those who are currently in economically stable circumstances, through the mother's own efforts. Thus, maternal life courses will influence the child's development. We believe that an understanding of maternal life decisions not only provides evidence of plasticity across the life span but also informs us as to why children of poverty are not all the same, and why some are more likely to benefit from intervention programs than others.

Fourth, environmental situations are not equally associated with outcomes across the childhood and adolescent years. In some cases, disadvantageous characteristics occurring in the preschool years are predictive of child deficits, and in others, characteristics occurring in the adolescent years are important. This suggests that models of development focusing primarily on early plasticity or on the equipotentiality of plasticity across the childhood years are both inadequate. Plasticity may be fairly specific to environmental

characteristics and to child outcomes. The challenge is to test models that take age of the child, behavior outcome, and environmental characteristic into account simultaneously.

Finally, constraints on plasticity do exist. As others have suggested, plasticity is a relativistic phenomenon (Gollin, 1981; Lerner, 1985; Scarr, 1982). Change is limited by the features of the individual, the present context, and, in some cases, by earlier experience. Additionally, plasticity is not inevitable given a change in environment. Whereas a change in maternal status, such as going off welfare, may alter the child's academic success, it is not guaranteed that success will be forthcoming.

CONCLUSION

The focus on the children of teenage mothers and the ways in which the children's developmental trajectories may be altered is critical. We still know relatively little about ameliorating developmental delays; we do know that environmental characteristics associated with poverty increase the likelihood of such delays. The percentage of children under 13 living in poverty has increased dramatically in the last decade, from 16% in 1970 to about 23% in 1982 (Preston, 1984). This increase is primarily due to two demographic trends: the increasing number of children born out-of-wedlock and the increase in marital disruptions. Both are associated with poverty. Based on the trends of the 1970s, we can expect 86% of black children and 42% of white children to live part of their childhoods in one-parent households, and if demographic trends continue, the percentage may rise as high as 94% and 70% respectively (Bumpass, 1983). Teenage mothers have more than their share of out-of-wedlock births and marital disruptions, and their children are at increased risk for school and societal failure.

REFERENCES

Baltes, P. B., & Brim, O. G., Jr. (Eds.). (1979). *Life-span development and behavior* (Vol. 2). New York: Academic Press.

Baltes, P. B., & Brim, O. G., Jr. (Eds.). (1980). *Life-span development and behavior* (Vol. 3). New York: Academic Press.

Baltes, P. B., & Brim, O. G., Jr. (Eds.). (1981). *Life-span development and behavior* (Vol. 4). New York: Academic Press.

Baltes, P. B., & Nesselroade, J. R. (1973). The developmental analysis of individual differences on multiple measures. In J. R. Nesselroade & H. W. Reese (Eds.),

Life-span developmental psychology: Methodological issues. New York: Academic Press.

Bloom, B. S. (1961). *Stability and change in human characteristics*. New York: John Wiley & Sons.

Brim, O. G., Jr., & Kagan, J. (1980). *Constancy and change in human development*. Cambridge, MA: Harvard University Press.

Bronfenbrenner, U. (1985, May). *Interacting systems in human development. Research paradigms: Present and future*. Paper presented for the Society for Research in Child Development Study Group, Cornell University: Ithaca, NY.

Brooks-Gunn, J., & Furstenberg, F. F., Jr. (1986). The children of adolescent mothers: Physical, academic and psychological outcomes. *Developmental Review, 6,* 224–251.

Brooks-Gunn, J., & Weinraub, M. (1983). Origins of infant intelligence testing. In M. Lewis (Ed.), *Origins of intelligence* (2nd ed.) (pp. 25–66). New York: Plenum.

Bumpass, L. (1983). *Demographic perspectives on the consequences for children of changing marital patterns*. Final report to NICHD, Contract #1-HD-02852- 82.

Cambell, A. A. (1968). The role of family planning in the reduction of poverty. *Journal of Marriage and the Family, 30*(2), 236–245.

Crissey, O. L. (1937). Mental development as related to institutional residence and educational achievement. *University of Iowa Studies on Child Welfare, 13*(1).

Furstenberg, F. F., Jr. (1976). *Unplanned parenthood: The social consequences of teenage childbearing*. New York: Cambridge University Press.

Furstenberg, F. F., Jr., Brooks-Gunn, J., & Morgan, P. (1987). *Adolescent mothers in later life*. New York: Cambridge University Press.

Furstenberg, F. F., Jr., Nord, C. W., Peterson, J. L., & Zill, N. (1983). The life course of children of divorce: Marital disruption and parental contact. *American Sociological Review, 48*(5), 656–668.

Garmezy, N., & Rutter, M. (1983). *Stress, coping and development in children*. New York: McGraw-Hill.

Gollin, E. S. (1981). Development and plasticity. In E. S. Gollin (Ed.), *Developmental plasticity: Behavioral and biological aspects of variations in development*. New York: Academic Press.

Hunt, J. Mc. (1961). *Intelligence and experience*. New York: Ronald Press.

Kagan, J., & Moss, H. (1962). *Birth to maturity: A study in psychological development*. New York: John Wiley & Sons.

Kellum, S. G., Ensminger, M. E., & Turner, R. J.

(1977). Family structure and the mental health of children. *Archives of General Psychiatry, 34,* 1012–1022.

Lerner, R. M. (1985). *On the nature of human plasticity*. New York: Cambridge University Press.

McCall, R. B., Hogarty, P. S., & Hurlburt, N. (1972). Transitions in infant sensorimotor development and the prediction of childhood IQ. *American Psychologist, 27,* 728–748.

McKey, R. H., Condelli, L., Ganson, H., Barrett, B. J., McConkey, C., & Plantz, M. C. (1985). *The impact of Head Start on children, families and communities*. Final report, Administration for Children, Youth, and Families, U.S. Department of Health and Human Services. Washington, DC.

Moore, K. A., & Burt, M. R. (1982). *Private crisis, public cost: Policy perspectives on teenage childbearing*. Washington, D C : The Urban Institute Press.

Piaget, J. (1937). *The construction of reality in the child*. New York: Basic Books.

Piaget, J. (1952). *The origins of intelligence in children*. London: International Universities Press.

Preston, S. H. (1984). Children and the elderly: Divergent paths for America's dependents. *Demography 21*(4), 435–457.

Rutter, M. (1979). Maternal deprivation, 1972–1978: New finds, new concepts, new approaches. *Child Development, 50,* 283–305.

Scarr, S. (1982). Development is internally guided, not determined. *Contemporary Psychology, 27,* 852–853.

Scarr, S., & McCartney, K. (1983). How people make their own environments: A theory of genotype environment effects. *Child Development, 54,* 424–435.

Skodak, M. (1939). Children in foster homes: A study of mental development. *University of Iowa Studies on Child Welfare, 16*(1).

Wachs, T. D., & Gruen, G. E. (1982). *Early experience and human development*. New York: Plenum.

Werner, H. (1948). *Comparative psychology of mental development*. New York: International Universities Press.

Werner, H. (1957). The concept of development from a comparative and organismic point of view. In D. B. Harris (Ed.), *The concept of development*. Minneapolis: University of Minnesota Press.

Zabin, L. S., Hardy, J. B., Streett, R., & King, T. M. (1984). A school-, hospital-, and university-based adolescent pregnancy prevention program: A cooperative design for service and research. *The Journal of Reproductive Medicine, 29*(6), 421–426.

PLASTICITY AND POLICY

Chapter 15

Science Policy and the Concept of Plasticity

Peter M. Vietze

Science policy in the United States is driven by the need to obtain information to solve problems of national significance and by individual scientists pursuing their own problem areas and interests. There are a number of ways in which science policy may be formulated. That is, there are different sources that originate changes or initiatives in science policy. One source is the President and the White House staff. The President can direct new initiatives in science policy by creating new agencies, suggesting legislation, or merely discussing certain issues. The President also may influence science policy by the appointments made to head science agencies and advisory groups. A second source of science policy is the Congress. Congress can enact laws directing studies, emphasizing particular areas, and appropriating and authorizing funds for scientific agencies and endeavors. In the federal government, the science agencies themselves can influence science policy by the studies they undertake and support, conferences they hold, and appointments they make to key advisory groups. Finally, various constituencies can influence science policy. This group includes both the lay public and the scientific constituencies that produce the science. Ultimately, however, there are two major sources that drive science policy: scientists and their findings, and the problems perceived to be of national significance.

In this chapter, each of the sources of science policy is briefly described and its relevance to the concept of plasticity discussed.

PRESIDENTIAL INFLUENCE ON SCIENCE POLICY

When it became obvious in the late 1950s that the Soviet Union had solved the problem of space travel before we had, there was a marked shift in science policy so that information necessary to solve the next set of problems relevant to travel beyond earth would be made available quickly. The change in science policy included formation of nationally visible federal agencies (i.e., NASA) with responsibility for development of resources necessary for space travel, availability of more or new funds that could be used to assist scientists in pursuit of the knowledge and information necessary to accomplish space travel, and availability of resources that would permit training of scientists in disciplines that contribute to research and development in the space travel industry. These disciplines included engineering, mathematics, astronomy, computer sciences, physics, chemistry, biology, psychology, medicine, nutrition, and so forth.

In the 1960s, when the Kennedy administration felt that prevention and treatment of mental retardation was a major problem that could not be solved without new information, there was a change in science policy so that the new information that was needed could become available in the future. This led to the formation of a new institute at the National Institutes of Health, the National Institute of Child Health and Human Development. (The original recommendation was for a national institute on mental retardation, but the scientific community felt that this would be too narrow a focus for a major research institute.) The mission of this new institute was to provide financial assistance to scientists studying issues relevant to the prevention or treatment of mental retardation. It also led to the development of a network of research centers at selected universities, where the most important research related to mental retardation and its prevention, and the training of scientists studying such problems were being carried out. In addition, the construction and support of facilities for training health care professionals who would treat retarded and developmentally disabled individuals was fostered.

These two examples are cases in which science policy was created or effected by the President and his staff, in order to solve a problem of national importance. There are other examples of how science policy was determined by the Chief Executive of the federal government to solve an immediate and important problem—the use of nuclear energy to make weapons such as the atomic bomb (the Manhattan Project) and actions taken as a result of the energy crisis of the 1970s come to mind. These sorts of occurrences require cooperation between the legislative and executive branches of the federal government, so that the resulting policy reflects a consensus of what is needed to solve the problem. An initiative by the President is usually an indication of deep, broad-based support for the policy issue at hand. However, the details of how the policy is to be expressed are often only found in the legislation passed by the Congress. Thus, it is possible that the original intent of the policy may be modified or obscured by congressional action with the President supporting measures that have little impact on the scientific enterprise. Finally, the details of a policy are ultimately expressed through the regulations written by the agencies of the Executive Branch in the process of implementing legislation.

CONGRESSIONAL IMPACT ON SCIENCE POLICY

A second source of initiative or change in science policy may be the Congress itself. Such initiatives may be the result of an immediate problem recognized by a legislator or they may come from some constituency that brings the problem to the attention of the senator or congressman. It should be noted that legislative action involves *authorization* to take some action first, and then *appropriation* of funds to carry out the activity. Thus, Congress may authorize establishment of a particular program but provide minimal funds to carry out the program. Three examples illustrate how specific problems may lead to pursuit of scientific goals.

The first concerns sudden infant death syndrome, or SIDS. Here, as a result of what some legislators perceived as an epidemic of infants dying mysteriously in their first year, Congress passed the Sudden Infant Death Syndrome Act of 1974 (PL 93-270). This law singled out SIDS for special emphasis. Congress also occasionally has "earmarked" some of the funds authorized for the National Institute of Child Health and Human Development (NICHD) to be spent only for research on SIDS. Despite the fact that it would appear that Congress itself originated the focus on SIDS, there is ample evidence that NICHD initiated the interest with major input from the scientific and clinical communities, through an international conference held in Seattle, Washington in 1963. The conclusion from this conference was that federally supported research on SIDS was needed. A second international conference sponsored by NICHD was held in 1969. Continued progress in identifying the causes and epidemiology of SIDS were noted by the second conference. This example illustrates that Congress may act to give emphasis to a research focus as a result of pressure and information from the scientific community. Congress continues to maintain oversight into research progress in SIDS by requesting an annual report specifically concerned with research on SIDS.

Another example of congressional action leading to a science policy came as a result of an intense lobbying effort by a parent group, mostly initiated by two mothers. In 1978 and 1979, a prominent drug company manufactured two soy-based infant formulas, Neo-Mull-Soy and

Cho-free, with insufficient chloride content. Some of the infants fed these formulas were diagnosed as having hypochloremic metabolic alkalosis, a disorder that produces symptoms similar to failure to thrive. The connection between the formula and the illness was made by several pediatric nephrologists in late 1978. The two suspect formulas were ordered to be taken off the market by the Food and Drug Administration in 1979.

In response to the clinical reports and the efforts of two mothers whose infants had been fed the chloride-deficient formula, the Infant Formula Act of 1980 (PL 96-359) was passed. One section of the act mandated that ". . . a study to determine the long-term effect on infants of hypochloremic metabolic alkalosis resulting from infant formulas deficient in chloride'' should be conducted. The Secretary of Health and Human Services designated NICHD the lead agency to respond to this mandate. As a result, several studies are being conducted to uncover the precise relationship between exposure to the deficient formula and any damage to the children exposed. Congress continues to maintain an interest in this problem until the final report of the NICHD is made.

The last example concerns acquired immune deficiency syndrome, or AIDS. This very serious public health problem has achieved epidemic proportions as of this writing. As a result of clinical and scientific reports, Congress has authorized hundreds of millions of dollars to be spent on finding the cause, treatments, and cure for this deadly disease. Over the past 4 years, great progress has been made in uncovering the cause and course of the illness. Originally thought to be of concern only to certain risk groups—homosexuals, Haitians, some hemophiliacs, intravenous drug users, and prostitutes—the disease is spreading to other sectors of the population. Although no specific set aside has been identified to study the course of AIDS in children, several research efforts have been focused on children because in some individuals the AIDS virus attacks brain cells.

The three examples given of Congressional focus were not selected at random. Each of these three examples has implications for the topic at hand—plasticity, specifically brain plasticity. In the case of SIDS, it is believed now that one cause of death among SIDS victims is sleep apnea—episodes when a baby stops breathing while sleeping and doesn't have the capacity to start breathing again on its own. Not all infants who have this tendency die as a result; some of them survive the period of greatest risk, ages 2 to 6 months. It is still not known what the effect of such episodes is on affected infants who do survive.

Because apnea means oxygen deprivation to the brain, the effects on the brain may depend on brain plasticity. For the infants exposed to the chloride-deficient formula, there is some evidence already that cognitive and motor skills may be affected. Perhaps the age of the infant and the length of exposure interact with the plasticity of the brain at these times. Finally, AIDS in children may produce pronounced effects on the developing brain. How does brain plasticity affect the way in which children with the AIDS virus develop? All three of these examples of how congressional action directed science policy—by either providing funding for research or by making laws that focused attention on general or specific areas for study—depend on the concept of brain plasticity for solving the problems.

These three examples of Congressional action in areas of science policy also show that in order to carry out science policy, the early involvement of the executive agencies most concerned with a particular area is essential. These agencies often provide scientific information to congressional staff persons and the general public. They may even indirectly stimulate the scientific community to effect congressional action, as in the case of SIDS, where the NICHD preceded the SIDS Act by more than a decade with the first international conference on SIDS.

HOW SCIENTIFIC AGENCIES SHAPE SCIENCE POLICY

There are many agencies of the federal government charged with the conduct of scientific investigation for the public good. Almost every branch of government has some scientific program that is necessary for the conduct of its business. However, not all of these scientific programs are large or support research in the general scientific community. Those that do provide assistance for scientific inquiry in the form of grants or contracts must engage in several activities in order to give out such support. They must decide on specific programmatic directions and then institute procedures to publicize the programs, receive applications, review the applications, and monitor progress once awards are made. In some agencies, the review of applications and the programmatic management of research are separate. Therefore, the policy influence of these two administrative functions are separate also. In addition, there are often advisory bodies appointed from the scientific community that have an opportunity to exert some influence also. Finally, the administrators of agencies have a great deal of authority to determine policy. Each of these functional units is discussed separately. Since they have the most complex and refined procedures, The National Institutes of Health serve as the model for the following sections.

Program Staff

Program staff have the greatest opportunities to influence science policy. By virtue of the fact that they are the initial contacts with scientists in the field, they may wield the most influence. Program staff engage in four major functions that may lead to policy determination in scientific endeavors. They propose and carry out initiatives, review progress, report findings, and provide information. In the area of initiatives, program staff engage in planning efforts for new directions, advising the agency administration of promising areas of investigation for the agency to pursue. They determine needs for research in areas that may be understudied. This can lead to issuing Announcements; Requests for Applications (RFAs), which ask for proposals to address a specific problem area; and Requests for Proposals (RFPs), which specify the design of the problem to be addressed, and ask for bidders willing to conduct a particular study. These three mechanisms declare areas of agency interest to the scientific fields. They highlight specific topics that are believed to be of high program relevance, and, in the case of RFAs and RFPs, announce the availability of funds for research grants or contracts, respectively.

A program officer will usually make a determination to issue such an announcement based on a number of activities. First, the program staff are expected to keep current in the fields of science they administer. This means reading journals, going to conferences and society meetings, obtaining expert consultation, and holding conferences and workshops. Conferences and workshops are a special category of activity in which the program staff have an opportunity to focus attention on a specific topic (e.g., identification of infants at risk for mental retardation, families with a mentally retarded member, intervention with high-risk infants) and convene a group of scientists to discuss research relevant to the topic and perhaps even to make recommendations about the agency's future directions in the area. At some agencies, these conferences or workshops will result in the publication of proceedings, which makes the information available to the broader scientific community. These activities are all focused on discovering and determining the most up-to-date information about the science and advising the agency regarding research priorities. In other words, although the individual program officer decides on topics and priorities, these must always be justified by reference to scientific findings, breakthroughs, and opportunities. The state of the science drives the setting of priorities.

Advisory Council

Once a grant application has been reviewed by an initial peer review group of scientists outside the agency, the advisory council has a chance to concur with the recommendations of the review group or to differ with their recommendations. At the time that the advisory council meets, the program staff may also make such recommendations for council approval. Thus, a program officer may recommend funding of a project that has especially high program relevance. Occasionally, an investigator who has submitted an application for grant support may differ with the results of the review with regard to the recommendation, priority score (the numerical rating given by the peer review group), or some detail of the summary statement. The investigator may register such differences by writing a rebuttal letter. Program staff are responsible for considering the merits of the protest. The program officer responsible discusses the points raised with the executive secretary who conducted the review and with an advisory council member to whom the application has been assigned for secondary review. Based on these discussions, the program officer decides on a course of action and responds to the applicant. The possibilities include bringing the rebuttal letter to the advisory council for action on the program officer's recommendation. The council may then take one of the courses of action open to them as detailed below. The program officer may inform the applicant that the best course of action is to revise the application and resubmit it at the next submission deadline.

In agencies where review of new proposals for funding and program staff are kept separate, program staff still have some review functions that may be more properly called oversight functions. A program officer is responsible for monitoring progress for ongoing funded projects. Here there are opportunities to communicate with scientists regarding direction of the research. With regard to research contracts, the program officer actually directs the research; whereas with grant-supported research, the program officer acts in an advisory and monitoring capacity. Program staff are also asked to make recommendations to the review staff regarding peer reviewers and consultants. Thus, there is some possibility to influence the outcome of reviews by recommending particular reviewers.

Program staff are expected to provide information about the research program to agency administrators as well as to the scientific community in general. This may include formal as well as informal communication. In addition, Congress makes inquiries about programs, and program staff are charged with providing such information. This may take the form of written reports or more informal interchange on particular topics. In some cases, Congress has standing orders for reports on topics such as sudden infant death syndrome, mental retardation, and nutritional research.

Program staff will select appropriate scientific information from funded programs and describe the progress in these fields. During budget hearings, congressional committees will ask specific questions about particular programs, and these are usually answered by program officials in the agency. Finally, program staff may also write articles for submission to journals or present papers at scientific meetings in which particular programs or scientific issues are discussed. Other written documents that may serve to determine or influence the direction of scientific inquiry in an area include annual reports, brochures, even reports in the written and electronic media. Program officers are responsible for all such communication.

In short, program staff are the focal point for initiating much of the activity regarding science policy and also for making operational policy decisions that are considered at other levels in the agency. However, it should be emphasized that most initiatives and activities carried out by program staff are expected to reflect the most up-to-date scientific information and findings. Again, the science drives the policy decisions.

Review Staff

Although it is not always obvious, review staff also have some influence on science policy. This influence is indirect rather than direct, however, because policy making is not officially the role of people on review staff. Nevertheless, people who run review committees, the executive secretaries, have the role of selecting reviewers and assigning them to review particular applications for research support. In this way, the executive secretary can have some influence over the way in which an application is reviewed. Following assignment of proposals to reviewers, the executive secretary conducts the review meeting during which the proposals are reviewed. Such factors as time of day, when the application is reviewed, and atmosphere may all have some influence on the review. These are all under the control of the executive secretary. In these times of highly competitive grant reviews, some of these factors may influence whether a proposal is given a favorable score or not. There is also opportunity to communicate with applicants during the review by the executive secretary.

Furthermore, the executive secretary is responsible for writing the summary statement that gives the results of the review. The summary statement serves the purpose of giving feedback to the applicant, program staff, and advisory bodies. Thus, although the program staff and advisory council may make the final decisions in advising an agency director whether to fund a particular project, the executive secretary can exert some influence over this decision by how the summary statement is written. Review staff thus have some indirect influence over what sort of research is supported, and this may contribute to the determination of science policy. Presumably, review staff exert their influence according to their reading of the scientific literature.

Advisory Groups

As indicated already most federal agencies that administer scientific programs have advisory groups often called boards or councils. These councils function much as boards of organizations in the private sector. They review decisions made by staff, and either concur or differ. In some cases they may also be empowered to make policy or initiate programmatic changes. In the case of advisory councils for scientific agencies, there are three specific functions that may determine the direction of science as administered by the agency. First of all, they are advisory to the agency director, who is actually the only individual authorized officially to give out grants or contracts. In this capacity, the council can recommend policy changes to the director with regard to specific topics for research priority or with regard to the operational aspects of grant support.

Most advisory councils are intimately involved in the planning efforts of the agency that they advise. They also are asked to review recommendations made by staff with regard to policy changes. In this capacity, they may also have considerable influence over specific plans brought to them for discussion by program staff. Finally, they serve as a secondary review body. They are asked to review the recommendations made by review groups and by program staff for funding of grant applications. They may concur with the recommendations or make their own recommendations. Thus, they may decide to recommend a particular application for funding when that application might not have otherwise been funded. Similarly, they may also recommend that an application that received a fundable priority rating not be funded. Finally, they may suggest that an application be sent back to an initial review group to be reviewed again, if they think it warrants such action. One of these actions may be the result of an applicant's submitting a rebuttal letter.

The council's decisions and actions may result in direct or indirect influence over science policy, depending on the topic of the action. However, here too, the science policy decisions are presumably driven by the science. Political considerations are not usually acceptable reasons for changes or initiations in science policy. The impact of the council's recommendations may only be felt if the director chooses to accept the recommendations, and the only pressures that the council may exert are by direct discourse or by communications outside the lines of communication with the director.

Agency Director

The director of a scientific agency that is a component of the National Institutes of Health is usually the official with the authority to expend funds to carry out the mission of the agency. The director has reporting responsibility to higher officials and is accountable to the secretary of the department under which the agency is located organizationally. Spending authority is legally passed to the agency director by the secretary.

The director has major responsibility for formulating science policy and has a number of mechanisms available to him or her to do so. These include the authority to initiate programs and program direction; to organize and reorganize staff or programs; to set priorities; to hire staff or terminate staff with good cause; and, of course, to fund grants, contracts, cooperative agreements or interagency agreements in order to conduct the science.

Usually program initiation is delegated to the program staff, and this has been discussed already. However, the director also can direct agency program staff to initiate or terminate programs and to emphasize some programs while deemphasizing others. Here again, the presumed impetus for changes in policy is the science itself. But the director is also the link between the scientific community, through the program staff, and the funding authority given by Congress through the President. The director is often directed by Congress to carry out specific programs or program initiatives and the director is then accountable to Congress for this.

The Director reports directly to Congress during budget hearings, responding to questions and probes about the program. The Director is also responsible for formulating the budget which goes to the Office of Management and Budget (OMB) and then to the President. This is where the OMB may exert its influence by deleting programs or items from the budget. The budget process is considered briefly next, because it is in that process that the most significant nonscientific influence of science policy may take place.

The Budget Process

The budget process begins after the agency director consults with staff in the agency. The agency director, after consulting with his key lieutenants, presents the budget for the next fiscal year to the secretary of the department, who transmits the budget request to the Office of Management and Budget (OMB). The OMB

is the "watchdog" of the President, designed to keep budget requests within the Executive Branch under control. The budget is then collated by the OMB and policy decisions are made based on the President's priorities. The President's budget is transmitted to Congress, which engages in its own budget process. Each branch of Congress conducts budget hearings through its committee structure. It is during these budget hearings that the agency director has an opportunity to present proposals for new initiatives and programs, and to report on ongoing programs. Following hearings there is a chance for response to questions, and then the Congress formulates its priorities for appropriations and budget authorization. Following these formulations, Congress eventually votes on the budget for the subsequent fiscal year.

Once the budget is passed, each agency takes the money it is allocated and proceeds to spend the funds in accordance with its authority. The director of the agency is responsible for carrying out the program within the guidelines set by Congress. At each stage of the budget process, there are policy decisions that can be made, some of which are responsive to the scientific community and some of which are responsive to other considerations including national need and political considerations. The scientific community has the opportunity to address these various considerations by communicating with the science agencies and with the Congress. Thus, even though there are many points at which decision-makers and elected officials are charged with responsibility, the scientific community may exert its influence.

The Case of Malleability or Plasticity

During the 1930s—when Skeels and his colleagues (e.g., Skeels & Dye, 1939) conducted a study in which they demonstrated that children raised in institutions under optimal caretaking conditions would not be retarded, whereas those who were not given adequate caregiving would be—the issue of the plasticity of intelligence was a focal one. At the time, there were few federal agencies that were able to influence science policy. However, if, as has been contended in this chapter, there had been a network of federal science agencies, they probably would not have supported the Skeels work because the dominant scientific community did not embrace the concept of intellectual plasticity. Since then, the evidence for plasticity has been accumulating; the work of Hunt (1961) and others established the scientific basis for early intervention during the 1960s. The fact that some of the early intervention and early experience experiments of the 1960s and 1970s did not fulfill some theoretical expectations led again to serious questions regarding the scientific basis for plasticity. The other chapters in this volume document the presence of some plasticity and the promise of more, given sharply changed environmental conditions.

We are also now on the edge of a revolution in neuroscience in which hard evidence for brain plasticity is becoming more and more evident. Nevertheless, it is the scientific discoveries of the last two decades that form the basis for this change. The latest discoveries in molecular genetics allow elaboration and modification of previous views about the absoluteness of hereditary endowment. The prospects for genetic therapy for modifying hereditary structure may lead to new conceptualizations about the malleability of brain structure and of behavioral capacity. Although alteration of genetic structure is presently in a very primitive state, the theoretical possibilities for such alteration are already being realized. Only time and scientific discovery will allow for the operationalization of some of these possibilities. As these discoveries accumulate, the finality of organic causes of various diseases including mental retardation will be called into question; these discoveries may show that many conditions previously assumed to be hopeless can be eliminated. The degree to which science policy permits or prohibits ex-

ploration of these lines of research will determine the limits of plasticity that may be discovered.

Science Policy and the Concept of Plasticity

Science policy is formulated at many different levels and is usually expressed as money spent on scientific investigation. Most of the scientific agencies are responsive and responsible to the whole continuum of the decision-making process in government. However, the scientific community seems to have ample opportunity to address this process from the agency itself to the decision-makers in the White House and Congress. Ultimately, there must be a match between the science as it is laid down in scientific writing and the policies that govern expenditures of funds in pursuit of scientific investigation. Those agencies that rely most heavily on the scientific community for direction of its programs are most responsive to the accretion of scientific information to determine science policy. Those agencies that are subject to nonscience pressures are the least likely to be embraced by the scientific community.

Because science is more than the mere accumulation of empirical data, the science policy of the nation is also determined by the conceptual models that scientists and philosophers create with the findings. Such conceptualizations may also determine science policy, usually through the efforts of scientists espousing particular views. The conceptualization that behavior and intelligence are malleable will lead to certain types of investigations, whereas alternative conceptualizations will lead to other sorts of studies. The fact that science is usually conducted in a public arena and that the most important criterion for scientific endeavor is that its tenets be falsifiable or open to challenge make it essential that science drive the formulation and modification of science policy.

REFERENCES

Hunt, J. McV. (1961). *Intelligence and experience.* New York: Ronald Press.

Skeels, H. M., & Dye, H. B. (1939). A study of the effects of differential stimulation on mentally retarded children. *Proceedings of the American Association of Mental Deficiency, 44,* 114–136.

Chapter 16

Public Policy and The Malleability of Children

James J. Gallagher

This chapter attempts to sketch the dynamics of the growing interest in public policy in the social sciences, present a multivariate model of intellectual malleability for young children, and show how that model applies to one of the most current of public issues—what is our responsibility for 4-year-olds in our society?

The interest in public policy and public decision-making on the part of social scientists has been a relatively recent phenomenon. Twenty years ago, social scientists who became involved with local, state, or federal government policy were seen as engaging in slightly disreputable behavior, and it was a clear sign that they could not make their way in the respectable academic community. Twenty years later, practically all professional organizations in education and the social sciences have a presence in Washington. Many of these professional societies include public-policy articles in their journals, and discussions of the implications of social science findings for public policy are heard at practically every professional convention.

One reason for this change has been the rapid development of social programs—stimulated largely by the Kennedy and Johnson administrations, and continued in subsequent administrations—that relied upon the social sciences for their rationale. Another reason is that a variety of prominent professionals have spent time as program administrators in Washington and have returned to academia with a great deal of knowledge about how decisions are made in the public arena. They have often been disturbed about the way in which the social sciences were misinterpreted or misused to forward or attack a particular policy (Gallagher, 1975).

There would appear to be four very specific bodies of knowledge or skills that need to be mastered in order to have a systematic impact on policy. The typical social scientist, individually and collectively, would seem to have clear capabilities in only one of these four areas:

1. *Knowledge base:* In order to establish effective policy, one must know the particular field or area that is being discussed. This is the area of expertise of the social scientist, who may know a great deal about families or young children, or the effects of poverty on individuals. Social scientists bring to the issue a deep understanding of the problem itself.

2. *Alternative strategies:* It is in the design of solutions to these problems that the social scientist has had a great deal of difficulty. In the past it has been traditional for Congress or the White House to form prestigious commissions, bringing together the most knowledgable and scholarly people on a given topic such as delinquency or handicapped children. These commissions are at their weakest in making suggestions about how institutions, such as public education or health delivery systems, should be modified to take into account new knowledge.

Although these experts who serve on such commissions have the knowledge about the target child or family that needs special attention, they often have a very incomplete appreciation or understanding of the social institutions, organizations, or systems they propose to change. The result is often an uncertain and unrealistic set of recommendations that results in a lack of confidence on the part of the practical decision-maker.

For example, the National Commission on Excellence in Education, in the report entitled *A Nation at Risk* (1983), put its collective finger on a major problem, the lowering of standards in the public school systems. When the time came for them to make recommendations, however, they contented themselves with recommendations that everyone should take 4 years of English, 3 years of mathematics, 3 years of science; and that the schools should lengthen the school year. None of these recommendations comes within a country mile of the fundamental problems of the schools, or even shows an understanding of why the schools have drifted away from standards of excellence.

3. *Public decision mechanisms:* The desire to modify existing legislation or regulations requires an understanding of how public decision-making and program implementation takes place. Even the most sophisticated social scientists in their own special field can be quite naive in understanding how the local school board, the state legislature, or Congress makes decisions. A thorough and effective utilization of these systems requires a greater appreciation of how the systems themselves work. Institutional reform, if it is not to be of the meat-axe style, would necessitate that we understand the complicated democratic systems that serve us.

4. *Media and communications:* The social scientists generally have not shown sufficient understanding of the role of the media as a communication bridge between public decision-makers and professionals. Few public decision-makers have, or will, read scholarly journals, monographs, or books. They have educated themselves over the years on a variety of topics through reading newspapers such as the *New York Times* and the *Washington Post*, *Time* and *Newsweek* magazines, and by watching television news. If the social scientist wishes to get a message across to the decision-maker, the most promising vehicle is the media. This again requires a broad understanding of the media and how that societal segment operates.

If social scientists collectively can master these four areas, then they will be able to have a significant impact on public policy. This chapter will discuss in more detail the knowledge base and will present a model of policy analysis by which alternative strategies are generated and reviewed—one which has been developed at the Bush Institute for Policy Analysis at the University of North Carolina at Chapel Hill (Gallagher, 1981).

THE CROSS-NATIONAL KNOWLEDGE BASE FOR INTELLECTUAL MALLEABILITY

In this context, the term malleability is used to describe the amount and kind of changes that take place in a child's development coincident with significant changes in the environmental context surrounding them.

One strategy for approaching the issue of malleability of intelligence is to examine the findings obtained from other societies. If such findings differ considerably from one another, there is the clear implication that socio-cultural factors have substantial impact on the development of this characteristic. Further, if there are differences across national groups, we may discover some clues about what causes them, and develop an explanatory or predictive model of how these various forces work.

Statistics that have comparability across nations are not easy to obtain, but data on the intellectual performance of children in Sweden, Scotland, and the United States do seem to have potential for interpretations on the malleability issue.

A variety of investigators have suggested, for example, that the prevalence of mental retardation in Sweden is considerably lower than what is indicated by the figures available in the United States. Grunewald (1979) found a prevalence rate of 0.44% for mental retardation in Sweden, which he suggested might be the lowest prevalence rate in the world. Before these figures can be accepted at face value, we have to decide whether we are discussing the same concept, mental retardation, and whether the method that Grunewald used to identify mentally retarded children was appropriate, or whether he might have overlooked some children.

The problem of defining mental retardation is a serious one in the first place. The American Association on Mental Deficiency (AAMD) offers this version (Grossman, 1983):

> Mental retardation refers to significantly sub-average general intellectual functioning existing concurrently with deficits in adaptive behavior and manifested during the developmental period. (p. 1)

If deficits in adaptive behavior are considered a part of the definition of mental retardation, then, the prevalence of mental retardation reflects the expectations and pressures of the society as well as the characteristics of the individual. If one wishes to intervene to improve this situation, it is unclear whether the target should be the individual child or the environmental forces impinging on him or her.

One example of how different environmental pressures can influence the concept of mild mental retardation is provided by Robinson (1978), during a visit to the People's Republic of China. She found Chinese educators unable to discuss the concept, and interpreters having difficulty finding words to communicate questions on the subject. Finally, the term *blunted child* seems to be some type of functional equivalent. Robinson commented:

> From all we could gather, Chinese society makes limited demands for intellectual competence, and usually provides natural support with the family and commune or the workers' residential district. There is a strong emphasis on helping one another, on minimizing individual differences (both positive and negative), and on group needs rather than those of the individual. (p. 295)
>
> At the same time one must recognize the advantages for retarded children and adults of living in a technologically rather unsophisticated society, one in which there is minimal value placed on independence, and individuality and maximal emphasis on cohesiveness and mutual support. (p. 298)

One does not have to go to China, however, to find the effect of differential expectations on the concept of retardation. Some years ago the President's Committee on Mental Retardation (1970) issued a report entitled the *Six Hour Retarded Child,* describing the child who is retarded when in school but not in his home or neighborhood, where the intellectual demands were not as great as in school.

Ogbu (Chapter 13, this volume) points out that different cognitive competencies (if not cognitive capacities) in cultural subgroups may be accounted for by the differential rewards and experiences societies provide for various cognitive skills. He notes studies that showed boys superior to girls in artistic competence in Southwestern Native American groups, where men were more involved in art than women; whereas among Japanese villagers where the women were more highly involved with art work, girls were superior to boys in artistic competence.

If differences in culture can cause differential interpretation of the concept of mental retardation itself, then what are we comparing in a cross-national comparison of mental retardation prevalence—individual cognitive differences or differences in cultural pressures for intellectual performance? A better question to pose would be: Are there differences across cultures in the rate of intellectual subnormality? Then we might be able to study the role that the culture might have played in the child's cognitive development.

The use of measures of cognitive abilities does not eliminate, of course, our concerns with environmental influences, because these measures also are vulnerable to such influences. As pointed out by Plomin (Chapter 2) and Scarr and Arnett (Chapter 6) in this volume, various adoption and twin studies show a strong genetic component to measures of intelligence; the effects of intervention deliberately designed to enhance cognitive performance consistently yield only a difference of ½ to 1 standard deviation, and that difference seems to decline with time (Lazar, Darlington, Murray, Royce, & Snipper, 1982). Overall, measures of intellectual development seem to be one of the most resistant of developmental indices to change or modification.

To return to Grunewald, we can now pose the question, is the prevalence rate for intellectual subnormality in Sweden different from that in the United States? In this way, we finesse the difficult question as to whether the more societally determined concept of mental retardation is different across cultures. Hagberg, Hagberg, Lewerth, and Lindberg (1981) studied over 24,000 children in Gothenberg, Sweden born between 1966 and 1970. All children suspected of mental retardation were examined, as well as those who had already been diagnosed as mentally retarded. In this instance, a prevalence rate of 0.81% was determined. This was larger than Grunewald's figures but still considerably below those from U.S. data.

Another approach to establishing a stable prevalence figure for Sweden was pursued by Granat and Granat (1975, 1978), who studied the prevalence of mental subnormality in populations of 18-year-olds reporting for military service. Approximately 2.2% were disqualified for military service, but it was not clear if the armed services used the same demarcation line for intellectual subnormality as was used in the educational settings.

A third country, Scotland, has provided a careful epidemiological study conducted by Birch and his colleagues (Birch, Richardson, Baird, Horobin, & Illsley, 1970). They sought mentally subnormal children, 8 to 10 years of age, who resided in a city in Scotland, and arrived at figures of 27.4 per thousand for intellectual subnormality. In the United States, Conley (1973) estimated the relative rates of intellectual subnormality by sex and race; he then applied these rates back to the more general population in the proportions in which the

race and sex factors occur across the total culture. Conley's estimates approximated the standard estimate of 3% often used in the past for intellectual subnormality (Robinson & Robinson, 1976), but not for mental retardation with its social adaptability component (Mercer, 1973; Tarjan, Wright, Eyman, & Keeran, 1973).

Gallagher (1985) pointed out one other factor to be considered. The Swedish investigators used the earlier norms of the Stanford Binet, although the renorming of the test in the United States seemed to set the demarcation line for intellectual subnormality at a higher level. Nevertheless, there were apparently some factors in Swedish society that created a somewhat different rate of intellectual subnormality. This anomaly has led the author to suggest a possible model of factors influencing intellectual subnormality by establishing conceptual confidence limits that estimate the relative contribution of individual and social variables to the development of subnormal cognitive functioning. This model includes, by implication, a statement on malleability.

A MODEL OF PROPORTIONATE INFLUENCES ON INTELLECTUAL SUBNORMALITY

One can obtain almost universal scientific agreement about the general proposition that intellectual subnormality is influenced by polygenic inheritance, language development, health status, and subcultural values, among other factors. However, the simple discovery of statistically significant relationships is neither sufficient nor explanatory. One goal of further scientific inquiry would be to establish the relative contributions of each of these factors and their interactions to the prevalence of intellectual subnormality.

Even those who stand at the far poles of controversy such as Jensen (1972) or Hunt (1979) will readily subscribe to the influence of all of the factors listed above. Jensen merely would maintain that the polygenic inheritance has a much greater influence upon the total

Intellectual Performance → f(A)(B)(C)(D)(E)(Z)(AB)(AC) . . . . (100%)

Components contributing variance	Estimated variance influence
A = Polygenic inheritance of intelligence	(30%–50%)
B = Adult-child linguistic interaction	(10%–20%)
C = Physical health re: attention, persistence, etc.	(5%–15%)
D = Subcultural values of child's family	(5%–10%)
E = Perception of child by significant others	(5%–10%)
Z = Significant pathology affecting central nervous system	(?)
AB, AC, BC, etc. = Interaction effects	(15%–25%)

Figure 1. Model estimating variance contributions to intellectual performance.

variance than do the other factors. Similarly, environmentalists, such as Hunt, still would give due deference to the role heredity plays in the emergence of such a condition, but would merely downgrade the amount of variance contributed by heredity. The essential scientific disagreement lies not in the presence or absence of these factors, but merely in the relative weights that are to be applied.

We have proposed in Figure 1 a series of variance estimates for these variables as a means of providing a hypothetical model that could be tested. Such variance estimates would be appropriate, if at all, for the current milieu. If there were major changes in that environment, then the relative contributions of the factors would be expected to change.

Factor A, *polygenic inheritance of intelligence,* although difficult to pin down because it cannot be directly observed, does seem, on the basis of twin studies and adoption studies (see Scarr & Weinberg, 1978), to suggest that there is a strong constitutional factor present that is influential in producing mental subnormality or superiority. The concept of *canalization,* introduced by Wilson (1978) and expanded upon by McCall (1983), has endorsed the powerful thrust of heredity in intellectual development. The fact that child intervention programs have had slight influence on the cognitive developmental patterns of the young child (Lazar et al., 1982) is additional evidence of the powerful contribution of this particular factor, contributing perhaps 30%–50% of the variance according to the estimates of behavioral geneticists (Plomin, DeFries, & McClearn, 1980).

Factor B, *adult-child linguistic interaction,* represents one of those variables that is specifically linked to the broader concept of environmental stimulation (Feagans & Farran, 1982). The degree to which adults communicate with their children on a concept level, or use language in a causal, "if . . . then" relationship ("If you touch the stove, then you will burn your hand.") is the degree to which youngsters learn to use language as a tool to understand and master their environment (Farran, Haskins, & Gallagher, 1980). Such a use of language seems critical to adequate school performance in later years. The relative presence or absence of this factor has been noted in comparing lower-class to middle-class family interactions, which suggested that such a factor is making a tangible contribution to the total of intellectual performance (Bernstein, 1970; Hess & Shipman, 1968). Let us estimate its influence on the total variance as 10%–20%.

Factor C, *physical health,* indicates that nutritional deficiencies and other health problems may interfere with the learning set of the individual and could be expected to have a cumulative effect influencing mental subnormality. Still, many children of high ability are in poor health. We are aware from the work of Sameroff and Chandler (1975), Zeskind and Ramey (1978), and others, that this factor of poor health may well interact with other variables, such as poverty and family disorganization, to result in more problems than when it is operating as an independent variable. Zigler and Trickett (1978) also commented on the link between physical well-being and motivation.

Health status appears more important in an interacting set of conditions, but not so important by itself. No more than 5%–10% would seem to be allocated to this factor operating alone.

Factor D, *subcultural values,* also seems to have a measurable, if minor, influence. The fact that there are, and have always been, differences in proportions of measured subnormality found in different American subcultures suggests that such a condition deserves inclusion in the set of important variables (Adler, 1963; Shonkoff, 1982). The further fact that there is a tremendous range of measured ability *within* any subcultural group also suggests that subcultural membership is not a dominant variable, and that its influence can be overcome by some of the other factors present. This allows us to conclude tentatively that this variable is contributing perhaps 5%–15% of the variance—hardly any more, hardly any less.

Factor E, the *perception of the child by significant others,* is estimated to contribute between 5% and 10% of variance. If that estimate is correct, then modifying that variable significantly (i.e., if other children and adults would not refer to the child as a "dummy," a "retard," or other characterizations that lower self-esteem) would still not yield dramatic improvements in measured mental subnormality, because 10% of the variance does not contribute that much to the total. The way to disprove the estimates provided in this model is to demonstrate how much a change in that variable can, in reality, modify intellectual performance.

Factor Z, *significant pathology affecting CNS,* would operate in a very different fashion; representing, as it does, a physical insult to the integrity of the central nervous system, resulting in demonstrable brain injury. The presence of this variable would affect all the other variables, when present. That is, if a significant CNS pathology exists, it can very well cancel out or suppress the effect of all of the other variables—thus operating as a suppressor variable.

The impact of these factors interacting with one another often has been a topic of discussion, but with few estimates as to what such interaction might mean quantitatively. Scarr and McCartney (1983) have presented a theory of genotype—environmental effects, which would suggest that interaction of variables has a strong impact over time, perhaps as strong as the 15% to 25% allocated in this model.

As one reviews these proposed cross-national differences, the implication of lower prevalence of intellectual subnormality is that the Swedish culture may be maximizing certain variables in this multivariate formulation of adult-child linguistic interaction, subcultural family factors, and physical health conditions, as well as minimizing significant infant pathology through good prenatal and postnatal care. By maximizing the variance contributed from those factors, they would be providing a rationale for a lower prevalence of intellectually subnormal children. The further assumption to be considered by public policy-makers would be that the application of comprehensive social programs, education, and health care could produce a lesser number of cases of mild mental subnormality in this country.

POLICY ANALYSIS AND 4-YEAR-OLDS

Whereas many of the chapters in this volume explore the concept of malleability for its scientific significance, malleability has importance for policy as well. If there is limited malleability on a particular developmental dimension, then there can be major questions raised about the appropriateness of expending large amounts of scarce resources in an attempt to change that dimension.

If, on the other hand, there appears to be substantial malleability present in children on other dimensions, then there is an increased responsibility placed on those whose task it is to optimize the development of such children. High malleability favors remediation; low malleability favors prevention, when the characteristic in question is unfavorable, as in intellectual subnormality.

The knowledge of the malleability of children can be applied to a variety of public-policy issues. One such issue at the present time involves the question of 4-year-olds, and what options are available in our society to provide appropriate care for them. Policy analysis should provide information to decision-makers who may have to choose between competing options on how to solve the public issues of the moment. The definition of social-policy analysis provided by MacRae and Wilde (1979) has merit: "Policy analysis is the use of reason and evidence to choose the best policy among a number of alternatives." However, we must also accept the additional criterion suggested by Moroney (1981) that few decisions are made in the public area that do not have a value base to them, either overt or covert.

Gallagher (1981) has presented a model of policy generation that includes six steps. That model will be applied here to the issue of malleability of young children and the specific issue of how we might plan, as a society, to care for 4-year-olds.

Restatement of the Problem

Public issues are rarely framed in a manner that the policy analyst would find workable. Therefore, the first step in the process would be to take the presented problem and restate it in a way that can yield useful information. For example, the public concern about 4-year-olds may be stated in this way: Why don't we have public school classes for 4-year-olds? Such a statement, in effect, provides a solution before we really understand the problem that we are trying to solve.

Instead, what is required is a statement of needs, goals, and objectives that will give some background and direction to the strategies that we might wish to apply. In the case of 4-year-olds, this issue has arisen in the past few years, in part, because of our concern for children who come from families heavily burdened by economic problems, with little tradition for proactive child development strategies (Feagans & Farran, 1982; Ramey & Haskins, 1981; Zigler, Kagan, & Klugman, 1983).

In part, this issue is a live one because of the rapidly growing number of mothers in the work force. Over 50% of mothers with children under the age of 5 are now in the work force part time or full time (U. S. House of Representa-

tives report, 1984). Since many of those mothers appear to be working predominantly for economic reasons, there would seem to be every reason to believe that such a situation will continue into the immediate future, if not beyond. This would mean that more than half of all 4-year-olds in this country will be cared for by someone other than their parents for a significant part of the day.

If children are malleable from an intellectual or personality standpoint, then what happens to them during childhood becomes a matter of significance to the society, and specifically to the public schools, who must shape their curricula accordingly. Since malleability can lead to negative as well as positive results, then we have a basis for concern that the policy analysis must address. How big a problem are we facing? What negative consequences will occur if we are not able to insert a useful policy that would increase the likelihood that the 4-year-old child will have a constructive experience during that away-from-parent period?

Establishing Goals and Objectives

What would we wish our policy initiatives to accomplish? Too often we don't ask that crucial question explicitly, so we become confused about what our programs are supposed to accomplish. If our major goals are to create experiences that would maximize the child's readiness for school and to promote the child's own feelings of worthiness and security, then we are at least somewhat closer to determining a program structure that would have a rationale for achieving those goals. If we then proceed further and establish a program objective such as, "The children will increase the number of prosocial interactions with peers by 50% by the end of the year," then the quantitative results of such a program should either confirm or disprove the achievement of that objective and establish a type of public accountability.

Generation of Alternative Strategies

In this stage, we should generate a range of viable policy options designed to meet the goals in the restatement of the problem. These options should represent a range of program

Policy options	Cost	Past record	Political feasibility	Personnel needs	Vertical equity	Start-up time
1. Public school for all 4-year-olds						
2. Public school for 4-year-olds with special needs						
3. Day care for 4-year-olds						
4. Negative income tax						
5. Tax breaks for industry day care						
6. Parental voucher						
7. Status quo						

Figure 2.   Policy options and decision criteria for 4-year-olds.

possibilities that extend beyond any one particular professional discipline.

Figure 2 provides a list of possible policy options that can be considered on the issue of the 4-year-old child. These options range from educational strategies, such as the downward extension of school for some or all of the students; to economic solutions, such as the negative income tax or tax breaks for industry; to the possibility of a larger level of support for day-care services; to a parental voucher that could be cashed in at the child-care facility of the parents' choice. This list is limited only by the range of information available to the analyst and his or her sophistication regarding the issue at hand. The status quo should always be included as one of the strategies and be analyzed for its effect along with the other strategies. One may wish to leave well enough alone, but one should know the costs of doing that as well as the costs of taking some form of new action.

Synthesis of Information

The analyst draws together all available information from a variety of disciplines to determine what is known about 4-year-olds, and about existing policy efforts to meet their needs. This is the type of activity that is most familiar to the scholar or academician. However, this is more than the traditional review of the literature. The analyst must seek informa-

tion from a variety of fields such as developmental psychology, economics, sociology, and cultural anthropology. Where policy issues clearly require input from a diversity of professional sources, a multidisciplinary-team approach is highly desirable.

Criteria for Strategy Choice

In this stage, the analyst is required to establish the various criteria that will be used to weigh one option against another. Some criteria are so often included in the analysis that they might almost be called universal criteria. Two examples of such criteria can be seen in Figure 2. These would be *cost* and *past history* of the various strategies or options. In any public policy issue, cost is a fundamental concern, often playing a determining role in the choice of options. Yet cost is a factor rarely considered in discussions by academicians, who are often more concerned with evidence of program effectiveness. The history of the program option is a criterion with which the scholar is particularly comfortable, but it is only one of a variety of criteria that the public decision-maker must consider in his or her decision-making.

As noted in Figure 2, some other criteria for decision-making between options would be *personnel needs* and *political feasibility*. For example, on the options that would include downward extension of school for all 4-year-olds, a key question from the decision-maker would be, where are all the trained personnel necessary to make these strategies work?

A particular strategy or option might have numerous supporters in the academic community because of its effectiveness, yet be ruled out by the decision-maker or the analyst on the grounds of virulent public opposition that would place a major barrier in the way of the adoption of that policy. The negative income tax strategy or the voucher strategy might well be such a strategy that could arouse strong negative public feelings, although the analyst would want to collect some information about the presence of such feelings by polling or using other attitude data, rather than making a subjective judgment. The number of people who would be offended by the awarding of money to families who are not working would seem to be large, but would need to be documented, as would the belief that parents might spend a voucher on frivolous options rather than for constructive services for their child.

A different type of criterion can be noted in Figure 2—*vertical equity*. This is a criterion that expresses a clear value, which is not necessarily shared by everyone, but one which the analyst might wish to pursue so that the decision-maker would be aware of its result on each policy option. In this instance, vertical equity means the unequal treatment of unequals in order to make them more equal. Many of the major social programs for children who are handicapped, or who may be lacking resources to develop their capabilities, have had this underlying value at the heart of the program. Head Start and Public Law 94-142 (The Education for All Handicapped Children Act) are two prime examples of policies that embody such a philosophy. It would seem important for the full review of these options that one could see how well this philosophy matches each option.

Implementation Plan

Once a choice is made as to which option or combination of options is the most desirable,

implementation of such a policy must be addressed. The process of implementation may present problems that impede the success of the policy itself. Laws are passed by lawyers but carried out by policemen. If the policemen are hostile or antagonistic to that law, the implementation of that law may have a rough road ahead. Similarly, a new educational policy may be established at the school board or superintendent level in the educational system, but it must be implemented by teachers who may have had little to do with its initiation and have even less sympathy for its execution. The ability to design an implementation strategy that will bring dissident groups to support the policy is a rare gift. Individuals or institutions that may not have been consulted, or whose judgment was ignored in the establishment of a policy, require that their own needs be satisfied in the implementation process. In a full-scale analysis, the matrix in Figure 2 would be completed quantitatively ($-$ or $+$) where subjective judgments were applied. This allows the analyst and others to view the relative merits of the available options.

Policy analysis, as described here, is a new field; the questions it poses, the methodology it employs, and the analytic techniques it applies are still in the formative stage. Still, this analytic framework can provide a bridge between the world of academia and the world of public decision-making. Something akin to the procedures and approach described here are likely to be used if one is to satisfy the initial description of policy analysis as the use of reason and evidence to choose between options. The alternative to this approach is the old-fashioned one of political log-rolling or power politics. We should have enough sense of history to be suspicious when decisions are made by political log-rolling or power politics, as these have been applied unsuccessfully in the past to the needs of our children.

REFERENCES

Adler, M. (1963). A study of the effects of ethnic origin on giftedness. *Gifted Child Quarterly, 7*, 98–101.

Bernstein, B. 1970). *Primary socialization, language and education*. London: Routledge and Kegan Paul.

Birch, H., Richardson, S., Baird, D., Horobin, G., & Illsley, R. (1970). *Mental subnormality in the community*. Baltimore: Williams & Wilkins.

Conley, R. (1973). *The economics of mental retardation*. Baltimore: The Johns Hopkins University Press.

Farran, D., Haskins, R., & Gallagher, J. J. (1980). Poverty and mental retardation: A search for explanations. In J. J. Gallagher (Ed.), *New directions for exceptional children* (Vol. 1). San Francisco: Jossey-Bass.

Feagans, L., & Farran, D. (Eds.). (1982). *The language of children reared in poverty: Implications for research and intervention*. New York: Academic Press.

Gallagher, J. J. (1975). Why the government breaks its promises. *New York University Quarterly, 6*, 22–27.

Gallagher, J. J. (1981). Models for policy analysis: Child and family policy. In R. Haskins & J. Gallagher (Eds.), *Models for analysis of social policy: An introduction*. Norwood, NJ: Ablex Publishing Corporation.

Gallagher, J. J. (1985). The prevalence of mental retardation: Cross-cultural considerations from Sweden and the United States. *Intelligence, 9*(1), 97–108.

Granat, K., & Granat, S. (1975). The generalizability of patterns of intellectual performance from institutionalized to nonlabeled intellectual subaverage adults. *Journal of Mental Deficiency Research, 19*, 43–55.

Granat, K., & Granat, S. (1978). Adjustment of intellectually below-average men not identified as mentally retarded. *Scandanavian Journal of Psychology, 19*, 41–51.

Grossman, H. (Ed.), (1983). *Classification in mental retardation*. Washington, DC: American Association on Mental Deficiency.

Grunewald, K. (1979). Mentally retarded children and young people in Sweden. *Acta Paediatrica Scandanavia, 275*, 75–84.

Hagberg, B., Hagberg, G., Lewerth, A., & Lindberg, U. (1981). Mild mental retardation in Swedish school children. *Acta Paediatrica Scandanavia, 70*, 1–8.

Hess, R. D., & Shipman, V. C. (1968). Maternal influences upon early learning. In R. D. Hess & R. M. Bear (Eds.), *Early education: Current theory, research, and action*. Chicago: Aldine.

Hunt, J. M. (1979). Psychological development: Early experience. *Annual Review of Psychology, 30*, 103–143.

Jensen, A. R. (1972). *Genetics and education*. New York: Harper & Row.

Lazar, I., Darlington, R., Murray, H., Royce, J., & Snipper, A. (1982). Lasting effects of early education: A report from the Consortium for Longitudinal Studies. *Monographs of the Society for Research in Child Development, 47*, 1–151.

MacRae, D., & Wilde, J. (1979). *Policy analysis for public decisions*. Belmont, CA: Wadsworth.

McCall, R. (1983). Environmental effects on intelligence: The forgotten realm of discontinuous, nonshared, within-family factors. *Child Development, 54*, 408–415.

Mercer, J. (1973). The myth of 3% prevalence. In R. K. Eyman, C. E. Meyers, & G. Tarjan (Eds.), *Sociobehavioral studies in mental retardation: Papers in honor of Harvey F. Dingman. Monographs of the American Association on Mental Deficiency, 1*, 1–18.

Moroney, R. (1981). Policy analyses within a value theoretical framework. In R. Haskins & J. Gallagher (Eds.), *Models for analyses of social policy* (pp. 78–102). Norwood, NJ: Ablex Publishing Corporation.

The National Commission on Excellence in Education. (1983). *A nation at risk: The imperative for educational reform* (A Report to the Nation and the Secretary of Education). Washington, DC: U. S. Government Printing Office.

Plomin, R., DeFries, J., & McClearn, G. (1980). *Behavioral genetics: A primer*. San Francisco: W. H. Freeman.

President's Committee on Mental Retardation. (1970). *The six-hour retarded child*. Washington, DC: U. S. Department of Education, Office of Special Education.

Ramey, C., & Haskins, R. (1981). The causes and treatment of school failure: Insights from the Carolina Abecedarian Project. In M. Begab, H. Haywood, & H. Garber (Eds.), *Psychosocial influences in retarded performance* (pp. 89–112). Baltimore: University Park Press.

Robinson, H., & Robinson, N. (1976). *The mentally retarded child* (2nd ed.). New York: McGraw-Hill.

Robinson, N. (1978). Mild mental retardation: Does it exist in the People's Republic of China? *Mental Retardation, 16*, 295–298.

Sameroff, A., & Chandler, M. (1975). Reproductive risk and the continuum of caretaking casualty. In F. Horowitz (Ed.), *Review of child development research* (Vol. 4, pp. 187–244). Chicago: University of Chicago Press.

Scarr, S., & McCartney, K. (1983). How people make their own environments: A theory of genotype—environment effects. *Child Development, 54*, 424–435.

Scarr, S., & Weinberg, R. (1978). The influence of "family background" on intellectual attainment. *American Sociological Review, 43*, 674–692.

Shonkoff, J. (1982). Biological and social factors contributing to mild mental retardation. In K. Heller, W. Holtzman, & S. Messick (Eds.), *Placing children in special education: A strategy for equity* (pp. 133–181). Washington, DC: National Academy Press.

Tarjan, G., Wright, S. W., Eyman, R. K., & Keeran, C. V. (1973). Natural history of mental retardation: Some aspects of epidemiology. *American Journal of Mental Deficiency, 77*(4), 369–379.

U. S. House of Representatives. (1984, March). *Children, youth, and families: 1983 a year-end report on the activities of the Select Committee on Children, Youth, and Families*. Washington, DC: U. S. Government Printing Office.

Wilson, R. (1978). Synchronies in mental development: An epigenetic perspective. *Science, 202*(1), 939–948.

Zeskind, P., & Ramey, C. (1978). Fetal malnutrition: An experimental study of its consequences on infant development in two care-giving environments. *Child Development, 49*, 1155–1162.

Zigler, E., Kagan, S., & Klugman, E. (Eds.). (1983). *Children, families, and government*. Cambridge, England: Cambridge University Press.

Zigler, E., & Trickett, P. K. (1978). IQ, social competence, and evaluation of early childhood intervention programs. *American Psychologist, 33*, 789–798.

Index

Page numbers followed by *n* indicate footnotes.